CHICAGO AND ILLINOIS

The
Spiritual Traveler

✸

CHICAGO
AND ILLINOIS

A GUIDE TO SACRED SITES AND PEACEFUL PLACES

MARILYN J. CHIAT

HiddenSpring

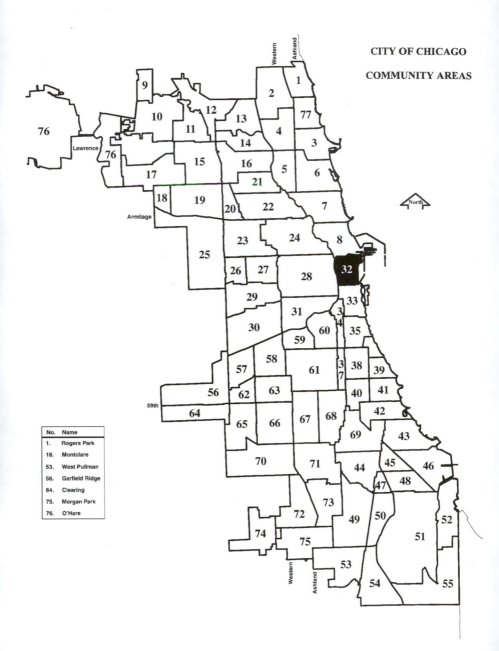

CITY OF CHICAGO

COMMUNITY AREAS

No.	Name
1.	Rogers Park
18.	Montclare
53.	West Pullman
56.	Garfield Ridge
64.	Clearing
75.	Morgan Park
76.	O'Hare

There are many community areas in Chicago. This key shows a sampling of them.

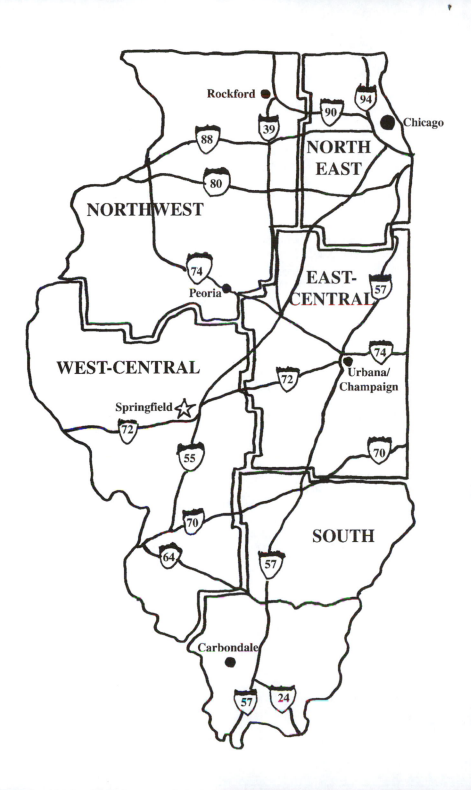

The Spiritual Traveler series editor: Jan-Erik Guerth

The cover image shows the Water Tower and the John Hancock Center in Chicago.

Cover photo: © Digital Vision
Cover design by Alexandra Lord Gatje
Book design by Saija Autrand, Faces Type & Design

Library of Congress Cataloging-in-Publication Data

Chiat, Marilyn Joyce Segal.
    The spiritual traveler [i]n Chicago and Illinois : a guide to sacred sites and peaceful places / Marilyn J. Chiat.
      p. cm.
    Includes bibliographical references and index.
    ISBN 1-58768-010-6 (alk. paper)
    1. Sacred space—Chicago.   2. Sacred space—Illinois.   3. Chicago (Ill.)—Religion.   4. Illinois—Religion.   I. Title.
    BL2527.C48C48 2004
    203'.5'09773—dc22

                              2004004170

Published by
HiddenSpring
An imprint of Paulist Press
997 Macarthur Boulevard
Mahwah, New Jersey 07430

www.hiddenspringbooks.com

Printed and bound in the
United States of America

Contents

A Note to the Reader *x*

CHAPTER ONE

The Story of Spiritual Life in Illinois *1*

A Brief History of Illinois *2*

A Brief History of Some Faith Groups in Illinois *33*

CHAPTER TWO

Visiting Sacred Sites and Peaceful Places *64*

Pathways *64*

Locations *65*

Architectural Elements *67*

Building Plans *78*

Church Interiors *83*

Synagogues *87*

Mosques *89*

Buddhist Temples *90*

Hindu Temples *91*

CHAPTER THREE

Chicago *93*

The Loop *95*
South Side *107*
Southwest Side *138*
Northwest Side *144*
North Side *161*
Chicago's Environs *183*

CHAPTER FOUR

Northeastern Illinois *207*

CHAPTER FIVE

Northwestern Illinois *218*

CHAPTER SIX

West-Central Illinois *260*

CHAPTER SEVEN

Southern Illinois *284*

CHAPTER EIGHT

East-Central Illinois *315*

Glossary *335*

Bibliography *339*

Acknowledgments *343*

Index *346*

Picture Credits *356*

The *S*piritual Traveler

❈

Sacred journeys and sacred sites have been at the center of humankind's spiritual life from the very beginning. The Spiritual Traveler invites seekers of every faith and none to discover and connect with these ancient traditions and to find—either for the first time or anew—unique ways of pilgrimage in today's world.

PLEASE BE IN TOUCH

We have worked very hard to make this edition of The Spiritual Traveler as accurate and up to date as possible. However, any travel information could change at any time. If you think you have come across errors or omissions, please let us know. In addition, we would love to hear about your spiritual discoveries—any sacred spaces or peaceful places that you have found along the way, but not in this book. We will try to include them in upcoming editions. You can reach us at:

thespiritualtraveler@hiddenspringbooks.com.

LAST, BUT NOT LEAST

Please understand that the author, editors, and publisher cannot accept responsibility for any errors in this book or adverse experiences you might encounter while traveling. We encourage you to stay alert and be aware of your environment while on your spiritual journey.

"I have seen many things in my travels, and I understand more than I can express."—Sirach (Ecclesiasticus) 34:11, 12

A NOTE TO THE READER

Every book has a "back story," a tale about how it came into being. This book is no different. For many years the focus of my research has been on America's religious architecture, on buildings that can be factually documented by religion, style, date, architect, and significance. I was interested in how America's places of worship, in all their great variety, reflect the diversity of people who came to settle here. But I was also aware that sacred sites could exist outside the confines of a built environment—there is not always a clear distinction between the sacred and the secular. The Spiritual Traveler series provides me with a venue to explore spiritual sites and peaceful places in all their embodiments in Chicago and Illinois, including buildings, cemeteries, battlefields, and landscapes, both natural and manmade. However, the limitations of a book's size also place limitations on the number of sites to include—Chicago alone could fill an entire book—so I had to leave out many sacred sites and peaceful places not because they were unimportant, but simply because of lack of space.

Driving through Illinois made me aware of how many sacred sites and peaceful places our nation is blessed with and how many of them remain relatively unknown to travelers. These are places steeped in history or graced with scenic beauty that imbues them with a spiritual or peaceful quality worthy of our contemplation.

Chapter 1 is a historic overview of the religious and spiritual life in Chicago and Illinois, and includes brief descriptions of selected faith traditions that will provide a perspective on a sacred building or site. Chapter 2 discusses what to look for in a house of worship and includes descriptions of various architectural styles, building plans, and symbolic and/or decorative artifacts and motifs. Chapter 3 describes Chicago's sacred sites and peaceful places by neighborhood. Each of the remaining chapters covers one region of Illinois, traveling counterclockwise from the northeast to the northwest, west-central, south and ending in the east-central region. Each chapter begins with a brief description of the region, followed by a suggested travel route and sites to visit. In all cases, major sites are listed first, and each includes—if it is a house of worship—its denomination or religion (unless clearly stated in the name); a complete address or location; the date of the building (usually its year of dedication unless otherwise indicated); the architect's name when known; the telephone number (☎)

and Web site (🖳). ➡ indicates "nearby" sacred sites or peaceful places worthy of a stop, and ✿ marks gardens, parks, and other natural environments, private 🍃 and public, that welcome visitors seeking peace and quiet in nature. Sidebars include additional information on various related topics of interest to the traveler. The appendices include a bibliography, glossary, and an index.

The initials NR identify buildings listed on the National Register of Historic Places, indicating they have been recognized by the secretary of the interior as having *regional* significance in American history, architecture, archaeology, engineering, and culture, and are worthy of preservation. The initials NHL identify a National Historic Landmark, a designation given by the secretary of the interior to sites that fulfill a stringent and distinct set of criteria that prove their *national* significance.

Visiting a House of Worship

Except at times of service, most houses of worship keep their main doors locked. To gain entry, either call ahead or inquire at the office, often in an adjoining building. When visiting during a service please always observe the customs and dress of the congregation. If unsure, call ahead and request information. Please respect these specific rules or traditions:

1. Women and men worship separately in mosques and Orthodox synagogues.
2. Men must cover their heads in Orthodox and Conservative synagogues; women must have head coverings in mosques and Orthodox synagogues.
3. Shoes are removed before entering a mosque and most Buddhist and Hindu temples.
4. Even when services are not being held, it is important to request permission to photograph or videotape the interior of a house of worship. Never take photographs or videos during a religious observance or service.
5. If you do not wish to participate in a service, either sit quietly or make arrangements to visit at a time when there is no service.

Obviously, sacred sites and peaceful places are not limited to the ones included in this book. As you travel, you will encounter many places and spaces that will provide you with a sense of peace and belonging. It is my hope that this book will enable you to becoming increasingly aware and accepting of the spiritual experience that transforms the ordinary into something that is clearly sacred.

ABOUT THE AUTHOR

Marilyn J. Chiat has taught at the University of Minnesota and has lectured extensively on religious art and architecture in this country and abroad. Her previous books include *America's Religious Architecture: Sacred Places for Every Community* and *Handbook of Synagogue Architecture*. She has also written encyclopedia entries on churches and synagogues and numerous journal articles. Awards for her work in preserving and documenting religious architecture include the Model Initiative Award from Partners for Sacred Places in Philadelphia and the Community Urban Environment Award from the city of Minneapolis. She has been a consultant on a number of television and radio programs, including the Emmy-nominated public television series *Country Spires*.

CHAPTER ONE

✶

The Story of Spiritual Life in Illinois

IT HAS BEEN SAID we are a nation of seekers, foraging in the wilderness for some sense of identity. Important clues to our identity can be found in the nation's heartland, in Illinois, a state shaped like an arrowhead clinging to the southwestern tip of Lake Michigan. If you listen closely as you travel along Illinois' highways and byways, you will hear the nation's heartbeat, its steady rhythm reflecting the timelessness of its hills and prairies, its rivers and lakes. Throughout the state you will see evidence of the toil and turmoil that transformed a vast wilderness into productive farmland and prosperous towns and cities. The effort did extract a toll in human suffering, in Native Americans forced from their land, in slaves who sought freedom and were often denied it, and in the countless others who risked all they had in an often futile effort to improve their lot in life. The struggle to succeed can be found in the words and deeds of many of the state's sons and daughters, revered leaders, heroes, writers, and artists, who gave voice to the country's greatest hopes and aspirations and exposed its most serious shortcomings. They have left their mark on the nation's character. Illinois is the heart of America. It does not belong to one region, but to all regions, combining within its boundaries most of the social, economic, historic, and geographic diversities found in this country.

A Brief History of Illinois

"God's meadow": That is how Father Jacques Marquette, the French Jesuit priest and explorer, described the territory he saw as he was paddling down the Illinois River in 1684 in search for a passage to the Pacific Ocean. He went on to report that he "had seen nothing like this river, for the fertility of the land, its prairies, woods, wild cattle, stag, deer, wildcats, bustards, swans, ducks, parrots, and even beaver, and its many little lakes and rivers." The land was a sea of grass scattered with dazzling wildflowers and groves of trees. The ground trembled under the hooves of thundering herds of buffalo, and flocks of carrier pigeons darkened the sky. Native Americans living in villages along the rivers harvested crops of corn, squash, and beans and hunted wild game. To Frenchmen who came from a world ravaged by internecine wars, its land and economy exhausted, this new world seemed a Garden of Eden where the land's bounty, particularly its furs, would replenish France's depleted coffers and Roman Catholic missionaries could save the souls of "noble savages."

FRENCH EXPLORERS AND MISSIONARIES

It was in 1671 that the Jesuit priest Claude Allouez, Sieur d'Aumont Sanite Lussan, proclaimed the Mississippi River and the Great Lakes region to be possessions of France. While exploration was one of the goals of the French in the New World, there were two others that were clearly intertwined: fur trade with the Native Americans and saving their souls. Jacques Marquette (1637–75), born in France where he was ordained as a Roman Catholic priest, arrived in the town of Quebec in 1666. After spending nearly two years studying the Algonquin and Huron languages, he accepted his first assignment at Sault Sainte Marie and later founded the Mission of St. Ignace at Mackinac, both in Michigan. Native Americans told him stories about a great river to the west that he and Louis Jolliet would later set out to explore.

Louis Jolliet (ca. 1645–ca. 1700), born near Quebec and raised in a Jesuit seminary, chose to become an adventurer rather than a priest. He was a mapmaker and fur trader and while exploring the Great Lakes region in 1668 became acquainted with Father Marquette. Because of his knowledge of the area, Jolliet was selected to be the leader and Marquette the chaplain of the expedition to explore the Mississippi River.

They left St. Ignace on May 17, 1673, in birch bark canoes and crossed Lake Michigan to the Door Peninsula (Green Bay, Wisconsin). They first canoed down the Fox River, then the Wisconsin River to where it enters the Mississippi River and followed it to the mouth of the Arkansas River. After concluding that the Mississippi did not flow into the Pacific Ocean as they had hoped, they retraced their steps northward. Both men kept copious notes of their observations of the landscape and of their meetings with friendly Native American tribes; however, Jolliet lost his journal when his canoe overturned.

Following his travels with Marquette, Jolliet continued his explorations. In 1697, he was named the royal hydrographer and mapped the waterways of New France.

Marquette stayed in the Lake Michigan region and continued his missionary efforts among the Native Americans until his death in 1675. On December 15, 1674, he performed the first mass at the site of what became Fort Dearborn and later Chicago (see p. 101). The following year he established the Mission of the Immaculate Virgin Mary near present-day Utica and the Mission of the Immaculate Conception at Kaskaskia (see p. 291).

Fathers Montigny and St. Cosme from the Quebec Seminary of Foreign Missions established the Holy Family Mission at Cahokia, east of the Mississippi River, in 1699. The log church there has been continuously occupied since then (see p. 285). As the eighteenth century progressed, Catholic missionary activity began to wane as religious dissension in France led to the French Revolution (1789–99). By that time France had already relinquished control of its holdings in North America to the British and missionary activity all but ceased in the Great Lakes Region.

Less than two hundred years later, Shabbona, chief of the Potawatomi, watched helplessly as his people's land and its natural resources were consumed by white settlers: "In my youthful days, I have seen large herds of buffalo on these prairies, and elk were found in every grove, but they are here no more, having gone towards the setting sun. . . . The red man must leave the land of his youth and find a new home in the far west. The armies of the whites are without number, like the sands of the sea. . . . " By

4 ● THE SPIRITUAL TRAVELER

1832, with the defeat of the Sauk leader Black Hawk (see p. 14), all Native Americans had been driven out of Illinois. All that remains today are library and museum exhibits, archaeological sites and a giant statue of Black Hawk (see p. 220) sadly surveying what once was his land. Ironically, Illinois' name now recalls a Native American nation that has vanished from its home.

Illinois received its name from French explorers encountering members of the Algonquin Nation who called themselves *Hileni* or *Illiniwek*, terms translated as "men." Numbering between eight and ten thousand people, the Illiniwek were a loose confederacy of five tribes known as the Illinois Confederation: the Kaskaskia, Cahokia, Peoria, Tamaroa, and Michigamea. The land they occupied was bountiful; the vast prairies provided ample game and buffalo; the rivers offered a steady supply of water and fish, as well as transportation routes for the flow of trade goods, technology, and culture; and the soil was rich. But it was not the "Garden of Eden" sought after by French Enlightenment intellectuals. The Illinois Confederation was often at war with its neighbors; periodic floods drove them from their villages, and fearful episodes of disease decimated entire communities. None of this was new; long before the coming of the first Europeans, large towns had developed in the Mississippi and Illinois River Valleys, especially at Cahokia (see pp. 282–83) and Dickson Mounds (see p. 253). They flourished for nearly five centuries, from 900 C.E. until about 1350 before their populations began to decline. They had disappeared entirely by the time of European incursions. The reasons for their disappearance remain unanswered.

PREHISTORIC NATIVE AMERICANS IN ILLINOIS

Evidence of Native American occupation of Illinois can be traced back to 13,000 B.C.E., the *Paleo-Indian Period*, when the first humans began to arrive on the North American continent. Sites dated to this era are scarce. One is at Kimmswick in Missouri, located on a small tributary of the Mississippi River across from the American Bottom. Spear points and other stone tools were found at the site, along with the bones of mastodons that became extinct in about 9000 B.C.E.

The *Archaic Period* dates from 8000 to 500 B.C.E. A Middle Archaic village dating approximately to 5100 B.C.E. has been uncovered in the Lower Illinois River Valley near Kampsville. Pottery began to appear at this time, as did the custom of burying the dead in mounds, often with grave goods.

During the *Woodland Period* (800 B.C.E.–1500 C.E.) people began to establish permanent settlements throughout the region. It was at this time that the bow and arrow came into use, as did the custom of burying the dead in mounds atop river bluffs.

The *Mississippian Period* (1000–1500 C.E.) was when the fertile American Bottom in Illinois began to be cultivated; crops, primarily corn and squash, helped to transform a foraging and hunting society into one that was more dependent upon agriculture. Settled communal life and a new social order that began to develop throughout the region flourished until about 1500 C.E. A network of ceremonial centers was built that spread from the Great Lakes to the Lower Mississippi Valley. The largest and most famous can be found at the Cahokia Mounds Historic Site (see pp. 282–83).

By the time the first Europeans reached this region, these sites were deserted and their inhabitants scattered, absorbed into other indigenous cultures. The reasons for their abandonment remain unknown, although archaeologists speculate that floods, disease, or intertribal warfare may have decimated the population. The remains of these great mounds and ceremonial centers puzzled early explorers who refused to attribute them to ancestors of the indigenous people of the region. Instead they invented wild tales to explain their existence, even suggesting they were built by people from India, China, or the Crimea who supposedly had crossed the ocean or the Bering Straits and arrived in the New World prior to Columbus. Others perpetuated the myth about a "race of Moundbuilders" that once lived in North America. It wasn't until the late nineteenth century that scholars began to seriously study the mounds; their conclusion was that Native Americans built them over a long period of time beginning in approximately 3000 B.C.E. But the antiquity of the sites and the awe they inspired did not prevent settlers from destroying them by the thousands to make way for farms, towns, and roadways. Over 3,000 mounds were destroyed in the American Bottom alone.

Aware of the value of the area's natural resources, especially fur, France laid claim to all of the land known then as Illinois Country, a vaguely undefined area extending from Lakes Michigan and Superior to the Ohio and Missouri Rivers. From 1673 until 1763, France prevented British expansion into the region by building forts along its waterways. The French also supported the Native Americans' efforts to confine European settlers east of the Appalachian Mountains; in gratitude tribal leaders agreed to support the French cause against the British.

The first French fort in Illinois Country was hastily built in 1680 on a cliff overlooking the Illinois River in present-day Peoria by Robert Cavelier, Sieur de la Salle, an ambitious French nobleman, and his faithful lieutenant, an Italian soldier of fortune, Henri de Tonti. Named Fort Crevecoeur, it survived for only a few months before the soldiers La Salle had stationed there deserted, stealing all the supplies and destroying the stockade (see p. 251). Undaunted, La Salle and Tonti continued their explorations on behalf of France and arrived at the mouth of the Mississippi River in April 1682. Anxious to cement the presence of France in the New World, LaSalle immediately claimed the Mississippi River and all the rivers that flowed into it, and all the land surrounding the rivers, for France, naming the entire vast area Louisiana in honor of his king, Louis XIV. Returning north, La Salle and Tonti built Fort St. Louis at Starved Rock, a former Native American campsite overlooking the Illinois River (see p. 6).

Fort de Chartres (see p. 289), erected in 1720 at the site of Prairie du Roche, a village named for nearby limestone bluffs, served as France's Illinois Country headquarters for over forty years. It, along with most of France's North American possessions, was surrendered to Britain in the 1763 Treaty of Paris that ended the "French and Indian War."

Evidence of French presence in the region endures, even though French control was short-lived and its impact modest in terms of economic and political development. There is Pere Marquette State Park (see p. 276), at the confluence of the Mississippi and Illinois Rivers; Holy Family Catholic Church, built in 1799 in Cahokia (see pp. 285–86); the elegant Pierre Menard home, built in 1802 for a French fur trader and entrepreneur at Ellis Grove (see p. 292); and Kaskaskia, the site of the Mission of the Immaculate Conception, founded in 1675 by Father Marquette, that was later transformed into a British fortification, known as Fort Gage, before it became Illinois' territorial and then state capital (see p. 289).

The British, in an attempt to appease the rebellious and suspicious tribes within their newly conquered territory, drew up a royal proclamation on October 7, 1763, that reserved as tribal hunting grounds the country west of the Appalachian Mountains. It directed all settlers to withdraw from unceded lands west of the mountains and ordered that in the future land could only be purchased if agreed upon by the Native American owners and the British government. These directives, along with the British decision in 1774 to make the territory north of Ohio part of the Province of Quebec, enraged colonists and contributed to the onset of the Revolutionary War.

1763–1818

The Union Jack flew over Illinois Country for only fifteen years before the flag of a new nation, the United States of America, replaced it. Although the Revolutionary War was mainly fought east of the Appalachians, one battle in Illinois did have an impact on the war's outcome. After 1763, some of the eastern colonies—Virginia, Massachusetts, Connecticut, North and South Carolina, and Georgia—had extended their reach westward, claiming land that stretched to the banks of the Mississippi River. These lands were vulnerable and difficult to protect from the British whom colonists feared would try and retain control of their western territories. In response to this perceived threat, Colonel George Rogers Clark, a Virginian, convinced his governor, Patrick Henry, that he could smuggle troops into the area and capture the British garrisons at Fort Gage (at Kaskaskia—see p. 289) and Fort Sackville (at Vincennes, Indiana). Clark's plan worked; he and his Kentucky frontiersmen known as "long knives" surprised the British at Fort Gage on July 4, 1778, and captured it without firing a shot. In joyous celebration, the town's inhabitants rang the parish bell given to them in 1741 by King Louis XV that is now known as the "Liberty Bell of the West" (see pp. 290–91). It took two tries for Colonel Clark to capture Fort Sackville, but following his victory there on February 25, 1779, the vast majority of the region that later became Illinois was proclaimed to be part of the Commonwealth of Virginia.

Following the Revolutionary War, Virginia ceded all its frontier holdings to the Continental Congress, and in 1787 the Northwest Territory, a region south and west of the Great Lakes, northwest of the Ohio River, and east of the Mississippi River was established. Congress stipulated that no less than three but not more than five states would be created from the Northwest Territory's 265,878 square miles. French Catholics in the Midwest who became part of the new nation forced the founding fathers to come to terms with the country's increasing religious diversity. Although most of the signers of the Constitution were Protestant churchgoers (two-thirds were Anglicans), they also believed that God was revealed in nature, reason, and law, and that these concepts were available to all thoughtful people. To avoid the religious warfare that had caused havoc in the Old World, they passed the First Amendment to the Constitution, which ensured that the U.S. Congress would "make no law respecting an establishment of religion, or prohibiting the free exercise thereof." This allowed, eventually, for Roman Catholics, Jews, and other minorities to openly practice their faiths and to compete for the souls of their fellow Americans.

The founding fathers also had to create order out of what they perceived as the chaos of the wilderness. At the time the Northwest Territory was established in 1787, it was criss-crossed by river networks and trails used for centuries by Native Americans and fur traders. The curves and forms of nature determined where people settled and the routes they traveled. To the Native Americans this represented the natural order of things, as eloquently expressed by Chief Luther Standing Bear (born in 1868) of the Oglala Band of Sioux (now known as Dakota or Lakota): "We do not think of the great open plains, the beautiful rolling hills, and winding streams with tangled growth as 'wild.' Only to the white man was nature a 'wilderness.' . . . to us it was tame."

The same rationalist Enlightenment philosophy applied to religion was used to divide up the Northwest Territory. Two ordinances passed by the first Congress were intended to avoid the chaotic division of land evident in the original thirteen colonies. Using the ancient grid pattern perfected by the Romans, the *Land Ordinance of 1785*, which encompassed the entire trans-Appalachian territory, divided up "Indian purchases" into townships of six miles square, each consisting of thirty-six sections, each one mile square, or 640 acres; the sections were to be divided as needed, with four sections in each township to be set aside for the U.S. government and one section for public schools. The *Northwest Ordinance of 1787* ordered the division of land north of the Ohio River and east of the Mississippi River into a similar grid pattern, using meridian (north-south) and base (east-west) lines to stake out towns, villages, and farms with spaces set aside for schools and churches. The township grid, a six-by-six-mile square, became standard in 1796. Surveyors were immediately sent out to divide the territory into its checkerboard pattern, a pattern that is familiar to anyone flying over the region or driving along its highways.

The Northwest Ordinance included provisions on the advancement of education, maintenance of civil liberties, and exclusion of slavery. Despite the founding fathers' declarations of civil liberties, however, these liberties were not to be enjoyed by all the territory's inhabitants. The Northwest Ordinance forbade slavery but recognized the rights of owners to reclaim fugitive slaves, a right that was to cause enormous pain and suffering in Illinois. Many settlers were slave owners from the Upland South, and the state's first six governors were slaveholders. And although the rights of Native Americans to remain on land they already inhabited were assured by the Northwest Ordinance, those rights could no more be enforced than the British proclamation of 1763 (see pp. 6–7). Settlers who illegally moved into the territory demanded that the military protect them from Native Americans fighting to save their land from encroachment. The war for supremacy raged until an army under the command of General Anthony Wayne soundly defeated the Miami Indians at the Battle of Fallen Timbers (in northwestern Ohio) on August 20, 1794. Tribal leaders were forced to cede millions of acres of land to the U.S. government, including almost all of the present state of Ohio, part of Indiana, and other parts of the Northwest Territory. Pioneers now began to arrive by the thousands, as did immigrants from the "Old World" lured by the news of cheap and available land.

The western frontier was a wild and wooly place that attracted saints, seekers, and sinners alike. "Sinners" were fleeing the civilizing effects of faith and government in the east in hopes of getting lost in the frontier's vastness. "Seekers" traveled the often perilous routes westward in search of a better way of life in a land envisioned as a new "Zion" overflowing with milk and honey. Itinerant preachers, mainly Baptist and Methodist and some Presbyterian, were the "saints" who would ride on horseback for miles through uncharted wilderness to bring faith, hope, and community to scattered settlers at camp meetings where, according to one observer, the religion was "red hot." Propelling the search for faith was a religious revival that began in about 1800 in the east and spread westward. Known as the Second Great Awakening (the first occurred prior to the Revolutionary War and had little effect on the west), its success resulted in Protestant Christianity's "conquest" of the midwestern and southern regions of the United States, and the emergence of Methodists (see pp. 49–50) and Baptists (see pp. 40–41) as the nation's two major Protestant denominations.

In 1803, the government agreed to purchase two million square miles of land from the financially strapped French (the Louisiana Purchase), thereby extending the nation's borders to the Rocky Mountains. Under orders of President Thomas Jefferson to find a new route to the Pacific Ocean and make contact with native tribes further west, Meriwether

THE SECOND GREAT AWAKENING

Visiting America in the 1830s, the French aristocrat and traveler Alexis de Tocqueville (1805–59) wrote: "There is no country in the world in which the Christian religion retains a greater influence over the souls of men" than in the United States. Apathy toward religion that had set in after the Revolutionary War forced clergy to devise new ways to fill their houses of worship in a nation where religion was voluntary. A series of chapel sermons by the president of Yale College, Timothy Dwight, a Congregational minister, inspired a number of students to become preachers. They carried the revival westward, but slightly changed the Christian message. While they continued to proclaim the sovereignty of God, they also emphasized the role individual Christians must play in their own salvation and the acceptance of personal responsibility for living a righteous and godly life. One such preacher was Peter Cartwright (see pp. 265–66), a Methodist minister born in Virginia in 1785, who moved to Illinois in 1824. He wrote in his autobiography: "Ten, twenty, and sometimes thirty ministers, of different denominations, would come together and preach night and day, four, five days together. . . . these camp-meetings last[ed] three to four weeks. I will venture to assert that many happy thousands were awakened and converted to God at these camp-meetings."

Lewis (1774–1809) and William Clark (1770–1838) began preparations for their famous expedition during the winter of 1803–1804 at Camp Dubois near Wood River, entering the uncharted Missouri River on May 14, 1804 (see p. 265).

In 1800 the U.S. government partitioned the Northwest Territory, including the Illinois region, into the Indiana Territory. The settlers in Illinois Country were not pleased with the situation and began lobbying Congress to establish Illinois as a separate territory. Their goal was reached on February 3, 1809, when the Illinois Territory was created. It consisted of almost the entire present state of Illinois, most of what is now Wisconsin, and part of present-day Minnesota.

The War of 1812 (concluded December 24, 1814) slowed settlement of the Illinois Territory. Potawatomi Indians who sided with the British attacked Fort Dearborn (the future site of Chicago—see p. 101), located at

EARLY PROTESTANTS IN ILLINOIS

River and land routes offered relatively easy access into southern Illinois for Upland southerners. According to Douglas K. Meyer (*Making the Heartland Quilt*), Protestantism in Illinois originated with these migrant families. Many were Primitive Baptists or "Old School" Baptists (see p. 41), who established small homesteads in the area known as "Egypt" (see p. 284). The first Baptist minister to arrive in Illinois Country was Elder James Smith, a Virginian, who in 1787 visited a small pioneer community on the Mississippi River named New Design. Elder David Badgley, also from Virginia, established a Primitive Baptist church in New Design in 1796, considered the first Protestant church organized in Illinois Country. According to one count, nearly 150 Primitive Baptist churches were organized in the state before 1840.

Methodists had their circuit-riding ministers who would travel throughout the territory holding camp meetings for people living in isolated areas. The first Methodist minister in Illinois arrived in 1793 from Kentucky and erected the territory's first Methodist church in the biblical-named town of Goshen. Jesse Walker, who began holding camp meetings in southwest Illinois in 1807, was known as the "Daniel Boone of the Methodist Church." He was responsible for organizing the First Methodist Church in Chicago in 1831 (see p. 103).

Presbyterian missionaries were in Kaskaskia (see p. 289) as early as 1797, while Cumberland Presbyterians (see p. 302) began to arrive at about the time Illinois became a state in 1818. The first Presbyterian congregation in Illinois Country was The Old Sharon Presbyterian Church in White County, organized in 1815 by pioneers from Kentucky (see pp. 313–14).

German-speaking pioneers from the Piedmont area of North Carolina, many of whom were Lutheran, settled in the Shawnee Hills area of southern Illinois in about 1810. They lived in close proximity to one another and built churches where they could maintain their language and practice their traditional customs and folkways. The oldest Lutheran congregation in Illinois is St. John's Lutheran Church near Dongola, organized in 1816 (see pp. 304–5).

the junction of the Chicago River and the then shoreline of Lake Michigan, massacring fifty-two settlers who were attempting to escape. Tecumseh, the charismatic Shawnee chief, and his brother, Tenskwatawa, "the Prophet," in an attempt to hold onto their lands, sided with the British during the war. Tecumseh and his men played an important role in the surrender of American militia to British forces at Detroit on August 16, 1812; however, subsequent British defeats on Lake Erie and elsewhere forced them to retreat into southern Canada, where Tecumseh was killed on October 5, 1813. His last words haunt people of good conscience to this day: "Where is the Pequot? Where are the Narragansetts, the Mohawks, the Pokanoket, and many other once powerful tribes of our people? They have vanished before avarice and the oppression of the White Man, as snow before a summer sun."

Following Britain's defeat, Fort Dearborn was rebuilt and Illinois began to develop in the center of a steadily expanding nation. However, the threat of dispossessed Native Americans and the vastness of the wilderness discouraged large-scale migration, except for frontiersmen seeking adventure and desperate Upland southern farmers forced off their land by wealthy plantation owners. Their point of entry was Shawneetown (see p. 307) on the Ohio River. Others journeyed along ancient paths such as the Buffalo Trace, created by migrating buffalo that went from near Owensboro, Kentucky, through Indiana into Illinois. Most of the Upland southerners were proslavery and members of Protestant denominations.

As the south developed, settlement began along and between rivers and waterways. The northern part of the territory became increasingly attractive to settlers from the East. Many were abolitionists and members of established Protestant denominations, Congregational, Episcopalian, and Presbyterian (see pp. 44, 46, and 52). The time was ripe for Illinois Territory to become a state.

1818–1860

The Northwest Ordinance of 1787 stated that a territory had to have at least sixty thousand "free inhabitants" in order to be admitted to the Union "on an equal footing with the original States in all respects whatever." By 1803, Ohio had the requisite number of inhabitants to become the first state to be carved out of the Northwest Territory. Indiana was admitted into the Union in 1816 by circumventing the antislavery clause in the Northwest Ordinance through the passage of a questionable "indenture" law that allowed blacks to be bought and sold and required they sign contracts to work for their masters for at least twenty years. This law was used as a model by Illinois when its delegates began to lobby Congress for admission into the Union. Slavery was a divisive and decisive factor in determining whether Illinois would be admitted into the Union, and it was an issue that had divided the territory from the time the first white settlers began to move into it.

Slavery was introduced into the area in 1720 when a French miner brought a number of slaves he had purchased in the Caribbean to work in his mines near Kaskaskia. When he moved he sold the slaves to local French families. Slavery was never an issue to the British or the Virginians when they controlled the area. When Virginia ceded the land to the federal government following the Revolutionary War it was with the understanding that its inhabitants would be allowed to retain all their property, including slaves. The Upland southerners and former French slaveholders were not about to capitulate to what they viewed as "Yankee" demands to give up their "rightful property." Furthermore, many feared freed blacks would compete for land and jobs.

Northern congressmen, concerned that Illinois would be admitted into the Union as a proslavery state, manipulated the state's boundaries to encompass fourteen counties that were to be part of Wisconsin, including a portion of the Lake Michigan shoreline and the site of Fort Dearborn (Chicago—see p. 101); these areas were largely settled by New Englanders opposed to slavery. But even with this additional land, the delegates struggled for several years to get the requisite number of residents, finally succeeding on December 3, 1818, when President James Monroe signed the act that created Illinois, the nation's twenty-first state. Like the nation, Illinois remained divided between proslavery forces in the south and abolitionists in the north. The slavery issue could not be ignored, and was addressed in the writing of the state's constitution.

Aware that Congress would not approve a proslavery state constitution, and to appease Yankee abolitionists, the delegates to Illinois' first constitutional convention included an antislavery provision similar to Indiana's. Within a year, however, the state's proslavery General Assembly passed the controversial "Black Laws" that remained in effect until the end of the Civil War. The laws ordered that slaves could not be brought into Illinois to be freed; freed slaves were required to carry certificates that proved they were free; and indentured servants had no civil rights and could be treated as property upon the death of their masters. The passage of the Black Laws set off a series of deadly encounters between proslavery advocates and abolitionists, including one in Alton in 1837 that resulted in the death of the crusading newspaperman and Presbyterian minister, Elijah Lovejoy (see p. 280). Swearing he would "never forsake the cause that has been sprinkled with my brother's blood," Owen Lovejoy, a Congregational minister, transformed his family's home in Princeton into the principal stop in northern Illinois for the Underground Railroad (see pp. 241–42).

In the years that led up to the Civil War, the last of the Native Americans were forcibly removed from Illinois. One last desperate attempt to retain possession of tribal land occurred in 1832, when the old warrior Black Hawk tried to rally tribes in northwestern Illinois to declare war against the new settlements. Black Hawk was known as *Ma-ca-tai-me-she-kia-kiak*, "Black Sparrow Hawk" in the Algonquin language of the Sauk. Born in 1767 in the village of Saukenuk, located a few miles north of the

THE UNDERGROUND RAILROAD

The Underground Railroad was a series of routes through the Northeast and the Midwest used by as many as 100,000 fugitive slaves trying to reach freedom in Canada. The name, "Underground Railroad" has been attributed to Tice Davids, a slave from Kentucky who escaped his owner in 1831. Tice allegedly swam across the Ohio River with his owner in hot pursuit. Unable to find him, the owner reported that Tice must have gone on an underground road. Since railroads had just been introduced, the term *road* was transformed into *railroad*, and railroad terms became part of the language and lore of the escape network. Slaves would hear about places in the North where they could own property, work for pay, and be free. For many the promise of freedom outweighed all risks and with nothing but the North Star to guide them, they would set off into the unknown. Some would follow land routes, and others traveled along rivers and waterways north to Chicago and the Great Lakes Region, and from there would try to find a friendly ship captain to ferry them to Canada. Traveling at night and knowing what would happen to them if they were caught, desperate men, women, and children would somehow find their way to homes of freed blacks or white sympathizers who could provide them with food, shelter, and directions to the next safe house. Some got no further than the region's growing cities like Chicago, where freed slaves who had organized Quinn Chapel A.M.E. Church in 1844 would offer them shelter (see p. 111).

confluence of the Rock and Mississippi Rivers, he was a fierce warrior and respected leader of the Sauk Nation who fought with Tecumseh (see p. 12) on the losing side during the War of 1812. The British defeat in 1814 dashed Black Hawk's hopes of stemming the tide of white settlement on his people's land. Pushed into what later became Iowa and then ordered to move even further west, he decided to make one last attempt to regain his people's land in Illinois. Other tribal leaders chose to stay out of the conflict, but Black Hawk and his men, although badly outnumbered, were able to fight off the U.S. militia for fifteen weeks before they were defeated at the Battle of Bad Axe, Wisconsin, on August 2, 1832. Black Hawk surrendered himself at Prairie du Chien, Wisconsin, on August 27, 1832, where he delivered a poignant speech: "Farewell, my nation. Black Hawk tried to save you, and avenge your wrongs. He drank the blood of some of the whites. He has been taken prisoner, and his plans are stopped. He can do no more. He is near his end. His sun is setting, and he will rise no more. Farewell to Black Hawk." After being paraded around the country by President Andrew Jackson, Black Hawk died in 1838; his body went on display in a museum in Burlington, Iowa, that was later completely destroyed in a fire.

With the last of the native peoples forced west across the Mississippi River, all of Illinois was now "safe" for settlers. Its natural resources were available for exploitation by easterners moving westward and by Europeans fleeing unrest in their homelands. But how could settlers get to Illinois? The overland trails were long and difficult; alternative routes were needed. One solution was the National Road (then known as the Cumberland Road for its starting point in Cumberland, Maryland), which reached Vandalia (see pp. 274–75), Illinois' first capital, in 1852.

Steamboats were another option. The first practical steamboat in the United States was launched in 1807, and within ten years there were sixty steamboats in service on the nation's waterways; however, there was no natural water route between the mid-Atlantic States and the Midwest. In 1816, DeWitt Clinton, governor of New York, suggested digging a nearly four-hundred-mile-long canal from Buffalo on the eastern shore of Lake Erie to Albany on the upper Hudson River, thus connecting New York City and the Great Lakes. After the Erie Canal opened in 1825, settlers could easily reach the Great Lakes Region, but the problem of journeying farther west from Chicago remained unresolved. To populate the state's hinterlands and to facilitate transportation for the region's agricultural and industrial products, Illinois joined the canal-building boom with the Illinois and Michigan Canal (see pp. 205–6).

HOLY TRAMPS

It was Yankees who conceived the idea of a canal linking Lake Michigan with the Illinois River and ultimately the Mississippi River, but it was Irish Catholics who dug it, often toiling under the most inhumane of conditions. "Holy tramps," priests assigned to the Mission of Chicago, would travel by horseback to where the Irish labored to tend to their spiritual needs. The canal's first mission was established in 1837 at Haytown, a temporary settlement located north of Lockport (see p. 205). The holy tramps would risk their own lives to ease the suffering of cholera victims, many of whom were buried in the peaceful cemetery surrounding St. James Sag Catholic Church near Lemont, completed in 1859 (see p. 203). For those workers unable to attend church services, the priests would pack their saddle-bags with a portable altar and other ritual objects used in the sacramental acts and conduct mass anywhere space could be found—in an open field, a storehouse, or a private home. As more settled communities began to develop, the holy tramps became resident priests in the area near the canal.

The ninety-six-mile canal, completed in 1848, transformed Chicago, incorporated in 1837, into the nation's leading trade center. However, the canals had their limitations (e.g., freezing over in winter), and another form of transportation was introduced that would radically change the character of the nation—the railroad. As one historian observed, it was the railroads that settled the prairies.

Although the Baltimore and Ohio Railroad was in operation in the East by 1830, railroads did not enter Illinois until the 1850s. Senator Stephen A. Douglas, Democrat from Illinois, sponsored a bill passed by Congress that awarded a 2.5 million–acre land grant to the Illinois Central Railroad, organized by eastern capitalists, to run tracks from Chicago to Cairo (see p. 305) and to establish a link connecting Cairo and Galena (see p. 228). The vast, largely uninhabited Illinois prairie was now accessible to settlers representing a great variety of religious and ethnic groups.

Unsettled affairs in Europe in the mid-nineteenth century propelled the first major wave of immigrants to seek a safe haven in the United States. Many were German speakers: Catholic, Protestant, and Jewish. Others were Irish Catholics fleeing the devastating potato famine, as well as Italians and Polish. Germans often formed farming communities, such as the one around Belleville (see p. 286) that has retained its German character. German-speaking Jews, mainly from Bavaria, began to settle in Chicago in the late 1830s. One of the first was Henry Horner, the organizer of the Chicago Board of Trade, whose grandson and namesake served as governor of the state (1933 to 1940). By 1860, there were fifteen hundred Jews living in Chicago.

Towns were platted and tracts of land were opened for farming, but the sticky rich prairie soil was difficult to till with iron plows. Three inventions manufactured in Illinois transformed the prairie into the nation's bread-basket. John Deere's self-polishing steel plow, invented in 1837 and dubbed by farmers the "singing plow," made breaking the prairie a far less arduous task (see pp. 219–20). Cyrus McCormick's mechanical reaper, patented in his native Virginia in 1834 and manufactured in Chicago, enabled farmers to harvest five times more wheat than was possible by hand (see p. 151). Less well known is the contribution of Joseph Glidden of De Kalb, who invented barbed wire in 1873, which was soon widely used to easily fence in properties (see pp. 208–9).

Advances were also being made at this time in construction that had an impact on Chicago's growth. Traditionally wooden buildings were framed with heavy timbers that were mortised, tenoned, and pegged together and then raised into position. It was a difficult and labor-intensive method that was replaced in the 1830s by "balloon framing." What made this method affordable was the availability of machine-made nails and precut boards. Conceived by George W. Snow, a Chicago contractor and jack-of-all-trades, the balloon frame consists of light, two-by-four studs nailed rather than joined in a basketlike manner that rises continuously from foundation to rafters. It was first used in Chicago for the erection of St. Mary's Church in 1833 and subsequently for many of the city's earliest houses.

Even with all of its growth and prosperity, a shadow continued to hang over Illinois: the growing split between Yankee abolitionists in the northern and central areas of the state and proslavery Upland southerners who were well entrenched in the south.

The political conflict that divided Illinois mirrored tensions elsewhere in the country, where heated disputes regarding slavery, especially in the newly acquired territories, tore at the nation's fabric. Illinois politicians were at the heart of the debate. Proslavery Senator Douglas reopened the issue in 1850 when he questioned the legality of the Missouri Compromise, an attempt by Congress to balance the number of free and proslavery

PREACHING FOR AND AGAINST SLAVERY

The issue of slavery was fought fiercely from pulpits throughout the United States. Three large Protestant denominations divided over the issue. In 1844 the Methodist Episcopal Church separated into two general conferences with the formation of the proslavery Methodist Episcopal Church, South. Organized in 1845, it had its headquarters in Louisville, Kentucky. The North and South Conferences reunited in 1939. Also in 1844, the Baptist Church split into the Southern Convention and the antislavery "American Baptist Missionary Union." The Presbyterian Church began to polarize as early as 1830, when conservative southerners of Scotch-Irish background formed the "Old School," and New England abolitionists organized the "New School." The Presbyterian Church in the Confederate States (also known as the Presbyterian Church in the United States) was formed in 1861.

While Lutherans were generally antislavery, each local and ethnic synod was allowed to make its own decision on the issue, as did the Disciples of Christ. Episcopalians eventually divided into two "national" churches over slavery, whereas the Congregationalists, Unitarians, and Universalists remained undivided and staunchly antislavery. The Catholic Church's official position was that although the slave trade was to be condemned, slavery as a principle of social organization was not intrinsically sinful. Irish Catholics, in particular, supported Senator Stephen Douglas's views on slavery, in fear that freed slaves would compete for jobs. Jews were few in number and assumed a neutral stance on the issue.

states entering the Union. A direct result was the emergence of the Republican Party, formed by antislavery Whigs and some Democrats that went on to gain control of Congress in 1854. States threatened to secede from the Union over the question of slavery. It was in the midst of all this turmoil that another son of Illinois took the political stage and dramatically changed the course of the nation.

Abraham Lincoln, then in private practice in Springfield, made a speech in Peoria in 1854 that gained him fame throughout the region. Lincoln declared: "Slavery is founded on the selfishness of man's nature— opposition to it on his love of justice." But it wasn't slavery alone that

Lincoln feared; it was the threat it posed to the Union, as he made clear in one of his most famous and prophetic speeches, delivered on June 16, 1858, in Springfield at the opening of his Senate campaign against Douglas: "A house divided against itself cannot stand. I believe this government cannot endure permanently half slave and half free. I do not expect the Union to be dissolved—I do not expect the house to fall—but I do expect it will cease to be divided."

Lincoln the Republican and Douglas the Democrat held seven debates in the summer of 1858 in towns located in each of the state's seven congressional districts: Ottawa (see pp. 214–15), Freeport (see p. 225), Jonesboro (see p. 303), Charleston (see pp. 317–18), Galesburg (see p. 248), Quincy (see p. 260), and Alton (see p. 279). Thousands of people and local dignitaries gathered in town squares bedecked with flags and banners to await the arrival of the two opponents. Douglas, short and stocky, resplendent in his Washington clothes, came by a special train provided by the Illinois Central Railroad; Lincoln, tall and lanky, arrived with his clothes wrinkled from the hours he spent on an ordinary passenger train. The contrast between the two men could not have been greater, but how they could debate! Douglas may have won the election, but Lincoln gained national recognition. In 1860, at the Republican Party's convention held in Chicago, he was nominated to be the party's presidential candidate. Southerners threatened that if Lincoln was elected they would secede from the Union, and beginning with South Carolina on December 20, 1860, they did.

While religious and racial conflicts erupted throughout the region, there were others who saw the wilderness as a place to find salvation. Away from the distractions of the materialistic world, idealistic utopians began to develop their own communal settlements where they could live in peace and harmony with one another and with nature, free to pursue their religious beliefs and practice their particular customs and traditions unfettered by the demands of society to conform.

Numerous utopian communities were established throughout the Great Lakes Region in the years prior to the Civil War, including several in Illinois. One of the most famous is Nauvoo, established in 1839 by Joseph Smith, Jr. (1805–44), the founder of the Church of Jesus Christ of Latter-Day Saints (see pp. 42–43). Forced to flee upstate New York State because of their beliefs, the Mormons trekked westward and settled for seven years in a small town in Illinois they renamed Nauvoo, transforming it into a nearly autonomous religious community (see p. 257). Smith and his brother

Hyrum were murdered by a mob while imprisoned in Carthage (see p. 256), but undeterred and under the new leadership of Brigham Young (1801–77), the Mormons set out to find their utopia further west. A splinter group, the Reorganized Church of Jesus Christ of Latter Day Saints (renamed the Community of Christ in 2001), remained in Illinois under the leadership of Smith's son and built a church in Plano in 1868 (see pp. 211–12).

Seven months after the departure of the Mormons, another group seeking spiritual perfection arrived in Illinois and settled less than one hundred miles northeast of Nauvoo. Led by their prophet, Eric Jansson (d. 1850) and fleeing persecution in Sweden, the Janssonites hoped to find religious freedom in the wilderness. Their community, named Bishop Hill, prospered, the first six years under the leadership of Jansson before he, like Smith, was murdered for his beliefs (see pp. 242–44).

1860–1900

On March 4, 1861, Abraham Lincoln left Springfield for his inauguration in Washington, D.C., with great fanfare but with few illusions about what lay ahead for him as president of a nation teetering on the brink of a civil war. Five weeks later, on April 13, 1861, his worst fears were realized when Fort Sumter was surrendered to Confederate forces. Although no battles of the Civil War were fought on Illinois soil, the state found itself in the midst of the struggle, geographically, politically, and militarily.

The Mason-Dixon Line, which separated northern and southern states, followed the Ohio River along a portion of Illinois' eastern and southern border. Kentucky to the southeast and Missouri to the west were slave states that didn't secede from the Union because of the presence of northern forces on their soil. Missouri, however, became the site of numerous guerilla battles that at times spilled over into southern and western Illinois.

Politically, Illinois gave the nation its president, a man of vision who saw the oncoming conflict as presenting "to the whole family of man the question whether a constitutional republic or democracy—a government of the people, by the same people—can or cannot maintain its territorial integrity against its own domestic foes." Lincoln's primary objective at the onset of hostilities was to preserve the Union. It wasn't until after the battle of Antietam in September, 1862, that Lincoln issued his famous Emancipation Proclamation that was to go into effect on January 1, 1863. Congress finally passed the thirteenth amendment to free the slaves in January 1865.

This state in the heartland also contributed the general who led the Union forces to victory, Ulysses S. Grant (1822–85), a merchant from Galena (see p. 228). It was at Fort Defiance (see p. 307), near Cairo, at the confluence of the Mississippi and Ohio Rivers, that Grant began his assault on the South. The fort was also where Confederate prisoners were mustered before being shipped to prisoner-of-war camps, including ones at Alton (see p. 281), on Senator Stephen Douglas's estate in Chicago (see p. 115), and on Rock Island (see p. 239). Outside Cairo is Mound City National Cemetery, where thousands of Confederate and Union soldiers are buried in a solidarity they did not share during their lives (see p. 307).

The North prospered during the war; one historian claims that the four years of battle witnessed one of the greatest business "booms" in American history. Crop failures in Europe led to demand for American wheat; industries in the North flourished, supplying provisions and equipment to the troops; and new natural resources such as coal and oil were discovered and exploited. Immigration into the northern states never ceased; enough people arrived during this period to replace the men who had gone to war. Outmanned and ill equipped, the Confederacy began to break up. Aware of the futility of prolonging the war, General Robert E. Lee surrendered to General Grant on April 9, 1865, at Appomattox Courthouse, Virginia. President Lincoln, seeking to heal the nation's scars, urged people to "extinguish their resentments if we expect harmony and union." Sadly, Lincoln didn't live to see those resentments extinguished; on Good Friday evening, April 14, 1865, he was assassinated at Ford's Theater in Washington, D.C., by an actor, John Wilkes Booth. With great ceremony, Lincoln was brought home to Illinois for burial. Today one can visit numerous sites in Illinois, Indiana, and Kentucky dedicated to Lincoln's memory, but none are more moving than his home and tomb in Springfield (see pp. 266–72).

Beginning in the 1820s with the network of canals, followed by the arrival of the railroad, and concluding with the Civil War, the nation's axis was reoriented from north-south (New York to New Orleans) to east-west, across the entire continent. In 1861 the total railroad track in the United States was less than 31,000 miles; by the turn of the century there were over 200,000 miles of main track, including the first transcontinental railroad completed on May 10, 1869. Vast expanses of land were opened for settlement; farmers were needed to till the soil and laborers to work in the factories and mines. Agents were sent abroad to search for workers. Making their task easier was Congress's passage of the Homestead Act of 1862, which allowed any citizen or intended citizen to claim 160 acres of unoccupied public land upon payment of a nominal fee ($1.25 an acre or less) after five years of residence. Land-hungry Europeans and Americans jumped at the opportunity and began to arrive by the trainload.

In the years following the Civil War the character of Illinois began to change dramatically, but not always peacefully. As industries and mining expanded, so did the need for additional laborers. Immigrants from Ireland and eastern and southern Europe were underpaid and overworked. Several of their more outspoken and rebellious coworkers tried to form unions to improve the lot of the "unskilled, unorganized and unwanted, the poorest and weakest sections of labor." Coal mining was particularly dangerous due to the attitude of mine owners who were indifferent to their workers' safety. The United Mine Workers of America, organized in 1890, lobbied to establish mine safety laws, but unions were anathema to the mine owners, and they went to often deadly extremes to prevent their workers from striking. Virden (see pp. 272–73), a small coal mining community near Springfield, was the scene of a particularly brutal strike in 1898 that resulted in the death of at least eleven men, union members and company guards. The dead miners were initially buried in the town cemetery, but their bodies were later moved to the Union Miners' Cemetery where Mother Jones is interred. The cemetery is a pilgrimage site for supporters of the labor movement (see p. 273).

Chicago was the scene of many bloody labor battles. One of the most violent confrontations, The Haymarket Riot of May 3 and 4, 1886, at the McCormick Harvester Company ended with deaths, arrests, trials, executions, and the denial of all the workers' demands (see p. 151).

WOMEN IN THE LABOR MOVEMENT: MOTHER JONES AND LUCY PARSONS

Two women from different backgrounds who lived in Chicago had a profound influence on the development of the labor movement in the United States and in the formation of the Industrial Workers of the World (the "Wobblies").

Mary Harris "Mother" Jones, born in Cork, Ireland, in 1830, immigrated to Toronto, Canada, with her family when she was five years old. She eventually moved to Chicago, where she worked as a seamstress for some of the city's wealthy families. After moving to Memphis, Tennessee, in 1861, she married an iron molder who was a member of the Iron Molders Union. Six years later, after she lost her entire family in a yellow fever epidemic, Jones returned to Chicago to work as a seamstress, only to lose all of her belongings in the Great Fire of 1871. It was at this time that she became involved in the "Knights of Labor" and began to travel to wherever there were labor troubles. Her battles on behalf of the workers earned her the nickname "Mother" Jones. She was a paid organizer for the United Mine Workers from 1890 to 1904 when she became a lecturer for the Socialist Party of America. In 1905, Mother Jones, along with Lucy Parsons, stood on the platform with Eugene Debs at the first meeting of the Industrial Workers of the World. Jones was the first woman to join the new organization founded by Debs; Parsons was the second. At the age of eighty-one, Jones left the Socialist Party to work again as an organizer for the United Mine Workers, a position she held until 1922. Mother Jones gave her last speech at a party celebrating her one hundredth birthday on May 1, 1930; she died on November 30, 1930, and is buried in the Union Miners' Cemetery, amongst the graves of men and women whose causes she championed all of her life.

Little is known about Lucy E. Parsons's early life except that she was born in Texas in 1853, possibly to slaves. She was of mixed ancestry, African American, Native American, and Mexican. She met Albert Parsons, a white man whom she could not marry because of miscegenation (marriage between races) laws, but whom she considered her husband. They were forced to flee Texas because of Albert's efforts to register black voters. They arrived in Chicago in 1873, where he worked as a printer and became involved in labor disputes. Identified as an anarchist, he soon lost his job and was blacklisted. To support their family, Lucy opened a dress shop and became involved in the International Ladies Garment Workers Union. The Haymarket Riot proved her family's undoing. Although Albert was not present when a bomb was thrown into a mob, he was arrested along with eight other anarchists. After being found guilty, he was hung in what has been called one of the worst violations of civil rights in the United States. This event galvanized Lucy's radical tendencies, and she became an eloquent spokesperson for the disenfranchised and downtrodden. She supported the tactics of the Industrial Workers of the World and edited their newspaper, *The Liberator*. Parsons continued to fight for workers' rights until her death at age eighty-nine in an accidental fire.

Chicago was the major beneficiary of the nation's new east-west axis. It was much closer than New York to the western frontier, where new farms and industries increased the demand for goods and services. As the city grew its character changed to reflect the diversity of the people who found jobs in its factories, stockyards, and mills. The devastating fire of 1871 could have spelled doom for Chicago, but instead the city rose like a phoenix from the ashes. Innovative architects using new technology began to design buildings that are associated with the Chicago School of Architecture (see p. 96).

Ethnicity and religion were important factors in determining where immigrants would settle; thus their houses of worship often defined the neighborhoods. These were havens of quietude and spirituality for underpaid and overworked workers—places where they could speak in their mother tongue and maintain their traditions.

An ugly byproduct of diversity was xenophobia. As the Catholic population in the United States increased in the second half of the nineteenth century from two million to over ten million people, it fueled anti-Catholic sentiment. At the same time as parishes were established along ethnic lines for non-English-speaking Catholics, such as the mother church of all Polish Catholic parishes in Chicago, St. Stanislaus Kostka (see pp. 153–54), anti-Catholic groups were calling for restrictions on immigration and demanding that Protestant employers fire Catholics; however, this did little to discourage their coming.

The completion of the Illinois Central Railroad opened the "Egypt" region of southern Illinois to further settlement, particularly by non-Protestant Christians. A land development company recruited settlers in Poland and in Polish American communities. Many of those who came chose to work in the region's coal mines rather than farm, and worshipped at St. Charles Borromeo Catholic Church, established in DuBois in 1868 (see p. 296). Carpatho-Russian Orthodox Christians from a region that is now part of Slovakia and Ukraine settled in Royalton and built Holy Protection Orthodox Church in 1914 (see p. 298). The arrival of the newcomers, with their unfamiliar languages, customs, and faiths led to predictable clashes with their Protestant neighbors. The situation was further exacerbated by the arrival of freed blacks seeking jobs in the mines. The Ku Klux Klan became an active force in the region, contributing to sporadic episodes of racial and ethnic violence.

The attacks against Catholics eventually decreased due to the arrival of new targets, the nearly two million Yiddish-speaking Orthodox Jews who were escaping the pogroms in eastern Europe. Most settled in urban areas such as Chicago, where they organized their own congregations and institutions separate from those of their more liberal coreligionists (see pp. 60–63). By 1910 there were over forty Orthodox synagogues in Chicago's West Side ghetto area. Anti-Semitic exclusionary policies affected all Jews and limited where they could work, live, go to school, and even vacation. This forced them to become "clannish," for which they were then condemned—an accusation leveled at other ethnic and religious minority groups as well.

Others who began to arrive at this time included Amish from Pennsylvania and Ohio (see pp. 39–40), who had settled in Douglas County in 1864, establishing the towns of Atwood, Arcola, and Arthur. They retain both their Amish character and community to this day (see pp. 318–19). Danes settled in Sheffield, Bureau County, where they founded the nation's first Danish Lutheran Church, St. Peter's, in 1867 (see pp. 240–41).

The American Social Gospel movement began in the mid-nineteenth century as Protestant congregations sought to expand their ministry beyond the church door. Its goal was to reconcile evangelical Christianity with social Christianity in order to serve people's spiritual as well as social needs. To that end the movement's leaders framed and sought legislation designed to close the gap between rich and poor. Churches were built that could accommodate a variety of activities such as social welfare programs and Sunday school, the latter a result of the increased importance in religious education. One of the movement's most successful preachers was Dwight Lyman Moody (1837–99), a layman who organized revival campaigns, first in Chicago, then worldwide. Moody Memorial Church in Chicago is named in his memory (see pp. 173–74).

According to Barry A. Kosmin and Seymour P. Lachman in *One Nation Under God*, "Black churches were among the most stable institutions to arise after the Civil War." It is estimated that African Americans comprised nearly half of the more than five million members of Southern Baptist and Methodist churches during the Reconstruction Period. African American churches played important roles in their communities that went far beyond the purely religious. They sponsored housing developments, business organizations, schools, and even the first black publishing house. Blacks also became active in politics. The Colored Convention held in Chicago in 1869 led to African Americans in Illinois receiving the right to vote in 1870 and the repeal of school segregation four years later. John Jones, born free in North Carolina, spearheaded the convention and went on to become the first black man to hold public office in Illinois when he was elected to Chicago's county board in 1871.

TWO PROMINENT
AFRICAN AMERICAN WOMEN

Amanda Berry Smith (1837–1915) and Ida B. Wells-Barnett (1862–1931) were black women with ties to Illinois who came to the forefront in the post–Civil War period.

Amanda Berry Smith, born a slave in Maryland, was a missionary for the African Methodist Episcopal Church in New York City before she settled in Chicago in 1893. She raised funds to open an orphan home for African American children in Harvey, located just south of Chicago, the state's first orphanage for black children. It was destroyed by fire in 1918.

Ida B. Wells-Barnett was born into slavery in Holly Springs, Mississippi. After moving to Memphis she began her lifelong battle for equal rights for African Americans by refusing to give up her seat on a train to a white man. She sued the railroad and won, but later saw the decision overturned by the Supreme Court of Tennessee. This event sparked her career as a journalist as she began to write about her exploits. The lynching of three of her friends, vividly described by her in a local newspaper, resulted in her having to flee Memphis. After settling in Chicago, she became active in many causes, including women's suffrage. Along with Jane Addams (see p. 148), she blocked the establishment of segregated schools in Chicago. She married F. L. Barnett in 1895, an attorney and the editor of one of Chicago's first black newspapers. She ran unsuccessfully for the Illinois State legislature in 1930, becoming one of the first black women to run for public office in the United States. A public housing development in Chicago is named in her memory.

The 1893–97 depression led to more unrest among workers and their families that often erupted into conflicts such as the Pullman Strike of 1894 (see pp. 136–37). But despite all the adversity of that period, including the Spanish-American War of 1898 and the enormous social and cultural changes brought by the influx of millions of immigrants, the nation continued to make steady progress toward becoming one of the world's great powers. Chicago celebrated its growth in 1893 with the World's Columbian Exposition, which was held at the same time as the Parliament of World's Religions, an event that exposed Americans to the diversity of faiths of many of the immigrants. In fact, it was the immigrants and their backbreaking labor that contributed greatly to the country's growth and prosperity. The nation's population steadily increased, from 31.4 million in 1860 to nearly 92 million in 1910, and at the same time its economy underwent a major transformation—from agriculture to industry. Isolation, long hours, hard work, and increased mechanization combined with steadily decreasing farm prices resulted in a drastic decline in the rural population—from over 80 percent of the nation's population following the Civil War to less than 40 percent by 1930. By 1900, industry surpassed agriculture in Illinois, although nearly three-quarters of the state still remains farmland. However, most of the land today is in the hands of a few large landholders who hire tenants to operate the farms.

The nineteenth century ended with most Americans looking back at over a century of growth and expansion. But Woodrow Wilson, speaking at his inaugural in 1913, recognized that the nation's success came at a cost: "The evil has come with the good, and much fine gold has been corroded. We have been proud of our industrial achievements, but we have not hitherto stopped thoughtfully enough to count the cost, the cost of lives, snuffed out, of energies overtaxed and broken, the fearful physical and spiritual cost to the men and women and children upon whom the dead weight and burden of it all has fallen pitilessly the years through."

The nation's bumpy road to religious, racial, and social equality would continue to be a challenge in the future, as it had been in the past.

1900–1950

The twentieth century began on a note of optimism, a sense of renewal and rebirth. The nation had survived the 1893 Depression and emerged victorious in the Spanish-American War. Prosperity had returned and all were allegedly united, reciting together the Pledge of Allegiance introduced at the 1893 World's Columbian Exposition in Chicago. The nation's motto was considered a reality: *E Pluribus Unum*, "from many one." The optimism took visible form in further experimentation in art, architecture, science, and technology.

In architecture, Louis Sullivan (1856–1924) (see p. 97) challenged tradition with his innovative designs for a variety of buildings, including Holy Trinity Cathedral (see p. 157), built in 1903 in Chicago, which he hoped would be one of "the most unique and poetic buildings in the country." Three years later, his former assistant, Frank Lloyd Wright (1857–1959) (see p. 98), designed Unity Temple in Oak Park, built of reinforced concrete and dedicated "For the worship of God and the service of man" (see pp. 194–96). The building's horizontal lines were inspired by the state's flat prairie lands and are associated with what became known as the Prairie School of Architecture (see p. 195).

In Detroit, Henry Ford (1863–1947) was tinkering with a new technology that would completely change the nation's transportation system, and ultimately its entire environment. At the turn of the century he organized the Ford Motor Company and in 1908 introduced the Model T, an affordable automobile for the working class; less than ten years later Ford had produced 700,000 vehicles. The American Federation of Labor, established in 1886, was achieving better wages and working conditions for its members. The expansion of industry in the heartland and the promise of better wages resulted in migrations of people from the Deep South and the crowded eastern seaboard. One of the largest was the "Great Migration" of African Americans moving north, who began to settle in older neighborhoods of the region's major cities. One of the most famous is Chicago's Bronzeville (see pp. 117–18) immortalized by Pulitzer Prize–winning poet Gwendolyn Brooks (1917–2000) in her collection of poems, *A Street in Bronzeville*.

The Social Gospel movement, which began in the mid-nineteenth century (see p. 25), motivated women like Jane Addams to establish Hull-House to aid immigrant families (see p. 148) and inspired men of great wealth to endow charities. The Chicago Community Trust was established in 1915 by civic leaders to award grants to institutions that "promote the well-being of our community." The Julius Rosenwald Fund, created in 1917 by the president of Sears, Roebuck and Company, was a major benefactor of African American and Jewish causes, and established many YMCAs. Their efforts, as well meant as they were, and those of city planners who had grandiose ideas about improving the urban fabric did little to end the growing disparity between the rich and poor.

City planning, introduced at the 1893 World's Columbian Exposition, was based on function and aesthetics. Efforts were made to set aside land for cultural institutions, government plazas, commerce, and industry linked together by grand boulevards. Space was left for parks and playgrounds to be free and open recreational areas for the working class. As automobiles became more common, additional roads were built to allow people easier access to sites of natural beauty. Yellowstone, the first national park, was established in 1872, but it wasn't until 1916 that the National Park Service was created to administer all existing and future parks. States, too, began to set aside or purchase land for parks, usually at sites of great scenic beauty and/or historic importance, such as Giant City State Park, where the remains of a Native American stone fort are still visible (see p. 300).

The bubble of optimism with which the century opened burst with the nation's entry into World War I. Industry, however, expanded to keep up with the war effort, so when the fighting ended, the nation's economy blossomed into the "Roaring Twenties." Building activities increased, including the erection of many new houses of worship, often motivated by congregations and parishes wanting to replace their older buildings with new, more stylistically up-to-date designs. St. Thomas the Apostle Parish in Chicago, designed in 1920 by Francis Barry Byrne (1883–1967), an associate of Frank Lloyd Wright, is considered the first modern Catholic church building in the nation (see pp. 133–34).

While the nation prospered, it was still divided by powerful issues, especially race and religion. The Ku Klux Klan, reorganized in Georgia in 1915, expanded its focus beyond blacks to target Roman Catholics and Jews, and its geographic reach was extended well into the Great Lakes Region. Newspapers published irresponsible and inflammatory editorials about the nation becoming "the cesspool of Europe." As hostilities toward certain ethnic groups grew, so too did the demand to restrict their entry into the country. Many states had racist and religious regulations designed to exclude those considered "undesirable." The same racism motivated Congress to enact the Immigration Act of 1921, which reduced the number of southern and eastern Europeans who could enter the country; most of them were Roman Catholic, Orthodox Christian, or Jewish. The Johnson-Reed Act, passed in 1924, effectively closed the nation's doors for over forty years. It wasn't until 1965 and the passage of the Immigration and Naturalization Act that the Statue of Liberty would once again hold out her light of hope to newcomers. This 1965 act has effectively transformed our nation from one that was perceived as Judeo-Christian to one that has become, in the words of Diana L. Eck in her book A *New Religious America*, "a Judeo-Christian, Islamic, Hindu, Buddhist, Jain, Sikh, Zoroastrian nation."

Two constitutional amendments passed in 1920 had an important impact on the nation: The eighteenth amendment prohibited the manufacture, transportation, and sale of intoxicating beverages (repealed in 1933), and the nineteenth amendment granted women suffrage. Chicago, due to its location on Lake Michigan and with easy access to Canada, became the headquarters for organized crime. Between 1920 and 1930 the city recorded over five hundred murders related to bootlegging, most committed by men under the leadership of Alphonse Capone, the "master of the Chicago bootleggers." The city was home to over ten thousand "speakeasies," and the police appeared to be powerless. Vigilante groups were formed to try to stop bootlegging, particularly in the southern reaches of the state.

Although labor unions began to gain power in the 1920s, many coal miners still worked for low pay under dangerous conditions. One of the nation's most violent labor disputes occurred in Herrin (see pp. 294–96) in June 1922, where union workers killed twenty unarmed strikebreakers. People who were outraged by the attack demanded that the miners be punished. Although hundreds were indicted and brought to trial, none was found guilty.

Also at this time, but receiving far less attention, were the violent attacks against African Americans who sought to purchase homes in Chicago's all-white neighborhoods. As increasing numbers of blacks settled in Chicago (between 1910 and 1920 their numbers rose from 44,000 to 110,000), white reaction became more violent. Race riots began to occur; according to one source, between July 1917 and March 1921, fifty-eight bombs were hurled at African American homes in Chicago. As whites increased their efforts to keep their neighborhoods segregated, black communities became more cohesive. While forced to live in tightly packed ghettoes, they united in a common cause to combat racism. It was a harbinger of things to come in the 1950s and 1960s (see pp. 31–33).

Throughout the roaring twenties the nation basked in the glow of prosperity that continued to shine brightly until the onset of the Great Depression. Black Thursday, October 24, 1929, was the day fortunes were lost and the poor became even more impoverished. Coal mines began to close, one-quarter of all factory workers were laid off, farm prices fell, trains were empty, and banks failed.

President Franklin D. Roosevelt's New Deal administration implemented many reforms, including a Works Progress Administration (WPA) and Civilian Conservation Corps (CCC). In Illinois, the CCC provided work for over a hundred thousand laborers, and the WPA employed more than one million more. Together they built or improved many of the state's roads and public recreational areas, such as Black Hawk State Historic Site and Hauberg Indian Museum, near Rock Island (see p. 239).

To counter the effects of the Depression, Chicago decided to mount a huge exposition similar to the one held in 1893. Named "A Century of Progress," its aim was to celebrate the many social, technological, and scientific advances of the past century. Opening in 1933, the exposition lasted two years and drew more than thirty-nine million visitors.

The onset of the Second World War proved to be the economic salvation of the country, but at an unfathomable human cost. Nearly one million men and fourteen thousand women from Illinois were in the armed services; more than twenty-four thousand never returned home. While the military mixed individuals from different ethnic and religious backgrounds within one unit, it remained racially segregated (until 1948). Even the enormous Great Lakes Naval Air Base in Chicago had an all-black training center that was named after a former slave, Camp Robert Smalls. Apparently the navy did not see the irony in the choice of name. Industries once again were operating at full capacity, and a patriotic fervor gripped the nation, uniting it in a single cause, the defeat of its enemy.

Following the war came a mass exodus to the suburbs; housing stocks in the inner cities deteriorated even further, and parks, once the pride of many communities, fell into disuse and decay. Minority groups who moved into the emptying neighborhoods to occupy homes and apartments left by whites reinvigorated sacred spaces that had been abandoned. Houses of worship built by European ethnic groups became home to Hispanic, African American, and Asian congregations. One of the earliest to be transformed, Kehilath Anshe Ma'ariv synagogue (see pp. 113–14) in Chicago, designed in 1891 by Louis Sullivan and Dankmar Adler, has housed an African American congregation, Pilgrim Baptist Church, since 1921. As Chicago's black population rose significantly, from 8 percent in 1940 to nearly 25 percent by 1960, the city's white leadership increased its efforts through urban planning and renewal to control where blacks could live. Expressways were constructed to make the city more accessible to suburban commuters, displacing black residents who already had limited housing options and demolishing many houses of worship. Public housing projects for displaced black families were built in established black ghettos far removed from new jobs that were opening up in the suburbs. Public transportation was inadequate, further ensuring that blacks would not impinge on white neighborhoods or compete for jobs. As a result, public schools were essentially segregated.

1950 TO THE PRESENT

An attempt in 1951 by blacks to move into Cicero triggered a riot that resulted in the governor calling out the National Guard. It was virtually ignored by the local press, who argued that its silence was based on the belief that to report the incident would inflame public opinion and draw more people into the fray. The 1960s saw racial unrest increase nationally as many blacks found their voice in Dr. Martin Luther King, Jr. (1929–68) and the civil rights movement. This happened at the same time that young people began to protest American involvement in Vietnam. The 1968 Democratic Convention in Chicago became the scene of one of the nation's most violent antiwar confrontations ever, with police attacking protestors who were disrupting the convention and trashing the city.

Dr. King visited Chicago in the summer of 1966 hoping to integrate housing. His efforts, although peaceful, led to several violent episodes that resulted in the cancellation of his march through Cicero. Two years later, when King was assassinated, African Americans on Chicago's South Side began to riot, convinced that King's nonviolent approach had failed them. Reverend Jesse Jackson, active in King's Southern Christian Leadership Conference (SCLC), was in Chicago at the time to head the city's branch of Operation Breadbasket, an organization dedicated to improving the financial position of the black community. Shortly after King's death, Jackson left Operation Breadbasket to organize Operation PUSH (People United to Serve Humanity) and the National Rainbow Coalition (see p. 128).

The suburbs, on the other hand, provided people with space—large lots for their homes, yards for their children to play in, double garages for their cars, and vast expanses of land for shopping malls and houses of worship, both set in the midst of asphalt parking lots. No longer did a religious building have to be squeezed into a tight urban setting; now architects had the space, and funding, to design large sprawling edifices that could serve a multitude of purposes. Examples include the Hindu Temple of Greater Chicago in Lemont (see p. 204) and North Shore Congregation Israel in Glencoe (see pp. 186–87). New houses of worship in a vast variety of styles are a hallmark of suburban America. They are also visual evidence of a renewed interest in spirituality that developed following World War II, affirmed by Congress, which passed a law in 1954 to add two words, "under God," to the Pledge of Allegiance.

The farm crisis in the last decades of the twentieth century has led to a decline in rural areas, especially evident in the nation's heartland. Main streets are lined with vacant buildings; houses of worship stand empty as congregations merge due to lack of worshipers and clergy. The countryside has changed, and the farms, market towns, and small, steepled, white clapboard churches are disappearing to be replaced by cookie-cutter super marts and houses of worship that more often resemble bowling alleys than sacred spaces.

Meanwhile, many cities are experiencing a renaissance, including Chicago. The city's population increased 4 percent between 1990 and 2000, and now numbers 2,896,000. Its civic and political leaders have made a concerted effort to improve the city. Parks have been revamped and beautified; vacant buildings renovated for new housing and businesses; streetscapes enhanced with plantings; and high-rise public housing projects are slowly being replaced. As David Perry, director of the Great Cities Institute at the University of Chicago recently remarked: "[Chicago] . . . has its own history of disparities that diversity brings, that it has yet to overcome." But, as anyone who has recently visited the city can attest, it has made enormous strides forward in its effort to become, for all of its citizens, the nation's most livable city.

A Brief History of Some Faith Groups in Illinois

In a letter sent to the Hebrew Congregation of Newport, Rhode Island, in 1790, George Washington pledged that "everyone shall sit under his own vine and fig tree and there shall be none to make him afraid" (Micah 4:4). This pledge became the law of the land with the passage of the First Amendment to the Constitution in December 1791 and has allowed our nation to be graced with a great variety of "vines and fig trees," each representing the beliefs of a group of people who found here the freedom to worship as they chose. The separation of church and state is one of the most revolutionary ideas set forth by the founders of this nation. The waves of people who came to these shores and moved westward with the frontier brought with them their cultures, traditions, and faiths that would have to find expression in a new environment. Many chose to settle with like-minded people, to form a community often centered on a house of worship that served a variety of communal purposes, both sacred and secular. These places provided security in an unknown and often unwelcome environment where indigenous peoples were desperately trying to protect and maintain their own land and spiritual traditions.

By the close of broad immigration in 1924, the nation's racial, ethnic, and religious diversity was well ingrained—a diversity that was unique in the world. Illinois was the recipient of many of the newcomers; the state's population doubled from four million to nearly eight million between 1900 and 1930. Today over twelve and a half million people live in Illinois.

The challenge of living in a new world and the freedom to worship produced an atmosphere where new faiths could develop and old ones could take on new forms. Some new faiths blossomed quickly and then faded; others have become a lasting part of the nation's religious landscape. The United Society of Believers in Christ's Second Coming (the Shakers) has virtually disappeared, but the Church of Jesus Christ of Latter-Day Saints, the Seventh Day Adventists, Jehovah's Witnesses, and the Church of Christ, Scientist claim millions of members. By the first half of the twentieth century, established religious bodies had splintered into numerous fragments, including seventy-five varieties of the Baptist denomination alone. Jewish immigrants in the nineteenth century brought with them Reform and Orthodox Judaism, and the seeds of the Conservative Movement. One other movement emerged in the twentieth century, the Reconstructionist. In the early years of the twentieth century, John Ireland, the first archbishop of the archdiocese of St. Paul and Minneapolis, was in the forefront of Americanizing the Roman Catholic Church. He argued that while the church must "be as thoroughly Catholic in America as it was in Rome . . . it must assume color from [the] local atmosphere, she must be American." To achieve this he would place Irish priests in ethnic parishes where, other than the Latin mass, the homilies, announcements, and devotions would be in English.

In the 1950s most Americans, when asked about their religious preference, said they were Catholic, Protestant, or Jewish. There were also a few Muslims and Buddhists, but immigration restrictions had prevented their numbers from increasing. This changed dramatically with the passage of the Immigration and Naturalization Act of 1965, which resulted in the number of foreign-born residents in the United States at the beginning of the twenty-first century to be greater than it was during the peak immigration years of 1880 through 1924. The fastest growing groups are Hispanics and Asians, who were most underrepresented during the first wave of immigration. At the beginning of the twenty-first century, there are more than fifteen hundred different religious bodies and sects in the United States, demonstrating that Americans take very seriously the rights granted by the First Amendment to the Constitution. All these traditions revitalize the nation's magnificent cultural mosaic, and their houses of worship enhance our communities.

NATIVE AMERICAN SPIRITUALITY

It might be considered inappropriate to refer to Native American beliefs as *religion*, since that term is clearly rooted in Western theology and sets up a distinction between the sacred and the profane. To most Native Americans, such a distinction does not exist; all of life's activities and all of nature, including humans, are interconnected. But just as it is impossible to generalize about any religious belief, so, too, is it impossible to generalize about Native American spirituality. As Ines Hernandez-Avila notes in her essay "Meditations of the Spirit" (in *Native American Spirituality: A Critical Reader*), "There are as many Native American spiritual traditions as there are distinct 'tribes' or nations in this hemisphere. . . . " Echoing other scholars of Native American spirituality, Hernandez-Avila points out that the one tradition Native people do share in common (and which is the basis of much of the discrimination they have faced at the hands of the U.S. government) is their complex relationship to and their reverence for their land that informs their belief systems. By forcibly removing Native Americans from their land, the government effectively undercut their ability to maintain their ceremonial and spiritual life. Four Acts by Congress since 1978 were necessary to give Native Americans the religious freedom promised to all Americans by the First Amendment to the Constitution.

Historically, Native American tribes in the Great Lakes Region share the belief in a supreme being or creator, a variety of lesser spirits, good and evil, and a hero figure that teaches survival skills. They participate in unison prayers for guidance and have shamans who communicate with the spirits and have the power to heal, divine, or prophesize. In some instances, shamans would perform their rites in a "shaking tent," or "conjuring lodge," made of bent saplings and only large enough to hold one individual. According to Peter Nabokov (in *Native American Architecture*), when the shaman enters the tent, he is at the center of the world, where he can make contact between the horizontal world of humans and the vertical world of mythological beings. Onlookers have reported hearing strange sounds issuing from the tent as it sways wildly from side to side. A mystical turtle inside the tent is said to then answer questions presented to it, such as the location of good hunting grounds or what the future holds.

Little remains of the villages encountered by the first Europeans who entered the region in the seventeenth century. Where sites have been discovered, for example, near Starved Rock State Park (see pp. 215–16) and

Kampsville, the government has decided to keep their locations secret to protect them from overzealous tourists. Most of our knowledge of the native people comes from reports written by French explorers and Jesuit and Franciscan missionaries. Although these writers attempted to be objective, it is important to remember that their reports are colored by their religious and cultural biases. They describe a loose confederacy of Algonquian-speaking peoples known as the Illiniwek, from the Algonquian word *illini*, meaning "man." Competing with the Illiniwek for land were refugee tribes, also Algonquian-speaking, who were fleeing south and west from tribal warfare and, later, white settlement. Among the spiritual traditions mentioned is a description of the Potawatomi offering sacrifices in honor of the sun for recovery from illness or for a particular favor. Another report depicts the "feast of dreams," in which dog meat was eaten and the tribe's special *Manitou*, an Algonquian term for "god," was selected. One writer describes a "feast of the dead," probably associated with a funerary ritual. What becomes obvious from these reports is that the explorers and missionaries had little understanding or respect for the spiritual traditions of the people they encountered. Only recently have objective scholarly efforts been made to fully understand the complexities of Native American spirituality and to attempt to explain it to non–Native Americans, but a great divide exists over whom should be teaching about it and how it should be presented.

The spiritual lives of *prehistoric* tribes in the region are better documented, thanks to excavations at two important sites, Cahokia (see p. 282) and Dickson Mounds (see p. 253), where interpretive centers have been built that include evidence of spiritual traditions. There are no known descendants of the indigenous people who occupied these sites; therefore the government is less hesitant to explore them and open them to the public.

In recent years, Native American traditions and rituals have been appropriated by some practitioners of so-called new-age religions. This is not too different from Christian groups who have begun to adopt certain Jewish traditions as a means of connecting to their historic past. However, as well intentioned as these appropriations may be, they remain simply that, appropriations, hollow echoes of hallowed traditions. To experience a true Native American event, you may attend one of the Native American powwows held at the D'Arcy McNickle Center for American Indian History in the Newberry Library, Chicago (see p. 164).

BAHA'I

The Baha'i faith traces its origins to Persia (Iran), where it was founded in 1863 by Mirza Husayn-'Ali (1817–92), known as Baha'u'llah, the "Glory of God." The word *Baha'i* derives from *baha* (glory or splendor) and means a follower of Baha'u'llah. The Baha'i faith is linked to the Babi faith, founded in 1844 by Mirza 'Ali-Muhammed (1819–50), known as the Bab (gate) who was executed for his beliefs by Persian authorities in 1850. Baha'u'llah picked up his mantle declaring he was the messenger of God prophesized by the Bab. He, too, was banished and imprisoned in various places in the Ottoman Empire, until his arrest in 1868 and imprisonment in 'Akka (Acre) for twenty-nine years. He died in 1892, but named his eldest son, 'Abdu'l-Baha (1844–1921) to lead the Baha'i community and to interpret the Baha'i writings. Shoghi Effendi (1896–1957) was his grandfather's successor. Today the affairs of the worldwide Baha'i community are administered by its Universal House of Justice in Haifa, Israel.

There is no clergy in the Baha'i faith. Meetings planned by local communities include devotional services, study classes, discussions, social events, the observation of nine holy days, and a period of fasting at the end of the Baha'i year that begins on the first day of spring. Its central belief is that certain individuals are "the door to divine truth"; these include Moses, Jesus Christ, Muhammad, and Baha'u'llah. The Baha'i faith seeks to bring about the unity of religion, mankind, world peace, and world order. For its members, the number *nine* symbolizes perfection; it appears often in the design of the Baha'i Temple in Wilmette (see pp. 184–85).

According to Baha'i records, the faith has approximately 110,000 adherents in 7,000 localities throughout the United States.

BUDDHISM

Buddha is not a proper name but an honorary title, which means "enlightened one," or "I am awake." Although anyone who achieves complete enlightenment becomes a Buddha, there is only one who is simply known as "the Buddha," Siddhartha Gautama, born around 560 B.C.E. in what is now Nepal. Pious Buddhists refer to him as either *Sakya Muni*, "teacher of the Sakyas," a particular clan, or as *Tathagata*, "Truth-revealer." The preferred name for what is called Buddhism in the West is *Buddhadharma*, "awakening to reality" or "teachings of enlightenment."

The Buddha's early life is masked by many legends, but most scholars believe he was a historical figure. Born into a wealthy family, he lived in luxury until he was twenty-nine, when he experienced what have become known as "the Four Passing Sights" that sent him on his search of enlightenment. First he saw a dying aged man, then a desperately sick man lying by the wayside, and then a funeral pyre that revealed to him that all people are subject to death. Unhappy with his life of empty pleasure, Gautama's fourth sight offered him an escape: It was of a monk whose calm demeanor appealed to him. He renounced his wife, family, and luxurious lifestyle, shaved his head, put on a monk's coarse robe, and vowed to live a religious life. After trying for six years to achieve enlightenment through asceticism, he sat down at the foot of a *bodhi* tree (meaning "enlightenment"), where he began a process of contemplation and meditation that produced his enlightenment. As the Buddha, he spent the rest of his life as an itinerant mendicant missionary preaching to others on how to obtain enlightenment.

The Buddha set forth his convictions about life in what are known as the Four Noble Truths: (1) all life is *dukkha* (suffering); (2) this suffering is caused by selfish desire or craving; (3) the elimination of craving ends suffering; (4) this craving and the suffering that it causes can be overcome by following the Noble Eightfold Path toward achieving Nirvana: right understanding, right thought, right speech, right action, right livelihood, right effort, right mindfulness, and right concentration. These in turn promote and perfect the three essentials of Buddhist training and discipline: ethical conduct, mental discipline, and wisdom. According to tradition, one is considered a Buddhist if "one takes refuge," or sanctuary, in the *Buddha* (the Teacher), the *Dharma* (the Teachings), and the *Sangha* (the Taught, considered the order of monks in the Theravada tradition, or all wisdom seekers who identify as Buddhist in the Mahayana tradition), and if one observes the Five Precepts that are considered the minimum moral obligations of a lay Buddhist. They are: (1) not to destroy life, (2) not to steal, (3) not to commit adultery, (4) not to tell lies, (5) not to take intoxicating drinks. There are no external rites or ceremonies that a Buddhist has to perform; it is a way of life that asks its adherents to follow the Noble Eightfold Path and the Five Precepts. For westerners it is often difficult to understand that Buddhists do not consider "enlightened beings" such as the Buddha, as divine. When the Buddha was asked by two wayfarers, "Are you a heavenly being? A God? An angel?" he responded, "No, I am awake."

Although Chinese and Japanese immigrants brought Buddhism to the United States in the nineteenth century, it wasn't until the 1893 World's Parliament of Religion that Buddhism was formally introduced here, thanks to Dr. Paul Carus, editor of the Open Court Publishing Company in LaSalle (see p. 217). Dr. Carus had attended the Chicago meeting, where he became acquainted with a number of Buddhist scholars whom he invited to La Salle to assist in producing English translations of Buddhist texts, the first to be published in the United States.

All three historical streams of Buddhism are practiced in the United States: the Mahayana of east Asia, which teaches its followers not to pursue Nirvana single-mindedly, but to show love and compassion toward others in order to bring them, too, to Nirvana; Theravada of southern Asia, which teaches that one should pursue Nirvana as the central goal of life; and the Vajrayana of Tibet and central Asia, described by religious scholar Diana Eck as a "complex skein of traditions" that has become popular in recent years because of the high visibility of the Dalai Lama.

Approximately 1.0 percent of the population of Illinois identify as Buddhist. Many more people may participate in Buddhist ceremonies and events but do not consider themselves to be Buddhists.

CHRISTIANITY

Generally, Christianity is divided into three major branches: Catholic, Protestant, and Orthodox. The term *Protestant* is often used as a catch-all to describe those Christian groups that are neither Catholic nor Orthodox. The National Survey of Religious Identification (NSRI), conducted in 1990, lists four types of Protestants: Lutheran; Calvinist or Reformed (e.g., Presbyterian); Episcopalian; and the independent, radical, or free type, which is predominant in the United States. The theological term *evangelicalism* is usually applied to denominations that emphasize an individualized experience of God, biblical centrality, proselytizing, and moral reform. Examples include certain Baptist groups, Adventists, and Pentecostals. During the nineteenth century, evangelicalism characterized many mainline Protestant denominations, including Congregationalist, Presbyterian, Methodist, Baptist, Disciples, and even some Unitarians.

There are hundreds of Christian denominations in the United States. Only those whose places of worship or spiritual spaces are included in this book are discussed here. They are presented in alphabetical order.

Amish

The Amish trace their origin to the late sixteenth century, when a group of Mennonites led by Jakob Amman, a Swiss pastor, split from their church over disciplinary issues. Those who agreed with Amman formed a conservative branch of Mennonites named for him, the Amish, or Old Order Amish. All Mennonites experienced terrible persecution in Europe. Many fled to the New World, where William Penn granted them asylum in his colony.

Amish and Mennonites oppose infant baptism and agree on two fundamental and distinctive beliefs. The first is nonresistance; therefore, most refrain from lawsuits and military service and avoid issues related to racial discrimination. Secondly, God's Headship Order is also a central principle. The practice of Headship Veiling, based on scripture that identifies God as the Head of Christ, Christ as the Head of man, and man as the head of woman, evolves from this principle. For that reason, men worship with their heads uncovered while women always wear a symbolic veiling, called a "covering" that signifies their submission to a "God-ordained order of authority."

The Amish hold formal church services biweekly on a rotating basis in their homes, which are built to double as congregational meeting places. There is no central church authority; each church district has a bishop, two ministers, and a deacon, all selected by lot. They receive no pay or special training. The bishop performs all religious rites such as baptism and marriage.

The first Amish in Illinois began to arrive in the waning years of the Civil War and settled in Douglas County (see pp. 318–19). There are about twenty-four hundred Amish in the area, divided into eighteen church districts.

Baptist

Baptist history is very complex, as expected in a denomination that believes in "theological individualism," where every believer has "absolute liberty under Christ." Baptist groups believe in adult baptism, congregational independence, and the separation of church and state. It began in England among English Separatist clergy who were against the Anglican Church and the divine right of kings and their bishops. One of the most outspoken critics was Roger Williams (1603–83), a former Anglican chaplain who had to migrate to America in 1630 because of his Puritan stance. Williams was a pastor in the Massachusetts colony, until he was banished for preaching in favor of full religious freedom, something Puritan authorities wouldn't tolerate. Along with a handful of his followers, he left to found a new colony, Rhode Island, where they were all rebaptized in 1639. It is from this date that most Baptists trace the beginnings of their movement in America. Today it is the country's largest Protestant denomination.

Baptists gained adherents during the Revolutionary War as the belief in religious freedom spread. Their major growth occurred in the early nineteenth century when the freedom and informality of their services appealed to large numbers of people on the frontier. Major tensions over slavery and missionary funds led to the formation in 1844 of the Southern and Northern Baptist Conventions. The antislavery Northern Baptist Convention, later called the American Baptist Convention (also known as "Missionary Baptist"), eventually split into several theological camps, with various ethnic groups forming independent divisions. The Southern Baptist groups tend to be more theologically conservative than those in the North. For instance, the Primitive or "Old School" Baptists claim to be the "original" Baptists because they still maintain the early Christian church's doctrines and practices.

Many African Americans are Baptist, including the founders of Chicago's Olivet Baptist Church on Martin Luther King, Jr. Drive (see p. 119), thanks to the efforts of Baptist ministers who actively converted former slaves following the Civil War. Autonomous local black churches formed the National Baptist Convention in 1880; it split in 1915 and again in 1961. There are now three national African American Baptist bodies: the National Baptist Convention of the U.S.A. (the largest of the three, with headquarters in Nashville, Tennessee); the National Baptist Convention of America; and the Progressive National Baptist Convention, formed in 1961 by Dr. Martin Luther King, Jr. According to the *Dictionary of American History*, published in 1996, approximately eleven million African Americans are Baptist.

The largest Baptist organization in the United States is the Southern Baptist Convention, numbering sixteen million members, primarily in the South. In Illinois, nearly 15 percent of the population today is Baptist.

Christian Science (Church of Christ, Scientist)

The idea of "mental healing," promoted after the Civil War by a German physician, Franz Anton Mesmer (1733?–1815) was popularized in America by Phineas Parkhurst Quimby (1802–66). One of his patients was Mary Baker Eddy (1821–1910), who consulted him in 1862 about a series of physical and nervous disorders she was experiencing. Mrs. Eddy (at the time she was Mrs. Patterson), however, credited God's healing power, not Quimby's, for her speedy recovery. She began to study spiritual healing, especially in the context of early Christianity, and wrote *Science and Health with Key to the Scriptures*, a book published in 1875 that she felt was divinely inspired. Mrs. Eddy's teachings found many followers and led to the establishment of a church in Boston in 1879. In 1892, the present organization of the church was adopted, and the First Church of Christ, Scientist, in Boston, became the faith's mother church. At the time of Mrs. Eddy's death, the Church of Christ, Scientist numbered over 100,000 members.

Christian Science has no creed or sacraments, but the six Tenets of Christian Science that Mrs. Eddy formulated in her book emphasize the need for both spiritual and physical healing. Mrs. Eddy was in Chicago for the 1893 World's Columbian Exposition, where she saw the beaux-arts style of architecture. The Merchant Tailors Building designed by Solon Beman particularly impressed her. She hired Beman to design the first Church of Christ, Scientist in Chicago (now the Grant Memorial A.M.E. Church) (see p. 120). Completed in 1897, it became the model for many Christian Science churches throughout the country.

The Church of Jesus Christ of Latter-Day Saints (Mormon)

In 1820, at a time of religious ferment and frontier revivalism, a fourteen-year-old boy, Joseph Smith, Jr., living near Palmyra, New York, beheld a vision of God and Jesus who told him that all churches were in error and that the true gospel would be restored through him. Mormons believe that Smith was guided by the Angel Moroni to a site where he discovered buried gold plates written with the history of two people, the Nephites and the Lamanites and their descendants, who were members of lost tribes of ancient Israel who had migrated to the North American continent long before the birth of Christ. Furthermore, according to Smith, the plates revealed that Christ had appeared to these people following his resurrection and established the true church in America. The Lamanites and Nephites ended up destroying one another, the only survivors being Mormon and his son Moroni, who wrote their history on the gold plates and buried them. Using seer stones named Urim and Thummim given to him by Moroni, Smith was able to translate the plates into what became *The Book of Mormon*, published in 1830.

Smith and his followers accept *The Book of Mormon* and the Bible as scripture, as well as two other documents, the *Pearl of Great Price,* and the *Doctrine and Covenants.* Mormons see America as the new Zion and consider it their duty to make this country the center of God's activity. Pioneers were attracted by the Mormons' optimistic beliefs that suggest people have a spiritual existence before earth-life, that life after death is a state of progress, first in the spirit world and later in the resurrected state, and that people may progress eternally and become perfected. The faith grew rapidly, too rapidly for some, resulting in their persecution and the destruction of their temple in Nauvoo (see p. 258), the site of Illinois' first Mormon community, and Joseph and Hyrum Smith's murder by an angry mob in nearby Carthage (see p. 256). Of the many millennial and utopian communities and movements formed in the nineteenth century, only the Mormons have survived and flourished. Credit for this must be given in great part to the missionary efforts of thousands of both young Mormon men who commit two years and women who commit eighteen months of their lives to evangelizing throughout the world. There are over five million Mormons in the United States; most live in Utah and neighboring states. Forty-five thousand are in Illinois, where they comprise .03 percent of the population.

Community of Christ (Reorganized Church of Jesus Christ of Latter Day Saints)

On April 6, 2001, the Reorganized Church of Jesus Christ of Latter Day Saints (RLDS) officially changed its name to "Community of Christ" in order to establish its identity separate from the Church of Jesus Christ of Latter-Day Saints, the Mormons. Both faiths trace their origins to Joseph Smith, Jr.; however, the founders of the RLDS believe that Smith had designated his eldest son, Joseph III, not Brigham Young, to be his successor as president of the church. Another major reason for the split was Joseph Smith's first wife's opposition to the practice of polygamy.

With its origin in Illinois, one of the faith's earliest churches is the Plano Stone Church, erected in 1868, which served as the headquarters of the RLDS church and its central house of worship until 1881 (see pp. 211–12). Since 1920, the headquarters of the church has been in Independence, Missouri. Today the Community of Christ ordains women and no longer requires that its president be a descendant of Joseph Smith; it has about 137,000 members, mainly in the United States.

Congregational (United Church of Christ)

The Congregational Christian Church and the Evangelical and Reformed Church merged in 1957 to form a new denomination: the United Church of Christ. Although the two denominations originated in different areas of Europe and have different Reformed traditions, both are covenanting rather than creedal denominations. This means that they emphasize personal commitments (covenants) to God and other people over binding statements of creed or belief. Each congregation elects a council (presbyters or elders) to deal with its affairs and, if it so desires, to formulate its own confession. There are three further levels of organization, with the highest being the General Synod. There is no set form of worship, with services ranging from nonliturgical to liturgical and generally including prayers, hymns, and music, sermons, offerings, and Bible readings.

Congregationalists are the direct ecclesiastical descendants of British nonconformist Protestants who agitated for reform of the Church of England in the late sixteenth century. Persecuted by the established church as Separatists, the Pilgrims (what they called themselves) fled to the Netherlands before crossing the Atlantic on the Mayflower to found the theocratic colony of Plymouth in 1620. Joining them in 1628 were Puritans who went on to establish the Massachusetts Bay Colony in Salem and later the city of Boston. The Puritans, unlike the Pilgrims, did not consider themselves Separatists, but rather reformers who wanted to "purify" the Church of England of elements of Catholicism. Once in the New World they set about to establish a new "Israel," a holy commonwealth that would welcome like-minded individuals. Those who did not share their views were ostracized, as was the case with Roger Williams (see p. 40). In the new Zion there was to be no distinction between church and state. Their houses of worship were "meetinghouses" to distinguish them from elaborate Anglican churches, and were used for a variety of purposes, sacred and secular. The congregation, not clergy or a board, were in control of affairs, thus the term "Congregational." Because of their autonomous organizational structure, the Puritans, later renamed Congregationalists, often found themselves in conflict with one another, as well as with other Protestant denominations. As a result, a series of schisms affected the denomination's growth.

The early histories of the Congregational and Presbyterian (see p. 52) denominations in Illinois are closely related. The migration of New Englanders into the Old Northwest Territory following the Revolutionary War resulted in "the first sustained church union efforts in American religious history." The Plan of Union (1801–52) joined together New England's two leading denominations, the Presbyterian and the Congregational, so their members in sparsely populated areas could establish congregations and have clergy of either denomination. The Union was not harmonious, especially when it came to the issue of slavery. The Presbyterians were far more tolerant of the practice than the Congregationalists. Ultimately the Union was rejected by both groups, mainly because the Congregationalists feared the Presbyterians were absorbing too many of their members.

There are 185,000 UCC members in Illinois today, constituting about 1.4 percent of the population.

Eastern Orthodox

Eastern Orthodoxy developed from the Church of the Byzantine Empire and the system of Pentarchy established at the Council of Chalcedon in 451. The five ancient patriarchates were Constantinople, Alexandria, Antioch, Jerusalem, and Rome. The Western church's addition of a clause to the Nicene Creed without the approval of Eastern Christian church authorities caused a schism that separated the Christian world into two entities: the Eastern Orthodox Byzantine Empire with its ecumenical patriarch in Constantinople, and the Holy Roman Empire led by the bishop of Rome, the pope. Any hope of uniting the two halves was effectively extinguished in 1204 when soldiers of the Fourth Crusade ransacked Constantinople just as violently as they had looted and destroyed non-Christian cities. The Catholic and Orthodox faiths still remain separate; however, steps have been made toward healing the rift. In 2001, during the first visit to Greece by a Roman Catholic pope in more than a millennium, Pope John Paul II formally apologized for the sacking of Constantinople.

The first Eastern Orthodox Christians in America were Greeks, recruited in 1763 to labor on a plantation in what is now Florida. Russian Orthodox missionaries who erected a church on the Kodiak Archipelago in Alaska in 1794 established the first permanent Orthodox community in North America.

The major migration of Orthodox Christians to America was a result of political and economic upheavals in Russia and the Balkans in the late nineteenth century. More Orthodox immigrants arrived following the

1917 Bolshevik Revolution, which all but extinguished their faith in their homelands. Many settled in Chicago where they found jobs in the stockyards and factories. Although most were poor, they pooled their resources to erect beautiful churches that still glorify many of the city's neighborhoods.

According to Jaroslav Pelikan (in his essay in *World Religions in America*), there are as many as twenty-five or more jurisdictions of Orthodox Christians in America; most echo their ethnic origins. They range in size from the Albanian Orthodox Diocese of America (with just over two thousand members in 2000), to the Greek Orthodox Archdiocese of North and South America with two million members. Accorded a special position of honor within all Orthodox churches is the ecumenical patriarch of Constantinople, although he has no authority to interfere with the governance of the many "autocephalous" (self-ruling) Orthodox churches.

Except for Greek Orthodox churches that remain bilingual, most Orthodox churches in America conduct their services in English and serve a mostly English-speaking constituency. In the years since 1970, when the newly established Orthodox Church in America (the former Russian Orthodox Greek Catholic Church of North America) ordered the transition from Old Church Slavonic to English, Orthodoxy in the United States has become a diverse religious movement.

The Orthodox Divine Liturgy portrays the splendor and mystery of heaven and appeals to all the senses: sight, hearing, touch, taste, and smell. Church interiors are beautifully decorated with icons, perfumed with incense, lighted with candles, and services are chanted or sung. Icons are perhaps the most notable feature in an Orthodox church and are considered a visual form of prayer and preaching. They are, to quote one Orthodox priest, a "window to heaven." Services can be several hours long; traditionally, worshipers stand, although most Orthodox churches in the United States now have pews. Most Orthodox congregations still follow the Julian calendar (replaced in 1582 in the West by the Gregorian calendar), which runs currently nearly two weeks behind the Gregorian. Thus they celebrate holidays such as Easter and Christmas at different dates than other Christian faiths.

Coauthored by Jana Riess

Episcopalian (Anglican)

A decade after Martin Luther (see p. 48) hammered his 95 Theses to the door of a church in Wittenberg, Germany, in 1517, King Henry VIII

(r. 1509–47) precipitated the English Reformation by demanding a divorce from his first wife, Catherine of Aragon. Because the pope would not grant one, Henry separated from the Roman Catholic Church to form the Church of England, or Anglican Church. As its "supreme head," Henry closed all English monasteries, confiscated church land, and cut all ties with Rome. Although his eldest daughter, Mary Tudor, tried valiantly to restore Catholicism during her brief reign (1553–58), it was the "Middle Way" of her sister Elizabeth I (r. 1558–1603) that consolidated the Church of England as a separate ecclesiastical body. Under Elizabeth's steady hand the spirit of the Reformation moved slowly forward and resulted in a simplification of the service, the translation of the Bible into English, and the creation of a new prayer book, *The Book of Common Prayer.* The Anglican Church condoned married clergy and altered the Catholic concept of transubstantiation (the miraculous transformation of the wine and bread into the blood and body of Christ).

Anglican colonists in the New World were not seeking asylum from religious persecution. While their individual motives may have varied, most compelling was their desire to exploit and control the New World. While some effort was made to evangelize Native Americans and African American slaves, clergy mainly served the colonists' own religious needs. Anglicans generally avoided settling in northern colonies occupied by the Puritans; instead they established colonies in the South, where the first Anglican church in the New World was organized in 1607 in Jamestown, Virginia. Most Anglicans remained loyal to the English king during the American Revolution (1776–83) and many fled to Canada and the Caribbean following the war's outcome. Those who remained had to redefine their faith and display their loyalty to the new republic. Anglican churches and institutions in the United States were renamed; King's College in New York, for example, named in honor of the king of England, became Columbia University, in commemoration of Christopher Columbus. Even the denomination's name was changed to the Episcopal Church of America. *Episcopal* comes from the Greek word *episkopos* meaning "bishop" and refers to the denomination's form of governance by bishops. Thus, they could assure Americans that this was a church ruled by bishops, not by a foreign king.

Services in Episcopal churches are considered "liturgical"—the focus of the Sunday worship is the eucharist (holy communion), which follows the pattern of the Roman Catholic mass, and can be fairly elaborate (see p. 53). Episcopal churches are generally adorned with stained-glass windows, elaborate altars and fonts, and other embellishments. Similar to their

Catholic counterparts, clergy wear symbolically colored vestments. Episcopalians accept two sacraments: baptism (infants and adults) and holy communion.

Many of Illinois' early civic leaders were Episcopalian, including those who erected the Cathedral of St. James, the oldest Episcopal Church in Chicago (see pp. 162–63). Although Episcopalians had a great deal of economic and political clout in the development of Illinois, today they comprise less than 1 percent of the state's population.

Coauthored by Jana Riess

Lutheran

Martin Luther (1483–1546) was ordained a priest in the Roman Catholic Augustinian order in 1507. As a young monk he journeyed to Rome, where he encountered what he viewed as the excesses of the papacy, including the building of a new St. Peter's Basilica. Luther was upset by the sale of indulgences (a certificate bearing the seal of the church, guaranteeing the purchaser absolution, that is, forgiveness of sins) by professional "pardon peddlers." To spark a public debate on the topic, in 1517 Luther posted on a church door in Wittenberg, Germany, his famed 95 Theses, stating in effect that indulgences were designed only to raise money for the church and could not provide absolution. Sin, Luther argued, could only be overcome through personal repentance, because only God grants forgiveness. It was this doctrine, "justification by faith," that became the basic teaching of Protestantism. It may not have been Luther's intention to pour new wine into old skins, but that he did, and subsequently set in motion the Christian church's second major schism. (The first major schism is discussed on p. 45.)

Luther was excommunicated in 1521, but many secular rulers in northern Germany and Scandinavia, eager to free themselves of the political influence of the pope and the Holy Roman Emperor, supported his "reformation." Before long, Lutheranism became the state religion of Denmark, Norway, Sweden, Finland, Iceland, Estonia, Latvia, and several northern German states, and gathered followers in other parts of central Europe.

While Dutch Lutherans were in the New World as early as 1619, it was not until the nineteenth century, with the arrival of large numbers of Scandinavian and German immigrants, that the Lutheran faith grew rapidly in the United States. The first Lutherans in Illinois were German Americans from North Carolina who settled in Union County, where they established St. John's Church at Dongola near Jonesboro, in 1816 (see pp. 304–5).

Lutheran worship is liturgical (see p. 83) and retains several of the sacraments of the Roman Catholic Church, including the two major ones: baptism (infants and adults) and holy communion (see p. 53). The church administration format is a mixture of Congregational, Presbyterian, and Episcopal concepts. That is, pastors are called and elected by the local congregation and administer the church with lay leaders. They meet annually in synods, which correspond to geographical regions, like states, chaired by an elected president or bishop. In 1900 there were twenty-four separate Lutheran church organizations in America. Today many have merged; among the most well known are the liberal Evangelical Lutheran Church in America and the more conservative Lutheran Church-Missouri Synod.

About 4.6 percent of the population of Illinois is affiliated with a Lutheran congregation.

Methodist

The founder of Methodism was John Wesley (1703–91), an Anglican priest who wanted to make the Church of England more responsive to the needs of the poorer classes. Wesley and his brother Charles formed the Holy Club at Oxford University in 1729, whose members were called Methodists because of their methodical study and prayer habits. Their goal was to achieve individual perfection through prayer and acts of charity, which would lead to a more perfect society, but these efforts left Wesley unsatisfied. He undertook a missionary journey to Georgia in the hope that contact with Native Americans would help him in his quest. Instead, he came under the influence of a group of Moravians (a reform movement that began in Prague in the fifteenth century), who told him that to be a true Christian it was necessary to personally experience inner conversion. Wesley returned to England, and on May 24, 1738, he (and several days later his brother Charles) had a religious experience in which Christ appeared to him and, as he described it, "I felt I could trust in Christ alone for my salvation . . . and that he had taken away my sins. . . ." The Wesley brothers immediately set out to persuade others, particularly the poor, to share in their religious experience. They preached in open fields or barns after being closed out of Anglican churches because the clergy distrusted their message. As the movement grew, Methodist societies were formed for prayer and strict religious living. A leader was selected for each society to supervise the members' spiritual growth. The separate societies constituted a circuit and were under the supervision of a lay preacher. This was the beginning of the circuit-riding minister, a custom that was later transferred to the American frontier. Wesley, who began to ordain ministers in 1784, preached a gospel of social justice and developed the "Methodist Discipline," which banned among other things smoking, drinking, theater-going, and dancing. By the time of Wesley's death, he left behind a movement that continued to grow in numbers and influence. Soon the Anglican Church denied Methodists the right of taking communion, and the movement then became a separate denomination.

Methodism in the United States has undergone many splits, mergers, and name changes since the ministry of Francis Asbury (1771–1816), considered the founder of American Methodism. The first Methodist Episcopal church in the New World was organized in Baltimore in 1784. Methodist circuit-riding ministers carried the gospel on horseback throughout the young nation, reaching out to isolated, and often unchurched, settlers along the frontier with their "tent meetings," which were part religious revival and part social gathering. They took place in Illinois as early as 1793, and by 1803 a regular circuit had been formed. Three years later the state's first Methodist church was built in Madison County. Although the early Methodists opposed slavery and demanded the gradual emancipation of slaves, Methodists from the South defended slavery and formed the Methodist Episcopal Church, South, in 1844.

In 1939 the Methodist Episcopal Church, the Methodist Episcopal Church, South, and the nonepiscopal Methodist Protestant Church united and organized the Methodist Church, which accounted for about 85 percent of all American Methodists at the time. The merger did not include the three major African American Methodist denominations (see below). Finally, in 1968, the Methodist Church and the Evangelical United Brethren merged to form the United Methodist Church. Now the second largest Protestant denomination in the United States with nearly nine million members, it accounts for 3 percent of the population of Illinois.

Personal religious experience is more important to Methodists than doctrine or creeds. Methodist churches vary from being somewhat liturgical to a much more informal type of worship. Most Methodists believe in the Trinity, the Virgin birth, and divine judgment after death. Two sacraments are observed: baptism (infants and adults) and holy communion. Methodist services emphasize preaching and music; thus the focus in a Methodist church is on the pulpit, organ, and choir.

AFRICAN AMERICAN METHODIST DENOMINATIONS

The independent African American church movement began soon after the Revolutionary War among freed slaves in northern cities. Because many established white congregations retained racist attitudes, African Americans established their own denominations. The African Methodist Episcopal Church (A.M.E.) was the nation's first independent black denomination. It dates back to 1787, when blacks in Philadelphia under the leadership of Richard Allen (1760–1831) and Absalom Jones withdrew from a Methodist church because they were not allowed to worship together with its white members. In 1793, Allen purchased an abandoned blacksmith shop and transformed it into Bethel Church, using its blacksmith anvil as a pulpit; the anvil has since become the symbol of the A.M.E. Church. A year later, Francis Asbury (see p. 50) dedicated the building as a church and ordained Allen. However, it wasn't until 1816 that Allen and his followers gained legal control over their property and independence over their internal affairs. It was then that the A.M.E. denomination was officially formed and Allen consecrated as its first bishop. Quinn Chapel is the first A.M.E. church in Illinois (see p. 111). In 1993 the A.M.E. Church had a membership of more than 2.5 million nationwide.

The African Methodist Episcopal Zion Church (A.M.E. Zion) began in 1796 in New York City, a result of racial segregation in the city's churches. The A.M.E. Zion Church became known as the "freedom church" because of the many black abolitionists who joined it, including Harriet Tubman and Frederick Douglass. Furthermore, it was the first Methodist church to ordain women. In 1993 it had a membership of 1.2 million nationwide.

In the south, the Colored Methodist Episcopal Church (C.M.E.C.) split off from the Methodist Episcopal Church, South in 1845 over the issue of slavery. In 1954 the denomination changed its name from "Colored" to "Christian." The C.M.E.C. has over 750,000 members.

All three denominations remain separate from the United Methodist Church.

Presbyterian

Presbyterians trace their origin to John Calvin (1509–64), a young Frenchman who wanted to become a priest but, influenced by the teachings of Martin Luther, chose instead to join the Reformation. Forced to flee France, he settled in Geneva, Switzerland, where he established his own religious community and wrote what has been described as "the masterpiece of Protestant religious thought," his *Institutes of the Christian Religion*. John Knox (1505–72), a Scotsman and a former Roman Catholic priest who was persecuted by Queen Mary for his "heretic" beliefs, fled to Geneva where he encountered Calvin's theology. Upon his return to Scotland in 1559 (after Mary's demise), he was able to convince the Scottish parliament to abolish Roman Catholicism and declare Presbyterianism the state religion.

The denomination's name reflects its system of government, since it is led by a group of elders, or presbyters. Scottish and Scotch-Irish immigrants who settled in the Upland South areas brought Knox's belief system to America. Several schisms occurred within the Presbyterian Church in the United States. One was a result of the Second Awakening (see pp. 9–10). A group of ministers who were not trained in a seminary formed the Cumberland Presbyterian Church, which not only stressed evangelism but also refuted having a centralized authority. A second schism was due to the battle over slavery and ultimately resulted in the formation of the Presbyterian Church in the Confederate States in 1861 (also known as the Presbyterian Church in the U.S.).

Presbyterians practice the sacraments of baptism (infants and adults) and holy communion. Preaching is emphasized, and several official publications provide suggestions and resources for worship. However, each local church can select its material and, as a result, there are wide variations in the way Presbyterian services are conducted.

Many of Illinois' wealthiest and most prominent families were Presbyterian; they now comprise 1.2 percent of the state's population.

Roman Catholic

Andrew Greeley, the well-known Catholic theologian and writer from Chicago, cautions: "A good rule of thumb for an outsider is that if you think you have finally figured Catholics out, you've almost certainly got it wrong." Even "insiders" often have a difficult time understanding their very complex faith—a faith that is truly global, embracing a vast variety of cultures and traditions under one very large umbrella, which is formally called the Holy Catholic Apostolic Roman Church.

Roman Catholics believe that Jesus founded the institution of the church when he gave the keys of heaven and earth to the apostle Peter. The Roman Catholic Church in general, and the pope in particular, is believed to be the successor of Peter. The great schism of 1054 split the church in two: Roman Catholic in the West and Eastern Orthodox in the East (see pp. 45–46). However, while most Roman Catholics today follow the Latin, or Western, Rite, there are about twenty jurisdictions of Eastern Rite Catholics. They hold identical beliefs and recognize the authority of the pope but differ in language, liturgy, customs, and tradition.

Although Catholicism was the first Christian faith to enter the New World (see pp. 2–3), Catholics were not welcomed in the original colonies, except for Maryland, which was founded in 1631 by a Catholic, George Calvert, first baron of Baltimore. It was through the efforts of John Carroll (1735–1815) of Maryland, the nation's first Catholic bishop, that more Catholics began to arrive. Their numbers increased dramatically in the nineteenth century, a result of the potato famine in Ireland and upheavals in continental Europe. Each ethnic group would establish its own national parish where its particular customs and traditions could be retained and the mother tongue spoken. In an effort to unify the Catholic Church in America, a change was made in canon law in 1918 that put an end to national or ethnic parishes. According to Greeley, five major ethnic groups account for 80 percent of the Catholic population in the United States today: Irish, German, Italian, Polish, and Hispanic (mainly Mexican, Puerto Rican, Dominican, and Cuban). There are more than 62 million Roman Catholics in the United States, by far the largest Christian denomination; over three million reside in Illinois.

Roman Catholics believe that God is one but is trinitarian in nature (the Father, Son, and the Holy Spirit are one being). There are seven sacraments: baptism (infants and adults), holy communion (the eucharist), reconciliation, confirmation, marriage, holy orders, and anointing of the sick. When Roman Catholics receive holy communion, they believe that Christ's body and blood are actually present. Catholic worship is liturgical; mass is the major service; its two central parts are the Liturgy of the Word (Bible readings, homily, Nicene Creed, Prayer of the Faithful) and the Liturgy of the Eucharist.

Priests are appointed by bishops or archbishops and have authority to celebrate mass and administer sacraments in a parish. A bishop rules a regional area called a diocese, and an archbishop rules a still larger area called an archdiocese. The Vatican appoints both bishops and arch-bishops.

Unitarian Universalist

The Unitarian Universalist Association was formed in 1961 by the union of two separate but parallel traditions—the Unitarian and the Universalist. Ethical living, humanitarianism, and cultural development are emphasized, with respect for human dignity and diversity. The Unitarians can trace their beginnings back to a sixteenth-century Spanish physician in Geneva, Switzerland, Michael Sevetus (1511–53), who maintained that the doctrine of the Trinity was wrong; there was only one God, and Jesus was simply a manifestation of God and the Holy Spirit. Thus the term *Unitarian*. He published his views and was attacked by both Catholics and Protestants. John Calvin (see p. 52) was responsible for his being burned at the stake in Geneva in 1553 for his Unitarian "heresy." Others took up his cause, including John Sigismund (1540–71), the ruler of Hungary. By 1600 that country had over four hundred Unitarian churches. From there Unitarianism spread throughout Europe.

In England the Crown persecuted its followers, including the scientist and Unitarian preacher Joseph Priestley, who fled to America in 1791 where he began to establish Unitarian churches in the Philadelphia area. Unitarianism found a receptive audience among followers of Deism and disenchanted Congregationalists (see p. 44). The Deists, who included Thomas Jefferson and Benjamin Franklin, believed in a "natural religion" that eliminated the so-called miraculous elements in Christianity. They argued that a rational God had established a world that operated according to reasonable "laws of nature." Deism, however, was limited to a small group of intellectuals. Unitarians found a much larger and receptive audience among liberal Protestants, especially in New England, where many Congregationalists disliked their denomination's increasingly conservative theology. In 1786, Boston's leading Anglican (Episcopalian) church, King's Chapel, changed its affiliation to become the first Unitarian congregation in America. By 1819, the Unitarians became a distinct denomination and in 1825 they formed the American Unitarian Association.

Unitarians were mainly well-educated, urban New Englanders, whereas the Universalists, who shared many of their beliefs, came from rural areas. Universalism began developing in Europe at the same time as Unitarianism. It, too, was a reaction to the Calvinistic belief that some people are "elected" by God to be saved. John Murray (1741–1815), an

English preacher who arrived in Massachusetts in 1770, was instrumental in gathering followers of Universalism into a distinct denomination in 1785 under the name of the "Independent Christian Society commonly called Universalists." The denomination's greatest leader in the nineteenth century was Hosea Ballou (1771–1852), who shared many theological views with Unitarians. It was said at the time that Unitarians believed "that man is too good to be eternally damned, while Universalists taught that God is too good to damn man eternally."

The first Unitarian church in Illinois was organized in Geneva in 1834 (see pp. 209–10); one of the earliest Universalist churches in the state is in Table Grove, organized in 1869 (see pp. 255–56); both remain active. Perhaps the nation's most famous Unitarian church is Unity Temple in Oak Park, designed by Frank Lloyd Wright and completed in 1909 (see pp. 194–96). Today about eight thousand Unitarian Universalists reside in Illinois.

HINDUISM

Americans were officially introduced to one of the world's oldest religions at the Parliament of World's Religions held in Chicago in 1893. Hinduism originated among sages in the Indus Valley region of ancient India around 4000 B.C.E. The origins of the faith's name remain unclear. One theory posits that the word *Hinduism* was something of a Western construct, used by Western tourists to describe the diverse religious traditions they observed while traveling in India. Another theory suggests the name was taken from the great Indus River, from which the name *India* is derived. Approximately 85 percent of India's population is Hindu, although exactly what *Hindu* means varies greatly from region to region.

Hinduism has been described as consisting of almost every form of religious expression and belief, while at the same time lacking many of the elements westerners associate with religion: a historical founder, a highly organized clergy or priesthood, and a required creed of beliefs. According to Hindus, their religion has no origin or beginning; it is eternal and is made up of the contributions of many cultures and peoples. New ideas and practices were absorbed into it and modified over thousands of years.

In its earliest form, Hindu practices included a respect for animals and plant life, a mother goddess cult that stressed the feminine element, and purification through water by bathing in a temple tank. Later, during what is called the Vedic Period (1400–500 B.C.E.), Aryan tribes who entered India introduced the concept of passage in one's life: birth, becoming an adult, marriage, and death. Considered the greatest contribution of this period are the *Vedas*, meaning "knowledge," sacred texts that are considered eternal. All Hindus accept them as authoritative. The most important section of the *Vedas*, the *Upanishads*, deals with questions about the meaning of life and the nature of the universe. They discuss the relation between *Brahman*, the life source (the ultimate reality or universal self) and the *atman* or inner self. The nature of this relationship has always allowed a variety of religious interpretations, including *samsara* (reincarnation, or the act of being born again) and *karma* (the effects that thoughts, words, and deeds have on a person's past, present, and future). The ultimate goal for Hindus is to gain release from the cycle of reincarnation and to achieve unity with Brahman. A variety of methods have developed to accomplish this goal, including meditation, ritual acts, and yoga. The *Bhagavad-Gita* (Song of the Blessed Lord) was written sometime between approximately 200 B.C.E. and 300 C.E. as a means of synthesizing these different methods, endorsing *bhakti* (devotionalism) as the best means to achieve salvation. However, Hindus will usually combine different elements from this sacred tradition to form their own personal religious devotion, thus the great variety of Hindu practices.

An important element in Hinduism is the worship of personal gods who are viewed as alternative aspects or manifestations of Brahman. Temples house images of these gods who are treated as living persons: priests clothe, feed, and bathe them, all symbolic acts that have an inner spiritual significance. Hinduism mixes ancient folk belief with a sophisticated hierarchy of deities. Besides Brahman, the creator god, there are two other chief Hindu gods: Vishnu, the preserver, and Shiva, the creator and destroyer. Together the three gods are referred to as the "three basic forms" of the Ultimate or Absolute.

The cow is considered a sacred animal (although it is honored, but not worshiped), and dairy products are believed to purify the body and the spirit. Hindus do not eat beef or wear leather clothing; many are complete vegetarians (vegans).

Swami Vivehananda, a disciple of the Hindu mystic of Calcutta, Sri Ramakrishna, spoke at the 1893 meeting in Chicago about the need for a unity of religions, and stated that "the Lord has declared to the Hindu in his incarnation as Krishna, 'I am in every religion as the thread through a string of pearls.'" These words resonated with those who were seeking religious harmony in a nation where xenophobia and prejudice were rampant. Vivehananda traveled throughout the United States, speaking to large, receptive audiences about Hindu spirituality and the practice of yoga. Two results of his travels were the formation of the Vedanta Society, the nation's first Hindu organization, and the erection in 1906 in San Francisco of the first Hindu temple in North America. A statue of Vivehananda can be found on the grounds of the Hindu Temple of Greater Chicago in Lemont (see p. 204).

Approximately 560,000 Hindus live in the United States.

Coauthored by Jana Riess

ISLAM

If the rapid growth of Islam in the United States continues, it will soon become the nation's second largest religion while remaining, perhaps, the most misunderstood. *Arab* and *Muslim* are not synonymous terms; not all Arabs are Muslims, and not all Muslims are Arabs. In fact, most Muslims are *not* Arabs; the majority are Asian and African, with the largest Muslim population found in Indonesia. Islam, like Christianity and Judaism, is a "revealed" religion, as God revealed himself to the prophet Muhammad through the angel Gabriel. Furthermore, Muslims worship the same God as Jews and Christians and also recognize the biblical prophets. Like the two other monotheistic faiths, Islam, too, has its origins in the Middle East and, likewise, it has spread throughout the world, embracing people of many races and ethnic groups. Like Judaism and Christianity, Islam includes several branches or sects (movements in Judaism; denominations in Christianity). The two major ones are the Sunni, who comprise about 85 percent of Muslims and who believe the caliphate should not be limited to the heirs of Muhammad, and the Shii (or Shiite), who account for 15 percent and believe only descendants of the Prophet can be the true spiritual leader. Sufism, the mystical tradition within Islam, has been called "the religion of the heart," since it places a paramount emphasis on the devotee's relationship with the divine. It is not a separate sect of Islam, but is suffused throughout the entire tradition. Except for followers of American Sufism, who often retain their own religious traditions, all Muslims share a common faith in Allah (God) and follow the teachings of his prophet, Muhammad (570–632 C.E.), who was born in Mecca, in what is now Saudi Arabia, and later was forced to move to Medina. The term *Islam* means "peace" or "submission [to God's will]" and the word *Muslim* means "one who submits [to God's will]."

A number of the African slaves brought to the New World by Spanish explorers were Muslim, making Islam, along with Catholicism, the first of two non-native religions to enter America nearly a century before the Puritans arrived. Scholars have estimated that as many as a tenth of the African slaves who were brought to North America from the sixteenth to the nineteenth centuries were Muslims. However, religions of any sort, including traditional African or Muslim, were discouraged among slaves, resulting in the suppression of many of their beliefs. It wasn't until the 1893 World's Parliament of Religions meeting in Chicago that Americans heard a Muslim speaker—an American, Mohammed Russell Alexander Webb, the son of an upstate New York newspaper publisher, who converted to Islam in 1887 after coming in contact with the faith while on an extended stay in the Philippines. In 1889 Webb began editing and publishing the periodical *The Moslem World*.

In the late 1890s, Arab immigrants, mainly Christians from areas of Greater Syria, began to arrive in the United States. Cedar Rapids, Iowa, became home to a small Christian Arab community that grew with the arrival of a group of Arab Muslims in about 1910. Other Muslim Arabs settled in the small town of Ross, North Dakota, where the nation's first known mosque was erected in 1925; it has since been demolished. The Muslims in Cedar Rapids formed the Rose of Fraternity Society in 1925 to maintain their religious and cultural traditions, and built a mosque in 1934 that is now considered the "Mother Mosque in North America." From this small beginning in two farm communities in the Midwest, Muslims have spread to every corner of the nation; their mosques and minarets add another silhouette to our nation's religious landscape.

In the 1930s a new generation of African Americans began to embrace Islam. One of many African American Muslim movements, the Nation of Islam, was founded by Wallace D. Fard, also known as Wali Farad or Farrad Muhammad, in Detroit in 1930. It was not considered to be legitimate Islam by Sunni Muslims until the 1970s when Wallace D. Muhammad reversed his father's stance and totally changed the tenor of the movement. He called it the World Community of Al-Islam in the West (this is no longer its name) and merged it into the larger rubric of Sunni Islam. The Nation of Islam also continued, although the vast majority of followers chose to follow Wallace D. Muhammad instead of Louis Farrakhan. Islam began to flourish in oppressed black communities, where it has undergone many changes over the years, due to internal conflicts and divisions. Today, according to Diana Eck, African Americans constitute somewhere between 25 and 40 percent of all Muslims in America.

Revelations received by Muhammad from the angel Gabriel and

recorded in the Qur'an, Islam's sacred book, assure believers of the reward of heaven by observing five duties, considered the "Five Pillars of Islam": (1) A profession of faith, the *shahada*: "There is no God but God and Muhammad is the Prophet (or messenger) of God." (2) Prayer or worship (*salat*): Muslims worship God five times each day at a designated time. They pray alone or in groups. Only on Friday are they expected to perform the noon prayer in a congregation. (3) Almsgiving (*zakat*): Those who have are expected to share with those in need. (4) Fasting (*sawm* or *siyam*): All adult Muslims who are physically able fast during the month of Ramadan. This is a time of reflection and discipline, to thank God for his blessings, repent, and atone for one's sins. There is no eating or drinking from dawn to dusk. (5) Pilgrimage to Mecca (*hajj*): Every Muslim who is capable is obliged to make at least one pilgrimage during his or her lifetime to the cities of Mecca and Medina in Saudi Arabia.

Islam has no clergy in the Western sense. The *imam* ("the one who proceeds") leads the congregation in prayer. There are particular ceremonies related to life-cycle events, including circumcision of all males. Animals are ritually slaughtered, and Muslims are prohibited from drinking wine or other intoxicating beverages or eating pork.

There are no accurate current population figures for Muslims in America; the numbers range from nearly four million to seven million. They worship in more than twelve hundred mosques. About two-thirds of the American Muslim population are immigrants or descendants of Muslims who came to America from overseas, most recently from areas in the Middle East, Pakistan, Bangladesh, and Malaysia. The Chicago area has approximately twenty-seven Islamic Centers serving more than 150,000 Muslims. Muslims comprise 1.0 percent of the state's population.

Coauthored by Jana Riess

JAINISM AND SIKHISM

Jains trace their origins back to the sages of ancient India who lived in the Indus Valley region of northwestern India over four thousand years ago. According to Jain belief, there were twenty-four great teachers, the last of whom was Lord Mahavira, who lived during the sixth century B.C.E. These teachers, called *Tirthankaras*, preached their acquired knowledge to the people; as a result Jains do not believe in one supreme being. They believe in reincarnation, with their souls taking on different lives in the continuous cycle of birth, death, and rebirth. The only way to break the cycle and to find eternal rest is to get rid of one's karma and to achieve all knowledge (Nirvana). To reach this goal, Jains must follow five rules: *ahimsa*: protect all life (nonviolence); *satya*: speak the truth; *asteya*: do not steal; *brahmacharya*: do not commit adultery; *aparigraha*: limit possessions.

Jains hold that all life is sacred; the teaching of *ahimsa*, or nonharming, is a central tenet of the religion. They are strict vegetarians. Jain monks, for example, will sweep the path before them with a broom so that they will not accidentally step on and kill an insect. Sacred rituals performed at the temple include *puja*, concentrating on one's soul through intense prayer, usually in the presence of images of teachers; *samayik*, a forty-eight minute ritual where one asks for forgiveness of sins; and *manokar mantra*, a short prayer that can be said anytime, which shows obeisance to the perfect souls that have achieved Nirvana.

There are approximately 25,000 Jains in America with more than sixty temples. Jains will worship in Hindu temples; however, whenever possible they prefer to erect their own building, as is the case in Bartlett, where the new Jain Center welcomes visitors (see p. 197).

Another faith that originated in India is *Sikhism*, begun in northern India by Guru Nanak (1469–1538) who wanted to bring about a kind of synthesis of the Hindu and Muslim faiths. Guru Nanak was a Hindu by birth but was against the Hindu caste system and what he viewed as their practice of idolatry and asceticism. He believed in the equality of men and women and in the worship of a personal God. In the seventeenth century, the Sikhs (the term means "disciples") became a religious military commonwealth, and the men were distinguished by five characteristics known as the five K's that remain visible today: *kesha* (hair), *kangha* (comb), *kada* (bracelet), *kirpan* (dagger), and *kachha* (underwear). Most Sikhs in the United States live on either coast; two *gurdwaras* (worship spaces) exist in Illinois.

JUDAISM

It was on August 3, 1492, that Christopher Columbus set out on his voyage of discovery; it was on this same day that Jews had to either flee Spain or convert to Christianity. Contrary to what some historians believe, there is no evidence to suggest Columbus was Jewish, but there is a consensus that several of his crew were.

The first permanent Jewish settlement in North America was started in New Amsterdam (New York City) in 1654 by a group of twenty-three

Sephardic Jews fleeing the Inquisition in Recife, Brazil, after that Dutch colony's capture by the Portuguese. The term *Sephardic* identifies them as Jews whose ancestors settled on the Iberian Peninsula (Spain and Portugal) in about the third century C.E. Their language was Ladino, or Judeo-Spanish, and many of their traditions, both cultural and religious, reflected their Hispanic heritage. They formed a congregation in New Amsterdam and worshiped in a storefront before erecting Shearith Israel in 1728, the American colonies' first synagogue (now demolished). About twenty years later, a second group of Sephardic Jews arrived, this time from Holland. They found a safe haven in Newport, Rhode Island, the colony founded by Roger Williams (see pp. 40–41) where they formed a congregation, Yeshuat Israel, and erected a synagogue in 1763, known as the Touro Synagogue, the nation's oldest continually used synagogue. It was to the members of this congregation that President George Washington wrote his memorable letter in which he outlined the new nation's support of religious freedom (see p. 8).

At the time of the American Revolution there were about 2,500 Jews in the American colonies, out of a total population of about two and a half million, prompting the American patriot and early supporter of George Washington, Haym Salomon, to write home to his family in Poland, there was "zer weining Yiddishkeit" (very little Jewish life) in America. Salomon was not Sephardic; rather he was one of the first Ashkenazi Jews to settle in the New World. *Ashkenazi* is the name medieval rabbinical authorities gave to lands along the Rhine River and is used to identify German Jewry and their descendants throughout central and eastern Europe. Ashkenazi Jews from central Europe spoke German, whereas those who arrived later from areas of eastern Europe were Yiddish-speaking, a dialect of German and other central European languages that emerged in the Middle Ages and is written using the Hebrew alphabet. It should not be confused with Hebrew, an ancient language used by Jews in prayer and the language of the *Tanakh*, the Hebrew term used for the threefold division of the Hebrew Bible.

In 1820 there were approximately five thousand Jews in America, most of them coming from German-speaking areas of central Europe. By 1850 their numbers had increased tenfold as thousands more fled war, famine, and persecution that was on the increase in the Old World.

Between 1880 and 1924, a "tidal wave" of impoverished Jewish immigrants entered the country, most of them escaping religious persecution in eastern Europe. Following the end of World War II, Jewish survivors of the Holocaust began to arrive, followed in the 1980s by Jews fleeing the collapse of the Soviet Union. The majority of the six million Jews living in America today are Ashkenazi. In Illinois, 2.2 percent of the population is Jewish.

According to Jacob Neusner, ". . . there is no single, uniform Judaism here or anywhere in the world. Like Islam and Christianity, Judaism comes to everyday expression in more than one way." And, as in Christianity, so too there are different movements within Judaism: Reform, Conservative, Reconstructionist, and Orthodox, with many subdivisions as well. What all Jews share in common are God, *Torah* (the Five Books of Moses), and Israel. They believe the God of Judaism is the one and only God, who created heaven and earth, who governs life with mercy, and who revealed the Torah to Moses on Mount Sinai. *Torah*, a Hebrew word that means "revelation" is "God's will and word to humanity." *Israel* is defined as the children of Abraham, Isaac, and Jacob, who assembled before Mount Sinai to receive the Torah from God, and their descendants through all time, including those who decide to figuratively "join them at Sinai" by accepting the Torah. The Hebrew Bible consists of the Five Books of Moses (Torah), the Prophets *(Nevi'im)*, and the Writings *(Ketuvim)* that include Psalms, Proverbs, etc. The three parts together are called *Tanakh*, a Hebrew word made up of the first three letters of the parts. Moses also received an Oral Law (the Talmud) that was handed down from generation to generation before it was written in two versions, one in Jerusalem, the other in Babylonia, between the third and sixth centuries B.C.E.

Orthodox Jews believe in the literal truth of the Torah and are committed to practice its commandments in every detail as the way of carrying out God's will. For example, dietary laws are carefully followed; they observe all restrictions regarding Sabbath activity; men and women sit separately in the synagogue at all services; only male choral music is allowed; and all men wear a head covering called a *kipot* (although any form of hat is acceptable) and a prayer shawl *(tallit)*. Married women are expected to cover their heads, and cannot be ordained as rabbis or be called to read from the Torah. Orthodox Jews comprise about 10 percent of the Jews in the United States who identify with a movement.

In the mid-nineteenth century, German-speaking Jewish immigrants brought with them a new form of Judaism. Known as *Reform Judaism*, its goal was to modify orthodox rabbinic Judaism so Jews could more fully participate in community life. It was a response to the dramatic improvements, political and cultural, that Jews began to experience in some western European countries following the French Revolution. In doctrine and practice, Reform Jews affirm that the Torah is holy, but read it as the work of man, and believe (as do all Jews) that what God wants is for people "Only to do justly, and to love mercy, and to walk humbly with thy God" (Micah 6:8). By the 1870s, the Reform movement introduced English into the service (in America), added Friday evening services, accepted the organ and mixed choir, allowed for the joint seating of men and women, and eliminated dietary restrictions and strict observance of the Sabbath. Head coverings are optional, as are the use of prayer shawls. Women have been ordained as rabbis since 1972, and participate fully in religious services. Thirty-five percent of affiliated American Jews belong to the Reform movement.

Conservative Judaism began in the mid-nineteenth century in Germany by rabbis who viewed the Reform movement as too radical. Many of the more progressive European rabbis who immigrated to America agreed that Judaism should make certain adjustments to modern life, but not all wanted to go to the extremes introduced by Reform Judaism. The Conservative movement in the United States attracted many second-generation Jews, children of Orthodox immigrants, who wanted to modernize their faith but not eliminate all of its traditions. Men and women sit together in a Conservative synagogue, and only men are required to wear head coverings and prayer shawls (increasingly, however, women choose to do so as well). Hebrew is used along with English in services, dietary laws are observed, and women have been ordained as rabbis since 1977 and participate fully in the service. Forty-three percent of American Jews are Conservative.

Reconstructionist Judaism is an American movement that grew out of the Conservative. It began in New York City as the Society for the Advancement of Judaism, formed in 1922 by an Orthodox rabbi, Mordecai Kaplan, who viewed Judaism as an evolving religious civilization that needed to change and adopt in a deliberate and planned fashion. Most unusual within Judaism is Kaplan's definition of God as the "power or process that works for human salvation or self-fulfillment." Similar to the Orthodox and Conservative movements, Reconstructionist Judaism emphasizes the importance of Hebrew and rituals, but allows for the ordination of women and the joint seating of men and women in the synagogue. Two percent of all American Jews identify with the Reconstructionist movement.

An additional 10 percent of the Jewish people in the United States are members of what pollsters describe as "miscellaneous" Jewish sects.

$\mathscr{V}$isiting Sacred Sites and Peaceful Places

Pathways

All journeys require a pathway, particularly those we take to "spiritual" spaces where we can encounter the peaceful or sacred. These pathways can take many forms—highways, trails, waterways, walkways through gardens and cemeteries, stations of the cross, labyrinths, and more. Pathways are part of our spiritual journey; as we move along them we observe changes in topography, vegetation, and settlement patterns. In Illinois the grid pattern established by the Northwest Ordinance (see pp. 8–9) greatly affects the way we experience the landscape and raises questions of how it may have looked before European culture imposed its enlightened view of "nature, reason, and law" upon it.

The concept of a pathway leading toward a spiritual or peaceful site is found in all cultures and religions. The ancient Greeks walked along the Sacred Way at Delphi to reach the Temple of Apollo; Israelites climbed the path up to the Temple on Mount Moriah in Jerusalem to witness the sacrificial cult; Christians trace Jesus' last steps along Jerusalem's Via Dolorosa; Muslims travel to Mecca and Medina to perform the *hajj* (see p. 59); Hindus visit the sacred city of Benares to ritually bathe in the holy Ganges River; and Native Americans have their ancient tradition of venturing into the wilderness on vision quests. Why are pathways so universal? Because just as life is a journey, a dynamic, ever changing, unpredictable experience filled with anticipation, so too is movement through physical space. All pathways are physical and psychological; the unexpected may appear at any time; they are not always smooth; their landscapes are ever changing, as are their shifting views. The journey along a pathway is a time of preparation, mentally and physically, for the spiritual or peaceful destination.

Long or short; circular, axial, or segmented; pavement, grass, rock, or stone; flat or inclined—paths of all types are included in this book. Some pathways, like the nation's "American Byways" have multiple stops along the way. One of the most scenic, the Great River Road (see p. 232) runs along the banks of the Mississippi River and forms Illinois' western border.

At times one pathway can lead a traveler to another. A journey to the birthplace of Carl Sandburg in Galesburg (see p. 248) provides insight into the early life of a famous American author-poet. In a small park behind his house is a path called Quotation Walk, created of stones incised with quotes from Sandburg's poetry that invite us to reconnect spiritually with this eloquent poet of the prairie.

Pathways can substitute for pilgrimage routes too distant or too difficult to reach. The stations of the cross in Roman Catholic churches serve this function, as do larger stations placed along pathways winding around the outside of churches, such as at St. James at the Sag Catholic Church (see p. 203). Introduced into different parts of Europe in the fifteenth century, the stations enable Christians to make, in spirit, a pilgrimage to the chief scenes of Christ's suffering and death in Jerusalem.

Labyrinths, a complex and circuitous path that leads from a beginning point to a center, have been in existence for thousands of years. In the Middle Ages labyrinths created with colored stone set in the floors of cathedral naves were walked as a devotional act that substituted for going on a pilgrimage to Jerusalem. Today labyrinths are often used as walking meditations, like the one found on the grounds of the National Center of the Theosophical Society in America near Wheaton (see p. 200).

Locations

The distance, design, and form of pathways leading to houses of worship are often predicated upon the building's location. Houses of worship can be found in many locations: on main streets, tucked away in neighborhoods, on the cusps of hills, amidst sprawling suburban asphalt parking lots, and adjoining rural cemeteries. Architecturally they range from simple storefronts to magnificent and monumental cathedrals, shrines, and temples. Some are adorned with religious symbolism, while others are plain, at times undistinguishable from neighboring buildings. Explore and experience a building's exterior before entering it; note its location, site, and architectural style. All these factors have an important impact on how you will experience the interior.

In selling real estate the mantra is "location, location, location." Location is equally important for a house of worship. Some locations are dictated by tradition: Hindu temples are oriented toward the east as are many churches; synagogues and mosques are aligned so their worshipers pray facing toward Jerusalem and Mecca respectively. Whenever possible, congregants will erect their houses of worship to conform to these traditions, but often their location is determined by other factors. Thus the location of a house of worship in a town or neighborhood can provide clues to a congregation's history and its status in the larger community.

A hundred years ago, throughout the country, the well-established Protestant denominations were often on or near the main street, while the Baptist and Catholic churches were in less desirable locations. Frequently, congregations had to settle for land that was affordable and available, and therefore *not* prime real estate.

At times the location of a house of worship, along with its architectural style (see pp. 67–78), was selected not only to fulfill a religious tradition, but also to achieve other, less spiritual goals. In many of Chicago's neighborhoods, it is still possible to view the monumental domes and towers of houses of worship of various faiths and denominations competing for the attention, and attendance, of passers-by. This happens even in small towns such as DuBois, initially settled by German Protestant farmers. Polish immigrants erected the monumental twin-towered Romanesque Revival St. Charles Borromeo Roman Catholic Church (see pp. 296–97) in 1908 that towers over its neighbor, St. Mark's United Church of Christ, built by German settlers, clearly illustrating change in the town's ethnic and religious dynamics.

In congested urban areas, houses of worship were often oases in the midst of decaying neighborhoods, or emblems of a neighborhood's particular ethnic identity. St. Nicholas Ukrainian Catholic Cathedral (see pp. 154–55) in Chicago was erected in 1913 in a Ukrainian neighborhood where its thirteen domes, visible for blocks around, continue to symbolize the identity and continued vitality of the neighborhood.

Architectural Elements

Buildings are like books—they can be read, and their stories can tell us a great deal about their history by providing clues that help us to understand their outward appearance. However, "you can't always judge a book by its cover," and the exterior architectural style of a house of worship does not always accurately portray what is to be found on the inside. Book covers and building façades are tools intended to attract people's attention. The exterior style of a well-located and well-designed building can be used to inform passersby of a congregation's success and good taste. This is particularly true for many of the houses of worship erected in the gamut of revival styles that became immensely popular in the United States in the nineteenth century. Vice versa, the severe, austere exterior of a building can enclose a poetic interior, as is the case with the deceivingly simple and innovative rusticated stone exterior of Kehilath Anshe Ma'ariv synagogue (now Pilgrim Baptist Church—see pp. 113–14) in Chicago, designed by Dankmar Adler and Louis Sullivan. Its interior has a spacious, well-lit, galleried auditorium decorated with a plethora of Louis Sullivan's famous ornaments: broad bands of gold-painted terra cotta in elaborate floral and geometric patterns.

Any discussion of architectural styles must begin with a caveat: America's religious architecture does not fit into neat stylistic categories based upon European prototypes such as Classical, Romanesque, Gothic, Renaissance, and Baroque. Many of these styles were revived in the nineteenth century and used to build houses of worship in the United States, but all were reinterpreted into an American idiom, often with regional variations dependent on the availability of materials, technology, funds, and perhaps most important, the vagaries of taste. **Vernacular** buildings, those built by local craftsmen who were often influenced by pattern books or memories of buildings left behind in the Old World, are even more difficult to categorize, especially if they were erected over a long period of time. However, a basic understanding of major architectural styles does allow a visitor to identify certain stylistic characteristics, or at least the sources of their inspiration. These clues may provide insight into why builders and congregants selected certain architectural and artistic details.

One of the first tasks undertaken by many pioneers arriving in the Midwest was to form a congregation and then pool their resources to erect a house of worship where they could gather to pray and socialize as a community. These buildings would allow them to make a statement about who they were—a statement they could not afford to make individually, but could do so collectively as a worshiping body.

There are no colonial era houses of worship in Illinois; the state's oldest surviving church is the Church of the Holy Family, erected by French Catholic missionaries in Cahokia in 1799 (see p. 285). Yankees moving westward in the first decades of the nineteenth century brought with them memories of the often grand churches they left behind. Rarely, however, did they have the material, time, or money to replicate them on the frontier; that would have to wait until later. Jewish settlers were few in number and worshiped in private homes or offices until they began to erect synagogues in the years following the Civil War. There were others, however, who had no desire to erect monumental edifices, satisfied instead with modest structures that served their purpose. These are the vernacular churches built by Upland southerners who were members of a variety of dissenting Protestant denominations, including Primitive Baptists, who built one of the state's first churches in 1796 in New Design.

[NOTE: Only those architectural styles and plans related to houses of worship in Illinois are discussed here. The Bibliography lists additional sources. Terms in **boldface** are in the glossary—see p. 335.]

NEOCLASSICAL

Neoclassical (sometimes rendered *Neo-classical*) describes a style of art and architecture that became popular in the seventeenth century. It was promoted by English aristocrats who had visited the continent to view ancient ruins and returned to England determined to replicate there "the glory that was Greece and the grandeur that was Rome." Architects began to borrow many features found in ancient architecture while adding others of their own invention. The result was a style that enjoyed great popularity in the eighteenth and nineteenth centuries, and still finds admirers today. In this country the Neoclassical style can be subdivided into two separate but related styles: **Georgian** and **Federal**. The Georgian style, also called English Colonial, dates from the reign of England's King George I, who ascended to the throne in 1733, to King George III, who reigned at the time of the American Revolution. The Federal style refers to the period following the conclusion of the War for Independence until about 1840.

While there are no churches dating to the colonial era in Illinois, it is still important to recognize the characteristics of the Neoclassical style because of its relationship to the Greek Revival (see below) that flourished in the state in the years immediately before and after the Civil War.

While many colonists abhorred the British monarchy and its treatment of the colonies, they still retained a link with England, often for economic reasons. Many also remained Anglicans, including two-thirds of the signers of the Declaration of Independence. Even among religious dissenters, the anti-English sentiment did not include English architecture. To them the Neoclassical style was devoid of British meaning; instead, it represented Greece's democratic ideals and republican Rome's constitutional form of government. America was the new Athens and the new Rome. For example, the First Baptist Church erected in 1775 in Providence, Rhode Island, is modeled after James Gibbs's Neoclassical St. Martin-in-the-Field in London, completed in 1726.

Gibbs published his plans and drawings for St. Martin in his *Book of Architecture* in 1728; it was brought to the New World by colonists and became a source of inspiration for many church builders. Following the conclusion of the War for Independence, Gibbs's plans and drawings were translated into an American idiom by Asher Benjamin in his "carpenter's bible," *The Country Builder's Assistant*, published in 1797. Benjamin's book provided carpenters and craftsmen with the architectural vocabulary needed to erect more sophisticated and elegant interpretations of the Neoclassical style that was identified in the new nation as Federal. The style had a profound impact on the country's religious architecture and on government buildings erected in Washington, D.C., including the Capitol building, whose Classical elements are attributed to the English architect Benjamin Henry Latrobe (1764–1820), appointed by President Thomas Jefferson in 1803 to take over the design of the building.

The outstanding feature of a Neoclassical church is its unique combination of a Classical **pedimented portico** (a porch with a triangular gable end) and a **multistage** (divided into telescoping sections) **tower** surmounted by a **steeple** (a tall structure usually topped with a spire) borrowed from earlier Gothic church architecture. Other features include arches (borrowed from Roman architecture) over doors and windows set with clear glass, and classical detailing, such as sculpted and painted garlands and wreaths. The extent of a church's adornment often depended upon a congregation's means and denomination, with Episcopal churches usually being the most elaborate. Federal-style churches, often clad in white clapboard or in red brick with white trim, are for many Americans a national "icon," the church on the village green, even though their stylistic source is firmly rooted in British soil.

GREEK REVIVAL

The Neoclassical interest, particularly in Roman antiquities, was soon eclipsed by a fascination with ancient Greece, sparked in part by Lord Elgin's "discovery" in 1804 of the Parthenon in Athens. Greece was the source for our nation's democratic principles; thus Americans also wanted to demonstrate their support for the Greek people's struggle for independence. The popularity of all things Greek gave impetus to the style that spread quickly throughout the expanding frontier. Soon even the most modest religious building would boast at least one Greek Revival feature, whether it be a simple **gable** (the triangular upper portion of a wall at the end of a pitched roof) front, corner **pilasters** (a rectangular column projecting only slightly from a wall), or a **colonnaded portico** (columns supporting a porch roof). As Carole Rifkind succinctly put it, "pagan Greece inspired Christian America."

In an attempt to replicate the appearance of Greek temples, the material of choice for a Greek Revival building was **ashlar masonry** (hewn blocks of stone). However, since this can be expensive, many were built of wood painted to mimic masonry. Greek Revival houses of worship are solid in appearance, rooted in the landscape. Some may have a tower atop the gable, but generally the emphasis is on the horizontal, a result of using the traditional Greek **trabeated** (post and lintel) method of construction (arches were unknown in ancient Greece) emphasized by horizontal elements such as the **entablature** and window and door moldings. Windows are set with clear glass, and a simple gable or portico runs along the front **façade** (the front or principal face of a building). Decoration is usually limited to **Greek orders** (Doric, Ionic, Corinthian) for columns and pilasters.

The Greek Revival was the first of the revival styles to reach Illinois. The small Unitarian Universalist Society building in Geneva, constructed in 1843 by New Englanders of local stone (see pp. 209–10), is a replica of Greek Revival churches they left behind in the East. Protestants dedicated to the principle of Christian unity erected a chapel in 1854 in the town of Godfrey (see pp. 278–79) that is considered one of the finest surviving early examples of Greek Revival architecture in Illinois. Even Swedish Lutheran immigrants, new to America, selected this style for their first church built in Illinois, the Jenny Lind Chapel in Andover, dedicated in 1854 (see pp. 245–47).

GOTHIC REVIVAL

The Gothic Revival style began to develop in western Europe in the mid-nineteenth century and went on to dominate architecture for nearly a century. The renewed interest in the medieval period (the eleventh to the fifteenth centuries) was an outgrowth of the Romantic movement that began in the late eighteenth century as a rebellion against the Industrial Revolution and the order, calm, balance, and rationalism of Classicism and the Enlightenment. Many influential intellectuals began to gaze back at past cultures with rose-colored glasses and sought ways to revitalize certain of their principles that they deemed to be more noble and moral than those of the "modern" industrial era. In order to replicate churches of the past, architects and designers began to graft historic decorative and stylistic elements onto modern buildings. Rarely was an effort made to revive the painstaking and time-consuming building techniques used in the Middle Ages. Rather, it was the revival of a particular style and its accompanying religious symbolism, not the revival of a historic building method, that was important to the congregations who commissioned Gothic Revival houses of worship.

The antithesis of Greek Revival, the Gothic Revival style expressed a newfound joy in the picturesque—the soaring verticality of spires and pointed arches, irregular roof lines, and large, colorful stained-glass windows. This style soon became, according to one historian, "the channel through which a strong current of genuine religious fervor found expression."

STAINED GLASS

Abbot Suger of the Abbey of St. Denis outside of Paris introduced the use of stained glass in the twelfth century. His purpose was to incorporate into the windows' designs biblical imagery and symbols that could be used to educate illiterate worshipers. Another purpose was more conceptual: He viewed the light filtering through the multicolored windows as a spiritual light that transformed the church's interior into sacred space. The practice quickly spread throughout Europe, where Romanesque, and then especially Gothic churches, were endowed with increasingly huge expanses of elaborately decorated stained glass. Stained glass lost popularity during the Renaissance, when the clear light of reason began to prevail over the diffused, colored light of theology. But in the nineteenth century, a combination of religious revivalism and romanticism, coupled with a renewed interest in the arts and crafts of the Middle Ages led by the English writer and designer William Morris (1834–96), rekindled interest in stained glass (see pp. 110–11). This coincided with Chicago's building boom following the Great Fire of 1871. Just as stained glass adorns the great churches and cathedrals of Europe, so too does stained glass adorn the great churches and synagogues in the modern metropolis of Chicago.

Artisans and craftsmen began to flock to the city in the late nineteenth century, where they established ateliers that transformed Chicago into a center for the production of stained glass. Most of the artisans looked to the past for their inspiration, often using fragments of antique glass in order to achieve an Old World effect. An outstanding example of this technique can be found in St. James Chapel's (see pp. 166–69), whose windows were designed by Robert Giles and installed by the John Kinsella Company of Chicago. Frank Lloyd Wright looked to the future, not only in his architecture but also in the designs he created for the stained-glass windows that adorn Unity Temple in Oak Park (see pp. 194–96). The placement of the windows and their geometric design and coloration are all intended to enhance the building's design and infuse the interior space with a sense of warmth.

The use of stained glass went into a second decline during the Great Depression in the 1930s. However, a renewed interest in the craft began to develop following World War II, when artists began to work in the media, including Abraham Rattner, who designed one of Chicago's most famous stained-glass windows for the Loop Synagogue (see p. 104), installed in 1960.

To view a wide variety of historic stained-glass windows from Chicago places of worship, residences, and other buildings, visit the **Smith Museum of Stained Glass Windows** at Navy Pier (700 E. Grand Avenue. ☎ 312-791-6049)

The Gothic Revival found a receptive audience in the United States. The Second Great Awakening (see p. 10) was sweeping the nation in the mid-nineteenth century, and with it came an increasing discontent with Greek Revival architecture that was viewed as too closely associated with pagan temples. Moreover, its cold formalism did not express the "red hot" faith being preached from the pulpits of many Evangelical Protestant Christian churches. Certain Episcopalians and Roman Catholics, too, seeking to "purify" Christianity of what they called "Reformation contamination," changes in liturgy and dogma introduced by various Protestant reformers, began to look back to the Gothic era (the twelfth to the fifteenth centuries), for inspiration. All of these factors contributed to the development of a new American "icon," the Gothic Revival house of worship, built in a variety of historic stylistic variations—French, Norman, English, and German, and two "modern" interpretations, Victorian, and neo-Gothic.

Characteristic of Gothic churches revived in the nineteenth century is the pointed arch. Stronger than the round arch developed by the Romans and featured in Romanesque architecture (see pp. 73–74), the pointed arch allowed builders to erect churches that soared toward the heavens, their walls pierced by large stained-glass windows framed by delicate **tracery** (ornamental stonework supporting glass in a window). Supporting the walls on the exterior are **flying buttresses** (arches that transmit the thrust of a vault or roof from the upper part of a wall to an outer support or buttress). In all their splendor, Gothic churches, with their towers and spires, elaborately sculptured façades, pointed arches, **ribbed vaults** (ceilings supported by arches), and stained-glass windows, came to represent the purity of faith of their builders and their devotion to Christian values that nineteenth-century religious leaders, artists, and architects wished to emulate.

Two British architects, Richard Upjohn (1802–78) and James Renwick (1818–95), who designed, respectively, the New York City landmarks Trinity Episcopal Church (1847) and St. Patrick's Cathedral (1853–80), were responsible for bringing the Gothic Revival style to the United States. Congregations selected the style to express not only their renewed interest in worship, but the fact that, by God's grace, they were able to erect an impressive church that reflected Christian values and was fashionable as well. This may have motivated the members of Second Presbyterian Church in Chicago to hire James Renwick to design their church (erected in 1872; see pp. 109–10) and to model it after fifteenth-century English Gothic churches. Chicago's neighborhoods offer Gothic Revival churches in all their stylistic, ethnic, and denominational variations, from Holy Family Church, erected in 1857 for Irish immigrants (see pp. 145–46), to the more recent Rockefeller Memorial Chapel on the campus of the University of Chicago, dedicated in 1928 and designed by the famed architect Bertram Grosvenor Goodhue (1869–1924 [see pp. 130–31]).

ROMANESQUE REVIVAL

Gaining popularity at about the same time as the Gothic Revival was the Romanesque Revival, a term used to identify buildings erected in western Europe between about 1000 and 1150 that were thought to resemble ancient Roman architecture. Like the Gothic, Romanesque architecture was a reflection of its era: the emergence of Christian Europe from the so-called Dark Ages, but still facing threats from Muslims to the south (the onset of the Crusades), and barbarian tribes to the north and east. Romanesque churches, in all of their massive grandeur, symbolize the might of Christianity in its battle against the forces of "darkness"—heathens and heretics. With their heavy stone walls and spacious **barrel-vaulted** (round-arched ceiling) interiors pierced with small windows set high in the walls, these churches were often the only places for people to seek sanctuary during times of attack, and their stone-vaulted roofs made them fireproof.

Romanesque Revival architecture has a solidity lacking in the Gothic, and a sobriety quite unlike the Beaux-Arts (see below). Usually built of ashlar masonry, the churches have thick, heavy walls pierced by deep-set round-arched doors and windows, the latter set with stained glass (not generally characteristic of medieval Romanesque churches), and are decorated on the exterior with relief carvings, usually of leaf or flowerlike forms. Massive towers may flank the main entrances or be placed off to one side. According to historian Jeanne Halgren Kilde, it was the militant character of the Romanesque style that made it especially attractive to many evangelical faiths in the nineteenth century who considered the turbulent urban milieu to be a kind of battleground. Building a church was seen within the context of a great battle between God's forces, now represented by Protestant Christians, and the unconverted that "had not experienced God's saving grace."

Most Protestant denominations favored an interpretation of the Romanesque style that became popular after 1870. Known as Richardsonian Romanesque, it is named after its creator, the Harvard and École des Beaux-Arts-trained architect Henry Hobson Richardson (1838–86). His highly influential Trinity (Episcopal) Church in Boston (begun in 1872) fused elements from Spanish and French Romanesque architecture with his own original decorative ornamentation. Although there are no Richardson-designed churches in Illinois, he did design two important buildings in Chicago: the Marshall Field Wholesale Warehouse (1885) and the John J. Glessner House (1886—see p. 108). His style also had an influence on local architects, including Solon Beman (see p. 120).

Other denominations, including Lutherans and Roman Catholics, also selected the Romanesque Revival style. For Catholics it represented the struggle they often faced for acceptance in the United States, which they perceived as similar to what Christians had experienced in the early Middle Ages. An important historic example is Old St. Patrick's Catholic Church (see pp. 146–47), built between 1852 and 1856 for Chicago's impoverished Irish immigrants; it survived the Chicago Fire of 1871 (see p. 94).

The Romanticism and eclecticism of the nineteenth century also had an impact on the appearance of houses of worship erected in the United States by two minority faiths, Orthodox Christians and Jews. In designing their churches and synagogues, both faiths looked back to their historic past for inspiration. However, their histories and motivations were quite different.

BYZANTINE "REVIVAL"

The Byzantine style, usually identified by its domed **Greek cross** (a cross with four equal arms) building plan (see p. 81), is associated with Orthodox Christianity (see pp. 45–46). Unlike the Romanesque and Gothic styles that were revived in the nineteenth century after centuries of disuse, it is not appropriate to refer to the Byzantine style as a revival, since it has been consistently used by Orthodox Christians, especially in Greece and in different variations elsewhere in eastern Europe, since the seventh century. An outstanding recent interpretation of this style is SS. Volodymyr and Olha Church, built in Chicago (1973–75) by Ukrainian Catholics, who still follow the Eastern Orthodox rite and the Orthodox Julian calendar (see p. 156). A variation in the Byzantine style has its origins in eastern Europe, in Russia and Ukraine, where Orthodox churches are divided into three sections in a linear fashion: **vestibule** (entryway), **nave** (great central space), and **sanctuary** (location of the **altar**). A small onion-shaped dome traditionally crowns the vestibule and a larger one the nave. An interpretation of this ancient design is Chicago's famous Holy Trinity Cathedral, designed by Louis Sullivan and built in 1903 (see p. 157).

MOORISH REVIVAL

The Jewish people's efforts to develop a distinctive architectural style for their synagogues went beyond the romantic yearning for an idealized religious past that characterized the revival movements associated with nineteenth-century church architecture. Living in the Diaspora, Jews, when permitted, built their synagogues in the vernacular style of the countries they lived in. The only exceptions were the unique wooden synagogues in the small Jewish villages and ghettos scattered throughout eastern Europe that were destroyed at the onset of World War II. This style of synagogue, however, was never revived in the United States. Following the French Revolution (ending in 1796), many European nations began to grant Jews civil rights, including the right to worship freely. The Jewish people now had access to Christian architects and could erect their synagogues outside the confines of the ghetto. This motivated a search for an architectural style that would distinguish their houses of worship from those of their Christian neighbors. Reform Jews living in central Europe were the first to adapt the Moorish/Islamic style that they associated with the golden age of Jewry in Spain, a time when Jews lived in relative peace under Muslim rule. This golden age came to an end with the Christian reconquest of the country and the final expulsion of all Jews in 1492. German-speaking Jewish immigrants brought the style to the United States, where the leader of American Reform Jewry, Rabbi Isaac Mayer Wise, adopted it for his congregation's synagogue, which now bears his name, erected in Cincinnati, Ohio, in 1866. The Moorish or Islamic forms found in these synagogues include horseshoe arches, brightly painted nonfigurative wall decoration interspersed with inscriptions (in Hebrew), domes and at times, what appears to be a minaret, such as the one adorning K.A.M.-Isaiah Israel Temple (pp. 126–28).

For Muslims, the Moorish style is not a revival but a continuation of a style that has its roots in Islam's formative years in seventh-century Arabia (now Saudi Arabia). As the Islamic population of the nation increases, so too will the number of its mosques. One of the most recent examples in Illinois is the domed Islamic Cultural Center of Greater Chicago, erected in 1988 in Northbrook (see pp. 187–88).

BEAUX-ARTS

The climax of nineteenth-century Romanticism is the Beaux-Arts style featured at the 1893 World's Columbian Exposition held in Chicago. It had its origins in the École des Beaux-Arts in Paris, founded in 1796 to expose artists and architects to the great monuments of the past and to encourage them to design equally great art and architecture for the new French Republic. The principles of the École were based on the belief that new architecture can borrow from *all* past sources (although the Gothic style was frowned upon), but ideally should be an extension of the Classical tradition, particularly that of Roman antiquity as it was reinterpreted by the great architects of the Renaissance and Baroque periods (the fifteenth through the seventeenth centuries). Furthermore, students were taught that churches "are the fullest statement of a society's values." Ethnic groups in America, many of whom were Roman Catholic, began to erect monumental churches in the Beaux-Arts style to link their historic past with their successful entry into American society. Many churches in this style can be found in Chicago, including Grant Memorial A.M.E. Church, built in 1897 for a Christian Science congregation (see p. 120). The Beaux-Arts style's greatest achievement, however, was in the design of monumental and imposing public buildings, like train stations, post offices, and museums, including the Field Museum of Natural History and the Shedd Aquarium, both in Chicago.

MODERN

While architects like William Le Baron Jenney (see p. 96) gave birth to the Chicago School of Architecture (see p. 96), which led to the erection of the nation's first skyscrapers, other architects were exploring ways to use modern building materials and technology to create a new architectural vocabulary to express ancient faith traditions. Louis Sullivan and Dankmar Adler's design for the K.A.M. Synagogue (now Pilgrim Baptist Church—see p. 113), built in 1890 and 1891, is one of the first houses of worship erected in the United States to achieve this goal. Its style anticipates the future, which became clearly visible when Frank Lloyd Wright began to develop his own style of architecture celebrating the flatness and openness of the Midwestern Prairie. Thus was born the Prairie School (see p. 98) of architecture, which received one of its finest expressions in Wright's Unity Temple in Oak Park, built between 1906 and 1909 for the local Unitarian congregation (see pp. 194–96). Wright's effective use of a new material, reinforced concrete, marks this building as an architectural milestone. Concrete can easily be molded into a variety of shapes and forms, and when used in combination with glass, brick, or stone, dramatic effects can be created, such as the soaring concrete vaults of North Shore Congregation Israel in Glencoe, designed by Minoru Yamasaki and built in 1964 (see pp. 186–87). Another famous architect who introduced new "words" into the architectural vocabulary is Ludwig Mies van der Rohe (see p. 99), who applied his famous philosophy that "less is more" to the only house of worship he ever designed, a campus chapel for the Illinois Institute of Technology, built in 1952 (see pp. 116–17).

As congregations moved to the suburbs, more land was available to build even larger religious and social complexes. Many of these buildings lack any particular architectural style, and from a distance, surrounded as they are by vast parking lots, could be mistaken for commercial establishments or schools. At the same time, other congregations began to explore their historical or mythical past for architectural inspiration, as did the members of Christ Church in Lake Forest, whose new church replicates a Federal era New England meetinghouse (see pp. 188–89).

The design of sacred space has challenged us humans since time immemorial; it is this ongoing quest that endows our landscape with some of its most beautiful and enduring buildings.

Building Plans

[Most of the building plans described here are for churches. Exceptions for synagogues are noted. Descriptions and plans of mosques and temples can be found beginning on page 87.]

A revival of an architectural style does not necessarily mean a revival of its traditional floor plan. Rather, new plans are often housed in old skins. For instance, a Romanesque Revival or Gothic Revival exterior may actually enclose an innovative (for its time) Akron or auditorium-style sanctuary (see pp. 81–82) rather than one in the traditional oblong, or **basilica**, plan (see pp. 79–80). An outstanding example of this is First Congregational Church (now First Baptist Congregational) erected between 1869 and 1871 in Chicago (see p. 149). Gothic Revival on the outside, the interior's design is not a corresponding basilica plan, but an amphitheater that functions well for a religious service that focuses on the preacher and choir.

While it is often possible to identify the historical source for the architectural style of a building, the style does not always reflect a congregation's religious affiliation. Symbols decorating a building can also be deceiving. A congregation may take over a building erected for another faith group and choose not to eliminate its symbols. Pilgrim Baptist Church in Chicago, formerly K.A.M. Synagogue, for example, retains Hebrew lettering over its main entry (see pp. 113–14). The exterior of a religious building promotes a congregation's public identity; its interior plan and decoration, however, have to function for a specific faith. The design of the interior worship space is called liturgical planning and refers to how the space is used in the ritual. This includes its furnishings, particularly where they are placed and how they relate to the function of the liturgy. There are four basic plans used for churches and synagogues: basilica, meetinghouse, central, and auditorium.

BASILICA PLAN

The term *basilica* as used here should not be confused with the honorific title presented by the pope to select Catholic churches, such as Our Lady of Sorrows Basilica in Chicago (see p. 152).

The basilica plan has an oblong or rectangular form based on a blending of two ancient building types, the Roman basilica, a large enclosed building often used as a storehouse or for public functions, and the Jewish Temple in Jerusalem, which was destroyed by the Romans in 70 C.E. In the years following the Temple's destruction, Jews began to adapt the enclosed public space of the Roman basilica for congregational worship. (For more on synagogue architecture, see pp. 87–89.) Following the legalization of Christianity in the early fourth century, Christians began to erect churches using a similar plan, except they added one important feature, the Jerusalem Temple's longitudinal axis, which was initially avoided by Jews for their synagogues because of its association with the sacred Temple. This axis travels through three spaces, each of increasing sanctity: porch, sanctuary, and the sacred Holy of Holies housing the Ark of the Covenant. The basilica-plan church favored by liturgical denominations echoes the Temple's plan: an enclosed **narthex** that serves as a transition from the secular world into the sacred and opens onto a main hall (nave), usually divided by aisles that provide pathways toward the church's most sacred site and its focal point, the raised **chancel** (the area that traditionally houses the altar). The chancel may terminate in an **apse** (projecting part of a building usually semicircular in plan) or a flat wall (see St. Patrick's Roman Catholic Church in Chicago, p. 146, and the Cathedral of St. Peter in Belleville, p. 286, respectively). Additional shrines or chapels may line the side aisles, or radiate out from an **ambulatory** (a semicircular aisle enclosing an apse or flat-ended chancel) that is an extension of the side aisles. There are several variations of the basilica plan, including the **cruciform** (cross-shaped) or **Latin-cross plan** that is created when **transepts** or cross-arms intersect the nave creating a **crossing** between the nave and chancel (see Chicago's Holy Name Cathedral, pp. 164–65). Another variation is the hall church, where the nave and aisles are of approximately equal height (see St. Michael's Catholic Church in Galena, p. 230).

Basilica-plan churches may have domes, towers, or spires. The building's architectural style may dictate the preference, as will a congregation's resources. A single dome or spire may rise above the crossing, while others may crown towers (see St. Stanislaus Kostka, p. 153, and St. Nicholas Ukrainian Catholic Cathedral, p. 154, respectively, both in Chicago). Churches with one or two spires piercing the sky are not uncommon; the spire of St. Alphonsus Catholic Church in Chicago is particularly dramatic, rising 260 feet above the street (see p. 175).

MEETINGHOUSE PLAN

Puritans were opposed to the use of the basilica plan favored by Anglicans. For them the very word *church* itself was anathema, not only for its association with the Church of England, but because its meaning was too limited. They preferred the term *meetinghouse*, which, along with the building's actual appearance, testified to their belief that civil authority and religious authority were one and the same and were to be housed under the same roof. Power rests in the pulpit and the minister's word; as Peter T. Mallary has observed, "The meetinghouse was the center for activities both secular and theological; and the pulpit, not the altar, was the centerpiece of the meetinghouse." While meetinghouses may vary in appearance, all are simple in plan and modest in size. Often built of wood painted white, the square or rectangular building may have up to four entrances: one in each wall so people can enter from all directions, or separate entrances for men and women. Three entrances symbolize the trinity. Galleries provide additional seating and box pews are arranged so worshipers have a good view of the pulpit, which is usually set on a raised **dais** or platform located against a broad wall opposite the main entrance. The table for the celebration of the sacrament is set below the pulpit. Decoration of any type is avoided and windows are set with clear glass. Bell towers are optional, but were added later to some meetinghouses. Early settlers in Illinois erected buildings similar to Puritan meetinghouses, particularly in the simplicity of their design and size. These include the followers of the Swedish dissident preacher, Eric Jansson, who erected the Old Colony Church in Bishop Hill in 1848 (see pp. 242–44).

CENTRAL PLAN

Orthodox Christians favored the centralized plan for well over one thousand years. Its source, like the basilica, dates back to antiquity, in this case to Roman mausoleums, and was later adopted by Christians for the tombs of saints. By the time of the first schism in Christianity (see p. 45), it had become the plan of choice for the Eastern Church. The plan's primary element is the dome that crowns its central space; in the Orthodox Church it symbolizes heaven and is often painted with an image of Christ Panto-crater (Triumphant). The most popular variation of the centralized plan is the Greek cross, where four arms of equal length radiate out from the central dome. A modern interpretation of this plan is SS. Volodymyr and Olha Greek Catholic Church in Chicago, dedicated in 1974 (see p. 156). In Orthodox churches, the central space under the dome was initially reserved for clergy and the altar; the laity gathered in galleries and circulating aisles (ambulatories), where they could view what was happening under the dome. However, this began to change in the fourteenth century when worshipers began to occupy the central space and the altar was moved behind a screen, known as an **iconostasis** (see p. 85).

Orthodox Christians are not the only faith to adopt the centralized plan. Jews living in eastern Europe worshiped in synagogues where the **bimah** (Greek for a raised platform) for reading Torah and preaching was set in the center of the hall. None of the surviving early synagogues in Illinois retain this plan. One of the more spectacular uses of the centralized plan is the Baha'i Temple in Wilmette, with its single circular auditorium rising into a hemispherical dome 138 feet in height (see pp. 184–85). In response to Vatican II, some Catholic and Episcopal congregations, in an effort to make their ritual more personal and participatory, also adopted the centralized plan by moving the altar table to the center of the hall, where it is in the midst of the people (see St. Benedict the African Catholic Church, 1990, p. 138, and Grace Episcopal Church, 1985, p. 106, both in Chicago).

AUDITORIUM PLAN

Acoustics and sightlines are of primary importance to Protestant faiths, whose emphasis is on the Word rather than the Act. As one Methodist minister complained in the nineteenth century, "[the basilica plan church] smacked of Catholicism and appealed to the eye and ear, rather than facilitating the direct reception of the preacher's message by the intellect." At the time of the Second Awakening (see p. 10), evangelical congregations were attracting large numbers into their churches by featuring passionate preaching, music, social programs, and Sunday schools. Clergy sought a plan that would accommodate large crowds but would still have excellent acoustics and sightlines. The answer was the auditorium plan, which was popular in the nineteenth century for secular venues like opera houses and theaters, and then was adopted for worship space. Unrelated to the Puritan meetinghouse, where the emphasis was on the authority and control of the preacher and the congregants were passive observers, the auditorium-plan church encourages congregational participation through music and impassioned sermonizing. The first auditorium church was designed in 1836 and built in New York City by a revivalist preacher, Charles Finney, whose experience preaching in a theater for four years led him to recognize that the goals of the theater, including making an audience comfortable and responsive, were similar to his goals as a revivalist.

Auditorium churches are generally square, circular, wedge-shaped (the Akron plan), or octagonal in plan. They are entered through a vestibule that opens onto a broad sanctuary space that has raked floors and pews arranged in semicircular arcs facing toward the pulpit stage. Galleries often wrap around three sides of the hall and are supported on slender columns, which do not obscure the view of the pulpit stage that is raised several feet above the main floor. Many auditorium churches feature moveable walls that open to adjoining spaces where additional people can hear the preacher's message.

An important early-auditorium-plan church in Chicago is First Baptist Congregational Church built in 1869 (see p. 149). It is an example of new wine in old skins—the innovative auditorium plan is housed in a Gothic Revival exterior. For many preaching faiths in the nineteenth century, the Gothic style continued to represent true Christian architecture, but the basilica plan usually associated with it did not serve the function of the evangelical liturgy. Synagogues, too, adopted the auditorium plan but generally avoided using the Gothic Revival style. One of the most innovative is the former K.A.M. Synagogue in Chicago (now Pilgrim Baptist Church) designed by Louis Sullivan and Dankmar Adler (see pp. 113–14).

Toward the end of the twentieth century, a new form of the auditorium church began to develop, the so-called megachurch. These huge complexes built in the suburbs not only have massive auditoria that seat thousands, but additional spaces set aside for a variety of other uses ranging from snack shops to bookstores.

Church Interiors

Although there is no such thing as a completely nonliturgical church, there is a tendency among scholars of Western Christianity to divide denominations into two groups based on their worship style. In **liturgical** (or ritual) denominations, which include the Roman Catholic, the Episcopal (Anglican), and the Lutheran churches, the focus is on the altar, the site of the sacrament (the **eucharist** or holy communion), usually located in a chancel. **Nonliturgical** (or nonritual) refers to Protestant denominations (including Baptist, Methodist, Presbyterian, and Congregational) that emphasize the Word over the Act. The focus in these churches is on the pulpit rather than on the altar. The interior arrangement of a church can tell a visitor a great deal about its liturgical practices.

Liturgical denominations have been affected by the rulings of the Second Vatican Council (1962–65) under the leadership of Pope John XXIII, which introduced liturgical reforms that led to the reconfiguring of the interior of many historic churches. Roman Catholic churches were no longer to be places where mysteries are celebrated or the Word dispensed, but rather places where the people of God assemble to worship together as a community. Barriers were removed that separated the clergy from worshipers and distractions (elaborate altars and statuary) minimized. This led to the removal of the communion rail, **reredos** (a screen behind the altar often decorated with images of saints and/or Christ), and **baldachin** (canopy over the altar representing the dome of heaven), and the turning of the altar so the priest could face worshipers to celebrate mass in their language, no longer in Latin. In many churches the modifications were thoughtfully conceived and completed, such as at St. Clement's Catholic Church (see p. 171) and St. Mary of Perpetual Help (see p. 141), both in Chicago. However, in other instances, decisions were made that resulted in churches losing their historic and architectural integrity.

All Roman Catholic churches, near the entrance, have a small font or fonts holding holy water for worshipers to dip their fingers in so they can genuflect while facing toward the altar and **crucifix** (cross with crucified Christ figure). Baptismal fonts, too, are commonly placed near the main entrance into the nave to symbolize a parishioner's entry into the church through the act of baptism (examples include St. Clement's, p. 171, and St. James Episcopal Cathedral, p. 162, both in Chicago).

Facing toward the chancel, to the viewer's left, is a pulpit for readings and homilies, and on the right a lectern typically used by cantors or announcers. In the chancel of a Catholic cathedral is the **cathedra** (throne) for the presiding bishop. Catholic mass is celebrated with clergy facing worshipers who view the rite of **transubstantiation,** the consecration of the host that changes bread and wine into the body and blood of Christ. Following mass, any consecrated hosts that are left are kept in a **tabernacle,** a decorated receptacle that traditionally was located on the high altar but now may be set off to one side of the chancel area or in a side chapel. A lit sanctuary lamp, usually red in color, indicates the presence of the host. The wide aisles of the nave provide worshipers with access to the altar to receive communion and for processionals before and at the end of mass. Worshipers can also use the church interior as a spiritual pathway as they follow the stations of the cross, which line the walls of the side aisles. Additional chapels or shrines dedicated to particular saints may be placed along the aisles, flank the chancel, or radiate off an ambulatory behind the apse. Prior to Vatican II, most churches were dimly lit by natural light filtering through stained-glass windows and smaller windows in the **clerestory** (clear story in upper story of wall) above the aisles. Since viewing the sacrament and participating in the liturgy now take precedent, churches have more elaborate lighting fixtures.

ORGANS IN ILLINOIS

After its physical building, the next most expensive item a congregation often owns is its organ. For many faiths organs are an important part of their worship. They support and lead congregational singing, accompany choral groups, and can be used for solo and instrumental performances.

Organs are known to have existed in the ancient Near East. Their origin can be traced back to the third century B.C.E., when a Greek engineer, Ktesibius of Alexandria, designed a *hydraulos,* which was used in pagan festivals. Initially, church fathers forbade the use of organs in Christian rituals because of their pagan association, but by the ninth century that memory had faded, and over the next several hundred years, organs began to increase in popularity to the degree that by the seventeenth century they were recognized as "the king of instruments."

The first documented use of an organ in North America was in Gloria Dei (also known as "Old Swede Church") in Philadelphia in 1703. Shortly thereafter organs began to be built in America; in Illinois the firm of Lancashire & Marshall was established in Moline in the mid-nineteenth century.

Today the organ remains the instrument of choice for most congregations responding to worship needs in a variety of styles and voices. The majority of churches do not use pipe organs regularly any longer; many are now electronic, but there is no special type of "church organ." Whether an instrument is German Baroque, French Romantic, or American neo-Baroque, it still must have the tonal resources necessary to support and lead congregational singing. If proper care is given, a pipe organ can last in operable condition for hundreds of years.

Chicago is home to many outstanding organs. According to Dennis Northway and Stephen Schnurr, authors of *100 Great Organs of Chicago*, among the city's most famous organs are: Fourth Presbyterian (see p. 165); Holy Family Catholic Church (two organs, one an 1879 Steinmeyer—see p. 145); Holy Name Cathedral (see p. 164); St. James Episcopal Cathedral (see p. 162); North Shore Congregation Israel (see p. 186); and First Baptist Congregational (see p. 149).

Great organ music can also be heard outside of Chicago, including the Casavant Freres organ in the Evelyn Chapel, Illinois Wesleyan University, Bloomington (see p. 328), and Kilgen Organ in the First Methodist Church in Urbana (see p. 323).

Orthodox Christianity is considered liturgical or ritual as well. While the reforms of Vatican II were designed to bring light into the Western church, literally and figuratively, by encouraging more congregational participation, Orthodox Christians have maintained their age-old rituals that transport worshipers into a world of mystery and awe that stirs all of the senses: the candlelight reflecting off icons, the wafting of incense, the murmuring of prayers and antiphonal singing of an all-male choir. Upon entering a church, Orthodox Christians bless themselves and light a candle. All Orthodox churches have a *bimah* that supports an **iconostasis** (a screen hung with **icons** that separates the sanctuary and altar from the nave). Holy Trinity Orthodox Cathedral in Chicago (see p. 157) has an elaborate gilded iconostasis; a more modest version can be seen in Holy Protection

Orthodox Church in Royalton (see p. 298). In the center of the iconostasis are the Royal Doors behind which stands the altar table. It is here that the priest performs the rites prior to bringing the consecrated host out through the Royal Doors to present it to the laity. Facing the iconostasis, to the immediate left of the Royal Doors is the icon of the Theotokos (Virgin Mary) and the Christ Child; to the immediate right is the icon of the Glorified Christ. On the Royal Doors are the icons of the four evangelists and, in some instances, the Annunciation. Above the doors is the icon of the Last Supper. The side doors of the iconostasis, or Deacon's Doors, have icons of angels or deacons; larger iconostases will have additional rows of icons of the apostles, prophets, and other holy people. Regardless of its size, the iconostasis is always crowned with a cross. An image of Christ Pantocrater (Christ Triumphant) often appears in the dome over the nave. Directly behind the altar table, visible when the royal doors are open, is an image of Christ in glory, usually enthroned or transfigured. In front of the iconstasis, at floor level, is a table and pulpit; the choir may be seated on either side of the *bimah*. Most Orthodox churches now have pews, but a few, such as Holy Trinity Orthodox Cathedral (see p. 157) in Chicago still retain the tradition of standing throughout the service.

Perhaps no form of religious art is so misunderstood by outsiders as the icon. It is not intended to be a pictorial representation, but rather the visual expression of the eternal and divine reality of the person or event depicted that is firmly rooted in the worship and piety of the Orthodox Church. An icon is not an idol but a symbol; taken out of their prayerful context, they cease to be icons in their proper sense.

Nonliturgical (or nonritual) churches provide visitors with quite a different experience. The first impression one has in a Protestant auditorium-plan church is a sense of airiness created by its broad, open plan and lighting. There is no mystery here; the entire space is well lit by chandeliers and natural light filtering through windows, often set with clear or stained glass. The preacher's message takes precedent over ritual; thus the auditorium's focus is the large pulpit stage that holds the pulpit, seats for clergy, the choir and, placed a step below, a simple communion table. Organ pipes may form the stage's backdrop (see Second Presbyterian, p. 109, and First Baptist Congregational, p. 149, both in Chicago). A small baptismal font may be set to one side; however, in Baptist churches, such as Pilgrim Baptist Church in Chicago (see pp. 113–14), a full immersion baptismal font is located toward the back of the stage. It is often kept covered except when baptisms are scheduled.

Synagogues

According to Jewish tradition, worship can take place anywhere ten Jewish men over the age of thirteen (known as a *minyan*) gather. (Reform congregations do not require a minyan; Conservative congregations do, but include women.) However, for nearly two thousand years, the Jewish people have been erecting specific buildings in which prayer services are held. The term *synagogue* provides a clue to the institution's origin; it is a derivation of the Greek word *synagoge*, which means "to gather," suggesting the first synagogues were built in the Greco-Roman world following the Temple's destruction in 70 C.E. Up until the fourth century, when Constantine the Great proclaimed Christianity to be the faith of the Holy Roman Empire, the Jewish people had taken the initiative in adapting the Greco-Roman basilica plan for congregational worship (see p. 79). However, with the growth and spread of Christianity the Jewish people found themselves increasingly marginalized and dispersed throughout the known world. As a result, their synagogues came to reflect their status as a minority group living on the fringes of society. Modest in size, they were erected by local craftsmen (usually not Jewish) in the vernacular style of their surrounding culture. But as varied as their outward appearance may be, the interiors of all synagogues share one feature in common: Located on the *bimah* and traditionally set against the wall facing toward Jerusalem, the direction of prayer, is the **Aron ha Kodesh,** the Holy Ark, a cabinet that houses the Torah scrolls, the Five Books of Moses (see p. 61). It is the presence of the Torah Scrolls that endows a synagogue with its sacred character.

The amount of adornment or use of figurative motifs found in a synagogue is usually related to a congregation's affiliation; Orthodox Jews usually avoid all figurative art and unnecessary decoration other than specifically Jewish symbolism, such as the Star of David. A depiction of a seven-branched **menorah** (candelabrum) that stood in the Jewish Temple is common in Conservative and Reform congregations; Orthodox Jews, however, do not replicate the Temple's accoutrements. Brief quotes from Hebrew texts may adorn the walls; one that is often inscribed above the Ark admonishes all who approach it to "Know before whom you stand." All congregations adorn their Torah scrolls with beautiful symbolic ornaments. The scrolls, written in Hebrew on parchment by an Orthodox scribe using a quill, are wound around wooden rollers known as **Etz Hayyim** (Tree of Life) and are encased in luxurious mantles, at times needlepoint made by women in the congregation. Torah finials, or *rimonim* (pomegranates), are removable ornaments often with bulbous midsections similar to pomegranates that are placed over the upper ends of the scroll's wooden rollers. Pomegranates represent the fruit of the Tree of Life and traditionally are eaten on Rosh Hashanah, the Jewish New Year. They are believed to hold 613 seeds, one for each commandment in the Torah. Hanging from the rimonim are gilded bells symbolizing the golden bells on the high priest Aaron's robe. At times, the rollers may be covered with a beautiful silver crown decorated with bells; this refers to **Keter Torah,** the Crown of Torah, one of the three crowns of Judaism; the other two are God and Israel. Silver breastplates decorated with Jewish motifs and remindful of the breastplate (**ephod**) worn by the high priest in the Temple, are hung over the front of the "dressed" scrolls, and a silver pointer, a **yad** (hand) in the shape of a hand with a pointed finger, hangs off one roller. The pointer is used when reading the Torah because according to Jewish Law, no one is to touch the scroll.

Synagogues require a plan that provides all congregants with a good, clear view of the *bimah* where the Torah is read and where the rabbi and cantor conduct the service. According to a famous Medieval talmudic scholar, Joseph Caro, the Torah was to be read in the midst of the people. This led to the erection of synagogues in the Middle Ages that had the *bimah* in the center of the hall and the Ark on the wall facing toward Jerusalem. However, by the mid–nineteenth century, following the emancipation of many European Jews (see pp. 60–63), that custom began to change, a result of exposure to the church plan. The *bimah* and Ark were now against the Jerusalem wall and theater-style seating was introduced. This coincided with the development of the auditorium plan in the United States, which was quickly adopted by many Jewish congregations, including Anshe Emet in Chicago (1910–12) (see pp. 176–77). The need for additional seating during the Jewish High Holy Days (New Year and the Day of Atonement) led to the design of expandable space, such as Temple Sholom's west wall that can be moved back to expand the seating capacity of the sanctuary (see p. 177). In some cases the cantor and rabbi share the same lectern; in others there will be two. Also on the *bimah* is a table for reading Torah and seats for clergy and others participating in the service. In some Orthodox synagogues, the *bimah* may extend out toward the center of the sanctuary in keeping with the tradition that the Torah should be read in the midst of the people, but the Ark is still against the eastern wall. The doors of the Ark may be covered with drapes or made in other media, but are usually embellished with Jewish symbols. Above the Ark hangs the **ner tamid,** a perpetual light symbolizing the light of the seven-branched golden menorah that stood in the Jerusalem Temple. The Ark remains closed except when the Torah is removed (it is read only on the traditional market days of Monday and Thursday, the Sabbath and holidays) or at certain times during the liturgy.

Reform and some Conservative congregations have organ or piano music, and both allow mixed choirs. Orthodox synagogues have unaccompanied male choirs. In Orthodox and Conservative congregations men are required to wear a head covering, either a *kippot,* a small skullcap, or a hat. Women must wear a head covering in Orthodox synagogues and are obligated to sit separate from men.

Mosques

The second pillar of Islam is prayer, *salat.* Muslims pray toward Mecca five times a day, either individually or in a group. On Friday, the noon prayer must be congregational and is said in a mosque, or *masjid,* an Arabic term that means "prostration"; it refers to one of the positions Muslims assume while praying. The others are standing, bowing, sitting, and kneeling. In Arabia, the birthplace of Islam, there was no tradition of building temples, so when the prophet Muhammad built the first mosque in 622 C.E. to house congregational prayer and to provide shelter from the elements, he erected a simple square enclosure surrounded by walls of brick and stone and partially roofed, which was similar to the region's vernacular architecture. As Islam spread throughout the Middle East and beyond, mosques were erected in a variety of architectural styles, a practice that continues to this day, although many mosques incorporate architectural and decorative elements indigenous to the Near and Middle East, such as domes, horseshoe arches, and arabesque designs. In America mosques vary from remodeled storefronts to magnificent new structures such as the Islamic Cultural Center in Northbrook (see pp. 187–88). Regardless of their size, all mosques share certain characteristics that are essential to Islamic ritual. A pool or fountain in an adjoining space is where worshipers perform a ritual ablution of face, hands, and feet and leave their shoes prior to entering the mosque. The mosque's orientation is of primary importance and is signified on the interior by the *mihrab,* an empty niche in the *qibla* wall that is oriented toward Mecca, the birthplace of the Prophet, and the direction of prayer. Looking toward the *qibla* wall, to the right of the *mihrab* is the *minbar,* a pulpit, usually in the form of a miniature flight of stairs that is sometimes canopied, where the imam preaches, leads prayers, and reads from the Qur'an. The worshipers, men separate from women, face the *mihrab*. Light filters through windows placed high in the walls and from lamps that hang from the ceiling and flank the *mihrab*. The lamps symbolize Allah as the light of the heavens and the earth. Careful to follow the commandment not to create figurative art, mosques are traditionally decorated with a complex web of geometric and abstract patterns, known as arabesques, or with quotes from the Qur'an executed in graceful Arabic script. Unlike Christianity and Judaism, there are no rituals other than prayer performed in a mosque.

Muslims' call to prayer, the **adhan** (or **azan**), is given by the imam or an official summoner (*muz'azzin*) from a balcony wrapped around a tall slender tower called a **minaret** that stands separate from the mosque itself. For many Muslims the vertical minaret and a dome (representing paradise) are signs that a building is a mosque, just as a steeple or spire signifies a church to most Christians. This is certainly evident when one visits the Islamic Cultural Center in Northbrook, which replicates in a modern idiom its ancient prototypes, the dome and minaret, each crowned with the crescent and star of Islam (see pp. 187–88).

Buddhist Temples

Buddhist temples rarely adopt the style of Western prototypes; most reflect the faith's origin in pre-Buddhist India. Common to all Buddhist temples is the **stupa,** a dome-shaped monument set on a square four-stepped base and crowned with a tapering towerlike structure. A stupa is a memorial and not a building. Adapted from an earlier form of Indian burial mound for use as a reliquary to inter the traditional relics of the Buddha in an inner chamber called the "cosmic egg," stupas later were constructed to hold the remains of other holy figures and offerings donated by worshipers. A stupa can be free-standing or take the form of a pagoda crowning a temple's roof, as is typical in East Asia, or small and enclosed within a temple. As a cosmological symbol, the stupa is fixed to the earth by a vertical post encircled by thirteen rings that emerge through its top that symbolize the thirteen steps of Enlightenment. Its squared base faces the four cardinal points and represents the underworld. Worshipers recite prayers while they walk around a stupa in a clockwise fashion and traditionally hang prayer flags on lines strung near it.

The Midwest Buddhist Temple in Chicago (see pp. 174–75) is a typical Japanese temple interpreted in a modern idiom. The focal point of its interior is the altar, a symbolic mountain, crowned with the figure of Buddha. Surrounding the altar are images of other sacred figures, bowls of offerings, candles and incense, and Holy Scriptures. All the décor is intended to encourage meditation. Few temples have pews; rather, worshipers traditionally sit on rugs or recline on pillows.

Hindu Temples

Hindu temples in the United States take on many forms and are usually designed to accommodate a variety of divine images and languages, and to serve as cultural or community centers. When funding is available, most Hindus, like the ones living in the Chicago area, will build a temple modeled after one in India. Each region of India has its own stylistic characteristics, but most share similarities in design and purpose. The sacred complex of the Hindu Temple of Greater Chicago in Lemont (see p. 204) consists of two temples modeled after south Indian prototypes.

The plan of a Hindu temple and its measurements are based on specific rules to ensure that it is a microcosm of the universe. To make certain a temple is built in harmony with the cosmos it is intended to replicate, its ground plan will include a geometric diagram called a **mandala** upon which it is erected. The mandala is square, a form considered by Hindus to be holy and perfect, and is based on a grid pattern of either sixty-four or eighty-one spaces of equal dimensions that, according to ancient Hindu texts, creates a "primordial cube of energy." The diagram may contain the drawing of the *Purusha,* the Universal Man, arranged in such a fashion so that a part of his body is in each small square. The temple is also considered a mountain where gods reside; thus the name given to its tower is *shikhara* (mountain peak). In India, Hindu shrines are also found in grottos cut into rock to create cavelike interiors.

Oriented toward the east, the temple's interior sacred space, called the *prasada,* contains a number of cubicles, also called temples. The largest cubicle, usually at the western end, is called the **garbha griha**, or womb chamber, and houses the temple's most sacred divinity. Other divinities, colorfully garbed and painted, are housed in other cubicles or adjoining rooms and can be identified by their attributes. Unlike Buddhist temples, the Hindu temple was never designed for congregational worship. The temple itself is considered sacred and an object of devotion as the dwelling place of the gods on earth, and as a result there are no pews. After circling the exterior of the temple, the worshiper enters the *prasada* through an outer hall or porch (*madapa*), and to the accompaniment of temple bells, walks in a circle clockwise (*pradakshina*) either to pray alone or with a priest in front of the presiding deity as well as other major shrines in the temple. Other worshipers come simply for meditation, peace, and solitude.

Similar to icons in Orthodox churches (see p. 46), the images of deities found in Hindu temples are symbolic. In Hindu belief, God is formless and shapeless; thus it is not the physical form of the god that is being worshiped, but the spiritual quality of the divine symbolized by the image. The temple, the imagery, the rituals and ceremonies are all intended to serve as channels for devotion to God and to foster spirituality. For Hindus, as with most seekers, spirituality is self-realization of one's union with God.

CHAPTER THREE

Chicago

CHICAGO'S MOTTO IS *urbis in horto*, the city in a garden, but most guidebooks on Chicago usually begin with a list of its many nicknames: "second city," "windy city," the "I will city," and Carl Sandburg's the city with "the big shoulders," or his less popular appellation: "hog butcher to the world." These names are not lightly given; each reflects one of the city's characteristics. In the nineteenth century, Chicago was the nation's second largest city; today it is third, but it still likes to think of itself as being second only to New York City. "Windy" refers both to the long-winded politicians who helped to shape the city and the winds that blow off Lake Michigan. "I will" reflects Chicago's attitude following the Great Fire of 1871, and it's a motto that still resonates today as the city continually reinvents itself. Its "big shoulders" describes those who labored in industry and the city's ability to shoulder whatever natural or political disasters play out on its streets. "Hog butcher" refers to Chicago's famous stockyards, today only a memory except for its Old Stone Gate and the many churches erected by those who toiled there. Together these nicknames describe a dynamic city that still retains its core identity as a city of neighborhoods.

Chicago's Historic Resources Survey lists seventy-seven community areas in the city, identifiable enclaves that have been home to a variety of ethnic and religious groups. Within these areas are over seventeen thousand buildings dating prior to 1940 that are considered architecturally and historically significant, including over three hundred houses of worship and nearly that many cemeteries or monuments. These plus numerous others built after 1940 are worthy of a visit by a spiritual traveler, but due to space limitations, not every worthwhile site is included in this book.

Sites were selected for their stories, their historical and aesthetic importance, and for their ability to provide visitors with quiet places to escape
the noise and stressful atmosphere of a large metropolis to find peace, spirituality, and sanctuary.

Chicago is laid out on a grid system overlaid with several major diagonal streets and expressways. The Loop is the city's center; State Street is
the east-west bisector and Madison Street the north-south bisector. All
addresses begin at the intersection of Madison and State Streets and are
given as east or west of State, or north or south of Madison. This chapter is
divided into six sections, The Loop, South Side, Southwest Side, Northwest Side, North Side, each encompassing a series of community areas,
and Chicago's environs.

A series of events in the late eighteenth and early nineteenth centuries
led to a swampland's transformation into a teeming metropolis. It began
with the arrival in 1772 of an African French fur trader, Jean Baptiste-
Point Du Sable, who became the area's first permanent settler in 1779 (see
p. 102). In 1803, the U.S. government erected Fort Dearborn on the site
(see p. 101), and a squatters' town began to develop. Its swampy location
led to the town being named *Chicagou,* meaning "wild onion" or "stinking
place" in some Native American dialects. Few settlers found the town
attractive at first, and when Chicago was platted in 1830 it had only four
hundred residents. The number had increased tenfold by the time the city
of Chicago was incorporated in 1837. Real expansion began when the
city's potential as a port became evident following the completion of the
Erie Canal in 1825 and the Illinois and Michigan Canal in 1848 (see pp.
204–5), along with the arrival of the first railroad, also in 1848, the Galena
& Chicago Union. Chicago was now positioned to become a major Great
Lakes port and rail center. By 1870 the city's population had risen to
334,000. A year later disaster struck when a hot, dry spring and summer
turned the entire Great Lakes Region into a tinderbox. Spasmodic fires
broke out, including one on October 8, 1871, that destroyed the town of
Peshigo in northern Wisconsin, killing eight hundred people. The Great
Fire that swept Chicago the same day overshadowed that tragedy. Over
one-third of the city, eighteen thousand buildings, was destroyed, three
hundred people lost their lives, and a hundred thousand more were left
homeless. The poet John Greenleaf Whittier lamented: "The City of the
West is dead!" His eulogy, however, was premature. Like a phoenix rising
from the ashes, Chicago emerged from the fire determined to fulfill its
destiny as a grand metropolis on the Great Plains. The City Beautiful
movement developed among influential social reformers and civic leaders

under the guidance of the architect Daniel Hudson Burnham (see p. 97). They argued that a beautiful city would inspire civic loyalty and "moral rectitude" in the lower classes, as well as stem the tide of the wealthy fleeing to the suburbs. The movement found its finest national expression at the World's Columbian Exposition, held from May to October 1893 in Jackson Park (see p. 124). Its chief of design was Burnham, who along with Edward H. Bennett later wrote the 1909 Plan of Chicago that included the creation of a beautiful park system along the lakefront that was to be "forever open, clear and free."

The Loop

"The Loop" identifies shopping districts of other cities, too, but the first "Loop" was in Chicago, where an elevated railroad, then known as the Union Loop Elevated, circling the city's business district, was built in 1897. It runs from Lake Street on the north to Wells Street on the west, then south to Van Buren Street and east to Wabash Avenue, and back up to Lake Street. The Chicago Historic Resources Survey has extended "the Loop" to an area that is bounded by the Chicago River on the north and west, Roosevelt Road on the south, and Lake Michigan on the east. The Great Fire of 1871, which leveled the downtown, gave architects an opportunity to rebuild it using the latest materials and technology.

CHICAGO ARCHITECTURE AND ARCHITECTS

(For additional sources on the city's architects and their buildings, the reader is referred to the books listed in the bibliography. For tour information contact: The Chicago Architecture Foundation, 224 S. Michigan Avenue, ☎ 312-922-8687. Parenthetical dates refer to styles' popularity in Chicago.)

Balloon-Frame Construction (1833–71): George Washington Snow (1797–1870), a Chicago contractor and jack-of-all-trades, started Chicago on its road to becoming a center for architectural innovation with his development of balloon-frame construction that replaced the expensive and labor-intensive building technique that used heavy pieces of lumber held together with mortise-and-tenon joints. The balloon frame consists of light, precut two-by-four studs held together with factory-produced nails that are joined in a basketlike manner that rises continuously from foundation to rafters. It was first used in Chicago for the erection of St. Mary's Catholic Church in 1833 (demolished) and subsequently for many of the city's earliest houses. These were the structures that went up in flames during the 1871 fire and led to the city's ban on the further construction of wooden buildings. Frame houses, however, continued to be built in the city's suburbs that were later incorporated into Chicago.

The Chicago School (1880–1910) The 1871 fire contributed to the development of the Chicago School of Architecture that was responsible for the design of increasingly taller buildings, first of masonry, and later in a new type of skeletal steel-frame construction. The early high-rises designed by these architects and others with their gridlike character and large "Chicago windows" helped to define this style, and in the process they transformed Chicago into the world's first vertical city.

William Le Baron Jenney (1832–1907) was born in Massachusetts and trained as an engineer at the École Polytechnique and École Centrale in Paris. He designed fortifications during the Civil War before moving to Chicago to take advantage of the city's building boom. His first work was to contribute to the design of the city's boulevard system and many of its parks, including Garfield (see p. 152) and Douglas. Jenney was instrumental in the development of "skyscraper construction," a method of carrying the external masonry cladding of a building on steel shelves bolted to an internal steel skeleton. His ten-story Home Insurance Building (1885, demolished) is considered the world's first true skyscraper. Jenney is also famous for training many young architects, including Daniel Burnham (see below) and John Wellborn Root who together designed the Montauk Block (1882, demolished) and the north side (1891) of the sixteen-story Monadnock Building (53 W. Jackson Boulevard), and Louis Sullivan who, along with his partner Dankmar Adler (see p. 97), designed the famed Auditorium Building, completed in 1889 (430 S. Michigan), which served as a transition to the Prairie style (see p. 98).

Daniel Hudson Burnham (1846–1912) born in Henderson, New York, moved to Chicago with his family in 1855. Burnham was a draftsman in Jenney's firm before forming a partnership in 1873 with John Wellborn Root (1850–91), a civil engineer from Georgia. Together they designed many significant buildings in Chicago, including the Rookery (1888, LaSalle and Adams Sts.), St. Gabriel's Church (1887–88), and the Union Stockyards Gate (1889) (see p. 140). Burnham and Root were selected to design the grounds for the World's Columbian Exposition in 1893, but Root's untimely death in 1891 left Burnham as the Exposition's sole designer. In 1906 he began work on his grand plan for Chicago (see p. 95).

Louis Sullivan (1856–1924) was born in Boston and educated at the Massachusetts Institute of Technology and the École des Beaux-Arts. He apprenticed under the famed Philadelphia architect Frank Furness before moving to Chicago in 1873. The Adler & Sullivan partnership produced more than one hundred buildings, including their first success, the Auditorium Building, which owed little to the popular historical eclecticism of the late nineteenth century. Its design and acoustics were by Adler, and its beautiful ornamentation was Sullivan's contribution. The building illustrates Sullivan's famous and oft-repeated dictum "form follows function," which grew out of his belief that architecture must evolve from and express the environment in addition to expressing its particular function and structural basis. The designs he did complete following his breakup with Adler in 1895 were quite modest, including several banks and Holy Trinity Russian Orthodox Cathedral (1903—see pp. 157–58).

Dankmar Adler (1844–1900), born in Stadtlengsfeld, Germany, arrived in the United States in 1854. His family settled in Detroit, where he began his study of architecture in 1857. He then moved to Chicago for further study and served in the Civil War. He returned to Chicago following the war and formed a partnership with Louis Sullivan in 1881. Adler and Sullivan were responsible for the design of a number of innovative buildings, including K.A.M. Synagogue (now Pilgrim Baptist Church) (see pp. 113–14). Adler, whose specialty was acoustics, acted as engineering designer and administrator, soothing clients who were put off by Sullivan's brusque manner. Sullivan was the planner and artist. The partnership ended unhappily in 1895 when Adler accepted a lucrative position as designer and agent for the Crane Elevator Company. Unsatisfied with this career move, Adler returned to architecture a year later, continuing to practice until his death in 1900.

The Prairie Style (1890–1917) was contemporary with the Chicago School, but rather than designing and constructing high-rises in the Loop, its followers focused mainly on designing residences that introduced a new vocabulary into domestic architecture. This style celebrates the Midwest's flat prairie landscape and promotes the use of natural materials. Although associated with the Chicago School because of his many contributions to Chicago's commercial architecture, the progenitor of the Prairie style was Louis Sullivan, whose early works, including the Auditorium Building and the Getty Tomb of 1890 (see p. 180), are harbingers of the style most closely associated with his apprentice and draftsman, Frank Lloyd Wright.

Frank Lloyd Wright (1867–1959), born in Wisconsin, attended the University of Wisconsin's engineering school for one year before being hired by Louis Sullivan. He left Sullivan in 1893 to open his own practice in Oak Park, where he began to develop his own unique architectural vocabulary that still resonates today. He was the driving force behind the Prairie style, which is characterized by low, horizontal houses inspired by the state's flat prairies and whose rooms flow into one another in a manner that is often referred to as "organic." Wright, considered among the nation's most famous and significant architects, has left a legacy of important structures in and around Chicago, including the Robie House (see p. 131), Unity Temple (see p. 194), and his Prairie style houses in Oak Park.

International Style (1940–70). This style is most closely associated with the Bauhaus, a teaching institution for the arts founded in 1919, in Weimar, Germany, by Walter Gropius (1883–1969). The Bauhaus moved to Dessau, Germany, in 1925 and three years later Mies van der Rohe was named director. The Nazi government closed it in 1933, and many of its instructors fled to the United States where they were to have an important impact on the nation's architecture and visual arts.

Ludwig Mies van der Rohe (1886–1969) was born in Aachen, Germany, where he worked in the family stone-carving business before joining an architectural firm in Berlin in 1908. Influenced by the modern aesthetics of Russian Constructivism and the Dutch De Stijl, he developed his dictum "less is more," which found expression in his spare, simplified architecture identified with the German Bauhaus and International movements. In 1937, Mies became director of the Illinois Institute of Technology, and in 1940 founded its School of Architecture. Mies was never licensed in Illinois to practice architecture, but by associating with licensed architects he was able to design the institute's campus and twenty-two of its buildings, including the Chapel of St. Saviour (see pp. 116–19). He also designed the steel and glass 860-880 and 900-910 North Lake Shore Drive Apartments, completed in 1951 and 1953 respectively, and the Farnsworth House in Plano (see pp. 212–13).

A Temple Dedicated to Art
THE ART INSTITUTE OF CHICAGO (NR)
111 S. Michigan Avenue at Adams Street. Original wing by Shepley, Rutan, and Coolidge, 1893. ☎ 312-443-3600 🖥 www.artic.edu/aic/

The museum houses many important works of art both secular and sacred; however, two galleries in particular evoke an atmosphere that is both spiritual and peaceful. The first is Tadao Ando's "Power of Sixteen Pillars." Winner of the prestigious Pritzker Architecture Prize in 1995, Tadao Ando was born in Osaka, Japan, in 1941. Self-educated, he has received widespread acclaim for his buildings and spaces that aim "to impart rich meaning through the use of natural elements and the aspects of daily life." Commissioned in 1991 to create a space to display the museum's Japanese screens, he drew upon his fascination with trees—how they grow and how the sun and shade alter their appearance. Ando placed sixteen pillars in this gallery, each one foot square and ten feet high, which, like trees in a forest, obstruct the view yet also suggest the depth and resonance of the space. Moving through the gallery, the visitor experiences different perspectives of space as well as the Japanese screens. According to the designer, the screens, known as *byobu*, embody the Japanese people's traditional love of nature and evoke an image of their way of life.

The second gallery is the reconstructed Trading Room of Louis Sullivan's 1894 Stock Exchange Building that originally stood at 30 North LaSalle Street. Sullivan, in collaboration with Louis J. Millet, created the room's decoration, a series of intricate stencil patterns that cover the walls and ceiling. The gallery also serves as a memorial to Richard Nickel, an architectural photographer who gave his life trying to salvage parts of the historic structure prior to its demolition. Nickel and his friend and fellow architect, John Vinci, were ardent preservationists who were among the first to recognize that the nation's historic buildings were threatened with destruction in the wake of post–World War II urban renewal programs. Nickel was killed when the building collapsed on him while he was retrieving artifacts; his body was found in the northwest corner of the Stock Exchange floor. It is thanks to his efforts, and others like him, that we are able to enjoy and experience important historic spaces like this one.

NEARBY

➥ **The South Garden of the Art Institute**, Jackson and Michigan Avenues. This tree-shaded oasis adjoining the Art Institute is watched over by Lorado Taft's (see p. 126) famous sculpture and fountain symbolizing the Great Lakes. The garden received a Millennium Medal from the American Society of Landscape Architects as one of the most significant landscapes in the United States.

Where City and Nature Peacefully Coexist
GRANT PARK (NR)

Framed on two sides by skyscrapers, the boundaries of Grant Park are Lake Michigan on the east and Michigan Avenue on the west, and it stretches from Randolph Street on the north to Roosevelt Road on the south. Its 319 acres are an inviting place to escape the city's noise and congestion. It is part of the twenty-four miles of lakefront parks connected by Lake Shore Drive that stretch from Lincoln Park (see pp. 172–73) in the north to Jackson Park (see p. 124) in the south.

Much of the original park, dedicated on April 29, 1844, was created from landfill dumped into Lake Michigan. Debris from the 1871 Great Fire was used to expand the park farther; its latest addition is the Millennium Park in the northwest portion, which was added in 2001.

One of the park's focal points is **Buckingham Fountain**, one of the largest fountains in the world. Created by the French sculptor Marcel F. Loyau, it is modeled after the Bassin de Latome at Versailles, France, and was donated by Kate Buckingham in 1927 in memory of her brother

Clarence, a director of the Art Institute. The fountain symbolizes Lake Michigan, while the bronze sea horses surrounding it represent its four bordering states: Wisconsin, Indiana, Michigan, and Illinois. A lovely way to spend a summer evening is to attend a music and light show that takes place nightly at the fountain. In the center of the park is the **Court of the Presidents**, dominated by a 1926 statue of Abraham Lincoln created by Augustus Saint-Gaudens. (An earlier Lincoln statue by Saint-Gaudens is in Lincoln Park—see pp. 172–73.) Other spiritual sites include the **Daniel H. Flaherty Rose Garden** and the **Wildflower Garden** adjacent to the **Cancer Survivors Garden** located at the north end near Lake Shore Drive.

A Fort on the Frontier
SITE OF FORT DEARBORN
Corner of E. Wacker Drive and N. Michigan Avenue. Founded in 1803.

Signs set in the sidewalk on the corners of Michigan Avenue and Wacker Drive outline the fort's perimeter; a plaque at the south end of the Michigan Bridge over the Chicago River commemorates its founding.

In 1779, on a swampy site at the junction of the Chicago River and what was then the shoreline of Lake Michigan, Jean Baptiste Point Du Sable, an African French trapper, established a profitable trading post, the first permanent settlement in what would become Chicago (see below). Fort Dearborn was erected in 1803, on the same site, to protect the lucrative fur trade from the British. Potawatomi Indians who sided with the British during the War of 1812 attacked the fort in 1812 killing fifty-two men, women, and children and forcing the American soldiers to flee. The site remained abandoned until 1816, when the fort was reestablished. For supporting the British cause, the Potawatomi tribe was forced to cede the land on either side of the mouth of the Chicago River to the United States.

NEARBY
➥ **Jean Baptiste Point Du Sable Homesite** (NR), 401 N. Michigan Avenue. Pioneer Court Plaza, an open space overlooking the Chicago River between the Equitable Life Insurance Company Building and the Chicago Tribune Building, partially occupies the site where Jean Baptiste Point Du Sable had his trading post. A large fountain in the center of the plaza is inscribed with the names of Chicago pioneers, including Du Sable.
➥ **Harold Washington Library Center** (1991), 400 S. State Street.
☎ 312-747-4999. Chicago's central public library is named for the city's first African American mayor. The Winter Garden on the ninth floor

WHO WAS
JEAN BAPTISTE POINT DU SABLE?

Du Sable, the son of fur traders in Haiti, was sent to New Orleans to purchase furs for his family's business. He then traveled up the Mississippi into Indian territory where, according to legend, he was befriended by Chief Pontiac. Du Sable took an Indian wife, Chikiwata, and in 1772 settled in a marshy area between what is now the Chicago River and Lake Michigan; in 1779 he built a cabin and trading post on the site. By the 1790s his settlement was known as Point Du Sable, and consisted of a large log house, poultry and dairy barns, and a sawmill. Fearful of his ties with the French, the British jailed him for a year at Fort Mackinac; however, thanks to political pressure, he was released and was allowed to continue his fur trading business. In 1800, dissatisfied with the U. S. government's land policies in the territories, Du Sable sold his business to Jean Lalime and left for Canada. Lalime quickly sold the land to John Kinzie, a trader and speculator from Detroit, who for years was credited with founding Chicago. It wasn't until 1968 that Du Sable was acknowledged as the city's first permanent resident. The Du Sable Museum of African American History is named in his honor (see pp. 125–26).

provides a restful haven where visitors can relax and read in the midst of greenery in a fifty-two-foot-high atrium. An exhibition hall adjacent to the Winter Garden houses the archives and collections of Mayor Washington.

➡ **The Illinois and Michigan National Heritage Corridor**, Navy Pier. Established in 1984 by Congress in recognition of the area's unique contributions to the nation's development, the Corridor's trail begins at Navy Pier, right off Lake Shore Drive, and travels along the Chicago River and the Sanitary and Ship Canal through twenty Chicago neighborhoods, with a stop along the way at the Chicago Portage National Historic Site. The corridor continues for ninety-four miles before ending at LaSalle/Peru on the Vermillion River.

➡ **Spertus Museum**, 618 S. Michigan Avenue. Established in 1968. ☎ 312-922-9012 🖳 www.spertus.edu/museum.html

Housed in the Spertus Institute of Jewish Studies, the museum offers its guests the opportunity to view Judaism as both a religion and a culture.

Visitors can pause and reflect on the Holocaust in the museum's memorial hall. A central marker stone symbolizes the tragedy of the Holocaust while displays and a film document its atrocities.

A Chapel in the Sky
THE CHICAGO TEMPLE, FIRST UNITED METHODIST CHURCH

77 W. Washington Street. 1922–24, Holabird and Roche.

☎ 312-236-4548 💻 www.chicagotemple.org

The spiritual can be experienced in many places, including atop a twenty-two-story Gothic Revival office building. As real estate values escalated in the early twentieth century, congregations in prime business areas began to develop dual-purpose buildings that would house sanctuaries as well as commercial office space. An outstanding example is the Chicago Temple Building's "Sky Chapel," described in the Guinness Book of Records as the "highest place of worship from street level in the world."

The Reverend Jesse Walker founded the First United Methodist Church in 1831, the first Protestant religious institution in Chicago. Since 1838, the congregation has occupied five churches on the same site, a prime piece of real estate in the heart of the Loop. In 1922 a decision was made to take full advantage of the site by erecting a twenty-two-story building that would house a sanctuary, two chapels, parsonage, meeting rooms and offices for the congregation on its first four floors, the twenty-second floor, and tower, while the remaining floors were used for tenants. Completed in 1924, the building's tower and spire are decorated in the French Gothic style, including buttresses, pinnacles, and arches often associated with religious architecture (see p. 71). However, unlike the city's other Gothic Revival skyscrapers, its spire is crowned with a twelve-foot-high illuminated gold cross that is visible throughout the downtown area.

Visits to the Sky Chapel are conducted following each worship service on Sunday. Additional tours are available on weekdays; call to verify times. The main sanctuary is on the ground floor; Dixon Chapel and the Rose Window Chapel are located on the second floor. To reach the Sky Chapel it is necessary to take an elevator to the twenty-second floor, where the Prince Memorial Gallery is located. From the gallery one can either walk up 173 steps to the chapel or take another small elevator. If you walk up from the gallery, note the *Shields of the Apostles* hanging on the stairway's walls. Created by Howard Walker Woodruff of Springfield, Missouri, they are designed for the blind so they may "see" the apostles' stories with their hands.

The idea for the chapel was conceived by Dr. Charles Ray Goff, minister of the temple from 1941 through 1961, and donated by Myrtle Norton Walgreen in memory of her husband, Charles. The oak used throughout came from the Walgreen estate near Dixon, Illinois. Sixteen stained-glass windows by the firm of Giannini and Hilgart of Chicago (who created all the Temple Building's stained glass) illustrate scenes from the Hebrew Bible, the New Testament, and the Old and New Worlds. The solid oak altar carving is by Alois Lang originally of Oberammergau, Germany. It is an unusual companion piece to the one he carved for the main sanctuary downstairs, which depicts Christ seated on the Mount of Olives gazing out over Jerusalem. Here Christ is shown gazing out over Chicago. The chapel is used for small weddings, prayer groups, and sunrise services on Easter.

Let There Be Light
CHICAGO LOOP SYNAGOGUE
16 S. Clark Street. 1957–58, Loebl, Schlossman and Bennett.
☎ 312-346-7370 🖥 www.chicagoloopsynagogue.org

A brochure describing the interior of the synagogue is available in the first-floor office, where you may request permission to visit the sanctuary. The congregation is described in its literature as "traditional."

Several blocks west of Michigan Avenue is bustling commercial Clark Street, an unlikely place to find a sacred space. Yet nestled among office buildings is Loop Synagogue, founded in 1929 to serve the religious needs of Jewish Chicagoans working in the Loop and the thousands of Jewish visitors who stay in the downtown area.

Chicago Loop Synagogue

What distinguishes the synagogue from its neighbors is the enormous stained-glass window on its façade and the sculpture over its main entrance, the *Hands of Peace*. Created by the Israeli sculptor Henri Azaz, the sculpture symbolically depicts the priestly hands raised in benediction, set against a background of the text of the ancient threefold priestly blessing rendered in Hebrew and English.

The sanctuary on the second floor has its *bimah* located on the broad north wall with pews directly in front of it and along the western wall below the balcony. The synagogue's focus, however, is its eastern wall, the direction toward Jerusalem, where the Ark containing the Torah scrolls is located under the great stained-glass window created by Abraham Rattner and installed in 1960, *Let There Be Light*, taken from the biblical text of Genesis 1:3: "And God said, 'Let there be light'; and there was light."

The window is divided into three panels: the one on the left is the key to the composition containing symbols of God's covenant with the Jewish people: The central panel shows the Twelve Tribes, the shofar or ram's horn, the *etrog* (citron) used in the harvest festival of Succoth, the menorah, and the Palm of "Shins." The panel on the right depicts the planets, sun, moon, and Star of David. Across the bottom in Hebrew is the *Shema*, the watchword of Israel: "Hear O Israel, the Lord our God, the Lord is One."

Henri Azaz designed the Ark and the Eternal Light. The Hebrew text (Proverbs 3:17–18) on the bronze doors of the Ark reads: "It [the Torah] is a tree of life to those who take hold of it, and happy are those who support it. Its ways are ways of pleasantness, and all its paths are peace." The decoration at the top of the Ark is an acronym composed of Hebrew letters of Numbers 24:5, "How goodly are thy tents, O, Jacob, thy dwelling places O, Israel", and the letters on the Eternal Light read *Ner Tamid*, "Eternal Light" in Hebrew.

A House of God in a Valley of Stone
ST. PETER'S CHURCH
Catholic. 110 W. Madison Street. 1951–53, Karl Vitzhum and John Burns.
☎ 312-372-5111

St. Peter's, on busy Madison Street, calls itself "An oasis in the Loop." Founded in 1846 as the city's first German Catholic parish, the original 1865 church was replaced by the present building in 1953. Situated in the midst of skyscrapers, St. Peter's is staffed by thirty Franciscan friars of the Province of the Sacred Heart of Jesus who live in a friary above the church. The church serves as a pilgrimage site for thousands of Catholics

working in the Loop and for visitors seeking a quiet retreat. The monumental marble façade of the five-story church is dominated by a giant crucifix, *Christ of the Loop*, designed by the Latvian sculptor Arvid Strauss and
executed by a Chicago artist J. Watts. Eighteen feet tall and weighing
twenty-six tons, the crucifix is set in front of a large stained-glass window
dedicated to Mary, Queen of Peace.

Other than this stained-glass window, the body of the basilica-plan
church is windowless. Instead, lining the walls of the nave are ten recessed
marble panels, five on each side, containing bas-relief scenes from the life
of St. Francis of Assisi by an Italian sculptor, Carolo Vinchessi, from
sketches by Louis Carraciolo, a Chicago artist who also painted the
church's stations of the cross.

A Place of Grace for Four Faiths
GRACE CHURCH AND COMMUNITY CENTER
Episcopal. 637 S. Dearborn Street. 1985, Booth Hansen Architects.
☎ 312-922-1426 💻 www.gracechicago.org

A former commercial building on historic Printers Row was transformed into GracePlace, a community center and sanctuary shared by four
different faith groups: Grace Episcopal Church (the founders of Grace-
Place), Makom Shalom, a Jewish Renewal congregation (unaffiliated with
the four major movements), Loop Christian Ministries (a ministry of the
Christian Reformed Church), and the World Outreach Conference
Center (a holiness congregation). Grace's mission statement, "We want to
nurture and grow our community life, and to grow ourselves and others
spiritually," is made visible in its outreach programs and its willingness to
share its space with other faiths.

The history of GracePlace began with the establishment of Grace Episcopal Church in 1851. The church had had four different locations before
the momentous decision was made in the early 1980s by its rector, William
L. Casady, to move into an empty building on Printer's Row. The architects were given the challenge to transform the space into a welcoming
spiritual environment. Their success is immediately evident upon entering
GracePlace's social hall on the first floor, which serves as a gathering place
for a variety of meetings and neighborhood events.

The chapel on the second floor is the heart of the building—a warm
and inviting space lit by exterior windows. In its center and lit from above
by a skylight is a circular platform where services are conducted; facing it
are pews arranged in a semicircle. A statement by the Jewish congregation

Makom Shalom, which means "grace place" in Hebrew, best expresses GracePlace's accomplishment: "We recognize that we are all part of a pattern, a oneness that transcends us."

South Side

Chicago's South Side stretches from Roosevelt Road to 138th Street and east to the Indiana border and encompasses twenty community areas. Discussed in this chapter are: Near South Side, Douglas, Oakland, Grand Boulevard, Kenwood, Hyde Park, Greater Grand Crossing, and Pullman.

The Near South Side (see p. 108) was the first area south of the Loop to attract settlers, including Henry B. Clarke, whose 1836 Greek Revival farmhouse is considered the oldest surviving house in Chicago (see p. 108). The arrival of the railroad and various industries in the 1850s attracted workers who moved into hastily built frame shanties that were destroyed in the 1871 fire (see p. 94). Construction following the fire ranged from mansions such as the 1886 John Jacob Glessner House (see p. 108) to more modest workers' homes. Others began to settle in a new subdivision on Senator Stephen Douglas's estate, which had served as a prisoner-of-war camp during the Civil War (see pp. 115–16). Jewish residents living there erected Kehilath Anshe Ma'ariv Synagogue, designed by Adler and Sullivan, in 1889 (see pp. 113–14). By the time the synagogue was sold to a black congregation in 1922 and transformed into Pilgrim Baptist Church, the Douglas Community Area had become part of a large, vibrant, African American community known as Bronzeville (see pp. 117–18).

Farther south are the formerly posh neighborhoods of Kenwood and Hyde Park, now undergoing revitalization and home to some of Chicago's most distinguished historic architecture, including Frank Lloyd Wright's famed Robie House (see p. 131), the University of Chicago (see pp. 129–30), and two beautiful parks, Washington Park (see p. 125) and Jackson Park, the site of the 1893 World's Columbian Exposition (see p. 124).

Most of the area south of 93rd Street developed as intensive industrial growth began in the late nineteenth and early twentieth centuries. Workers' housing is interspersed among the area's railroad yards and various industries. The one exception is the planned industrial and residential community of Pullman, which was deliberately situated to be isolated from the rest of the city and the labor unrest that was rocking it in the late nineteenth century (see p. 136).

Near South Side

The Near South Side is bounded on the north by Roosevelt Road and on the south by the Stevenson Expressway; it stretches west to near I-90/94 and east to Burnham Park. The area has been transformed over the years from a sparsely settled wilderness to the site of some of the city's most opulent mansions. It was once home to "brothels and gambling dens" in "the Levee" (see p. 111) and car showrooms along Michigan Avenue. Burnham Park, to the east, is the site of Soldier Field and several of the city's most famed institutions (see p. 113).

Two Historic Houses

HENRY B. CLARKE HOUSE (NR)

1855 S. Indiana Avenue. 1836. Access from Glessner House.

Henry B. Clarke moved from Utica, New York, to Chicago in 1835 to take advantage of the new city's opportunities. He purchased land near 16th Street and Michigan Avenue and built a substantial house in a style then popular along the East Coast, the Greek Revival. The house survived Clarke's business failures as well as the Chicago Fire of 1871. Following his death from cholera in 1849, Clarke's widow completed the house's elaborate Italianate cupola and much of its interior. The home served for a time as a location for the St. Paul Church of God in Christ, which was responsible for preserving the building.

JOHN JACOB GLESSNER HOUSE (NR)

1800 S. Prairie Avenue. 1885–87. ☎ 312-326-1480

In 1885, John J. Glessner, one of the founders of International Harvester, and his wife Frances commissioned Henry Hobson Richardson (1838–86), the architect of Chicago's Marshall Field Wholesale Store (1885, demolished in 1930), to design a house that would emphasize privacy. Glessner's neighbors decried Richardson's plan as a fortress. Indeed, the house's front façade of heavily rusticated granite stones pierced with only a few windows on the first level does make it appear unwelcoming. Its interior, however, presents a totally different impression: Large windows along the back façade look out on a restful enclosed courtyard. The Glessners lived in the house until their deaths in the 1930s, long after the neighborhood's ethnic mosaic had changed from a haven for wealthy industrialists to a working-class African American community. The restored house is Richardson's last surviving work in Chicago. Furnished in the Arts and Crafts style, Glessner House reflects the taste of Chicago in the years immediately following the 1871 fire.

The Spotted Church

THE SECOND PRESBYTERIAN CHURCH (NR)

1936 S. Michigan Avenue. 1872–74, James Renwick; 1900–1901, Howard Van Doren Shaw. ☎ 312-225-4951 🖳 www.2ndpresbyterian.org

Guidebooks are available in the church office.

Many of the people who lived on Prairie Avenue worshiped in this church designed by the architect of St. Patrick's Cathedral (1859–79) in New York City, James Renwick (1818–95). Rich in history and famous for

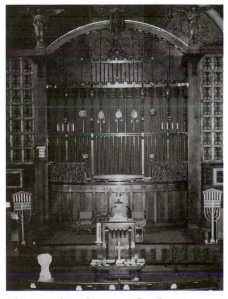

The Second Presbyterian Church

its architecture and array of art, Second Presbyterian offers visitors a welcome oasis.

The church's history reflects how the slavery issue began to tear apart the nation's fabric in the first decades of the nineteenth century. Presbyterians first met in a small cabin at Fort Dearborn in 1833 and incorporated as the First Presbyterian Church and Society of Chicago in 1835. Two years later the congregation split over the issue of slavery. Those opposed to the emancipation of slaves organized Second Presbyterian Church. In 1851 the congregation hired James Renwick to design a Gothic Revival limestone structure that was destroyed twenty years later in the Great Fire. In 1872 work began on this church located in what was the city's most exclusive neighborhood. This time Renwick designed an edifice modeled after fifteenth-century English Gothic churches. Situated on a corner lot and over six stories high, Second Presbyterian has a monumental presence on Michigan Avenue, a testament to the wealth and prestige of its builders, who included the influential Chicago families of Armour, Swift, Field, Pullman, and Kimball.

Flecks of black on the limestone blocks on the exterior have given the building its nickname, "the spotted church." The bituminous mottled limestone, known as "fairy," was cut from a quarry just southwest of the site.

Following a devastating fire in the spring of 1901 that gutted the nave, the congregation called upon one of their own, Howard Van Doren Shaw (1869–1926), a well-known and honored Chicago architect, to redesign the interior. Shaw collaborated with his close friend Frederic Clay Bartlett (1873–1953), a European-trained painter, and completed the project in one year. Influenced by the English Arts and Crafts movement (see below), Shaw and Bartlett transformed the interior of the church into a celebration of this very romantic style. The church has one of the nation's most significant Arts and Crafts interiors and was selected by the National Park Service and the White House to be one of the Save America's Treasures sites.

The first impression upon entering the nave is the warmth of its buff-colored walls and the earth tones of its beautiful murals and dark oak paneling, all infused with light filtering through stained-glass windows. Fourteen windows in the sanctuary are by Louis Comfort Tiffany or created in his studios. Tiffany's *Jeweled Window* on the north wall, completed about 1895, receives its name from the effect created by the thousands of tiny, irregularly chipped and faceted pieces of glass, each separately leaded, that cause the light to diffuse in all directions.

Centered high in the east wall of the balcony are two windows designed by William Fair Kline and executed in Tiffany's studio: *The Ascension* and *The Five Scourges*. Both display stained-glass techniques that were developed in Tiffany's studio, such as the sculptural appearance of the robes and the subtle shading of skin and hair of the figures.

Behind the organ screen on the west wall is Bartlett's thirty-by-forty-foot *Tree of Life* mural that includes the *Rainbow of Hope*. Above it is a

ARTS AND CRAFTS MOVEMENT

The Arts and Crafts Movement developed in late nineteenth- and early twentieth-century England under the leadership of William Morris (see p. 72) and grew out of a renewal of interest in handcrafted everyday objects. (In painting it is known as the Pre-Raphaelite Movement.) Its followers urged a return to the ideals of the Medieval craftsman, a response to what they viewed as a decline in design and aesthetics brought on by the Industrial Revolution. The movement resonated throughout Europe and the United States, primarily among the wealthy who could afford hand-wrought objects.

choir of angels floating in a star-studded heaven. Other church treasures include its beautifully carved limestone baptismal font created in Florence, Italy, and donated in the 1880s.

Second Presbyterian, built by the wealthy, is now an inner-city church located in a neighborhood that is evolving from commercial and industrial to residential. It draws its diverse congregation from surrounding neighborhoods and continues to fulfill its role as a place of worship and peaceful refuge for those living and working nearby.

Chicago's First African American Congregation
QUINN CHAPEL A.M.E. CHURCH (NR)
2401 S. Wabash Avenue. 1891, Henry F. Starbuck. ☎ 312-791-1846
💻 www.tourblackchicago.com/Quinn.htm

The Near South Side changed in the last decade of the nineteenth century as warehouses and buildings housing light industry were built near the railroad tracks. The area around Clark and Dearborn Streets and Roosevelt and Cermak Roads, known as the Levee and now part of Chinatown, was home to many African Americans, including those who worshiped in Quinn Chapel A.M.E.

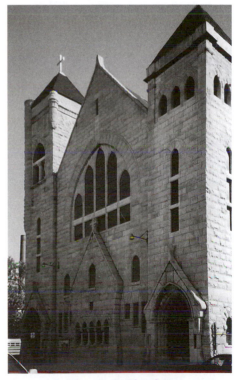

Organized by ex-slaves in 1844 as a nonsectarian prayer group that met in members' homes, the chapel became an affiliate of the African Methodist Episcopal Church in 1847. Shortly after Congress passed the Fugitive Slave Act in 1850, the congregation's first church, erected in 1853, became a way station on the Underground Railroad (see p. 14). A resolution passed by its members stated they would "stand by our liberty at

Quinn Chapel A.M.E. Church

the expense of our lives, and we will not consent to be taken into slavery or permit our brethren to be taken." The first church at the corner of Jackson and Federal Streets, now the site of the Monadnock Building, was destroyed in the 1871 fire, and a new church was built five years later on Federal Street just south of Van Buren Street. It was replaced in 1891 by the present Quinn Chapel, named for William Paul Quinn, fourth bishop of the A.M.E. Church, who was born in Calcutta, India, in 1788. Quinn was present at the A.M.E. founding conference in 1816 and was named a deacon two years later. Defying slavery organizations, Quinn set out to do missionary work in New Jersey, Pennsylvania, Ohio, Missouri, and Kentucky, and became a church elder in 1838, bishop in 1844, and senior bishop in 1849. He died in 1873.

Quinn Chapel was designed by Henry F. Starbuck (1850–1935), an African American architect, one of only a few practicing at this time, and built by African American workers. The combined Gothic and Romanesque Revival brick and rusticated gray-stone building has remained virtually unchanged since its construction. The spacious chapel on the second floor has pews fanning out from the chancel area, providing all congregants with good sightlines. A balcony provides additional seating. The sanctuary contains the pulpit, choir seating, and a historic William H. Delle pipe organ that was an exhibition piece in the German pavilion at the World's Columbian Exposition of 1893. Behind the organ is a mural *The Risen Christ*, painted in 1904 by Proctor Chisholm, a member of the congregation.

Presidents William B. McKinley and William Howard Taft spoke in this church whose members have included Adelbuy H. Roberts, the first African American elected to the Illinois State Senate, and Robert R. Jackson, who served twenty-one years as a Chicago alderman.

NEARBY
➥ **National Vietnam Veterans Art Museum**, 1801 S. Indiana.
☎ 312-326-0270 🖳 http://www.NVVAM.org

The museum houses an art exhibition, *Reflexes and Reflections*, created by military personnel from all nations who fought in the Vietnam War, including those from North and South Vietnam. The art dramatically illustrates the highly charged personal responses the artists had to their individual experiences in the conflict. Ironically, the museum also displays memorabilia and artifacts from the war, including medals, uniforms, and weapons.

The Last Link Added to Chicago's Chain of Parks
BURNHAM PARK

Stretching along the lakeshore for five miles from Grant Park and Solidarity Drive south to Hyde Park, this lakeside park is named for Daniel Hudson Burnham (see p. 97). The Park's "Museum Campus" is home to the 1929 **John G. Shedd Aquarium**, 1200 S. Lake Shore Drive, ☎ 312-939-2438; the 1915 **Field Museum of Natural History**, 1400 S. Lake Shore Drive, ☎ 312-922-9410; and the 1929 **Adler Planetarium**, 1300 S. Lake Shore Drive, ☎ 312-322-7827. All three are named after their major donors, influential and important nineteenth-century developers and entrepreneurs who generously endowed the city with much of its grandeur.

Douglas

The area from 26th Street south to Pershing Road and west to the Dan Ryan Expressway is named for Illinois Senator Stephen Arnold Douglas (1813–61). Settlement began with Douglas's purchase of a sixty-acre estate in 1852 that he named Oakenwald. His decision to have the tracks of the Illinois Central Railroad run along the lakefront adjacent to his estate increased its value and encouraged the area's development. During the Civil War, part of his estate became an infamous prisoner-of-war camp where thousands of Confederate soldiers and sailors perished. After the war, Douglas's sons transformed the land into the Groveland Park subdivision, which soon became an upper-class neighborhood. Douglas is buried in an elaborate tomb on his former estate (see pp. 115–16).

A Catalyst for Change
PILGRIM BAPTIST CHURCH (KEHILATH ANSHE MA'ARIV) (NR)

3301 S. Indiana Avenue. 1890–91, Louis Sullivan and Dankmar Adler. ☎ 773-842-5830

This is the fourth synagogue occupied by Kehilath Anshe Ma'ariv (Congregation of the Men of the West, K.A.M.) that was founded in 1847, the oldest Jewish congregation in Illinois. Dankmar Adler was a member; his father-in-law, Abraham Kohn, was one of its founders; and his father, Liebman Adler, was for a time its rabbi. These associations help explain how the congregation obtained the services of one of Chicago's most famous and pioneering architectural firms to design its building. Adler contributed the plan and designed the building's famed acoustics; Sullivan was responsible for the ornament.

The building's appearance comes as a surprise to a visitor; it is unlike any other synagogue built up to this time and stands as a tribute to both of its designers and the congregation who had the farsightedness to encourage them to explore a new vocabulary for synagogue architecture.

The only indication of this building's original identity is a Hebrew inscription above its entryway. Other than that, nothing about its architectural style or decoration suggests its function. Among its more visible exterior characteristics are its rusticated Bedford-stone walls that support a clerestory and steeply pitched roof, and a large recessed tunnel-arch over the entrance. The austere exterior does not prepare the visitor for the grandeur of its spacious auditorium, which occupies the second floor. A great parabolic vault formed by metal girders rises up in the clerestory that originally had stained-glass windows. One can only imagine how the filtered light must have flickered off Sullivan's organic designs and the gold-painted plaster ornament that remains intact. Other changes made when

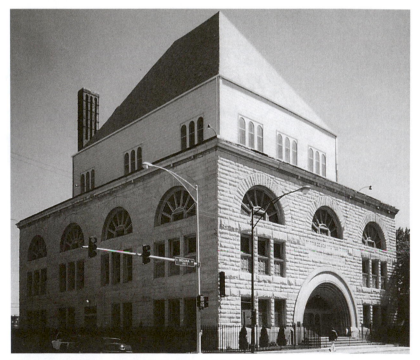

Pilgrim Baptist Church (Kehilath Anshe Ma'ariv)

A NEW ARCHITECTURAL LANGUAGE
FOR SYNAGOGUES

Many of Chicago's churches are either in the Gothic or Romanesque Revival styles, which appealed to nineteenth-century worshipers because of their association with medieval Christian ideals and their immigrant European roots (see pp. 71–75). Jews, understandably, were reluctant to adopt these "Christian" styles for their synagogues. Living for centuries in the Diaspora, the Jewish people were never in a position to develop their own style of religious architecture. Until well into the nineteenth century, building restrictions in the Old World forced them to adopt and adapt their host country's vernacular style of architecture, with the result that synagogues were often modest in size and hidden from view (see pp. 87–89). America offered them an opportunity to erect more visible structures, but what style should they choose? The search for an answer can be seen in the variety of architectural styles selected for synagogues throughout Chicago. K.A.M. is one of the more dramatic efforts. A shortage of funds prevented Adler and Sullivan from carrying out all of their ideas, but those that they brought to fruition were indeed groundbreaking. This building looks forward to what its congregants believed was a promising future in the New World.

the synagogue was transformed into a Baptist church include the opening of the semidome on the east wall to accommodate a baptistery and choir.

The neighborhood began to undergo a change shortly after the synagogue was built, and by the first decade of the twentieth century it was the heart of what is known today as Bronzeville, Chicago's Black Metropolis (see p. 117). The building was sold in 1922 to Pilgrim Baptist Church, a black congregation founded in 1915. It was here that Thomas Dorsey first incorporated gospel music into a church service (see next page).

NEARBY

➡ **Douglas Tomb State Historic Site (NR)**, 636 E. 35th Street, 1881. Senator Douglas was one of the most distinguished statesmen of his day, and the Lincoln-Douglas Debates remain one of the most important political battles in our nation's history. Although he was an opponent of Lincoln, Douglas was one of the first supporters of the Union

THOMAS DORSEY

Born in 1897 in Villa Rica, Georgia, Dr. Dorsey is considered the father of gospel music. He played the blues with many of the greats, including Ma Rainey, before he started to compose religious music in 1921. Gospel music was introduced at the National Baptist Convention Jubilee Meeting held in Chicago in 1930, where Dorsey performed his piece, "If You See My Savior." Soon gospel choirs were formed in many Baptist churches, including Pilgrim Baptist, where Dorsey was a member. He became director of the church's gospel choir and, along with Theodore R. Frye, Sallie Martin, and Marion Pairs, organized the National Convention of Gospel Choirs and Choruses, Inc. Dorsey composed one thousand songs and was the first African American introduced into the Nashville Hall of Fame. He died in 1993 at the age of ninety-six.

at the outbreak of the Civil War. The Douglas Tomb Monument is a ninety-six-foot-high pylon surmounted by a bronze figure of Douglas by sculptor Leonard W. Volk.

The International Style Is Introduced in Chicago
THE ROBERT F. CARR MEMORIAL CHAPEL OF ST. SAVIOUR (IIT CHAPEL)
Nondenominational. 65 E. 32nd Street. 1952, Ludwig Mies van der Rohe. ☎ 312-567-3160

Located in the heart of the Douglas neighborhood is the campus of the Illinois Institute of Technology (IIT), whose establishment was a bit unusual. The story goes that Philip Armour, the founder of the meatpacking company, heard a young minister preach a sermon entitled, "What I Would Do with a Million Dollars." Armour gave him a million dollars and together they built a technical school, the Armour Institute, that opened in 1893. In 1940, it merged with the Lewis Institute to form the Illinois Institute of Technology, and Mies van der Rohe (see p. 99) was named its director.

The chapel, known on campus as the God Box, is the only religious building designed by Mies and is considered an outstanding example of

BRONZEVILLE

Bronzeville is the name given to an African American neighborhood on Chicago's South Side that runs from 26th to 51st Streets, and from the Dan Ryan Expressway east to Cottage Grove Avenue. Originally called the Ghetto by outsiders, it began to be known as Bronzeville in the 1930s, when a contest was sponsored by the *Chicago Bee* to elect a "mayor of Bronzeville."

By 1920, the Douglas community had become part of Chicago's Black Metropolis, which developed as a result of the "Great Migration" (1915–25), the first major wave of African Americans to arrive in Chicago. The Illinois Central Railroad, one of the few north-south railroads in the nation, provided African Americans with an escape from the South, where segregation and discrimination plagued their existence and boll weevils destroyed cotton crops. Many began to settle in the city's Near South Side as its affluent residents began to leave for the suburbs. Even though they were forced to live in segregated neighborhoods and the jobs available were poorly paid, Chicago was still considered the Promised Land, a vast improvement over conditions in the South. The city was the destination for a second wave of African Americans in the 1940s, partly a result of the invention of a mechanical cotton picker that put an end to the southern sharecropper tradition that had kept many African Americans in a state of semislavery. Ironically, many of them found employment at International Harvester, the manufacturer of the cotton picker. For nearly half a century, Bronzeville was a thriving economic and cultural center for the city's African American community, ranging from migrant workers to millionaires who were restricted from living in most of Chicago's other neighborhoods. It was here that the first black-owned businesses were opened and Duke Ellington and Louis Armstrong found receptive audiences. Chicago's first housing project was erected between 37th and 39th Streets along Martin Luther King, Jr. Drive. Following World War II, many African Americans began to move into other neighborhoods. Those that stayed found themselves without employment as industries and the stockyards began to close. Bronzeville went into a decline, but has since rebounded.

the International style. Unadorned on the exterior, its function remains obscure to passers-by. In plan it is a thirty-seven-by-sixty-foot rectangle with solid brick walls on the north and south. The east and west walls are brick on the sides with glass doors and floor-to-ceiling windows. The glass on the west wall is frosted, while that on the east façade is clear, inviting nature into the sanctuary. The interior is equally austere. A curtain frames a solid rectangular altar of travertine surmounted by a six-foot chromium cross. Tapestries depicting biblical scenes that once hung on the south wall have been removed.

In Honor of World War I African American Heroes
VICTORY MONUMENT (NR)
3500 Martin Luther King, Jr. Drive. 1926 and 1936. Sculptor: Leonard Crunelle. Architect: John A. Nyden.

Victory Monument commemorates the heroic World War I achievements of the African American Eighth Regiment of the Illinois National

Guard, who served in France under the 370th U.S. Infantry. In the mid 1920s, the black community of Bronzeville proposed the erection of a permanent monument in honor of the regiment on what was then Grand Boulevard. Their proposal was met with stiff opposition from the South Park Commission, which controlled that portion of the boulevard system. Only after intense lobbying by the black community did the commission finally relent and agree to the monument.

Its circular granite shaft is set with three bronze bas-relief panels by Leonard Crunelle that portray an African American soldier, an African American woman symbolizing motherhood, and a female figure of "Columbia" holding a tablet engraved with the locations of the regiment's principal battles. The monument was dedicated on Armistice Day, November 11, 1928. Crunelle also created the large sculpture of a uniformed World War I African American soldier that was placed at the top of the monument in 1936. One of the most famous African American landmarks in Chicago, the monument is the site of an annual Memorial Day ceremony.

Victory Monument

A Historic African American Congregation
OLIVET BAPTIST CHURCH
4101 S. Martin Luther King, Jr. Drive. 1875–76, Wilcox and Miller.
☎ 312-528-0124 💻 www.olivetchurch.org

Originally built for First Baptist Church of Chicago, this building was sold in 1917 to Olivet Baptist Church, which was organized in 1861 through a merger of two African American congregations. The congregation's first building was destroyed in the 1871 fire, but a decision was made to immediately rebuild it on the same site. That building remained in use until this church was purchased. At that time, Olivet Baptist laid claim to being the world's largest African American congregation, as well as the largest Protestant congregation in the world. By the 1940s its membership had grown to more than twenty thousand. The congregation's pastors have assumed important leadership roles in the National Baptist Convention, USA, and in the Civil Rights movement.

While the exterior of this church is in the Gothic Revival style, its interior is an auditorium plan. Rows of pews and a gallery curve to face the pulpit, located against the eastern wall. Behind the pulpit is a large tank used for full immersion baptisms and a three-manual pipe organ. Although the auditorium seats approximately fourteen hundred people, it has a sense of warmth and intimacy due to its plan, which brings all worshipers close to the pulpit, and the soft natural light filtering through amber opalescent stained-glass windows set behind the balcony.

Olivet Baptist Church remains a vibrant and active congregation and provides many programs for its members and neighbors.

Oakland

Oakland, located south of Douglas and abutting Lake Shore Drive, is bounded by 35th and 43rd Streets, Cottage Grove Avenue, and the Illinois Central Railroad tracks. When it was established along the old Vincennes Trail, Oakland was centered on a slaughterhouse, soap factory, and lard-rendering works operated by Charles Cleaver, a successful butcher who built a now demolished mansion, Oakwood Hall. As transportation improved following the Civil War, more expensive homes were built in Oakland, with the most lavish ones lining Drexel Boulevard, an important link in the South Parks Boulevard system. Some homes that date to the 1880s survive and remain privately owned; these include the three-storied limestone-clad houses at 4131-4137 S. Drexel Boulevard (1886–87) and the **Eliel House** at 4122 S. Ellis Avenue (1886) designed by Adler and Sullivan. Many lakefront homes were replaced by high-rise public housing projects in the 1960s and 1970s while others were demolished. In recent years several public and private agencies have worked to redevelop the area and to preserve what is left of its historic architecture. Grant Church (see below) erected a six-story building at 4161 Drexel Boulevard in 1991 to house senior citizens.

The Prototype for Christian Science Churches
GRANT MEMORIAL A.M.E. CHURCH
(FIRST CHURCH OF CHRIST, SCIENTIST)
4017 S. Drexel Boulevard. 1897, Solon S. Beman. ☎ 773-285-9760

The influence of the Beaux-Arts style (see pp. 76–77) introduced at the 1893 World's Columbian Exposition remains visible in Christian Science churches modeled after this building. Solon S. Beman, the architect responsible for the Merchant Tailors Building at the exposition, was hired by Christian Science founder Mary Baker Eddy to design the First Church of Christ, Scientist in Chicago, as well as five others in the city. (Still standing: **Second Church of Christ, Scientist,** 2700 N. Pine Grove Avenue; **Fifth Church of Christ, Scientist,** 4840 S. Dorchester Avenue; and **Sixth Church of Christ, Scientist,** 11321 S. Prairie Avenue.) Ms. Eddy associated the Greek Revival elements visible in the Beaux-Arts style with ancient Greek democracy, a style she viewed as appropriate for her new American church, which she based on the principle of equality for all members (see pp. 41–42).

Built of Bedford, Indiana, limestone, the church's relatively narrow classical façade belies its spacious auditorium, which seats approximately fifteen hundred people. The large domed space decorated with classical motifs has raked curved rows of seats that face the north wall, where the reader's desk is located.

Organized in 1914, the members of Grant Memorial A.M.E. Church have worshiped here since 1950. It is thanks to their efforts that this historic building still graces its neighborhood, continuing its service to all who require it.

NEARBY
➡ **Metropolitan Community Church,** 4100 S. Martin Luther King, Jr. Drive. 1889, Solon S. Beman. ☎ 773-536-2046. Solon Beman designed this Richardsonian Romanesque Revival church for the Forty-first Street Presbyterian Church. It was sold to the Metropolitan Community Church in 1926. The auditorium-plan building retains many of its historic features including a 4,500-pipe E. M. Skinner organ installed in 1916.

Grand Boulevard

Next to Oakland is the neighborhood of Grand Boulevard, the original name of Martin Luther King, Jr. Drive, which bisects this community. Laid out in 1869 by landscape architects Frederick Law Olmsted and Calvert Vaux (see p. 125), the boulevard was designed to connect Washington Park with downtown Chicago. The area is bounded on the north by Oakwood Boulevard and on the south by 51st Street; its eastern border is Cottage Grove Avenue and its western is State Street. It wasn't until after the 1871 fire and improved transportation that the neighborhood began to attract upper-class residents, including German Jews, Irish Catholics, and Yankees. The rapid pace of construction found the neighborhood reaching residential maturity by 1910. One of the most famous homes in the area is the Gothic Revival **Elam House,** a Chicago Landmark at 4726 S. Martin Luther King, Jr. Drive, built in 1903 and designed by Henry Newhouse.

The monumental houses of worship built in the area confirm its original residents' economic and social status and represent a variety of faiths and denominations. They illustrate how the nation's freedom of worship fuels a competition for souls often fought on the "battlefield" of religious architecture. A number of these historic buildings have survived, but most reflect changes that began to occur in the first decades of the twentieth century, when the neighborhood became part of Bronzeville (see p. 117). African Americans adapted Grand Boulevard's places of worship for their own use and built new ones as well. Thanks to their efforts it is still possible to visit and enjoy many of these historic structures that continue to serve as havens of hope, renewal, and beauty for those living in the area.

An African American Catholic Community
HOLY ANGELS
Catholic. 607 E. Oakwood Boulevard. 1991. ☎ 773-624-5375
🖳 www.holyangels.com

Irish Catholics who lived around 37th Street and Cottage Grove founded Holy Angels parish in 1880. Facing the anti-Catholic sentiments of their neighbors, the Irish had to secretly buy land in order to build their church. Dedicated in 1897, the beautiful Romanesque Revival church served its Irish members until the 1930s, when they began to be outnumbered by African Americans who had moved into the neighborhood. The Irish parish priests welcomed the newcomers and by the mid-twentieth century thousands of African Americans had joined the parish. Sadly, Holy Angels burned to the ground in 1986. Five years later a new church was dedicated on the site. It gained fame for being the first church to rely solely on solar power. Since then auxiliary power units have been added.

While the new building is uninspired architecturally, it is worth a visit to see an altar painting by Father Englebert Mveng, a prominent African priest, artist, and author who was brutally murdered in his home in Yaounde, Cameroon, in 1995, shortly after the mural was completed. The painting depicts ten roles and interventions that angels have performed throughout biblical history. They are: St. Michael the Archangel; Meshak, Shadrak, and Abednego as they were thrown into the fire by King Nebuchadnezzar; Peter visited by an angel in prison (Peter's face resembles Nelson Mandela); the Virgin Mary as a Nigerian woman visited by the angel Gabriel; the resurrection and ascension; the agony in the garden; the four angels of judgment day; Abraham, Sarah, and three angels; Tobit visited by the archangel Raphael; the star of Bethlehem at the birth of Jesus.

Dankmar Adler's Last Hurrah
EBENEZER BAPTIST CHURCH
(TEMPLE ISAIAH SYNAGOGUE)
4501 S. Vincennes Avenue. 1898–99, Dankmar Adler. ☎ 773-373-6144

This building was Adler's last major commission and represents his fourth effort to design a synagogue (two others have been demolished). Unlike Kehilath Anshe Ma'ariv (Pilgrim Baptist Church—see pp. 113–14), where Adler and his partner Louis Sullivan demonstrated their ability to develop a *new* architectural vocabulary, this building borrows from the past. Its Greek-cross plan is derived from Greek Orthodox churches dating back over one thousand years, except Adler chose not to crown this building with the usual dome. Rather, as becomes clear on the interior, a great north-south barrel-vaulted ceiling spans the auditorium.

While changes have been made to the sanctuary, it retains the excellent acoustics, sightlines, and adequate lighting that are characteristic of all of Adler's auditoriums. The sanctuary has rows of raked individual seats curving toward the eastern wall, where the pulpit, choir, and baptistery are located. Additional seating is available in the balcony, which runs along three sides of the auditorium.

In 1921, Ebenezer Baptist Church, founded in 1902, moved to this location from its second building at 35th and Dearborn Streets. The Jewish congregation built a new synagogue in 1923 and 1924, now the K.A.M—Isaiah Israel Temple (see pp. 126–27).

NEARBY

➡ **Corpus Christi Church,** Catholic, 4900 S. Martin Luther King, Jr. Drive. 1914–16, Joe W. McCarthy; 1975 renovation, Paul Straka. ☎ 773-285-7720; 773-285-2572

This parish, established in 1901 by Irish Catholics, had by 1904 outgrown its modest church. With his parishioners' blessing, the Reverend Thomas O'Gara made plans to erect a new church and rectory "whose splendor and beauty would eclipse all surrounding buildings." His goal was achieved when this handsome Renaissance Revival church was dedicated in 1916. The building has experienced a turbulent history, including being closed on two different occasions due to declining membership and the need for repair. Following renovations in 1975, it was reopened and continues to serve as a strong presence in its neighborhood. This parish is among the earliest Roman Catholic African American congregations in Chicago.

➡ **Mt. Pisgah Missionary Baptist Church,** 4600 S. Martin Luther King, Jr. Drive. 1910–12, Alfred S. Alschuler. ☎ 773-373-0070

Three different faith groups have used this classically inspired building since it was first erected in 1910. Initially built for the Chicago Sinai Congregation, organized in 1861 as the city's first Reform synagogue, it was sold in 1944 to Corpus Christi Parish, who used it as a Catholic high school until 1962, when it was sold to Mt. Pisgah Missionary Baptist Church, organized in 1929. Martin Luther King, Jr., spoke at this church on February 4, 1968.

The building was the first synagogue designed by Alfred S. Alschuler, who had worked for a year in the office of Dankmar Adler. Alschuler designed several other notable synagogues in Chicago, including Anshe Emet (see pp. 176–77) and K.A.M.—Isaiah Israel (see pp. 126–27).

Hyde Park/Kenwood

The neighborhoods of Hyde Park (see p. 129) and Kenwood (see p. 126) are home to some of the city's most distinguished and historic architecture, the University of Chicago, and two beautiful parks, Jackson and Washington, as well as the Midway Plaisance that connects them. The South Parks Commission, created in 1869, established the string of parks that encircles the Hyde Park community area and hired the Olmsted and Vaux Company to draft plans for their development. Their plans were lost in the 1871 fire, and another landscape architect, H.W. S. Cleveland (1840–1900), was asked to develop a less costly plan. Olmsted and Vaux were again hired by Daniel Burnham to be the site designers for the 1893

World's Columbian Exposition on land that now includes the two parks and the Midway Plaisance. Following the Exposition, Olmsted and Eliot drew up another plan for the park in 1895.

Six Hundred Acres of Lush Vegetation
JACKSON PARK

Jackson Park encompasses more than two square miles of parkland bordering Lake Michigan. Originally a treeless marsh with a lagoon, Olmsted transformed the site into what many consider Chicago's most beautiful park. Today it is filled with mature trees, reflecting ponds, lagoons where fishing is permitted, a perennial garden, and the tranquil **Osaka Garden,** reached by footbridges and a path made of red granite blocks taken from Chicago's streetcar tracks. This Japanese garden is carefully landscaped with rocks, flowers, and shrubs around a replica of the Phoenix Temple in Kyoto. Spectacular lakefront vistas and cityscapes are visible from **Promontory Point** at 55th Street. The **Golden Lady,** the popular name for *The Republic,* a sculpture originally created by Daniel Chester French (1850–1931) for the World's Columbian Exposition and recast in a smaller version in 1918, can be found on East Hayes Drive. The other visible evidence of the exposition is the monumental Palace of Fine Arts, now the **Museum of Science and Industry** (57th Street and Lake Shore Drive; ☎ 773-684-1414). Behind the Museum is the **Clarence Darrow Memorial Bridge,** named for the famous lawyer whose ashes were deposited in the parkland across from the lagoon.

Osaka Garden, Jackson Park

FREDERICK LAW OLMSTED

One of the greatest champions of the City Beautiful movement was Frederick Law Olmsted, the founder of American landscape architecture and its leading exponent. Born in 1822 in Hartford, Connecticut, he later moved to New York and became a farmer. Olmsted was named the superintendent of labor for New York City's Central Park in 1857, when he met Calvert Vaux who was in the process of designing the park. Olmsted became a collaborator and went on to design New York's Prospect Park, Boston's Emerald Necklace of parks, and the World's Columbian Exposition in Chicago, one of his last major commissions. He died in 1903.

A Companion to Jackson Park
WASHINGTON PARK AND
THE MIDWAY PLAISANCE

Olmsted originally designed the Midway Plaisance, a mile-long divided boulevard that runs through the University of Chicago campus, as part of his South Park plan and redesigned it in 1893 for the World's Columbian Exposition, and again in 1895. At its western end, where it merges with Washington Park, is one of Lorado Taft's greatest works, the **Fountain of Time,** (erected in 1922), an expansive statuary group of over one hundred figures that represent humanity passing before a monumental figure of Father Time, who watches them from the other side of a pool. Washington Park is similar in many ways to Jackson Park, including its green fields, lagoons where fishing is allowed, footbridges, and streams, but it lacks the lakefront. Instead, where beautiful homes and apartments once surrounded it, Washington Park is now in the midst of boarded-up buildings. However, it continues to provide its neighbors with a peaceful oasis.

NEARBY

➥ **The Du Sable Museum of African American History,** 740 E. 56th Place. ☎ 773-947-0600 🖳 www.dusablemuseum.org

The museum, housed in the South Parks Commission's former headquarters in Washington Park, is a Classical Revival building designed by D. H. Burnham and Company and built in 1910. It is named in honor of Chicago's first permanent resident, Jean Baptiste Point Du Sable (see

LORADO TAFT

Lorado Z. Taft (1860–1936) is one of Chicago's most important sculptors. He grew up in Elmwood and Champaign and was educated at the Champaign/Urbana campus of the University of Illinois and the École des Beaux-Arts in Paris. Taft was superintendent of the sculptural program for the 1893 World's Columbian Exposition, for which he won the Designer's Medal. Some of his most significant commissions were public sculptures commissioned during the City Beautiful movement and include the Fountain of the Great Lakes, dedicated in 1913, and the monumental *Fountain of Time*. Taft's **Midway Studios** at the University of Chicago are listed as Chicago and National Historic Landmarks (see p. 130).

p. 102). The museum's mission is to preserve and interpret the historical and cultural experiences and achievements of people of African descent.

Kenwood

Kenwood is bounded on the east by Lake Michigan, 43rd Street on the north, Cottage Grove Avenue on the west, and Hyde Park Boulevard on the south. The creation of Drexel Boulevard and nearby Washington Park in 1869, as well as the Great Fire of 1871, spurred its development. The area's impressive mansions built in styles ranging from Romanesque Revival to Prairie style earned Kenwood the reputation of being the "Lake Forest" of the south (see p. 188). As early as 1892, two homes built in Kenwood anticipated the Prairie style; Frank Lloyd Wright designed them when he was Sullivan's apprentice: **4852 S. Kenwood Avenue** and **4858 S. Kenwood Avenue.** Nearby are two Prairie-style homes: the **Julius Rosenwald House** (1903) designed by Nimmons and Fellows at 4901 S. Ellis Avenue, and the **Ernest Magerstadt House** (1908) at 4930 S. Greenwood Avenue, a Chicago landmark designed by George Maher.

A Synagogue with a Minaret
K.A.M.—ISAIAH ISRAEL TEMPLE
Reform Jewish. 5045 S. Greenwood. 1923–24, Alfred S. Alschuler.
☎ 773-924-1234 🖳 www.kamii.org

The search for an appropriate architectural style for synagogues (see pp. 87–89) included the adaptation of Byzantine and Moorish art and architecture, and at times, as in this instance, a combination of the two.

Since Judaism originated in the Middle East, it was thought appropriate to use styles indigenous to that area. This synagogue, with its combination of a massive dome and a minaret puncturing the sky above it, may puzzle an uninitiated visitor who would have difficulty fathoming the building's identity without its accompanying signs and symbols.

Designed by a well-known local Jewish architect, Alfred S. Alschuler (1876–1940), the synagogue now houses two congregations that merged in 1971: Kehilath Anshe Ma'ariv (K.A.M.) and Isaiah Israel. K.A.M. is the congregation that commissioned Adler and Sullivan to build the ground-breaking synagogue now occupied by Pilgrim Baptist Church (see pp. 113–14). Isaiah Israel, founded in 1852, the city's second-oldest Jewish congregation, originally commissioned this synagogue.

Stairs on the Greenwood Avenue façade lead to three arched solid oak doors. Above each door is a relief sculpture that depicts a different Jewish motif: the menorah, Star of David, and the Hebrew word "truth." Above the arch of the central door are the tablets of the Ten Commandments flanked by the name of the congregation.

A huge dome supported by eight freestanding pillars covers the octagonal sanctuary. Curved rows of seats and a balcony face toward a semicircular *bimah* upon which is an Ark of travertine and colored mosaic that holds the Torah scrolls. The Hebrew inscription on the Ark reads: "Know before whom you stand." On the arch above it and framing the tablets of the Ten Commandments is the Jewish call to prayer, the Shema, "Here O Israel, the Lord our God, the Lord is One." Above that is space for a choir and organ. Light filters into the space from seven large stained-glass windows and a series of smaller ones all created by Emil Frei Art Glass Company of

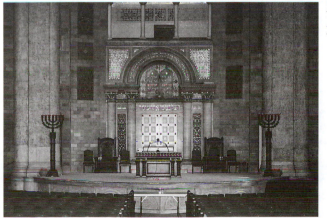

K.A.M.—
Isaiah Israel
Temple

St. Louis, Missouri. The minaret, incidentally, does have a practical function; it disguises the building's tall chimney. The synagogue also houses the
Morton B. Weiss Museum of Judaica that displays artifacts and memorabilia related to the congregation's history.

For an earlier example of a synagogue designed by Alschuler, see
Anshe Emet (see pp. 176–77), erected in 1910 and 1911 for Temple
Sholom, a congregation who built a domed Byzantine-style synagogue in
1930 (see p. 177).

NEARBY

➥ **Rainbow Push Coalition (K.A.M. Synagogue),** 4945 S. Drexel Boulevard. 1923–24, Newhouse and Bernham. ☎ 773-373-3366
🖳, www.rainbowpush.org. At the time Isaiah Israel was erecting its
Moorish/Byzantine–style synagogue, K.A.M. was moving into its new
building, one that did not look to the future like its famous predecessor in
Douglas (see pp. 113–14), but rather to the distant past: a Neoclassical
temple complete with a freestanding **colonnaded portico.** The use of this
style may be the congregation's response to the recent discovery of ancient
synagogues in the Galilee that date to the Greco-Roman period, although
none of them resembled a Greek temple, or it may be due to a renewed
interest in Greek democratic ideals that unfolded following the dedication
of the Lincoln Memorial in Washington, D.C. in 1922. The building was
sold to Operation PUSH (People United to Serve Humanity) in 1971,
when K.A.M. merged with Isaiah Israel.

Founded by the Reverend Jesse Jackson in 1971, PUSH grew out of
Operation Breadbasket, an organization dedicated to improving the financial position of the black community and headed by Jackson from 1966
through 1971. With the motto: "I am Somebody," Jackson attracted large
and enthusiastic crowds to his weekly PUSH prayer meetings, and became
a powerful voice for minorities and the disenfranchised. In 1986 Jackson
founded the National Rainbow Coalition. The two organizations merged
into a multicultural and multiracial human rights organization that is a
leader in the fight for racial and social justice.

Edgar Lee Masters Prayed Here
**KENWOOD UNITED CHURCH OF CHRIST
(KENWOOD EVANGELICAL CHURCH)**
4600-4608 S. Greenwood Avenue. 1887, William W. Boyington.
☎ 773-373-2861

Edgar Lee Masters was a successful lawyer in Chicago long before he
became famous for his 1915 book, *Spoon River Anthology* (see p. 254),

which he wrote while living at 4852 Kenwood Avenue and attending this church. Many prominent Chicagoans were members of this congregation, and they were the ones that selected William W. Boyington (1818–98), a respected Chicago architect famous for his design of the Chicago Water Tower and Pumping Station (see p. 162), to design a well-appointed, distinguished place of worship.

The church, built of granite from the demolished Chicago Board of Trade building, is in the Romanesque Revival style. It includes typical features of this style such as an asymmetrical façade, a single corner tower, round arches and arcades, and ornamental relief carvings. In contrast to its Revival-style exterior, the interior is in the auditorium plan (see pp. 81–82) favored by many Protestant denominations where the focus is on the pulpit.

Hyde Park

Named after Hyde Park communities in New York State and London, Chicago's Hyde Park is located directly south of Kenwood. Bordering it on the east is Jackson Park, on the west Washington Park, and the Midway Plaisance forms the southern border. Paul Cornell, a New York attorney, started the suburb in 1853 and assured its success by securing an agreement with the Illinois Central Railroad to build a station at 53rd Street. The suburb was incorporated in 1861, and eight years later Cornell established the South Parks Commission, which set aside land for Washington and Jackson Parks and the Midway Plaisance. Two factors led to Hyde Park's further expansion: the founding of the University of Chicago in 1891 and the 1893 World's Columbian Exposition. Many of Chicago's leading architects were commissioned to design houses in the area, including Frank Lloyd Wright, whose famed Frederick C. Robie House, completed in 1909, is open to the public (see p. 131).

Hyde Park began to decline in the 1950s, spurring the University of Chicago to spearhead an ambitious urban renewal program, the largest in the nation, that demolished about a thousand acres of buildings that were replaced by modern apartment buildings, townhouses, and commercial structures.

A Bastion of Scholarship
THE UNIVERSITY OF CHICAGO
☎ 773-702-1234 💻 www.uchicago.edu

The American Baptist Educational Society founded the University of Chicago in 1890; it was opened to students two years later. The university is built on land partially donated by Marshall Field and funded with a six-hundred-thousand-dollar endowment from John D. Rockefeller. Inspired by Oxford and Cambridge, the university's first buildings were designed in the Gothic Revival style, giving the campus the appearance of a medieval fortress set in the midst of an expanding urban neighborhood. The **Main Quadrangle** occupies four blocks between 57th and 59th Streets and Ellis and University Avenues and was designed by different architects over a period of fifty years. The 1959 **Laird Bell Law Quadrangle** (1111 E. 61st Street), designed by the Finnish architect Eero Saarinen (1910–61), is a modern complex of three buildings grouped around a six-story office-library building, an open court, and a reflecting pool with a bronze sculpture, *Construction in Space in the 3rd and 4th Dimension* by Antoine Pevsner (1886–1962). On Ellis Avenue between E. 56th and E. 57th Streets is a twelve-foot-high sculpture by Henry Moore (1898–1986), *Nuclear Energy.* It commemorates an event that occurred beneath the west stands of Stagg Field on December 2, 1942, when Enrico Fermi and his team of physicists who were part of the secret Manhattan Project "initiated a self-sustaining nuclear chain reaction and controlled it." The sculpture, dedicated on the twenty-fifth anniversary of this significant step in the development of the atomic bomb and nuclear power, resembles either a skull or mushroom cloud supported by what may be arches of a church.

Lorado Taft's **Midway Studios,** 6016 S. Ingleside Avenue, are used by the university's Department of Art and can be visited during academic sessions.

NEARBY
➥ **Rockefeller Memorial Chapel,** 5850 S. Woodlawn Avenue. 1928, Bertram G. Goodhue. ☎ 773-702-2100
💻 www.rockefeller.uchicago.edu

John D. Rockefeller, the University of Chicago's Baptist founder, requested that the campus's central and dominant feature be a chapel that could be used for a variety of events. Designed by Betram Grosvenor Goodhue (1869–1924), a leading proponent of the Gothic Revival style and dedicated in 1928, the chapel's 207-foot tower is a campus landmark. Above the chapel's arched entryway are life-size statues of biblical and historical figures that range from Abraham to Zoroaster with Christ at the arch's peak. The chapel is entered through a narthex that leads into a spacious nave that seats nearly two thousand people. Massive stone piers and arches help to support the vaulted ceiling that rises seventy-nine feet above the floor. The chapel includes a statue of Goodhue holding a model of the building.

➡ **Hyde Park Union Church,** United Church of Christ, 773 Woodlawn Avenue. 1906, John Gambel Rogers. ☎ 773-363-6063

🖳 www.hpuc.org

Organized in 1874 as the First Baptist Church, the congregation had close ties with the University of Chicago, where many of its members were on the faculty. It affiliated with the United Church of Christ in 1963. The Romanesque Revival structure has been described as "a rare blend of high and low church sensibilities." Amply decorated with impressive stained-glass windows created in the studios of Louis Comfort Tiffany, Franz X. Zettler, and Charles Connick, the sanctuary also contains a carved Celtic cross, a Sabbath menorah, and a raised Communion Table. A large formal baptismal pool is located at the southwest corner of the chancel.

➡ **Frederic C. Robie House (NR),** 5757 S. Woodlawn Avenue. 1906–9, Frank Lloyd Wright. ☎ 773-702-8374

🖳 www.wrightplus.org/robiehouse

Considered the culmination of Wright's Prairie style (see p. 98), it is furnished with both reproductions and originals of its Wright-designed furniture.

➡ **The David and Alfred Smart Museum of Art,** 5550 S. Greenwood Avenue. 1974, Edward Larrabee Barnes. ☎ 773-702-0200

🖳 www.smartmuseum.uchicago.edu

Located on the University of Chicago's campus, the museum houses over eight thousand works of art that span over five thousand years of artistic creation. It also has special exhibitions and a variety of educational programs.

➡ **The Oriental Institute,** 1155 E. 58th Street. 1931, Mayers, Murray and Phillip. ☎ 773-702-9514; 773-702-9520

Founded in 1919 by James Henry Breasted, the first American to receive a Ph.D. in Egyptology, the mission of the Oriental Institute is to document and study the languages, history, and cultures of the ancient Near East. Its galleries display many of the objects discovered in the course of the institute's many archaeological and survey expeditions to every country of the Near East.

➡ **The Joseph Bond Chapel,** 1050 E. 59th Street. 1925–26, Charles A. Coolidge, Charles Hodgdon. ☎ 773-702-8200

🖳 www.divinity.uchicago.edu/student/bond.html

The chapel is the worship space for the Divinity School and various campus ministries at the University of Chicago. Connected to Swift Hall by a beautiful stone cloister, the Gothic Revival chapel was given by Mrs. Joseph Bond in memory of her husband. The chapel's interior, designed by Charles J. Connick of Boston, is elaborately decorated with stone sculptures, polychrome angels, and stained-glass windows, including a large one in the chancel by Connick that is described as a "comprehensive spectacle of the whole New Testament."

"A Distinctly Different Seminary"
CHICAGO THEOLOGICAL SEMINARY
United Church of Christ. 5757 S. University Avenue. ☎ 773-752-5757

The seminary is the oldest of a cluster of seminaries in Hyde Park. Since its establishment in 1855 by Congregationalists, the seminary has emphasized "field education," sending its students out to learn firsthand about the facts of community life and the church's needs. Its faculty and students were active in the Underground Railroad prior to the Civil War, and the seminary has given honorary degrees to Martin Luther King, Jr., and Bishop Desmond Tutu. Located on the seminary's campus are the Funk Cloister and Hilton Chapel.

A Peaceful Place for Meditation and Prayer
THORNDIKE HILTON MEMORIAL CHAPEL AND CLARENCE SIDNEY FUNK CLOISTER
United Church of Christ. 5757 S. University Avenue. 1926, Herbert H. Riddle. ☎ 773-322-0246

The cloister is named for Clarence Sidney Funk, chairman of the Building Committee, under whose direction the seminary was built. Mr. and Mrs. Henry H. Hilton donated the chapel in memory of their son Thorndike, a classical scholar who died at the age of twenty-one.

The cloister and chapel are in the Gothic Revival style, and both are endowed with many symbolic embellishments. For example, the cloister's **corbels** (projecting blocks supporting a beam) are carved with various religious images including a dove representing the holy spirit and a pelican symbolizing sacrificial love. Memorial stones set in the walls and pavement include a fragment of the original Plymouth Rock and a small stone from Solomon's Quarries near the Damascus Gate in Jerusalem.

The chapel is at the 58th Street entrance to the cloister. It is an intimate space measuring thirty feet long by sixteen feet wide that has been described as a "refuge from noise and confusion, an isle of quietness in the ebb and flow of bewildering life." Its glory is its stained-glass windows modeled after those found in the thirteenth-century Gothic Cathedral at Chartres, France. The windows include scenes from the life of Christ and biblical stories.

The First Modern American Catholic Church
ST. THOMAS THE APOSTLE CATHOLIC CHURCH (NR)
5472 S. Kimbark Avenue. 1924, Francis Barry Byrne. ☎ 773-324-2626

In the early 1920s, Francis Barry Byrne, a former employee of Frank Lloyd Wright, collaborated with the parish priest, Father Thomas Vincent Shannon, and his parishioners to design this church whose distinct style has been variously described as a reinterpretation of Gothic mixed with Art Nouveau or a "modern evocation of a Spanish mission church." What is immediately noticeable is the building's richly decorative terra-cotta sculptural program that pays homage to, but doesn't replicate, the Gothic style. The sculptor was Alfonso Iannelli, an Italian American artist who collaborated with Wright and Byrne on other buildings, including Wright's famed Midway Gardens. Rising above the pointed arch over the main entry is a soaring figure of the crucified Christ on an unusual Y-shaped cross; below are images of Noah's Ark and Columbus's three ships: the Nina, Pinta, and Santa Maria, which bind together biblical and American history. Byrne interpreted the scalloped ornamental molding along the top of the church as representing fingers reaching toward heaven.

The church's plan reveals Byrne's and Father Shannon's awareness of the early liturgical reform movement within the Catholic Church that antici-

St. Thomas the Apostle Catholic Church

pated the reforms of Vatican II (see p. 83). Traditionally Catholic churches are based on a basilica plan with the altar located deep in the sanctuary opposite the main entrance (see pp. 79–80). This building's nave is almost as broad as it is long. At the time of its construction, the roof, unsupported by pillars or arches, was considered the largest of its type in the world. The lack of pillars or arches provides all parishioners with a clear view of the sanctuary and altar, which reach into the nave. The fourteen stations of the cross and the *Pieta,* both designed by Alfeo Faggi, an Italian sculptor born and educated in Florence, are among the church's many artistic treasures. The tall, richly colored stained-glass windows by Valentine D'Ogiers depict sacred and secular figures. The faces of the fathers of the Latin West and Eastern Orthodox churches are actually portraits of contemporary church figures, including Monsignor Shannon, the parish's priest, and Cardinal Mundelein, archbishop of Chicago at the time of its construction. Also depicted are secular figures like Calvin Coolidge and George Washington. Other religious art and artifacts can be found in the Chapel of St. Anne and the Chapel of St. Vincent.

Committed to Its Neighborhood
CONGREGATION RODFEI ZEDEK

Conservative Jewish. 5200 S. Hyde Park Boulevard. New addition 2000, Philip Kupritz and Associates. ☎ 773-752-2770
🖳 www.uscj.org/midwest/chicagorz/

    The congregation was founded in 1874 by Orthodox Jews who settled in a shantytown known as Canaryville in what is now part of Chicago's South Side. The name they chose for their congregation, Rodfei Zedek, is from the Book of Isaiah and means "pursuers of righteousness." Initially the congregation worshiped in a variety of rented quarters until it was able to purchase a Baptist Church in the Grand Boulevard neighborhood. After continual growth and prosperity, land was purchased in Hyde Park and a new synagogue was erected in 1926. A year later the congregation voted to join the Conservative Movement (see p. 63). Following World War II, when many congregations began to move to the suburbs, Rodfei Zedek made a conscious decision to stay in this neighborhood. Land was purchased at 5200 S. Hyde Park Boulevard for a community hall, educational center, and sanctuary that were completed in 1965. The congregation's commitment to its neighborhood remains unchanged, as seen in its erection of a new sanctuary and community center on the site in 2000. The red brick and white masonry building has a 320-seat sanctuary that can expand to 700 seats, and includes offices, classrooms, and a gymnasium.

Greater Grand Crossing

Paul Cornell, the developer of Hyde Park, established this community in 1871. Its irregularly shaped area is bounded by the communities of Woodlawn and Washington Park on the north, South Shore to the east, Englewood to the west, and Chatham on the south. It received its name from the site of a famous train accident (see p. 136).

An "American Lawn Plan" Cemetery
OAK WOODS CEMETERY
1035 E. 67th Street. ☎ 773-288-3800

Established in 1853 and developed under the supervision of Adolph Strauch (1822–83), Oak Woods is one of the city's oldest cemeteries. Its design is based on the "American lawn plan," which differs from earlier garden cemeteries (see p. 179) in that Strauch would not allow walls, curbs, or fences to be built along roadways or around gravesites. Oak Woods is the burial place of Harold Washington (1922–87), the city's first African American mayor. An inscription on his simple but elegant mausoleum reads, "Remember me as one who tried to be fair." Overlooking a lake is a monument marking the grave of Jesse Owens (1913–80), the African American track and field gold medalist and hero of the 1936 Olympic games in Berlin. A simple headstone marks the grave of physicist and Nobel Prize winner Enrico Fermi (1901–54), who created the first self-sustaining nuclear chain reaction at the University of Chicago (see p. 130).

Eternal Light, Oak Woods Cemetery

Oak Woods has the dubious distinction of being the site of the largest northern burial ground for Confederate prisoners of war. A large monument surmounted by a figure of a Confederate infantryman dedicated in 1895 marks the site where the remains of six thousand prisoners who died at Camp Douglas are buried (see p. 113). Another commemorative memorial is the **Eternal Light Monument,** dedicated to victims of the Holocaust. Unfortunately its light, created by radioactive material that absorbs the sunlight, can only be seen after dark, when the cemetery is closed.

NEARBY

➥ **Grand Crossing Park,** 7655 S. Ingleside Avenue. ☎ 312-747-6136
The park is named for a train wreck that occurred nearby. Many railroad lines once ran through this area, including the Illinois Central and the Michigan Southern Railroads, whose trains collided at an intersection in 1853 causing eighteen deaths and forty injuries. Even though signal lights were installed, the intersection remained dangerous until the tracks were elevated in 1912. The South Parks Commission created the neighborhood park for the area's many working-class families.

Pullman

Further south is the planned community of Pullman, named for its founder, George Pullman, and designed by Solon S. Beman (1853–1914) and landscape designer Nathan F. Bartlett. Pullman purchased four thousand acres on the east side of Lake Calumet between 95th and 115th Streets in 1877 for an experimental company town that would attract workers for his railroad-car factory. Designed in 1880, the town became the largest and most complete nineteenth-century planned industrial community. The houses, mainly row and double houses in the Queen Anne style, were all equipped with modern indoor plumbing, sewage, and gas, unusual features in workers' houses at that time. Because of the town's isolation, Pullman built a shopping arcade, market hall, stables, and a church, all revenue-producing because he owned everything, including the church. In 1896, Pullman received an award for creating the "World's Most Perfect Town," but it was anything but perfect.

Pullman's motives were complex. Undoubtedly, he believed that an aesthetically pleasing and well-ordered environment would attract hard workers, grateful for their employer's largesse. But his paternalistic attitude had another goal, to remove workers from the inner city, where labor organizers were attempting to form unions. On the surface, his ideas seemed to work, but there was an undercurrent of dissatisfaction that boiled over during the Depression of 1893–94, when Pullman laid off thousands of workers and cut the wages of those that remained, while still demanding they pay him high rents. The angry workers organized a strike in May 1894 that received support from Eugene Debs, the president of the American Railway Union. The Union members' refusal to move trains carrying Pullman cars brought railroad traffic nationwide to a halt. The strike ended after President Grover Cleveland, under the pretense of protecting the United States mail, ordered in fourteen thousand federal troops to break up the strike. Pullman won the strike, but after he died in 1897 a series of lawsuits related to the strike forced the Pullman Company to eventually sell the town to its residents. Pullman's grave in Graceland Cemetery is a peaceful place to visit (see pp. 178–81), but the method of his entombment speaks volumes about his life. The town he founded was threatened with demolition in 1960, but its residents formed the Pullman Civic Organization and defeated the plan. Pullman has since undergone restoration and the Pullman Historic District is on the National Register of Historic Places. For information on tours, call ☎ 773-785-3828 or e-mail 🖥, PullmanIL@aol.com.

A Place of Prayer for All People—That Failed
PULLMAN UNITED METHODIST CHURCH (NR) (THE GREENSTONE CHURCH)
11201 S. St. Lawrence Avenue. 1882, Solon S. Beman. ☎ 773-785-1492

Pullman's ideal town needed an "ideal" church where all workers, regardless of denomination, could gather to worship and develop a sense of community. What sounded good in theory didn't work in practice. Each denomination wanted its own clergy and service, but since no group alone could afford to pay the rent that Pullman demanded for the church's use, it remained essentially empty until it was sold to the Methodists in 1907. The Romanesque Revival limestone building has a corner tower with a tall steeple and a high gabled roof, which covers an open-timbered ceiling. The interior is warmed by light filtering through a large rose window on the west façade and through stained-glass windows along its walls.

✹

We leave behind the neighborhoods along and near Lake Michigan and the planned town of Pullman, and turn west to an area that is divided into fifty-two communities. It is separated into two major sections—south and north—by Roosevelt Road. The southern section is bordered by I-90/94 on the east and Harlem Avenue on the west; 63rd Street forms its southern edge. The northern section stretches to Howard Street on the north and is bordered by the North Branch of the Chicago River on the east and LeClaire Avenue on the west. Communities on Chicago's west side described here are, south to north: Englewood, New City, Bridgeport, Lower West Side, Near West Side, East Garfield Park, West Town, and North Park.

Southwest Side

Englewood

Englewood, named by its early Protestant settlers after their hometown in New Jersey, is located west of Washington Park and the Dan Ryan Expressway and south of Garfield Boulevard. The area's ethnic makeup changed after German and Irish Catholic packinghouse workers moved here from the Back of the Yards neighborhood (see p. 138) and began to build monumental churches. By 1920, Englewood was a bustling commercial center, but it experienced a decline in the 1930s. By the 1980s five of the neighborhood's Catholic churches closed and were replaced by St. Benedict the African, signaling another change in the area's demographics.

"There's a Sweet, Sweet Spirit in This Place"
ST. BENEDICT THE AFRICAN

Catholic. 340 W. 66th Street. 1990, Belli and Belli. ☎ 773-873-4464

The church named for St. Benedict the African, the patron saint of farmers, born in about 1522 in Sicily to slaves from Ethiopia, was designed

St. Benedict the African

to be an urban oasis. Set in the midst of a landscaped garden, it is a welcome sight in a blighted neighborhood. An inscription engraved on its cornerstone is an invitation to all who walk by: "There's a Sweet, Sweet Spirit in This Place," the title of a popular gospel song.

Upon entering the church the visitor walks down along a spiral ramp. One of its walls is actually the side of a huge baptismal pool, twenty-four feet in diameter and three and one-half feet deep, that contains ten thousand gallons of water. The ramp continues to curve around the walls of the pool toward the nave that is subtly shaped to recall the scalloped walls of an African hut.

The church's central plan allows for chairs to be arranged in a circle; in the center of the gathering are the altar table, pulpit, and chair, all carved out of walnut. Light pours in through skylights and narrow vertical windows by Robert Harmen set with bright reds and clear glass that are intended to evoke the dancing flames of the Holy Spirit.

New City

New City and its neighbor Bridgeport developed near the Illinois and Michigan Canal (see p. 202) and the stockyards. They were not desirable places to live, but for many it was their only choice. Relieving the squalor were the churches that still identify the neighborhoods, reminders of the city's original ethnic mosaic. According to one source, by the early twentieth century, Bridgeport alone had twelve Catholic churches, each representing a different ethnic group.

A century ago the streets were teeming with people who spoke in a myriad of languages, lived in overcrowded housing, and made their way along unpaved roads strewn with sewage and debris and lined with stalls, small stores and sweatshops, and dozens of saloons. Immigrants labored long hours under the most deplorable conditions, to dig the Illinois and Michigan Canal, slaughter and butcher animals, or work in lumber mills and factories for minimal pay. The churches played a crucial role in their lives, not only as places of worship, but as community centers and places of refuge from the ugliness that surrounded them. They provided immigrants with a sense of identity—a place where they could speak their mother tongue, share news from home, and keep alive their culture and traditions. Although the neighborhoods' mosaic has changed, the lofty domes, towers, and spires of many of these churches continue to beckon to those who live there.

New City, a heavily industrial area located southwest of the Loop, is bounded by Pershing Road to the north, Garfield Boulevard (55th Street) to the south, Stewart Avenue to the east, and Western Boulevard to the west. It was incorporated in 1865 as the town of Lake, the same year the Union Stockyards and Transit Company was organized. By 1884, it had more than thirty packinghouses and countless immigrants in need of housing in an already overcrowded residential district known as "Back of the Yards." The neighborhood gained notoriety in Upton Sinclair's book, *The Jungle* (1906), where he describes it as a filthy slum inhabited by exploited workers. This book's exposé led to the adoption of the Pure Food and Drug Act.

An Impressive Entry to a Slaughterhouse
OLD STONE GATE (NR)

850 W. Exchange Avenue at Peoria Street. Ca. 1879, Burnham and Root.

While the workers' houses may have been deplorable, visitors to the stockyards were greeted by an elaborate limestone gate, designed by the prestigious firm of Burnham and Root, that still stands at the original entrance to the Union Stockyards. This is all that remains of nearly five hundred acres of slaughterhouses that at one time were located east of Halsted Street between 39th and 47th Streets. Closed in 1971, the remaining meatpackers now do business in the area of the Fulton Market (west of the Loop).

A French-Style Church with an Irish Soul
ST. GABRIEL CATHOLIC CHURCH (NR)

4501 S. Wallace Avenue. 1887–88, Burnham and Root. ☎ 773-268-9595

This church is a reminder of the impoverished Irish immigrants who came to dig the Illinois and Michigan Canal (see p. 202) and later worked in the stockyards and local factories. Unable on their own to raise sufficient funds to build a church, the parish's first pastor, Father Maurice Dorney, befriended the stockyard's owners, Gustavus Swift, Philip Armour, and John Sherman, and convinced them not only to hire members of his flock, but also to finance the construction of their church. The fact that the parishioners had little to do with the church's construction may explain its style. It was built for Irish immigrants, but the architects, Burnham and Root, took as their model a medieval Romanesque church in Toulouse, France. It is uncertain why this particular style was selected, except that Root is quoted as saying that the simplicity of the Romanesque style was appropriate for a "home of the people." Note in particular the church's massive bell tower; originally 160 feet tall, it later had to be shortened for structural reasons by fourteen feet.

Proud to Be Lithuanian
HOLY CROSS CHURCH

Catholic. 1736 W. 46th Street. 1913–15, Joseph Molitor.
☎ 773-376-3900

In the first decades of the last century, the towers of Holy Cross and those of its now closed neighbor, St. Joseph's Catholic Church (1729 W. 48th Street), would compete for the attention of passers-by. Each was established as a national parish (see p. 53): St. Joseph's for the Poles and

Holy Cross for Lithuanians. As the century progressed, the neighborhood underwent a change; today most of Holy Cross's parishioners are Hispanic, but the appearance of the church remains unchanged. Its Classical Baroque style and sculptural program on the exterior reveal its Lithuanian heritage. According to the monograph published in celebration of the church's Golden Jubilee in 1954, "the poor, hard-working Lithuanians wanted not only a place to pray in their neighborhood, but they wanted God's house, the house of prayer, to be beautiful." A lofty dome covers the church's vast interior that was richly decorated in 1951 by Lithuanian artists who had sought refuge in the United States from the Soviets. Among them was Adolph Valesko, who executed four oil paintings that depict scenes from Lithuanian and American history. Valesko had been the planner and director of the Lithuanian Church Art Museum and Art Galleries of Vilnius, Lithuania. The brightly colored stained-glass windows installed in 1943 and 1944 by the Chicago firm of Arthur Michaudel depict scenes from the lives of Christ and a number of saints. When the church was built, electricity had been introduced and houses of worship began to use electric light for both practical and decorative purposes. Holy Cross carried this to an extreme: over two thousand lights, each set in a rosette, illuminate its interior.

Bridgeport

Bridgeport, north of New City, originally known as Hardscrabble, is one of the city's oldest communities. It is located south of the Chicago River's south branch and east of the river's south fork, and was the staging area for the construction of the Illinois and Michigan Canal. The eastern end of the canal located at Archer and Ashland Avenues survives and is a Chicago landmark.

Krakow in Chicago
ST. MARY OF PERPETUAL HELP CHURCH
Catholic. 1035 W. 32nd Street. 1889–92, Henry Engelbert.
☎ 773-927-6646

Founded as a mission church of St. Adalbert's (see p. 144), St. Mary's was established in 1886 as a parish for Polish immigrants. The church's style is Polish Baroque with elements borrowed from eastern and western European traditions, a reflection of Poland's position in central Europe. Its central dome rising 113 feet above the pavement and the flanking towers on its façade make a strong impression on any passerby. The interior is

St. Mary of Perpetual Help Church

even more overwhelming. Pilasters, arches, columns, and a succession of domes all lead to the chancel area. The rich array of paintings in this space culminates with the central art over the main altar depicting Our Lady of Perpetual Help. Other paintings are of Polish saints including St. Stanislaus Kostka, who was slain while at prayer in 1052, and St. Casimir of Poland (died in 1484), who was known as the Peacemaker because of his conviction that war was unjustified. Living in the midst of slaughterhouses and factories, this building provided its parishioners with a sanctuary where they could renew their spirits and their souls, and reaffirm their pride in being Polish.

Lower West Side

The Lower West Side is comprised of four communities: Lawndale, Little Village, Heart of Chicago, and Pilsen. The Stevenson Expressway is the Lower West Side's southern border and 16th Street its northern. On the east is the south branch of the Chicago River; California Avenue forms its western border. The area began to attract a number of industries following the 1871 fire, including the McCormick Reaper works. The company's new plant, built in 1873 near the Chicago River at 27th Street and Western Avenue, attracted so many Czech immigrants that the area soon became known as "Pilsen," after a city in what is now the Czech Republic.

Today Pilsen is in the center of Chicago's Hispanic community, the largest in the Midwest.

The Church Built without a Nail (Ripley's Believe It or Not)
ST. PAUL CATHOLIC CHURCH
2234 South Hoyne. 1897–99, Henry J. Schlacks. ☎ 773-847-7622

In the Middle Ages parishioners often built their own churches. In doing so, the people not only constructed a house of worship, but they were also participants in a spiritual act: the creation of a sacred space in which future generations would gather to worship. Congregants in rural America were often forced by circumstances to erect their own small churches, but this was rarely the case for monumental urban churches. St. Paul's, however, is an exception; it was indeed built by its parishioners under the guidance of its architect, Henry J. Schlacks, who was trained in the studio of Adler and Sullivan. Unlike his mentors, Schlacks preferred looking to the past for inspiration. This Latin-Cross church is allegedly modeled after medieval Gothic churches familiar to the congregants, who were mainly German immigrants from the Moselle Valley. Its twin towers are copied after the thirteenth-century Gothic-style St. Corentin Church in Quimper, France, located near the border with Germany.

While the church's design is not unique in the United States, its method of construction is. Schlacks was familiar with the brick interiors of German churches, so he proposed that the parishioners build an all-brick Gothic Revival church using Medieval techniques that would render it completely fireproof. It would require no wood and therefore no nails. Since he could not find a local builder familiar with this type of construction, he asked the parishioners to supply the labor, working under his supervision.

The church's stately façade and two towers, whose spires rise 245 feet above street level, make a powerful statement about the faith of the people who built it. While the interior has undergone some changes, it still retains its white Carrara marble furnishings, including an altar designed by Schlacks and executed in Italy. The elaborate mosaic in the chancel arch portraying the twelve apostles flanking Christ is considered one of the finest in the country. It was commissioned in 1922 and created in Venice, Italy, shipped to Chicago in pieces, and then installed in the church in 1930. The stained-glass windows are by F. X. Zettler, Munich, Germany, and depict scenes from the life of Christ and the life of St. Paul, the church's patron saint.

NEARBY

➡ **St. Matthew Lutheran Church,** 2100 W. 21st Street. 1888, Frederick Ahlschlager. ☎ 773-847-6458

German immigrants under the leadership of the Reverend Herman H. Engelbrecht, who later became the first president of the Lutheran Church Missouri Synod, Northern Illinois District, founded the congregation. Today, this Gothic Revival church is home to Chicago's first Hispanic Lutheran congregation, organized in 1976 by the Reverend Julio A. Loza as the "Latin American Lutheran Church." It provides a wide variety of religious and social services to its largely Mexican congregation.

➡ **St. Adalbert Catholic Church,** 1656 W. 17th Street. 1912–14, Henry J. Schlacks. ☎ 312-276-0340

Henry Schlacks also designed this church, which illustrates his continued mining of the past for ideas. Named after St. Adalbert, the evangelizer of Poland, it is modeled after San Paolo fuori le Mura (St. Paul Outside the Walls), a fourth-century pilgrimage church in Rome. The congregation, founded in 1874 as the city's third-oldest Polish parish, is now primarily Hispanic. A mural with the image of Our Lady of Czestochowa opposite Our Lady of Guadalupe illustrates this dual heritage.

➡ **Mexican Fine Arts Center,** 1852 W. 19th Street. ☎ 312-738-1503

The museum has a permanent collection that includes works by Diego Rivera, David Alfaro Siquerios, and Rufino Tamayo. It presents special exhibitions, sponsors performing arts, and serves as a community educational center. Check when the Del Corazon Performing Arts Festival, the Sol Juana Festival (honoring women), and the Dia de los Muertos Festival (Day of the Dead) are scheduled. The Fiesta del Sol takes place in July.

Northwest Side

Near West Side

The Near West Side is due west of the Loop and north of Roosevelt Road. It began to develop in the 1840s, when lumberyards, foundries, and flour mills were built along the south branch of the Chicago River. The spot where the 1871 fire began is now marked by a modern sculpture (see p. 151). After the fire, the area became densely populated with immigrants seeking work in nearby factories and the stockyards. Aiding their adjustment to the New World was the Hull-House, the city's first settlement house (see p. 148). The neighborhood was also the site of the Haymarket

Riot of May 4, 1886 (see p. 151). The Near West Side is bounded by Kinzie Street on the north, 16th Street to the south, the Chicago River on the east, and stretches to approximately California Avenue on the west.

Ellis Island of the Midwest
HOLY FAMILY CHURCH (NR)
Catholic. 1080 W. Roosevelt Road. 1857–59, Dillenburg and Zucher; interior and façade, 1860, John M. Van Osdel; tower and steeple, 1874, John Paul Huber; south addition, 1886. ☎ 312-432-0986

While New York City may have been where many Irish immigrants were first introduced to America, for those who traveled west to Chicago, Holy Family Church was where they were given the necessary tools to begin life in a new world: jobs, housing, and faith. Dedicated in 1860, Holy Family is the first Jesuit parish in Chicago. The fire of 1871 couldn't destroy this monumental church, one of only two Catholic churches to survive the fire. This was a miracle in the eyes of its pastor, Father Arnold Damen, S.J., who vowed that if the church was spared seven candles would always burn before the shrine in the east transept dedicated to Our Lady of Perpetual Help. Those candles continue to burn to this day, even though the parish has dwindled in size.

When it was built, Holy Family was in the midst of an Irish ghetto on the city's outskirts. Father Damen was roundly criticized by civic leaders for wanting to build a huge church when what they believed his parishioners really needed were orphanages and reformatories. For Father Damen, however, building a church meant building a community. He was right; by 1890, Holy Family had become the largest English-speaking parish in the nation, serving nearly 25,000 people.

For years the church's 226-foot tower was Chicago's tallest structure. Its interior was equally impressive; its original altar, reredos, statues, and confessional are all hand-carved walnut. More recently pews were removed to build a raised platform for a freestanding altar table. The stained-glass windows, made and installed by the Von Gerichten Art Glass Company of Columbus, Ohio, depict scenes from the lives of Jesuit saints, the nativity, and the annunciation.

Each ethnic group who came to worship here has donated its own religious art and statuary. Following the Irish in the 1890s were the Italians, who transformed Holy Family into one of the largest Italian parishes in the country. They donated the statue of Mother Frances Xavier Cabrini (1850–1918), the first American citizen to be proclaimed a Catholic saint (see p. 147). She was a parishioner here at the time she established the

Columbus Hospital in 1905. By the 1940s, the parish served a mixed community that included Slavs, Hispanics, and African Americans. At that time a painting of the Black Risen Christ by James Hasse, S.J., and a picture of Our Lady of Guadalupe were added to the church's collection of religious art.

After the parish membership declined drastically in the 1980s, the archdiocese closed the church and made plans to have it demolished. The parishioners protested the decision, and in 1988, the parish, the Jesuit owners of the property, and community leaders formed the Holy Family Preservation Society, a secular not-for-profit organization that collects funds to restore and maintain the building. Thanks to their efforts, the building continues to serve the neighborhood, which is now Hispanic and African American.

NEARBY

➦ **St. Ignatius College Prep,** 1076 W. Roosevelt Road. 1866–74, Toussaint Menard; additions in 1895 and 1990s. ☎ 312-421-5900

Directly adjacent to the Holy Family Church is St. Ignatius College Prep, the first home of Loyola University. The French Second Empire–style building features a mansard roof and an elaborate five-part façade with a columned entry atop a double-axial staircase. Its new additions are decorated with architectural reliefs from demolished historic Chicago buildings.

A Bit of Ireland in Chicago
OLD ST. PATRICK'S CHURCH (NR)

Catholic. 140 S. Desplaines Street. 1852–56, Carter and Bauer; towers, 1885; 1990s renovation, Booth Hansen Architects. ☎ 312-782-6171
🖥 www.oldstpats.org

St. Patrick's, Chicago's oldest surviving church, and Holy Family (see above) are the only Catholic churches to have survived the 1871 fire. It is the second-oldest Catholic parish in the city (St. Mary's is the oldest, founded in 1833), established in 1846 to serve Irish immigrants. What distinguishes the church are its unusual octagonal towers that were deliberately designed not to match. The south tower, surmounted by a tall belfry and spire, represents the church in the West, whereas the north tower, crowned with an onion dome, represents the Eastern church. Together they symbolize the Universal Catholic Church, a reminder, perhaps, that in this nation with all its ethnic diversity Catholics must remain united.

Unlike St. Gabriel's (see p. 140), St. Patrick's interior decoration leaves

MOTHER FRANCES XAVIER CABRINI, PATRON SAINT OF IMMIGRANTS

Born in Sant'Angelo Lodigiano, in the Lombardy region of Italy on July 15, 1850, Maria Francesca Cabrini devoted her life to helping the less fortunate. She founded the Missionary Sisters of the Sacred Heart in 1880 and became known as Mother Frances Xavier Cabrini. In 1889, Pope Leo sent her to aid Italian immigrants in New York. With six members of her community, she opened an orphanage in the city's Little Italy. Ten years later she opened the first free Italian immigrant school in Chicago. Aware of the impoverished immigrants' need to have a hospital in Chicago, she obtained financial help from the city's wealthy, purchased the North Shore Hotel near Lake Michigan, and transformed it into the Columbus Hospital. A chapel in the hospital was dedicated to her and became a pilgrimage site for many people. In her lifetime, Mother Cabrini founded hospitals, houses for the poor, orphanages, and other institutions throughout the United States, Europe, and South America. She spent the last years of her life in Chicago helping orphans. She died in this city on December 22, 1917, now her feast day. Pope Pius XII celebrated her canonization in Chicago's Soldier Field on July 7, 1946, in the presence of over 100,000 people. She is buried in the Shrine of Mother Cabrini in New York City.

little doubt as to the nationality of its original parishioners. The famous Book of Kells, illuminated by monks in Iona in the eighth century, and the Celtic art exhibit at the World's Columbian Exposition inspired the design of the church's twelve stained-glass windows. Designed and fabricated by Thomas A. O'Shaugnessy, the windows were installed in 1912. However, the triptych window that dominates the eastern façade, *Faith, Hope, and Charity*, also designed by O'Shaugnessy, is in the Art Nouveau style.

The construction of the Eisenhower Expressway and the decline of the neighborhood threatened the church's future. By 1983 the parish had only four registered members. A new priest assigned to the parish, Father John J. Wall, unveiled a plan to transform the church into what he described as a "church for the marketplace," with a strong outreach to young adults. His plan succeeded, and today St. Patrick's membership is over 2,500 households.

The City's First Settlement House
JANE ADDAMS'S HULL-HOUSE MUSEUM (NR)
800 S. Halsted Street. ☎ 312-413-5353
💻 www.uic.edu/jaddams/hull/hull-house.html

Churches could only do so much to help immigrants living in over-crowded, impoverished neighborhoods. Discontent, lawlessness, and the decline of the urban fabric motivated men like Daniel Burnham (see p. 97) to try and improve the city's physical appearance as a way to inspire moral rectitude in its residents. Women like Jane Addams (1860–1935) and Ellen Gates Starr (1859–1940) recognized that many urban problems began in the homes of overworked and underpaid men and women struggling to survive under the most desperate circumstances. Their solution was to provide families with a refuge, a place they could go to for help. In 1889, they took over an aging Italianate-style mansion built in 1856 for Charles J. Hull, a real estate developer, and transformed it into Hull-House, a haven for the dispossessed. It quickly became an important institutional anchor in the neighborhood. Hull-House could provide services and programs for immigrants that were not available elsewhere, like infant and child care, English language and Americanization classes, and vocational training—all the tools they needed to become self-sufficient, con-

JANE ADDAMS

Jane Addams (1860–1935), born in Cedarville, Illinois (see p. 226), graduated from Rockford College in 1882, and died in Chicago on May 21, 1935. She is buried in her hometown. Among her most lasting accomplishments was Hull-House, the birthplace of social work. Other projects undertaken by Addams and her staff include the establishment of the first public gymnasium in Chicago and the first juvenile court in the nation. They worked to have a strong child labor law passed by the Illinois legislature in 1903 that became a federal law in 1916. Addams was a prolific writer and speaker, and officiated over a number of social and cultural organizations. She became involved in the peace movement prior to World War I and served as the first president of the Women's International League for Peace and Freedom in 1919. Jane Addams was awarded the Nobel Peace Prize in 1931 for her efforts on behalf of world peace.

tributing members to American society. Addams's concepts went on to influence the settlement-house movement throughout the United States. All that remains of the thirteen-building complex is the Hull mansion and dining hall; the rest was demolished in the 1960s to make room for the University of Illinois at Chicago campus. Even in its diminished state, Hull-House still has much to say to visitors who want to understand the immigrant experience. The museum, operated by the University of Illinois, displays period furnishings, an exhibit about the neighborhood's ethnic groups, and other rotating exhibits.

An "American" Church Plan
FIRST BAPTIST CONGREGATIONAL CHURCH (UNION PARK CONGREGATIONAL CHURCH)
60 N. Ashland Avenue. 1869–71, Gurdon P. Randall. ☎ 312-243-8047

One of Chicago's finest residential neighborhoods began to develop along Washington Boulevard, between Halsted Street and Ashland Avenue. Many of its affluent residents attended Union Park Congregational Church.

The congregation was founded in 1851 by forty-eight abolitionists who had left Third Presbyterian Church over the issue of slavery. Their small wooden chapel served as a way station on the Underground Railroad until this monumental Gothic Revival–style church with a soaring tower and steeple was erected. It survived the 1871 fire and served for a short time as the center of city government, housing the mayoral and city council offices and the General Relief Committee.

While the church's Gothic Revival exterior is not unique, its interior plan was considered revolutionary for its time. Randall is credited with designing one of the first church interiors to use the auditorium plan (see pp. 81–82), with curving amphitheater style seating. The auditorium, almost square in plan with transepts extending slightly out from the nave, seats fifteen hundred people. A curved balcony is cantilevered out from all four walls and is supported on cast-iron columns. The auditorium's focal point is the pulpit set in front of a monumental organ built by W. W. Kimball and Company and installed in 1927. Known as the Andrew R. Dole Memorial Organ, it is among the largest enclosed pipe organs in the nation. Adjacent to the auditorium is the 1869 Carpenter Chapel designed by Otis Wheelock for the Chicago Theological Seminary.

With most of its members living elsewhere, the church was sold in

1970 to Mozart Baptist Church, an African American congregation founded in 1944. The congregation later changed its name to First Baptist Congregational Church.

An Important Example of the Richardsonian Romanesque Style
CHURCH OF THE EPIPHANY
Episcopal. 201 S. Ashland. 1885–86, Francis Whitehouse.
☎ 312-243-4242

Considered one of Chicago's most important examples of Richardsonian Romanesque church architecture, the Church of the Epiphany displays many of the features associated with this style (see p. 74). Built of rusticated Lake Superior sandstone, the church's thick walls are decorated with delicately carved patterns and pierced by round-arched windows and doors. A massive tower standing at one corner houses three bells.

The main door on the façade opens onto a narthex that leads into the almost sixty-foot-square sanctuary. Light filtering through stained-glass windows reflects off the church's beautifully polished cherry wood pews. The spectacular ceiling, supported on four piers, is composed of large-beamed open wood trusses that meet at the center; it conveys a sense of spaciousness to the auditorium. An altar in the design of a sarcophagus, intended to be the tomb of the church's first rector, dominates the east wall. Above it are a series of mosaics: The large center mural by M. C. Darst, installed in 1912, depicts the resurrection; it is flanked on either side by mosaics dating to 1885 of two kneeling angels. On the far left is a mosaic, *The Mother and Child* (1896), and to the right, *Jesus Bearing His Cross* (1897), both executed by Charles Halloway. Sadly, many of the church's original stained-glass windows were stolen in the 1970s; several new ones have since been installed.

NEARBY
➥ **Metropolitan Missionary Baptist Church,** 2151 W. Washington Boulevard. 1901, Hugh M. G. Garden. ☎ 312-733-9447

Originally built as the Third Church of Christ, Scientist, the building reflects the classical detailing favored by that denomination (see pp. 41–42), such as the entrance portico's two marble columns. Nearly square in plan, the church has a spacious auditorium on the second floor. In 1945, the building was sold to the Metropolitan Baptist Church, founded in 1920.

➥ **Notre Dame Catholic Church,** 1336 W. Flournoy Street. 1887–92, Gregory Vigeant; 1929, sanctuary enlarged. ☎ 312-243-7400

This Romanesque Revival church, founded as a French-speaking parish, celebrates the memory of the city's early French settlers. Crowning the church is a distinctive ninety-foot dome and cupola. In 1918, Cardinal Mundelein made the church the center for devotion to the Holy Eucharist.

➥ **Chicago Fire Academy,** 558 W. DeKoven Street. 1960, Loebl, Schlossman and Bennett. ☎ 312-744-4730

The "I Will" spirit of Chicago led to the city's decision to erect its Fire Academy on the site of Patrick and Catherine O'Leary's barn, where a cow allegedly kicked over the lantern that started the 1871 fire. The actual site is marked on the academy's floor. Dedicated in 1961, the academy trains the city's firefighting personnel. Standing in its courtyard is the *Pillar of Fire*, an abstract bronze sculpture of a flame by Egon Weiner.

➥ **Haymarket Square,** at Desplaines and Randolph Streets.

Cyrus McCormick's (1809–84) 1834 invention of the reaper improved the lives of farmers, but it did little to improve the lives for those who labored in the McCormick Reaper works. On May 3, 1886, a strike for an eight-hour day erupted into violence after police killed several workers who were protesting against the hiring of strikebreakers. Angered by the killings, the workers gathered again the next day, but this time there were 176 policemen waiting for them. A bomb thrown into the crowd killed a policeman. In the chaos that followed gunfire killed six more policemen, and four workers and sixty policeman were wounded. Although the identity of the bomb thrower was never known, the eight organizers of the meeting were arrested; seven were found guilty and sentenced to hang; one committed suicide in jail. Two sentences were commuted to life imprisonment; the other four were hanged on November 11, 1887. A plaque at the site is a quiet reminder of the violence that once occurred here as workers fought for the rights that many now take for granted. A monument in Forest Home Cemetery (see p. 193) marks the site of the common grave of the men who were hanged.

East Garfield Park

East Garfield Park is directly west of the Near West Side. Its western boundary is Independence Boulevard, and its southern is Taylor Street. The northern boundary is north of Garfield Park (see p. 152) approximately at Ferdinand Street. The completion of the Lake Street elevated line and streetcar electrification led to the area's rapid growth between 1880 and 1915.

Chicago's First Basilica
OUR LADY OF SORROWS BASILICA
Catholic. 3121 W. Jackson Boulevard. 1890–1902, Henry Engelbert, John F. Pope, William J. Brinkman. ☎ 773-638-5800

The parish, founded in 1874 by the Servite friars for Irish and Italian immigrants, is now predominantly African American. The church is the first in Chicago raised to the rank of a basilica. Pope Pius XII bestowed the honor in 1956 in recognition of its architectural and artistic value and its role as a center of devotion to the Virgin Mary. In the late 1930s, the church had thirty-eight services every Friday night attended by over seventy thousand worshipers.

The church's artistic and architectural detailing is based on Italian Renaissance models. For example, the balconies on either side of the high altar are modeled after those in the Sistine Chapel in the Vatican, and the coffered barrel-vaulted ceiling over the nave echoes that of St. Peter's in Rome. The basilica's lower shrine has a remarkable replica of Michelangelo's famed *Pieta* that is housed in St. Peter's in the Vatican.

NEARBY
➡ **Garfield Park,** 300 N. Central Park Boulevard. ☎ 312-746-5100

The East Garfield Park area was primarily flat and undistinguished farmland when it was annexed to Chicago. Designers William Le Baron Jenney (1869), Oscar F. Dubuis (1877–93), and, later, Jens Jensen transformed it into a spectacular park with winding lagoons and picturesque vistas. A suspension bridge built in 1874 is one of the park's original structures. The conservatory, built in 1907 and designed by Jensen, is considered the world's largest enclosed garden under one roof. Its eight glass-domed rooms allow visitors to experience a variety of environments, including the tropics in the Palm House; the cool, shaded Fernery; the American southwest in the Cactus House; and the beautiful, welcoming environment of the practically named Warm and Economic House, complete with waterfalls and sculptures by Lorado Taft (see p. 126). Adjacent to the conservatory is a very thoughtful addition, the Sensory Garden for the visually impaired. The Horticultural Hall houses a variety of seasonal flower shows held throughout the year, ranging from azaleas in February to poinsettias in December.

West Town

West Town is bordered on the east by the north branch of the Chicago River, Kinzie Street on the south, and approximately Bloomingdale Avenue on the north. It has an irregular border on the west with its neighbor, Humboldt Park. West Town's development in the late 1860s and 1870s began when industries built along the north branch of the Chicago River attracted Polish, German, and Scandinavian immigrants who settled in workers' housing built along Milwaukee Avenue. Today, Milwaukee Avenue, which cuts diagonally across the neighborhood, is home to a number of Hispanic businesses. The area around Wicker Park (Milwaukee Avenue and North and Damen Avenues) developed as an exclusive residential neighborhood; several mansions north of the park on the 2100 block of West Caton Street attest to the wealth of its original inhabitants.

The Mother Church of Polish Parishes in Chicago
ST. STANISLAUS KOSTKA CATHOLIC CHURCH

1300 N. Noble Street. 1876–81, Patrick C. Keeley; 1892 towers, Adolphus Druiding. ☎ 773-278-2470 🖥 www.stanislauskostka.org

Established in 1867 by Polish immigrants, the church was designed by Patrick C. Keeley (1816–96), a well-known Brooklyn, New York, architect who designed over six hundred churches in the United States, including Holy Name Cathedral (see pp. 164–65). He allegedly modeled St. Stanislaus Kostka after an unidentified church in Krakow, Poland. The church was dedicated in 1882; the twin towers that flank its monumental Renaissance Revival façade were dedicated ten years later. Only one tower has a cupola; lightning destroyed the other in 1964. The grandeur of the church's interior reflects its parishioners' ethnicity. The focal point is the Baroque altar standing at the end of a long central aisle. Above the altar is a painting of Our Lady placing the baby Jesus in the arms of Stanislaus Kostka, a Polish nobleman who died at age seventeen in 1568 after being instructed by the Virgin Mary to join the Society of Jesus. A large painting in the dome of the apse by the Polish painter, Thaddeus Zukotynski, depicts the resurrected Christ accompanied by the saints in heaven. The stained-glass windows by F. X. Zettler of the Royal Bavarian Art Institute in Munich illustrate the mysteries of the rosary.

By 1897, St. Stanislaus Kostka parish was the largest in the nation and perhaps in the world, numbering eight thousand families with a total of forty thousand parishioners. Its number diminished dramatically after the building of the Kennedy Expressway in the 1950s, which destroyed much of the neighborhood and forced parishioners to move elsewhere. By 1981, the parish served only 850 families, many of them Hispanic. Symbolizing the duality of its heritage is a wooden statue recently given to the church. Carved in Mexico, it's entitled *The Divine Mercy*, an image of Christ as seen by St. Faustina, a Polish nun who was canonized in 2000.

NEARBY

➥ **Pulaski Park,** 1419 W. Blackhawk.

Located in front of St. Stanislaus Kostka, this park is named for Brigadier General Casimir Pulaski, a Polish nobleman who served heroically under George Washington in the Revolutionary War. He was killed at the battle of Savannah in 1779. Jens Jensen designed the landscape in 1912, and William Carbys Zimmerman was the architect for the park's three-story field house, built in 1914, in a style described as "emulating Eastern European architecture."

➥ **Polish Museum of America,** 984 N. Milwaukee Avenue.
☎ 773-384-3352

One of the largest ethnic museums in the nation, it is housed in the headquarters of the Polish Roman Catholic Union. The museum contains manuscripts of famous Poles, including Thaddeus Kosciuszko and Casimir Pulaski, who fought valiantly in the Revolutionary War, and Ignace Jan Paderewski, famed pianist and diplomat. The museum displays art, costumes, religious objects, coins, stamps, and other memorabilia that tell the story of Polish culture in the New and Old Worlds.

Kiev in Chicago
ST. NICHOLAS UKRAINIAN CATHOLIC CATHEDRAL

2238 W. Rice Street. 1913–15, Worthmann, Steinbach and Piontek; renovation, 1974–77, Zenon Mazurkevich. ☎ 773-276-4537
💻 www.stnicholaseparchy.org

A Ukrainian community began to develop in the late nineteenth century in a section of West Town still known as Ukrainian Village. It is centered on two monumental churches, St. Nicholas and SS. Volodymyr and Olha (see below). As followers of the Eastern Rite, which acknowledges the pope but practices a Byzantine-Slavonic liturgy, Ukrainian immigrants were unlikely to join one of the many Polish national churches in the neighborhood. They established their own parish in 1905, and a year later purchased a small Danish church. As their numbers increased, so too did the need for a new church, one that would honor their devotion to their faith as well as match the monumental churches being built by their Polish neighbors. The same architectural firm that designed St. Mary of the Angels (see p. 158) was hired to design St. Nicholas. The architects, undoubtedly at the parishioners' urging, modeled the church after the eleventh-century Cathedral of St. Sophia in Kiev, the capital of Ukraine.

Religious imagery and symbolism abound throughout St. Nicholas, on the exterior as well as the interior. The thirteen domes rising above the neighborhood symbolize the twelve apostles and Christ. Above the entrance is a mosaic of Our Lady of Pochaiv that depicts the Virgin's appearance near Pochaiv, in the Ukraine, where her footprint is venerated. Above it is an icon of St. Nicholas the Wonderworker,

St. Nicholas Ukrainian Catholic Cathedral

also known as Santa Claus. The interior, renovated in the 1970s, is a feast for the eyes and soul, richly decorated with wall paintings, mosaics, icons, and stained-glass windows created in the Munich Studio of Chicago. From the center dome hangs a huge nine-tiered golden chandelier with 480 lights; the ceiling is painted blue and sparkles with stars. The artwork was done by Boris Makarenko, an expert on Ukrainian Byzantine painting, who used the mosaics in Kiev's St. Sophia as his models. Only the painting on the rear wall of the sanctuary that depicts Christ and the apostles with Mary was retained from the original 1928 decoration of the church. The iconostasis is brass and hung with traditional icons. Its openwork allows a visitor to see into the cathedral's most sacred area, the apse, housing the sanctuary and altar.

The arrival of Ukrainian immigrants following World War II revitalized the neighborhood. Ukrainian is spoken on the streets and many neighborhood stores advertise their wares in Ukrainian. But not all Ukrainians attend St. Nicholas; others prefer its neighbor down the block, SS. Volodymyr and Olha.

NEARBY
➡ **SS. Volodymyr and Olha,** Eastern Orthodox, 739 N. Oakley Boulevard. 1972–75, Jaroslaw Korsunsky. ☎ 773-276-3990

A golden dome of anodized aluminum crowns the beautiful church named for Ukrainian saints, Volodymyr the Great, who accepted the Orthodox faith in 988, and Olha, a ruler of Kiev who became a Christian in 937. The parish was founded in 1968 by former congregants of St. Nicholas who protested the cathedral changing from the Julian to the Gregorian calendar (see p. 46). Whereas St. Nicholas looks back at St. Sophia's in the Ukraine for its model, SS. Volodymyr and Olha is in the style of Greek Orthodox churches built in Byzantium (Constantinople, now Istanbul)—a Greek-cross plan crowned with a monumental gold dome; four smaller domes are at each corner of the roof. A large mosaic over the main entrance portrays St. Volodymyr the Great baptizing the people of Kiev in the Dnipro River in 988 C.E., an event that marks the Ukrainian people's acceptance of Christianity.

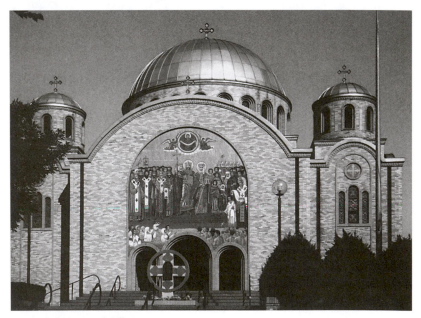

SS. Volodymyr and Olha

A Provincial Russian Orthodox Church Designed by Louis Sullivan
HOLY TRINITY CATHEDRAL (NR)

Orthodox Church in America. 1121 N. Leavitt Street. 1899–1903, Louis H. Sullivan. ☎ 773-486-4545

Located on a corner in an inner-city neighborhood is a church (designated a cathedral in 1923) built in the style of a small provincial Russian Orthodox church in the rural Carpathian mountains of southern Russia. Unlike the monumental churches built by their Ukrainian and Polish neighbors, the Russian immigrants who settled in Chicago were determined to erect a church that was remindful of the small, intimate, rural buildings they left behind in the Old World. What is surprising is the architect they selected for their church: Louis H. Sullivan, known for his inspired forward-looking designs that are associated with the famed Chicago School of Architecture (see p. 96). The building reflects Sullivan's ability to synthesize traditional Orthodox and Byzantine architecture and iconography with his modern sensibility; it is important to note, however, that he did not design the building's interior, which reflects the congregation's memories of their homeland's churches.

Sullivan worked closely with the congregation to develop a plan that not only illustrates his famous dictum that form should always follow function, but carries that dictum further in that the appearance of the building should be an expression of its function, in this case the Orthodox liturgy. The cathedral's traditional three-part division—an entry tower housing a narthex and topped with a belfry, the square nave crowned with an octagonal dome recently gilded, and an apse housing the altar in the Holy of Holies separated by the iconostasis—are all typical elements of a Russian Orthodox Church. The exterior is essentially undecorated, common for rural Orthodox churches, except for Sullivan's simple organic ornament around the door and windows.

As plain as the exterior is, the interior is elaborately decorated, its walls covered with icons, paintings based on nineteenth-century murals on the walls of St. Volodymyr's in Kiev, stenciling, glittering gold trim, banners, and, of course, the traditional iconostasis that reaches to the top round arch of the apse. The iconostasis was fabricated in Russia and presented to the church in 1912 by Charles R. Crane, the American ambassador to China at the time. As is traditional in Orthodox churches but often abandoned in the United States, the church lacks pews.

Czar Nicholas II contributed $4,000 to the congregation's building fund, as did Cyrus McCormick, who had investments in Russia. The church was consecrated by Patriarch Tikhon from Moscow in 1903 and became his base in the United States; he was recently beatified. The congregation's members now represent many ethnic groups.

A Guiding Light
ST. MARY OF THE ANGELS CATHOLIC CHURCH
1850 N. Hermitage Avenue. 1914–20, Worthmann and Steinbach; 1992 renovation, Holabird and Roof. ☎ 773-278-2644
▉ www.smachicago.org

A blue light glowing from a gilded cupola atop an immense terra-cotta dome (modeled after Michelangelo's dome over St. Peter's in the Vatican) surrounded by twenty-six nine-foot angels visible from the Kennedy Expressway has beckoned worshipers for nearly a century. For a time, the light was extinguished, but thanks to the efforts of its parishioners and concerned citizens, it again sends out its welcoming glow.

Constructed when Polish immigrants populated the neighborhood known as Bucktown, the parish began to experience a downturn following the construction of the Kennedy Expressway in the 1950s, which tore through its base of parishioners. The first serious sign of deterioration came in 1985 when a section of painted plaster fell from the church's dome and grazed a parishioner's forehead. By January 1988, the archdiocese had closed the church and declared it a health and safety hazard, but the congregation was determined to save it. A committee was formed, and a series of widely publicized and successful fund-raising affairs were organized. St. Mary's plight attracted the attention of Chicagoans of all faiths and ethnic groups who didn't want to lose what is considered one of the nation's finest examples of Renaissance Revival architecture and the largest Roman Catholic church building in Illinois. Restoration started in 1991 and was completed ten years later. Once again visitors can experience its glorious barrel-vaulted nave and dome that rises 135 feet above the floor. Each of its twelve stained-glass windows has an image of one of the apostles. At the base of the dome is an inscription that expresses the yearnings of all people of faith: "Glory to God in the Highest and Peace on Earth to Men." The church is the American headquarters of Opus Dei, founded in 1928.

NEARBY
➥ **Humboldt Park,** 1400 N. Sacramento Avenue.
The park was created in 1869 when West Town was annexed to Chicago. It is one of three parks that comprise Chicago's West Park system, designed in 1871 by William Le Baron Jenney. The other two are Garfield Park (see p. 152) and Douglas Park. Jens Jensen, general superin-

tendent of the West Park Commission, planned many of the park's naturalistic features, including a long "prairie river." The park has several important buildings, including the 1914 Natatorium designed by William Carbys Zimmerman. A parade held on Norwegian Independence Day (May 17) starts at the Norwegian Lutheran Memorial Church (see pp. 168–69) and ends at the park's statue of Leif Erickson.

North Park

North Park's boundaries are Devon Avenue to the north, Foster Avenue to the south, the north branch of the Chicago River on the south, and the North Shore Channel on the east. The neighborhood is named after North Park College (now North Park University), founded in 1891 by members of the Swedish Evangelical Mission Covenant (now the Evangelical Covenant Church). The campus's first building, **Old Main** (3225 W. Foster Ave.) was erected in 1894. The area is home to a number of cemeteries, including Montrose (see p. 160), St. Lucas, and the Bohemian National Cemetery.

A Place of Rest for All Bohemians
BOHEMIAN NATIONAL CEMETERY
5255 N. Pulaski Road. 1877. ☎ 773-478-0373

A Bohemian Catholic woman died in 1876 before receiving last rites and was denied burial in a Catholic cemetery. This event so outraged the Bohemian community that a national cemetery was established in 1877 that would accept anyone of Bohemian ethnicity. The cemetery honors Bohemian culture and its contributions to the United States. The entry to the cemetery is through an 1893 gate designed by John Krivanek and still houses its original funeral bell, the only one of its kind left in Chicago. Immediately ahead is a large flagpole dedicated in 1952 as a memorial to the two world wars. Other memorials include a Civil War Memorial, dedicated in 1889, paid for by contributions from various Czech organizations, and a United Spanish War Veterans Memorial dedicated in 1926, erected by the Bohemian American Camp No. 30, United Spanish War Veterans. Life-size statues of figures in American military uniforms as well as tombstones with photographs of the deceased in military uniform abound. A large open space in the cemetery is used for commemorative services on Memorial Day, and Mother's and Father's Days.

In front of the cemetery's chapel (1910) and crematorium (ca. 1890) is a statue simply named *Mother* (1927) by the Czech artist Albin Polasek. He also created one of the cemetery's most haunting images, a gaunt,

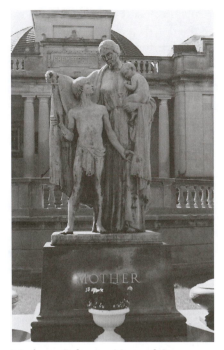

Mother—*Bohemian National Cemetery*

hooded figure popularly known as the Grim Reaper, which appears about to enter the mausoleum of the Stejskal-Buchal family; the sculpture's actual name is *Walking Death*. The chapel/crematorium houses the cemetery's columbarium (niches that hold ashes of the deceased) and a chapel whose focal point is not an altar, but a large American flag. Two empty containers stand on pedestals outside the chapel. These are sad reminders of human maleficence, past and present. At one time these pedestals held urns; one contained ashes from the Czech village of Lidice, destroyed by Germans in retaliation for the assassination of Reinhard Heydrich, Hitler's chief of the occupation forces in Czechoslovakia. The other contained a mixture of soil and ashes from Poland's Auschwitz concentration camp, where, along with thousands of Jews, hundreds of members of Czechoslovakian *sokols*, gymnastic societies, were executed. For reasons that go beyond comprehension, someone stole both urns.

In most columbaria the fronts of the niches are covered with wood or stone, but here they are glass revealing not only urns, but displays of photographs, artificial flowers, coins, medals, jewelry, and other objects related to the deceased. This makes it possible for one to walk through the columbarium's halls and view traces of people's lives and see, too, how decorative styles have changed over time, from elaborate Victorian Art Nouveau, the 1920s' and 1930s' flirtation with Art Deco, to the more stark modernism of the latter half of the twentieth century.

NEARBY

➡ **Montrose Cemetery,** 5400 N. Pulaski Road. This cemetery was selected in 1935 by Chicago's Japanese American community to be their communal burial ground. Set in the center of a Japanese garden is a mausoleum, erected in 1937, with a rising sun motif over its entry.

➠ **Beth-El/Ridgelawn Cemeteries,** 5736 Pulaski Road.

Just north of Montrose Cemetery are two small Jewish cemeteries separated by a fence. Dating back to approximately 1895, the tombstones face east, as is traditional for Jewish burials.

North Side

Chicago's North Side stretches from the Loop (see p. 95), where the Chicago River enters Lake Michigan, to the city's northeasternmost area, Rogers Park; its western border is the north branch of the Chicago River. The North Side has nine community areas; the ones discussed here are: Near North Side, Logan Square, Portage Park, Lincoln Park, Lake View, Uptown, and Lincoln Square. The approximate borders of the North Side's famed Old Town are: Wells Street on the west, Larabee Street to the east, Armitage Avenue on the north, and North Avenue to the south.

The North Side is where Chicago began (see p. 94) and where many of its most historic and stunning buildings are located. The area grew rapidly in the years following the 1871 fire, attracting many wealthy people who settled in the exclusive and fabled "Gold Coast." Laborers began to move near the factories that developed mainly along the Chicago River and rail lines.

Near North Side

The area's boundaries are North Avenue to the north, the Chicago River to the south and west, and Lake Michigan on the east. When the 1871 fire jumped the Chicago River it all but devastated the entire area save for a handful of buildings, but it quickly began to rebound. The city's famed "Gold Coast," a residential district north of Oak Street and east of Clark Street, is located here. The **Archbishop's Residence** (1555 N. State Parkway) and the Charnley House (see p. 168) still attest to its prosperous history. Contributing to the area's development was the construction of the Michigan Avenue Bridge in the 1920s, which transformed Michigan Avenue into an important commercial venue. Its "Magnificent Mile" is the site of a number of famous buildings, including the **Wrigley Building** (400–410 N. Michigan Avenue, 1921–24, Graham, Anderson, Probst and White) and the **Tribune Tower** (435 N. Michigan Avenue, 1922–25, Howells and Hood). Other acclaimed buildings erected after World War II include the twin apartment towers designed by Ludwig Mies van der Rohe (860–80 N. Lake Shore Drive, 1949), the **John Hancock Center** (875 N.

Michigan Avenue, 1965–69, Skidmore, Owings and Merrill), and the **Sears Tower** (233 S. Wacker Drive, 1968–74, Bruce Graham of Skidmore, Owings and Merrill; Fazlur Rahman Khan, engineer).

Also part of the Near North Side are Streeterville, immediately east of the Magnificent Mile, and River North, one of Chicago's oldest areas and now home to numerous art galleries.

A Symbol of Chicago's "I Will" Spirit
THE WATER TOWER (NR)

845 N. Michigan Avenue. 1869, William W. Boyington. ☎ 312-744-2400

When you ask a Chicagoan what are the most important and beautiful structures along North Michigan Avenue, the "Magnificent Mile," many will point to the Water Tower and its companion across the street, the **Pumping Station** (1866). These are the city's most cherished landmarks embodying its famed "I Will" spirit.

William W. Boyington, an esteemed and prolific architect, designed the Water Tower and the Pumping Station in a style that has been described as castellated Gothic, a whimsical and picturesque decorative style that hid their mundane but important functions. The tall Water Tower is now a visitors' center, but it originally housed the standpipe for the city's water system; the Pumping Station has remained in use since before the 1871 fire. Together the two structures appear to be part of a medieval fortress dropped in the midst of a modern city. Designed to be fireproof and constructed of local Joliet/Lemont limestone dug out of the Illinois and Michigan Canal, both buildings did indeed survive the 1871 fire.

Alongside the area's soaring skyscrapers, exclusive hotels, expensive shops, homes of the wealthy and those who labored in their industries are places of worship built as testaments to both faith and the rewards of commerce. Many of these monumental structures are cathedrals or mother churches of a particular denomination. Unlike the houses of worship in working-class neighborhoods, these churches were not built with small donations from poor congregants, but rather were erected in the heart of downtown by wealthy civic leaders.

Chicago's First Episcopal Parish
EPISCOPAL CATHEDRAL OF ST. JAMES

Episcopal. 65 E. Huron Street. 1856–7, Edward J. Burling; 1875, Burling and Adler; restoration Holabird and Roof. ☎ 312-787-7360
💻 www.saintjamescathedral.org

Among the first people to settle near Fort Dearborn were Yankee Episcopalians, many of whom became the city's civic and business leaders. They organized St. James parish in 1834 and three years later built a small brick church that served them for twenty years before a new church was erected. The second church is where Abraham Lincoln worshiped the day after his election to the presidency in 1860, even though he was neither an Episcopalian nor a regular churchgoer.

The walls and bell tower of the 1857 church were included in the design of the congregation's third church, dedicated in September 1871. At the base of the bell tower was an ornate memorial designed by Frederick Law Olmsted (see p. 125) dedicated to church members who died in the Civil War. To guarantee the memorial would survive all disasters, Mayor William B. Ogden insisted it be fireproof. His prescience was remarkable: One month after the church's dedication, it was destroyed in the Great Fire of 1871, but the bell tower and its memorial survived. Following the fire the church was rebuilt according to its original plan and was rededicated in 1875. The memorial, used as an altar while the new church was being constructed, now stands at the north end of the narthex. Augusta Freeman carved the beautiful marble font in 1874 that stands at the nave's entrance. A large marble altar and a cathedra (bishop's chair) in the chancel are the cathedral's focal point. The carved wood and painted reredos showing Christ in majesty was given to the church in 1884. Beautiful stained-glass windows in a variety of American and European art glass dating from the late nineteenth century light the interior that has recently had all of its original Victorian stencil work restored, designed originally by Edward Neville Stent in 1888, a student of William Morris.

The cathedral's St. Andrew's Chapel, designed by Bertram G. Goodhue and completed in 1913, is modeled after an ancient abbey chapel in Scotland. It was erected for the Brotherhood of Saint Andrew, founded in 1893 by young men in the church's Bible class. The intimate spiritual space has stained-glass windows depicting saints prominent in the British Isles, and a beautiful altar, reredos, and baldachin that are copied after a Scottish original.

NEARBY
➥ **Episcopal Church Center and Cathedral House,** 65 E. Huron Street. 1968, James W. Hammond and Peter Roesch. ☎ 312-751-4200

Completed in 1968, the center is the headquarters of the Episcopal Diocese of Chicago. The building and its adjoining plaza are used for a variety of religious and community activities. Summerfest performances are held on the plaza stage Wednesdays at noon, weather permitting. The cathedral has an extensive sacred music program and has been the site of a number of world and American premiers of sacred music.

Five Red Cardinal Hats
HOLY NAME CATHEDRAL

Catholic. 735 N. State Street. 1874–75, Patrick C. Keeley; 1890–93 renovation, Willett and Pashley; 1914 addition, Henry J. Schlacks; 1968–69 renovation, C. F. Murphy Associates. ☎ 312-787-8040
🖳 holynamecathedral.org

Rebuilt following the destruction of the original cathedral in the 1871 fire, Holy Name has undergone numerous renovations and additions since its original construction. A monumental building, it has been witness to many momentous events that include the International Eucharistic Congress in June 1926, the largest liturgical celebration in any American church up to that time; a visit from Eugenio Cardinal Pacelli in 1936, who later became Pope Pius XII; and more recently two visits in October 1979 by Pope John Paul II.

The nave's vaulted ceiling bears the coat of arms of John Cardinal Cody, archbishop of Chicago during the cathedral's 1968 renovation, surrounded by the official seals of the city of Chicago, the state of Illinois, the United States, and the Papal See.

Among the cathedral's many beautiful ritual objects and artifacts is the wooden resurrection crucifix suspended above the main altar. The altar is made from a six-ton monolithic block of red-black granite that rests on a pedestal encircled by bronze relief carvings depicting biblical scenes of

Holy Name Cathedral

sacrificial offerings and their preparation. Behind the altar is the cathedra, the bishop's throne, and above it are five bronze panels by Attilio Selva representing the Holy Name of Jesus. Above the panels and suspended from the ceiling are five red, broad-brimmed, ornamental hats, or *galeros*. Since the thirteenth century, the red hat, the symbol of a cardinal, is raised to the ceiling of his cathedral upon his death, where it is left to hang until it turns to dust, a symbol that all earthly glory is passing. The center hat belonged to Chicago's first cardinal, George Mundelein. Left to right, the others represent Cardinals Meyer, Bernardin, Cody, and Stritch.

The cathedral houses two important organs, a sanctuary organ handmade by Casavant Freres in 1981 that is modeled after seventeenth-century French organs, and a gallery organ handmade in the workshops of Flentrop Orgelbouw in Zaandam, Holland, and installed in 1989. With its 5,558 pipes, 71 stops, and 4 keyboards, it is considered the largest mechanical-action organ in the Chicago area.

Athens in Chicago
ANNUNCIATION GREEK ORTHODOX CATHEDRAL
1017 N. LaSalle Drive. 1910, N. Dokas. ☎ 312-664-5485

The third cathedral in the area is Annunciation Cathedral, built by Greek Orthodox immigrants from Sparta, Greece, who settled in Chicago in the last decade of the nineteenth century. The congregation worshiped in a rented hall and a Masonic temple until they erected the cathedral in 1910, which is modeled after the cathedral church in Athens, Greece. Two square towers frame the church's main entrance and large stained-glass window that depicts the annunciation to Mary by the angel Gabriel. A narthex leads into the nave that is divided by two rows of columns into three aisles. At its eastern end is an apse that houses the altar. As is traditional in Orthodox churches, the altar is separated from the nave by a beautiful wooden iconostasis hung with traditional icons (see pp. 85–86). The opalescent stained-glass windows installed in 1938 depict saints of the Eastern Church.

Dedicated to Social Activism and Art
FOURTH PRESBYTERIAN CHURCH (NR)
876 N. Michigan Avenue. 1912–14, Ralph Adams Cram.
☎ 312-787-4570

Located across the street from the John Hancock Center, Fourth Presbyterian is as famous for its long history of social activism as it is for its historic building, designed by one of the leading proponents of the Gothic Revival style, Ralph Adams Cram (1863–1942). Founded in February 1871, the congregation dedicated its new church on October 8 of that year; it was destroyed that very same night in the Great Fire. Undeterred, its members immediately raised enough funds to erect a new church, dedicated in 1874, which remained in use until the current building was erected.

Michigan Avenue was a muddy road called Pine Street at the time the congregation purchased land for its third church. The decision to erect such an expensive building in such an undesirable neighborhood was questioned by some members, but the gamble paid off. Except for the Water Tower, Fourth Presbyterian can proudly claim to be "the oldest surviving structure on Michigan Avenue north of the river."

Cram's design displays all of the architectural and decorative features associated with the Gothic Revival style. From its ornate spire piercing the sky to its pointed arches, stained-glass windows (by Charles J. Connick of Boston) framed in tracery, elaborately carved tympanum over its front doors, and long, narrow nave, Fourth Presbyterian proudly looks back to the Gothic Era when the church was triumphant (see pp. 71–73). Blair Chapel, west of the sanctuary, designed by J. J. Sherer of Milwaukee and dedicated in 1971, is in the thirteenth-century Gothic style.

In 1994 the sanctuary restoration project was started with the goal of restoring the church back to Cram's original design. Except for the subtle introduction of improved acoustics and lighting, Fourth Presbyterian appears today much as it did when it was constructed nearly a century ago. Among other buildings in the complex that surround a garth (an open courtyard) are the cloister, manse, and parish house, all designed in 1914 by Howard Van Doren Shaw (see pp. 109–10). A fountain in the center of the garth was also created and donated by Shaw.

The congregation has an active progressive art program that commissions works on religious themes and provides gallery space for exhibitions.

Chicago's Crown Jewel
ST. JAMES CHAPEL

Catholic. 103 E. Chestnut Street. 1917–20, Gustave Steinback, New York, and Zachary Davis, Chicago. ☎ 312-787-8625

Enter a space bathed in otherworldly light. That was the effect Abbot Suger hoped to achieve by introducing the use of stained glass into French churches in the early Middle Ages (see pp. 71–72). Nowhere is this more successfully achieved then in La Sainte Chapelle in Paris, completed in

1248 by King Louis IX to house a relic from Christ's crown of thorns. One could argue that a close second was built nearly seven hundred years later in Chicago for the chapel of Archbishop Quigley Preparatory Seminary, erected at the behest of then archbishop, later George Cardinal Mundelein, to honor his predecessor Archbishop James Quigley. Like its Parisian model, the walls of St. James Chapel are almost completely transparent, one of the largest and most spectacular displays of stained glass to be found in any religious building in the Midwest. Created under the direction of the architect Gustav Steinbeck and designed by the artist Robert Giles, the windows were constructed and installed by the Chicago-based John Kinsella Company. Each window is made of 20,000 to 45,000 pieces of antique English stained glass. The sanctuary windows set into a curved wall in front are thirty feet high by seven feet wide. Each has ten medallions set in two vertical columns that illustrate the life and parables of Christ. The windows on the south wall are forty feet high and ten feet wide and contain scenes from the Hebrew Bible. Those on the north wall depict the Acts of the Apostles and moments in the lives of martyrs and founders of religious orders. The Rose Window measures twenty-eight feet in diameter and contains scenes from the life of the Virgin Mary; it was inspired by the twelfth-century Notre Dame Cathedral in Paris.

NEARBY

➥ **Washington Square Park (LR),** 60 W. Walton Street and 915-29 N. Dearborn Street. A developer, Orasmus Bushnell, donated the land for Chicago's oldest surviving park in 1842. By the late nineteenth century its location was in the heart of the city, and it became a popular place for soapbox orators, thus its nickname, "Bughouse Square." Once a year the tradition is revived when would-be orators are invited back to the park to "bug" the public. The park is also used for Native American powwows sponsored by the D'Arcy McNickle Center for American Indian History, housed across the street in the famed Newberry Library. Check at the library for dates and time.

➥ **The Newberry Library,** 60 W. Walton Street. 1890–93, Henry Ives Cobb; 1981 addition, Harry Weese and Associates. ☎ 312-943-9090

The Romanesque Revival structure, modeled after the twelfth-century Provencal French Church of Saint-Gilles-du-Gard, houses an extensive collection of rare books, manuscripts, and reference materials focusing on history and the humanities, including the D'Arcy McNickle Center for American Indian History. In addition, its galleries feature changing exhibitions.

➥ **Charnley-Persky House (NHL),** 1365 N. Astor Street. 1892, Offices of Adler and Sullivan. ☎ 312-915-0105 🖥️ www.sah.org

The Charnley-Persky House, now the national headquarters for the Society of Architectural Historians, was described by Frank Lloyd Wright as "the first modern house in America." It was designed in 1891 by the firm of Dankmar Adler and Louis Sullivan at the time Frank Lloyd Wright was working for them. Wright liked to credit himself with its design, although there is no evidence to support his claim. The client was James Charnley, a lumber merchant, which may account for the house's magnificent oak and mahogany interior, including a large oak stairway with its noteworthy wood grill. The house's design does reflect the forward-looking ideas of Adler and Sullivan, which were further developed by their young apprentice, Frank Lloyd Wright.

Logan Square

Further north and west is Logan Square, named for Civil War General John Logan of Illinois. It is bounded by the Chicago River on the east, Diversey Avenue on the north, approximately Bloomingdale Avenue on the south, and the Hermosa community area to the west. The area remained largely rural until after the 1871 fire, and experienced its largest expansion in the late nineteenth and early twentieth centuries, following the opening of the Logan Square elevated line in 1895.

The Last Remaining Norwegian Language–Church in Chicago
NORWEGIAN LUTHERAN MEMORIAL CHURCH (MINNEKIRKEN)
2614 N. Kedzie Boulevard. 1908–12, Charles F. Sorensen.
☎ 773-252-7335; 708-867-7051

When the church was dedicated in 1912 as Christ Church (Kristuskirken), it was located in the midst of a heavily Scandinavian neighborhood. Financial woes forced the congregation to close its doors at the onset of the Depression, but thanks to the return of Pastor Johan B. Meyer, the founder of the congregation, its doors were reopened in 1934. The church was renamed Den Norske Lutherske Minnekirken, "Norwegian Lutheran Memorial Church," a reflection of the congregation's dedication to preserving Norwegian tradition and culture.

According to the congregation's history, the Gothic Revival church with its soaring steeple is modeled after the nineteenth-century Bragenes Kirke (church) in Drammen, Norway. Its white and gold-leaf altar, reredos (screen behind the altar), chancel rail, and baptismal font also reflect the congregants' Norwegian heritage. The church is graced with beautiful stained-glass windows that depict biblical scenes.

NEARBY
➡ **Illinois Centennial Memorial Monument,** 2600 N. Kedzie Boulevard, ca. 1910.

Created by Henry Bacon (1839–1912; see p. 181), with sculpture by Evelyn Beatrice Longman (1874–1954), the monument commemorates Illinois' centennial. It is a Classical Revival–style column set atop a cylindrical base decorated with carved images of Native Americans, French explorers, pioneer farmers, and other workers. Bacon also designed the Lincoln Memorial in Washington, D.C.

Portage Park

Located northwest of Logan Square, Portage Park was the site of a portage between the Chicago and the Des Plaines Rivers that was used by Native Americans. These portages followed the trails that are now Cicero and Narragansett Avenues. It is bounded by Cicero Avenue to the east, Belmont Avenue on the south, Narragansett Avenue on the west, and Gunnison Avenue on the north. The area became part of Chicago in 1889. Commercial and residential development began following the extension of the Milwaukee Avenue streetcar line in 1894.

NEARBY
➡ **St. Bartholomew Catholic Church,** 4949 W. Patterson Avenue. 1937–38. ☎ 773-545-2119

St. Bartholomew's looks like a New England Colonial church without the village green. Modeled after Protestant prototypes and built for an English-speaking parish, its style signals the Americanization of the Catholic Church. The church's bright and spacious interior has a simplicity usually associated with Puritan and Yankee values. More characteristic of Catholic churches are its cruciform plan, marble altar, and stained-glass windows.

➡ **St. Pascal Catholic Church,** 6149 W. Irving Park Road. 1930–31, B. J. Hotton, Raymond Gregori. ☎ 773- 725-7641

This is the boyhood church of Chicago's Francis Cardinal George. Greeting worshipers on the church's exterior is a monumental cross set within an arch that rises above its main entries. Upon entering the cruciform-plan church one faces the apse, whose half-dome is covered with glittering gold glass mosaic. Changes made after the Second Vatican

Council include the removal of the communion rail and side altars. The marble and wrought-iron pulpit set on a small platform has been in the church since its dedication.

Lincoln Park

The Lincoln Park area extends from Lake Michigan west to the Chicago River, north to Diversey Parkway, and south to North Avenue, and includes a portion of "Old Town." The area was acquired in 1830 by the trustees of the Illinois and Michigan Canal, who then sold parcels to farmers to finance the canal. Not well suited for farming, the area became the city's common burial ground. Prone to frequent flooding, the cemetery rapidly became an overcrowded eyesore and posed a health risk to the city's water supply. A decision was made in the 1850s to dig up all the graves, move them elsewhere, and transform the unsightly land into a beautifully landscaped lakeshore park known initially as Lake Park until it was renamed Lincoln Park (see pp. 172–73) following the president's assassination. This set in motion the development of rural garden cemeteries such as Oak Woods (see pp. 135–36), Graceland (see pp. 178–81), and Rosehill (see pp. 181–82). One family refused to move its mausoleum and won a lawsuit that allowed it to remain in Lincoln Park. Not easily visible, the **Ira Couch Mausoleum** is hidden behind bushes just to the north of the Chicago Historical Society (see p. 173). The Lincoln Park area was not spared from the 1871 fire, which destroyed everything in its tracks, but in the process cleansed the neighborhood of its funereal associations and set in motion its redevelopment as a desirable place to live.

The Bells of St. Michael's
ST. MICHAEL'S CHURCH
Catholic. 455 W. Eugenie Street. 1866–69; 1872–73, August Wallbaum.
☎ 312-664-1511

German immigrants who settled in the Old Town Triangle District of the Lincoln Park area founded the parish in 1852. The church, built by the Redemptorist Fathers, was badly damaged in the 1871 fire that also destroyed many of the parishioners' houses. They quickly set out to rebuild their homes and church, but this time in brick and stone. The neighborhood prospered for nearly a half century, but by the 1940s, it had begun to decline. Community concerns about its future evolved into one of the nation's first neighborhood revitalization programs, resulting in the preservation of its tree-lined streets and distinctive architectural character, all centered on St. Michael's Church.

Following the fire, St. Michael's was described in the *Daily Tribune* as the city's "most imposing ruins on the north side." Two years later the church was rebuilt, and in 1876 five great bells were installed in its belfry. According to a local tradition, anyone who can hear the bells of St. Michael's is considered a resident of Old Town. On the church's tower, which rises 290 feet above the ground, is a four-sided illuminated clock, an Old Town landmark. While the church's exterior is a mélange of Gothic and Romanesque Revival styles, the traditional off-white, gold, and light blue color scheme on the interior reflects its founders' Bavarian heritage. One of the church's cherished possessions is a painting of Mary, Mother of Perpetual Help that survived the 1871 fire. Pope Pius IX gave it to the church's Redemptorist Fathers in 1865

The Largest Private Institution in Chicago
DEPAUL UNIVERSITY
Lincoln Park Campus. ☎ 312-362-8000

Vincentian priests associated with St. Vincent de Paul Church (see below) established St. Vincent's College in 1898. It was chartered as DePaul University in 1907. The university now serves over twenty thousand students and has eight campuses. The Lincoln Park campus is the largest, sprawling over thirty-six acres in the heart of the neighborhood. St. Vincent de Paul Church serves DePaul University students.

NEARBY
➡ **St. Vincent de Paul Church,** Catholic. 1010 W. Webster Avenue. 1895–97, James J. Egan. ☎ 773-327-1113

The parish, founded in 1875 for German and Irish Catholics, worships in a beautiful Romanesque Revival–style church that seats over a thousand people. Its stained-glass windows are original and were designed and executed by the Mayer and Company Studio in Munich, Germany. The window in the west transept honors St. Vincent de Paul, the church's patron saint and founder of the Congregation of the Mission and the Sisters of Charity in 1660. The church's worship space was reconfigured in the 1980s and recently has undergone a major renovation.

➡ **St. Clement Catholic Church,** 642 W. Deming Place. 1917–18, George D. Barnett; renovation, Holobird and Roche. ☎ 773-281-0371
🖥 www.stclementchurch.org

Founded in 1905 as a German-speaking parish, St. Clement's is modeled after the Byzantine Romanesque–style St. Louis (Missouri) Cathedral and borrows many of its elements from the twelfth-century San Clemente

Church in Rome. Its outstanding feature is its huge central dome that is typical of many early Byzantine churches, such as the sixth-century Hagia Sophia in Istanbul, Turkey. The church underwent extensive renovation and remodeling in the 1980s that included transforming the apse into the baptistery and placing the altar table in the center of the transept.

➠ **Church of Our Saviour,** Episcopal, 530 W. Fullerton Parkway. 1888–89, Clinton J. Warren. ☎ 773-549-3832 💻 www.coschurch.org

Families living on Chicago's north side organized this congregation in 1867. A church was built on Lincoln Avenue in 1869 that remained in use until 1889, when the present building was completed. The Romanesque Revival church is built on the site of an earlier church, Fullerton Presbyterian, erected in 1864. Some argue that portions of that building's chancel area were actually incorporated into the present church. The baptismal font and the window over the altar are from the congregation's earlier building. The use of unglazed terra-cotta wall tiles in the nave is unique in Chicago churches. Tiffany Studios made some of the sanctuary's stained-glass windows.

Something for Everyone
LINCOLN PARK

There is something for everyone in Lincoln Park, from its **conservatory** where a visitor can experience spring or summer in the dead of winter, to its famous **zoo.** The park, covering over twelve hundred acres, stretches nearly six miles along the Lake Michigan shoreline. A series of talented landscapers were responsible for transforming a cemetery and landfill into a place of beauty. Swain Nelson and Olaf Benson created the park's first design in 1865. Over the years as more land was acquired, other landscapers made their contributions, notably Ossian C. Simonds (1903–21), Ernst G. Schroeder (ca. 1920–60), and Alfred Caldwell (1936–38).

Montrose Harbor offers panoramic views of Lake Michigan and the city, and along with **Belmont Harbor,** is a great place to see birds. Scattered throughout the park are statues of famous people, including an 1886 bronze statue of Abraham Lincoln (*The Standing Lincoln*) by Augustus Saint-Gaudens (see p. 101), located east of the Chicago Historical Society, and a thirteen-foot bronze statue of Alexander Hamilton by John Angel (1881–1960) that is set in front of a seventy-eight-foot pylon of black granite. In 1981, Ellsworth Kelly (born 1923) created the park's first contemporary sculpture simply named *I Will* in celebration of the city's spirit following the 1871 fire. Markers identify significant ancient sites in the park. One marks a beach that was near the sidewalk east of the center of North

Pond and another identifies a stand of bur oak trees near the South Field House that many believe survived the Chicago Fire. Recently restored and reopened to the public is the beautiful **Café Brauer,** the South Pond refectory. Built in 1908 and designed by Perkins and Hamilton, the building has been described as "an outstanding example of the Prairie School style in a public building." Rent a paddleboat at the refectory and enjoy the remarkable serenity available in the midst of one of the nation's busiest cities.

NEARBY
➡ **The Elks National Memorial and Headquarter,** 2750 N. Lakeview Avenue. ☎ 773-755-4700

Designed by Egerton Swarthout (1870–1943) of New York City and dedicated in 1926, the memorial is a palatial space that has been described as "befitting a coronation." Built as a monument to Elks who died during World War I and subsequently in memory of veterans of all wars, the recently restored structure features marble from quarries in the United States and Europe. Its exterior is modeled after the ancient Pantheon in Rome, and its interior decoration includes sculptures by James Earle Fraser (1876–1953) and his wife Laura Gardin Fraser (1889–1966), and allegorical murals by Edwin H. Blashfield (1848–1936) and Eugene Francis Savage (1883–1978). Savage received the Architectural League of New York's Gold Medal of Honor for his twelve panels that decorate the one hundred–foot tall rotunda and reception room.

➡ **Chicago Historical Society,** 1601 N. Clark Street. ☎ 312-642-4600

Located in Old Town at the southern end of Lincoln Park, the museum has exhibits that trace American history from the time of Columbus to the present. Every aspect of Chicago's development is covered. Period rooms provide a glimpse into the lives of Chicagoans; the Great Fire is documented, as is the 1893 World's Columbian Exposition and the 1933 Century of Progress Fair. The society houses an extensive library and archive that is open to researchers.

A Forerunner of the Modern "Megachurch"
THE MOODY MEMORIAL CHURCH
Nondenominational. 1630 N. Clark Street (Old Town). 1925, John R. Fugard. ☎ 312-943-0466 🖳 www.moodychurch.org

Across the street from the Chicago Historical Society is a formidable-appearing building whose identity is not immediately apparent. Displaying features borrowed from Byzantine and Romanesque Revival architecture, the building could be an auditorium or a basketball arena, but its name tells us it is a church. For many years the Moody Memorial Church was the nation's largest Protestant church building, seating four thousand people. It is named for its founder, Dwight L. Moody (1837–99), a charismatic preacher born in Northfield, Massachusetts. Although he claimed to be related to some of the nation's most famous people, including Harriet Beecher Stowe and the Roosevelts, his family was very poor. Moody moved from Boston to Chicago in 1856 and found work as a shoe sales-man; his real goal, however, was to preach the word of God. The nation was in the midst of a religious revival (see p. 10) and untrained, charis-matic preachers like Moody found receptive audiences. He first preached from a rented pew in a Chicago church and then in a beer hall. His thun-derous sermons began to attract large crowds that included Abraham Lincoln, who came by to hear him on his way to Washington, D.C. for his first inauguration. Moody's interest in young people led to the formation of the Young Men's Christian Association and later the Young Women's Christian Association. Returning from the Civil War where he served as a volunteer chaplain, Moody decided to build a church in Chicago, the Illinois Street Independent Church, which was lost in the 1871 fire. He quickly built the Northside Tabernacle and turned it into a relief center for those who had lost everything in the fire. His reputation as a charismatic speaker spread, and by the time he died he had traveled thousands of miles to preach to millions of people; this huge church is his memorial.

In spite of its vast size, the church's interior conveys a sense of welcome and warmth. A narthex encircles an oval-shaped auditorium with a can-tilevered balcony that sweeps along three sides and down to the level of the podium; everyone has an unobstructed view of the pulpit and choir. Light filtering through stained-glass windows and seven large chandeliers illuminate the interior.

A Temple of Enlightenment
MIDWEST BUDDHIST TEMPLE
435 W. Menomonee Street (Old Town). 1971, Hideaki Arao.
☎ 312-943-7801 💻 www.bcmw.org/directory/temples/midbudte (Note: Chicago and its environs are home to many Buddhist centers and organi-zations. A list can be found at 💻www.manjushri.com/TEMPLES/illinois.)

Japanese Americans who were discharged from internment camps where they were confined during World War II founded the Midwest Bud-dhist Temple in 1944, one of the first Buddhist centers in Chicago. It is affiliated with the Jodo Shinshu, or Pure Land School, which was founded in Japan by Shinran Shonin (1173–1262), who introduced Buddhist teachings to ordinary people.

Midwest Buddhist Temple

The tolling of the temple's bells has become a familiar sound in the Old Town Triangle district. Mayor Richard J. Daley hailed the temple, constructed of wood, concrete, and plaster, as a new Chicago landmark at its dedication in 1971. Designed by Japanese architect Hideaki Arao and known as the "Temple of Enlightenment," it is a replica of temples found in Japan. The sanctuary's focal point is an altar housing an imposing figure of Buddha surrounded by candles and other ritual objects. Two popular festivals sponsored by the Midwest Buddhist Temple are the Obon Dance Festival in July and the Ginza Holiday Festival in August. Call the temple for dates and time.

Lake View

Bounded on the east by Lake Michigan and on the west by Ravenswood Avenue, Lake View stretches from Diversey Parkway north to near Montrose Avenue. Prior to the 1871 fire, wealthy Chicagoans had built estates along the lakefront, but the area's character began to change after the fire with the arrival of many middle-class German immigrants who were fleeing the devastation in their Old Town neighborhood, which included the loss of their church, St. Michael's (see p. 170).

Out of the Ashes
ST. ALPHONSUS CHURCH
Catholic. 1429 W. Wellington Avenue. 1889–97, Adam Boos and Josef Bettinghofer, Chicago; Schrader and Conradi, St. Louis. ☎ 773-525-0709

German immigrants who had worshiped in St. Michael's established St. Alphonsus, named for the founder of the Redemptorist order, in 1882.

Their first church, a small wooden building, was destroyed by fire and was replaced by this monumental stone Gothic Revival structure that features a 260-foot-high tower similar to St. Michael's. Built to replace a church destroyed by fire, this church almost experienced a similar fate. On October 23, 1950, a fire accidentally set by workmen destroyed the church's roof and damaged its interior. The parishioners immediately set about to restore their historic building, which included replicating its elaborately rib-vaulted ceiling, except this time steel was used instead of wood. The church is endowed with many beautiful ritual objects, including the main altar made of Italian marble that survived the fire and collapse of the roof. Many of the statues are of Redemptorist saints, including St. Alphonsus, the church's patron. Note the shrine to the left of the nave dedicated to Our Lady of Guadalupe, an indication of change in the area's ethnicity. In 1999 the Redemptorist order turned the parish over to the Archdiocese of Chicago.

A Conservative, Egalitarian Synagogue
ANSHE EMET SYNAGOGUE
Conservative Jewish. 3760 N. Pine Grove Avenue. 1910–11, Alfred S. Alschuler. ☎ 773-281-1423

Alfred S. Alschuler (1876–1940) was a prominent Chicago architect who designed several of the city's synagogues, including the Byzantine/Moorish K.A.M. Isaiah Israel Synagogue built in 1923 (see pp. 126–28). Anshe Emet is far less exotic. Its exterior façade is relatively plain with a colonnaded portico supporting an entablature inscribed with words from Isaiah 56:7, "For my House shall be called a house of prayer for all people." The only other clue to the building's identity is a stone six-pointed Star of David set in the gable. The synagogue was originally built for Temple Sholom (see below) whose members worshiped in it until a new synagogue was built on Lake Shore Drive. Anshe Emet (Men of Truth), founded in 1873, acquired the synagogue in 1928, later adding a complex of buildings to house its many religious, social, and educational activities.

The synagogue is in the auditorium-plan style with amphitheater seats that face west toward the *bimah* and Ark. Although Jews traditionally pray facing toward Jerusalem, the availability of land often made this impossible, as is the case here. The auditorium's beautiful stained-glass windows designed by Todras Geller and A. Raymond Katz, which portray Jewish historic and religious themes, were installed in 1935 to replace ones removed by Temple Sholom for reuse in its new building. Adjoining the auditorium is the Hall of Memories, lit by twelve large stained-glass windows designed by Archie Rand and installed in 1981, representing the Twelve Tribes of Israel.

A Monumental Synagogue Designed by Students
TEMPLE SHOLOM OF CHICAGO
Reform Jewish. 3480 N. Lake Shore Drive. 1928–30, Loebl, Schlossman and Demuth, with Coolidge and Hodgdon. ☎ 773-525-3502

This synagogue has an unusual genesis. Three students at the School of Architecture at Armour Institute (later the Illinois Institute of Technology; see pp. 116–17) were given an assignment in 1921 to design a synagogue. Seven years later, with the professional assistance of two architects, Charles A. Coolidge of Boston and Charles Hodgdon of Chicago, their plan became a reality. The monumental building is remindful of Alschuler's design for K.A.M. Isaiah Israel (see pp. 126–28) in that both borrow from Byzantine and Moorish sources for their plan and decoration. Each is octagonal in shape and crowned with a dome, and each has 1,350 seats arranged in a raked, amphitheater style that face toward the *bimah* and Ark. Temple Sholom differs, however, in how the architects solved the problem of expanding the sanctuary's seating capacity. Here the entire western wall (with *bimah* and Ark) is mounted on wheels and can be moved back into the adjoining social hall to almost double the sanctuary's size. Light filters into the social hall through stained-glass windows moved from the congregation's former synagogue (now Anshe Emet; see above). Unlike K.A.M. Isaiah Israel, where monumental stained-glass windows pierce the walls of the sanctuary, Temple Sholom's main sanctuary walls are walnut-paneled. A complex lighting system set in the dome reflects indirect light throughout the interior.

Uptown

Uptown, immediately north of Lake View, is bounded by Lake Michigan on the east and Ravenswood Avenue on the west. Its northern boundary is Foster Avenue and its southern is Montrose Avenue from Ravenswood east to Clark Street, and Irving Park Road from Clark Street east to Lake Michigan. Initially part of Lake View, both areas were annexed by the city of Chicago in 1889. Between 1890 and 1920 Uptown developed into a popular residential area with a well-known entertainment district that was home to several theaters and the very popular **Aragon Ballroom** (1100 W. Lawrence Avenue, 1926).

A Roman Pilgrimage Site in Chicago
ST. MARY OF THE LAKE CHURCH
Catholic. 4200 N. Sheridan Road. 1913–17, Henry J. Schlacks.
☎ 773-472-3711

The church once overlooked the shoreline of Lake Michigan that has since changed. That is where St. Mary is depicted as standing in a painting located in the nave's south side altar. The campanile in the painting is the church's actual campanile that Schlacks modeled after the freestanding fourteenth-century bell tower at the Church of St. Pudenziana in Rome. Details from other famous Roman churches are incorporated within this single building: Its east façade and interior colonnade are modeled after San Paolo fuori le Mura (St. Paul Outside the Walls), and its paneled ceiling trimmed with gold leaf is similar to Santa Maria Maggiore (St. Mary Major); both date back to the fourth century and are famous Roman pilgrimage sites. The church's beautiful high altar is carved from white Carrara marble, the same Italian marble used by Michelangelo for his famous sculptures, including the *Pieta* in St. Peter's in the Vatican.

St. Mary's was built for a wealthy parish whose members may have actually visited the ancient churches used as models for their building. Today St. Mary's serves a far more diverse congregation that represents the city's ethnic mosaic.

A Garden of Eternal Rest
GRACELAND CEMETERY
4001 N. Clark Street. 1860. ☎ 773-525-1105

Graceland Cemetery, founded in 1860, is probably Chicago's most famous cemetery and one of the most historically, artistically, and architecturally significant cemeteries in the nation due to its landscape and monuments. It is where the City Beautiful movement, the Chicago School of Architecture, and the Art Nouveau style converge, with Daniel Burnham buried at its heart.

Check at the cemetery office for a guidebook. Only a few of Graceland's many highlights can be discussed here. Significant buildings include the original part of the Chapel (1886–88), as well as the Administration Building (1896) and Waiting Room (1896), all by Holabird and Roche, and more recently, the Chapel Hill Columbarium (1997) by John Eifler and Associates.

Interred here are some of the city's most important civic leaders and artists, people who literally transformed a swampland into a metropolis. The cemetery's earliest visionary founders and presidents, Thomas Barbour

Graceland Cemetery

Bryan and Bryan Lathrop, set the stage for a magnificent integration of art, architecture, and landscape at once apart from the city and at the heart of the city. As one of the country's first "garden" cemeteries, Graceland became a popular tourist destination in the late nineteenth and twentieth centuries; it remains so to this day.

What once was a wilderness area was transformed by a series of architects and landscape architects into a beautiful garden. Its design reflects the Victorian Age's belief that cemeteries were no longer to be frightening, blighted, overcrowded, disease-ridden eyesores where the dead were quickly placed in the ground. Instead, they were to be beautiful gardens where the deceased went to their eternal rest, and their descendants went for renewal and spiritual awakening, all in the presence of Mother Nature, carefully manipulated for effect. Mausoleums, monuments, statuary, gardens, lagoons, groves of trees, curving paths and roadways, beautiful buildings, including crematoriums carefully disguised as chapels or temples, all contribute to a peaceful and spiritual ambience.

Family plots with names of entrepreneurs and philanthropists like Field, Palmer, McCormick, Pullman, Armour, Getty, and Kimball are here, as well as the names of the architects who designed their homes, places of worship, businesses, and, at times, funerary monuments. These include William Le Baron Jenney, Louis Sullivan, Ludwig Mies van der Rohe, Daniel Burnham and his partner John Wellborn Root, Thomas Tallmadge, John Holabird, Howard Van Doren Shaw, Fazlur Rahman Khan, Bruce Goff, and the architectural photographer Richard Nickel (see p. 100).

One of the most interesting plots is the Pullman Family monument

(1897), a single tall Corinthian column flanked by benches, designed by Solon Beman, the architect who designed Pullman's ideal town (see p. 136). What cannot be seen completes Pullman's story. Fearful that workers still angry over Pullman's handling of the 1893 strike would try to dig up his body, his family had his coffin wrapped in tar paper and asphalt and sealed in a concrete vault the size of a room. More concrete was laid over the vault, which was then overlaid with railroad ties. Pullman's enemies were not able to enter his tomb, nor could his restless ghost depart it.

Another significant monument is the one designed by McKim, Mead, and White for the Palmer family. Modeled after a Greek temple and housing twin sarcophagi, the monument is dramatically situated on a hill overlooking the cemetery and Lake Willowmere. McKim, Mead, and White also designed the Honore (1906) and Kimball (1907) monuments.

When Louis Sullivan died in 1924 his accomplishments as an architect were all but forgotten, except by a few of his disciples. Thomas Tallmadge (1876–1940), the architect and historian, led the drive to finance a monument for Sullivan and then designed the simple granite stone that was placed over his grave in 1929. The sides of the stone are cut to represent Sullivan's contributions to the development of the skyscraper. On one face of the monument is a bronze plaque decorated with a profile image of Sullivan set against one of his beautiful geometrically patterned designs; on the reverse is a statement written by Tallmadge attesting to Sullivan's many contributions to architecture.

More lasting memorials to Sullivan's genius can be found nearby: the tombs he designed for the Ryerson and Getty families. When Martin Ryerson died in 1887, his son commissioned Sullivan to design a family tomb. A year later Ryerson's business partner, Henry Harrison Getty, requested that Sullivan design a tomb for his recently deceased wife, Carrie Eliza Getty. The two monuments, designed a year apart, could not be more different. The Ryerson tomb (1889), modeled after an Egyptian pyramid, looks to the past, while the Getty tomb anticipates the future. An inscription in front of the tomb sums it up: "The Getty Tomb (1890) marks the maturity of Sullivan's architectural style and the beginning of modern architecture in America."

Lorado Taft (see p. 126) created two monuments in Graceland. *Eternal Silence*, also known as the *Statue of Death*, was completed in 1909 and marks the grave of Dexter Graves (1789–1844), one of Chicago's first settlers. The hooded and heavily draped figure with a shadowed face has a haunted appearance. According to legend, a vision of the afterworld is rewarded to those who can gaze unflinchingly into its shrouded eyes. The other figure, *Crusader* (1931), is very different; it represents a knight with sword and shield standing guard over the tomb of Victor Fremont Lawson (1850–1925), the publisher of the *Chicago Daily News*, a newspaper that took pride in its political independence. Lawson's many good deeds, all done anonymously, include the establishment of the Fresh Air Fund, which supported a sanitarium at Lincoln Park for sick, poor children. His tomb is unmarked; instead, there is a quote engraved on the statue's base: "Above All Things Truth Beareth Away the Victory."

Marshall Field is commemorated by *Memory* (1906), a sculpture crafted by Daniel Chester French and Henry Bacon, the team who later designed the Lincoln Memorial in Washington D.C. The mythical figure Memory's seated pose before a reflecting pool anticipates that of Lincoln. Adjacent to this elaborate monument and set in a large L-shaped plot is the simple headstone that marks the grave of Cyrus McCormick (1884), the inventor of the reaper. The vast empty expanse of grass echoes the vast prairies that his reaper conquered.

Lincoln Square

Lincoln Square is located between the north branch of the Chicago River on the west and the Chicago and North Western Railway on the east, and stretches from Montrose Avenue north to Bryn Mawr and Peterson Avenues. In its northeast corner is Rosehill, the city's largest nonsectarian cemetery.

A Place of Rest for All People
ROSEHILL CEMETERY
5800 N. Ravenswood Avenue. 1859. ☎ 773-561-5940

(Check at the cemetery office for a guidebook. Only a few of Rosehill's many highlights can be described here.)

When the cemetery was established in 1859, it was in the midst of a wilderness reached by a spur of the Chicago and North Western Railway; today it is surrounded by a busy city. In 1867, Dr. I. Chronic, a German-born Reform rabbi, requested space in the cemetery for Jewish burials. In granting his request, Rosehill secured its identity as a nonsectarian cemetery.

William W. Boyington designed Rosehill's castellated Gothic Revival entrance gate in 1859, anticipating by ten years his design for Chicago's Water Tower and Pumping Station (see p. 162). Just inside the gates is a statue of Charles Hull, who made a fortune in real estate. He achieved immortality through the achievements of a woman, Jane Addams, who transformed his mansion into Hull-House (see p. 148), a haven of hope for many immigrant families.

Rosehill is where many of the city's leaders are interred. Included are Aaron Montgomery Ward (1843–1913) and Richard Warren Sears (1863–1914), competitive merchants whose remains are in the cemetery's foreboding community mausoleum, originally designed in 1914 by Sidney Lovell. According to legend, Sears's ghost, dressed in top hat and tails, is said to walk the mausoleum's dimly lit hallways. Also in the mausoleum is the burial site and family room of John G. Shedd (1850–1926) of Shedd Aquarium fame. Shedd died before the aquarium opened, but his love for the coast off his native New Hampshire and Lake Michigan compelled him to commission a stained-glass window from Tiffany that would bathe his crypt in a blue light. Adorning the room's furniture is a variety of aquatic images, including seahorses and shells.

Two famous monuments in the cemetery memorialize women. A marble sculpture of a reclining mother and child encased in protective glass marks the graves of Frances Pearce (d. 1864) and her infant daughter. Designed by Chauncey Bradley Ives (1810–94) for the grieving husband and father, Horatio Stone, the sculpture is typical of the dramatic, heartrending imagery favored during the Victorian Era. Also encased in glass is the statue of Lulu Fellows, seated and holding a book, who died in 1863 at age sixteen. Her monument, inscribed, "Many Hopes Lie Buried Here," is a pilgrimage site for people who have found comfort and hope in her image and have left behind money and other memorabilia as a token of their gratitude.

Another sculpture that evokes a sense of sadness is of a robed, hooded woman holding what appears to be a scarf or a scroll. The sculptor was Nelly Verne Walker (1874–1973), a student of Lorado Taft. Walker was born in Iowa and studied with Taft in Chicago, where she achieved some fame before her realistic style of art went into disfavor. The inscription on this monument could refer to her own life: "That best portion of a good man's [sic] life is his little nameless unremembered act of kindness and of love."

Chicago's Environs

Evanston

Evanston is located directly north of the city. The first Europeans to visit the site were Father Jacques Marquette and Louis Jolliet, who landed in its natural harbor in 1674. Today, Evanston is best known as the home of Northwestern University, founded in 1851 by a group of devout Methodists under the leadership of John Evans, for whom the city is named. The city has many extraordinary houses of worship; space allows for only two to be described here.

An Important Navigational Marker
GROSSE POINT LIGHT STATION (NHL)
2601 Sheridan Road. 1873. ☎ 847-864-5181
🖳 www.laddarboretum.org/light.htm

The light station is located at Lighthouse Landing and includes, besides the lighthouse, the Dr. Margery Carlson Greenhouse and the Lighthouse Nature Center. The U.S. government built the Grosse Point Lighthouse in 1873 as a navigational aid following a series of deadly shipwrecks on Lake Michigan near the promontory on which it stands. It remained in use until 1935, when it was decommissioned and the property deeded to the city of Evanston. The light was relit in 1946 and continues in operation as a navigational aid to small craft.

Restoration work that began in 1973 on the lighthouse and adjacent buildings that comprise the light station was completed in 1981. People can now visit the 113-foot-tall brick tower and adjoining keeper's home and the two foghorn houses. The one on the north is a Visitor/Maritime Center where exhibits interpret Great Lakes heritage; the south foghorn house is the Nature Center, which features plants, birds, animals, and minerals that are native to this area. The Carlson Greenhouse displays garden settings that use indigenous plants.

NEARBY

➡ **First Congregational Church of Evanston,** 1445 Hinman Avenue. 1927, Tallmadge and Watson. ☎ 847-864-8332

Founded in 1869 by settlers from New England, this, the congregation's third church, reflects its members' heritage. Reminiscent of the New England churches inspired by St. Martin-in-the-Fields (see p. 69) in London, First Congregational features a **pedimented portico** and a multistage tower surmounted by a steeple.

➡ **St. Luke's Episcopal Church,** 939 Hinman Avenue. 1906–14, John Sutcliffe. ☎ 847-475-7932

St. Luke's is a large Gothic Revival basilica-plan church that is intended, according to one writer, "to arouse a sense of splendor, and evoke a consciousness of God's presence among us." Upon entering the nave, the worshiper is facing the chancel that is subdivided into a choir and sanctuary. Flanking the choir's rood cross is the pulpit and lectern. The high altar, bishop's throne, and rector's chair are in the sanctuary. The church is richly adorned with stained-glass windows and woodcarvings of saints, including the national saints of the British Isles on the reredos behind the altar.

➡ **Frances E. Willard House Museum,** 1730 Chicago Avenue. 1865; enlarged 1879. ☎ 847-864-1396

This Victorian wooden house trimmed with Gothic Revival detailing is the home of Frances E. Willard (1839–98), best remembered as the founder of the National Women's Christian Temperance Union. The house contains many of her furnishings and personal items. Three rooms serve as a temperance museum. When she died, Congress voted to put a statue of her in the rotunda of the United States Capitol, where she is memorialized as "the first woman of the 19th century, the most beloved character of her time."

Wilmette

Just north of Evanston is Wilmette, named after Antoine Ouilmette, a French-Canadian fur trader who was the husband of Archangel Ouilmette, a Pottawatomie Native American who received the land under the Treaty of Prairie du Chien in 1829. The land remained virtually uninhabited until 1908, when landfills created by a new waterway system transformed a small village along Lake Michigan into an exclusive residential district.

"The Light of Oneness" (Baha'u'llah)
BAHA'I HOUSE OF WORSHIP (NR)
100 Linden Avenue. Dedicated in 1953; plan by Louis Bourgeois; interior design by Albert Shaw. ☎ 847-853-2300

Set in the midst of formal gardens in a six-acre tract, this large domed circular building made of white quartz-concrete is the North American seat of the Baha'i faith. Its dome, rising 191 feet above the surrounding landscape, is a navigational beacon to Lake Michigan ships and a landmark to airplanes flying overhead. The architect borrowed from an array of past architectural styles ranging from Egyptian to Italian Renaissance, and transformed them into a composite style that is a visual statement of the Baha'i faith (see p. 37). When the building's plan was unveiled in 1920, the *New York Times* described it as "the [architect's] conception of a Religious League of Nations."

Baha'i was introduced into the United States at the 1893 Parliament of World's Religions. The following year, Thornton Chase of Chicago became the first American Baha'i. As early as 1903, the few Baha'i living in Chicago began to discuss building the faith's first place of worship in the Western world. The architect selected for the project was Louis Bourgeois (1856–1930), a French Canadian, who devoted over ten years to the development of a plan that would be symbolic of a new faith. Construction began in 1920, but various problems delayed its completion for over thirty years. Bourgeois did not live to see his vision become a reality.

The building is nine-sided, as is the nine-point Baha'i star that symbolizes the nine messengers of God worshiped in the Baha'i faith. The number nine is repeated throughout the building: nine entrances reached by nine walkways that lead through its nine gardens. The building's lacy appearance that has been described as having the "airy substance of a dream," is created by delicate sculptured designs and symbols in a precast white Portland cement developed by architectural sculptor John Earley. The main floor of the building, a single circular auditorium with nine radiating alcoves, seats twelve hundred people. Downstairs are offices, reception areas, a display area, and a large hall.

NEARBY

➥ **Gilson Park,** Michigan and Lake Avenues. ☎ 847-256-6100

Landfills by the Chicago Sanitary District's new waterway system created Gilson Park. The **Wilmette Wildflower Garden** in the park is a peaceful place to stroll along a winding pathway that provides views of Lake Michigan.

➥ **The Church of Jesus Christ of Latter-Day Saints, Chicago Illinois Temple,** 4151 W. Lake Avenue, Glenview. Dedicated 1985, Wight and Company. ☎ 847-299-6500

🖳 www.chicagolds.org/Chicagolds_Temple.html

A Mormon Temple is only open to members of the church in good standing. However, the temple does allow visitors to walk around its beautifully landscaped grounds. It is one of three Mormon temples in the United States to be built in a six-spire design. The tallest spire (112 feet) supports a figure of the angel Moroni. Although it is spacious (37,000 square feet), the temple's interior is not designed for communal worship. It is divided into a series of rooms that are used for particular religious practices, including baptism. The temple is closed on Sundays so members can attend a Sacrament Meeting held in tabernacles that are congregational buildings.

Glencoe

Six miles north of Wilmette is the city of Glencoe, home of both the Chicago Botanic Garden and a well-known synagogue.

The Synagogue of Light
NORTH SHORE CONGREGATION ISRAEL

Reform Jewish. 1185 Sheridan Road. 1962–64, Minoru Yamasaki; south wing, 1982, Hammond, Beebe and Babka. ☎ 708-835-0724

Minoru Yamasaki, a Japanese American architect (who designed the original World Trade Center in New York City), knew little about Judaism when he was asked to design a synagogue for the North Shore Congregation Israel. In preparation, Yamasaki spent considerable time studying with the congregation's rabbi and attending religious services. He was particularly impressed by the beautiful descriptions of nature he found in the high holiday services that harmonized with his own interests in plant morphology. The result is a white concrete synagogue that has been described as a "huge exotically sculptured plant soaring skyward." The sanctuary's vaults appear to open upward like a Calla lily, and its windows have been described as both "flamelike" and resembling the tips of palm fronds. Light into the sanctuary filters through amber glass skylights and leaded-glass panels; the latter are intended to represent hands in prayer. The focus of the enormous sanctuary, measuring 80 feet wide, 126 feet long, and 50 feet high, is its *bimah* located against the eastern wall. The Ark, designed by Lee DeSell, is made of teak wood covered with gold leaf and appears to represent either a flame or leaf. The white wall surrounding the Ark is intended to symbolize the white prayer shawl worn by the rabbi and cantor. The sanctuary seats eight hundred people; its size can be increased to eighteen hundred by expanding into the adjoining memorial hall.

Many members felt the sanctuary's overwhelming size, scale, and grandeur did not contribute to a warm, intimate, spiritual atmosphere, particularly when there were only a few hundred people in attendance. Aware that the building was a Late Modern movement icon, a decision was made not to remodel or renovate it. Rather a small, adjoining sanctuary was built in a style described as traditional that fills "worshipers with a sense of intimacy, warmth, and community." The architects borrowed elements from a wide array of historic synagogues to create a sanctuary that reconnects the congregation with the Jewish people's historic past.

NEARBY
➡ **Chicago Botanic Garden,** 1000 Lake Cook Road. ☎ 847-835-5440 This 385-acre preserve offers an elaborate series of gardens and greenhouses that range from the **Japanese Garden** with its three islands, the Island of the Auspicious Cloud, the Island of Pure, Clear Breezes, and the Island of Everlasting Happiness, to the **Waterfall Garden** and the **Learning Garden for the Disabled.** You can walk or take a narrated tram ride through all types of natural habitats including marshes, woodlands, and prairie. A statue of Carolus Linnaeus (Karl von Linne), who established the system of classifying plants in the eighteenth century, can be found in the midst of greenery in the **Heritage Garden.**

Northbrook

West of Glencoe and I-94 is the community of Northbrook, home of the Islamic Cultural Center of Greater Chicago.

A Minaret on the Prairie
THE ISLAMIC CULTURAL CENTER OF GREATER CHICAGO

1810 N. Pfingsten Road. Phase one 1976; phase two 1984–85, Rowe, Abplanalp and Johnson Architects; Aziz Tohk, consulting architect.
☎ 847-272-0319 (Note: For information on additional Islamic centers in Illinois see 🖥 www.imbn.com/masjid)

The history of the center dates back to 1906 when a group of Bosnian Muslim immigrants formed the Bosnian American Cultural Association in Chicago. A building was purchased in the 1950s, and the association's name was changed to the Islamic Cultural Center to reflect the increasing ethnic diversity of its members. In the 1960s the decision was made to build a mosque and school in Northbrook. Funds were raised from members, as well as from the late King Faisal of the Kingdom of Saudi Arabia and the Kuwaiti Embassy. The first phase of construction included classrooms, library, offices, nursery, and a social hall that held four hundred people. A prayer hall and minaret were added in 1985.

Above the entrance to the prayer hall is a drawing of a mosque and minaret and an inscription in Arabic that reads: "There is no God but

Allah, and Muhammad is his messenger." This verse from the Qur'an is the basic creed of Muslims (see pp. 57–59). The walls of the prayer hall are covered with other Qur'anic verses, all executed in beautiful Arabic calligraphy. The hall does not have pews; Muslims use prayer rugs and pray facing in the direction toward Mecca that is marked by an empty niche in the wall called a *mihrab* (see pp. 89–90). The tall minaret next to the prayer hall has a role similar to bell towers in churches; from its balcony the *muezzin* calls the people to prayer.

Lake Forest

Located thirty miles north of Chicago and situated high on bluffs overlooking Lake Michigan is the very elite suburb of Lake Forest, platted in 1857 by St. Louis landscape architect Almerin Hotchkiss (the designer of Chippiannock Cemetery in Rock Island—see p. 237). It was the second development in the nation planned according to the picturesque principles of a garden city, where streets are not laid out in a grid pattern but take into account the land's natural features. (The first was Forest Hills Gardens in Queens, New York.) A later example in Illinois is Riverside (see p. 196). Lake Forest is home to several colleges, including Lake Forest College, established by Presbyterians as Lind University in 1857.

A Modern Meetinghouse
CHRIST CHURCH LAKE FOREST
Nondenominational. 100 N. Waukegan Road. 1989, Hammel, Green and Abrahamson, Inc. ☎ 708-234-1001

The people who organized the congregation in 1980 wanted to create a "nondenominational, congregational church" that would return to the "simple focus" of those considered its forefathers, the Puritans. When the decision was made to build a church, the key question asked of the architects was, "What would the American Puritans build today with their theology and our technology?" Congregants and architects alike studied the layout and plans of eighteenth-century New England villages and meetinghouses prior to designing a complex that consists of simple, steel-framed buildings clustered around a steepled meetinghouse. Thus far the meetinghouse, bell tower, and two parish houses have been completed; two more parish houses are planned.

The white clapboard meetinghouse is entered through a 153-foot-high freestanding campanile that is modeled after the 1771 steeple of the First Church of Christ in Farmington, Connecticut. A glass-walled narthex links the tower to the meetinghouse and serves as a gathering space. The spacious sanctuary is modeled after a small meetinghouse in Brewster, Massachusetts. Its focal point is a raised pulpit crafted by a local artisan. The communion table, however, dates to the eighteenth century. Twin staircases radiate from the chancel area and lead to a gallery. Oversized windows set with clear glass allows light to pour into the sanctuary, where white walls and dark woodwork create an effect described as "white, light, bright, and minimalist."

A Daughter of Chicago's "Spotted Church"
FIRST PRESBYTERIAN CHURCH
700 N. Sheridan Road. 1887, Charles Sumner Frost. ☎ 847-234-6250

In 1856, a group from Second Presbyterian Church (see pp. 109–10) came to this area to look for a place to establish a Presbyterian school, Lind University. Several found the setting so inviting that they moved here from the city and established the community that would become Lake Forest. A Presbyterian congregation was organized in 1859, and a church was dedicated in 1862. It was replaced in 1887 by the present building.

The church is built in the Shingle style, which was then considered appropriate for the suburbs and resorts. Less formal than many of the nineteenth-century revival styles, the Shingle style is characterized by its heavy stone foundation and substantial use of wood shingles. Tying this church to its mother church is its use of the spotted limestone that was salvaged from the Chicago church after it was badly damaged in the 1871 fire. Several stained-glass windows by Louis C. Tiffany were installed in the church soon after its construction, and Tiffany redecorated the entire sanctuary in 1902. A brochure available at the church office describes the stained-glass windows. The sculptor Sylvia Shaw Judson, born in Lake Forest in 1897 (d. 1978), created the statuary. Judson's best known sculpture is *The Bird Girl*, which appeared on the cover of the best-seller *Midnight in the Garden of Good and Evil*. Another copy of the statue stands in front of the Visitors' Center at the **Ryerson Conservation Center,** on the outskirts of Lake Forest.

Libertyville

Located west of Lake Forest and I-94, Libertyville, blessed with mineral springs and four lakes, was a summer retreat for Native Americans, and later, wealthy Chicagoans. It is home to St. Sava Monastery, the headquarters of the Serbian Orthodox faith in North America.

King Peter II of Yugoslavia Is Buried Here
THE CHURCH OF THE ST. SAVA SERBIAN ORTHODOX MONASTERY (NR)

32377 N. Illinois Route 21. 1925, architect unknown. ☎ 847-367-0698

A series of paths are laid out so that the Church of the St. Sava is at the center of a landscaped cross in the midst of the Serbian National Cemetery. King Peter II (1923–70) of Yugoslavia found sanctuary here after the Communists forbade him to return to Yugoslavia at the end of World War II, and this is where he is buried. 550 American airmen who were rescued by a Serbian underground fighter during World War II erected a memorial to this brave man immediately outside the church.

The monastery and church were built to train priests to serve Serbs who were working in Chicago's slaughterhouses and factories. As additional Serbs arrived following World War II, the importance of the monastery increased; today it is the largest diocese of the Serbian Orthodox Faith in the United States.

The church is an excellent example of eastern European church architecture reinterpreted in the Midwest. Although built in 1925, the church is firmly rooted in the historical past of its worshipers. It is a small structure, as are most Serbian rural churches, and is essentially square in plan. Built of brick trimmed with white limestone, each of the church's four large stepped gables faces one of the cardinal points of the compass. The east gable marks the site of the altar; the entrance is under the west gable. Thirteen domes crown the small building; the main dome represents Jesus; the other twelve represent the apostles. The interior is quite small, and in typical Orthodox fashion, there are no pews. An iconostasis, hung with traditional icons, separates the sanctuary from the altar; King Peter gave it to the monastery in 1926.

A Place of Pilgrimage and Peace
THE MARYTOWN EUCHARISTIC ADORATION CHAPEL

Catholic. 1600 W. Park Avenue. 1932, Joseph McCarthy.
☎ 847-367-7800

Designed by the architect of St. Mary of the Lake University in Mundelein (see below), Joseph McCarthy, the chapel was built by the Benedictine Sisters of Clyde, Missouri, at the invitation of Cardinal Mundelein. Located on the grounds of the Marytown Friary, the chapel's exterior is in the American Colonial style, but the interior is modeled after the fourth-century Roman basilica, San Paolo fuori le Mura (St. Paul

Outside the Walls). It is divided into a central nave and flanking aisles by arches supported on columns made of Greek, Italian, Spanish, and French marble. On the ornate altar is a monumental monstrance (which holds the Blessed Sacrament) made from donated gifts of jewelry. Light flowing through stained-glass windows reflects off art works made of enamel and mosaic that depict biblical scenes.

The chapel's Maximilian Kolbe Shrine honors the Conventual Franciscan priest and Polish saint Maximilian Kolbe who died in Auschwitz, a German concentration camp, in 1941. It is the English-speaking home of Maximilian's Militia Immaculata that he founded in 1917, an evangelization movement devoted to the Virgin. The chapel was an official pilgrimage site for the Jubilee Year 2000.

Mundelein

West of Libertyville is a town that has had several names, before it became Mundelein. The town's site was originally occupied by Pottawatomie Indians who were forced out by white pioneers who named their settlement Mechanic's Grove, before changing it to Holcomb. The town floundered, and in an attempt to generate revenue, the inhabitants renamed it Rockefeller after John D. Rockefeller, president of the Wisconsin-Central Railroad. Rockefeller wasn't impressed, but the Sheldon Business School in Chicago did buy six hundred acres and renamed the town Area, an acronym for the school's motto: "Ability, Responsibility, Endurance, and Activity." In 1919, the school sold the property to the Archdiocese of Chicago, and George Cardinal Mundelein (1872–1939), archbishop from 1915 to 1939, transformed it into the St. Mary of the Lake Seminary, reviving a charter given to the diocese by the state of Illinois in 1844 that had been allowed to lapse. The seminary became a university in 1986. Grateful for the presence of the seminary, the village's board changed the name to Mundelein; in return the cardinal presented the village with a new fire truck!

A Catholic Chapel Modeled after a Protestant Church
CHAPEL OF THE IMMACULATE CONCEPTION
100 E. Maple Avenue. 1926, Joseph McCarthy. ☎ 847-566-6401

St. Mary of the Lake University looks like a New England village transported to the Midwest, the exact effect Cardinal Mundelein hoped to achieve. Its style symbolizes the Americanization of the Roman Catholic Church. The chapel is modeled after a historic Congregational church in Old Lyme, Connecticut, a Georgian-style structure modeled after London's eighteenth-century church St. Martin-in-the-Fields (see p. 69). By the nineteenth century, this style had become an American icon, its classical details symbolizing the nation's democratic ideals. The seminary was the site of one of the major events of the 1926 Eucharistic Congress held in Chicago. At its conclusion, hundreds of thousands of people journeyed to the new chapel for a eucharistic celebration and dedication.

Throughout the chapel can be found images and symbols associated with its patron, the Virgin Mary. A sculpture of the Immaculate Conception in front of the chapel is a replica of one that stands in Rome's Piazza d' Espagna (Spanish Square). Above the chapel's main entrance is a statue of the Virgin; to the right is a figure of St. Charles Borromeo, patron saint of seminarians and clergy; to the left is St. Aloysius Gonzaga, patron saint of Catholic youths. The three shades of blue on the walls and ceiling of the interior are colors associated with the Virgin Mary, and the Latin inscriptions around the ceiling are from the *Litany of Loretto*, which relates how the Virgin's birthplace was miraculously transported to Loretto, Italy. The wall behind the altar is called *The Doorway to Eternal Life*. Beneath the altar is Cardinal Mundelein's crypt. Beautiful crystal chandeliers, a gift from the government of Austria, are modeled after a set in the White House.

Many other buildings on the campus are worth a visit, and the grounds provide many peaceful and contemplative places to rest and reflect.

NEARBY

➟ **Feehan Memorial Library** To the right of the chapel is the Feehan Memorial Library, modeled after Independence Hall in Philadelphia. Its interior is copied after the Renaissance-era Barbarini Palace in Rome, which later became the Propaganda Fide College, where Cardinal Mundelein studied. The golden bees decorating the interior are found on the Barbarini family coat of arms and were adopted by Mundelein for his own coat of arms when he was elevated to cardinal. Bees are symbolic of thrift, industry, and social order.

➟ **The Cardinal's Villa** The villa, modeled after George Washington's Virginia home, Mount Vernon, is not open to the public, but it can be viewed from the northeast shore of the lake.

➟ **The Cemetery** Wooden stations of the cross encircle the cemetery, located behind the seminary residence hall and faculty building. A statue of Gabriel, the angel of the resurrection, marks the site of the tomb of

Albert Cardinal Meyer (1903–1965), archbishop of Chicago from 1958 through 1965. Other seminarians and faculty are also interred here.

Forest Park

The Potawatomis occupied the area that is now Forest Park and buried their dead in mounds along the Des Plaines River in an area now partially occupied by Forest Home Cemetery. Forest Park began to develop when the first public transportation, the Galena & Chicago Union Railroad, came to the area in 1856. In 1870 the Free Sons of Israel was established as the area's first cemetery. The area is now home to five major cemeteries that together are known as Forest Home Cemetery: Jewish Waldheim, Woodlawn, Concordia, Altenheim, and Forest Home/German Waldheim.

The Haymarket Martyrs' Monument
FOREST HOME CEMETERY
863 S. Desplaines Avenue. ☎ 708-366-1900
💻 www.graveyards.com/foresthome/hmarket.html

Founded by German immigrants in 1876, the cemetery was first named Waldheim and then later changed to its English translation, Forest Home. It is the final resting place of the men convicted for their roles in the infamous Haymarket Riot on May 4, 1886 (see p. 151). They are buried in a common grave marked by the Haymarket Martyrs' monument, a National Historic Landmark, erected in 1893 by the Pioneer Aid and Support Association. Created by Albert Weinert and based on a verse from the French national anthem, the "Marseillaise," which was sung by the men on the way to their hanging, the sculpture depicts a powerful hooded female figure of Justice placing a crown of laurels on the brow of a fallen worker while at the same time about to draw her sword. On the front of the monument are the last words of one of the men, August Spies: "The day will come when our silence will be more powerful than the voices you are throttling today."

Nearby is the tomb of Emma Goldman (1869–1940), an anarchist and radical who fought on the side of workers and the underprivileged. When she died in Toronto, Canada, she requested that her body be returned to the United States for burial near the Haymarket monument. (Note: The date of her death is wrong on her tombstone.)

Twice a year union members make pilgrimages to Forest Home Cemetery to pay tribute to their entombed heroes: on the Sunday closest to May 4, the day of the Haymarket Riot, and on November 11, the date the men were hung for their role in the riot.

Oak Park

A twenty-minute drive west from Chicago's Loop is Oak Park and its neighbor to the west, River Forest. Both communities are home to a number of famous Prairie School buildings (see below). The architectural historian Paul E. Sprague, in his book *Guide to Frank Lloyd Wright and Prairie School Architecture in Oak Park* (Oak Park Bicentennial Commission, 1976), writes, "Surely there can be no question that, so long as these famous buildings stand, they will continue to be regarded with pride and respect by the nation, and sought out as sacred shrines by architectural pilgrims from the world over." Besides Wright's famed Unity Temple, Oak Park is home to many other historic churches. Contact the Oak Park visitors' bureau for information about tours to these buildings:

☎ 708-848-1500 💻 www.visitoakpark.com

The Home of a Genius
FRANK LLOYD WRIGHT HOME AND STUDIO (NHL)
951 Chicago Avenue. 1889–90; playroom and dining room, 1895; studio 1897. ☎ 708-848-1976

A self-guided map, audio-cassette tour, and guided exterior walking tours of the neighborhood are available in the office.

Frank Lloyd Wright was only twenty-two years old when he borrowed money from Louis Sullivan to purchase a lot in Oak Park to build a home. The house is in the Shingle style (see p. 189) but includes features that later came to characterize Wright's architecture, including the use of natural materials, geometric forms, and the fireplace as the heart of the home. Wright later added a nursery and dining room, and in 1898, added a four-room studio on Chicago Avenue, where he employed fourteen apprentices and associates. Wright left Oak Park in 1909, and his home and studio were divided into apartments. The site was opened to the public by the Frank Lloyd Wright Home and Studio Foundation in 1974 and subsequently restored to its 1909 design. It is now owned by the National Park Service and is a National Trust for Historic Preservation property.

Dedicated to "the Worship of God and the Service of Man"
UNITY TEMPLE (NR, NHL)
Unitarian Universalist. 875 Lake Street. 1906–8, Frank Lloyd Wright.
☎ 708-383-8873

Unity Temple is a National Historical Landmark, signifying that it is one of the nation's most important buildings. The inscription above its main entrance sums up its dual focus: "For the worship of God and the

PRAIRIE SCHOOL ARCHITECTURE

Considered to be the "most thoroughly American architectural expression," the Prairie School is identified with a generation of architects who worked in the Chicago area between 1890 and 1917; they include Frank Lloyd Wright, Walter Griffin, William Purcell, George Elmslie, Francis Barry Byrne, and Louis Sullivan. These men saw themselves as living at the dawn of a new age that required its own style of architecture free of any reference to the past. In opposition to Daniel Burnham (see p. 97) and other influential architects who viewed the Beaux-Arts style (see pp. 76–77) as the finest expression of architectural ideals, the Prairie School architects sought to express the place and period in which they lived. Similar to what was occurring in the art world (for example, the Cubist Period of Pablo Picasso and George Braque), these architects sought to reduce architectural masses to their most essential geometric forms, such as cubes, squares, rectangles, circles, and straight lines. Buildings that feature horizontal lines, bands of stained glass, and low projecting profiles distinguish the style. Decoration was either stylized floral abstractions or geometric patterns. Buildings were to have an organic quality, in harmony with their natural environment, built of materials derived from nature, and decorated with natural colors, such as shades of brown, green, and yellow. Interior rooms were to flow into one another, and the main living area was to be centered on the hearth, which Wright considered the heart of a home. The Prairie School was a short-lived architectural phenomenon; by the second decade of the twentieth century it was no longer "in style" because the public clamored once again for buildings that looked to the past.

service of man." Although volumes have been written about Unity Temple, less is known about what inspired its design. The American Unitarian Association published a pamphlet in 1903 that set aesthetic standards for Unitarian missions. Its main theme was that the design of a Unitarian temple must promote the unity of secular ethics found in the home with religion observed in the church. Frank Lloyd Wright's uncle, Jenkin Lloyd Jones, head of the Western Unitarians, declared there would be no "Gothic pretentiousness" in a Unitarian temple, for it was both costly and promoted a sense of individual insignificance. Rather, Unitarian temples would be simple in design and built to human scale. These words resonated with his nephew, who had already rejected historic prototypes in the houses he was designing for Oak Park clients, and inspired him to think anew about the design and appearance of religious architecture.

Built of reinforced concrete and using the geometry of the cube and square, Wright created three spaces that are based on Unitarian principles and Louis Sullivan's philosophy that form must fit the function. The two main spaces consist of the dominating cubical sanctuary or auditorium at the north, and the lower, rectangular social hall at the south, linked by the third still lower space, the entrance hall. The sanctuary, framed by recti-linear balconies, sits four hundred people, all no more than forty-five feet from the pulpit. It is bathed in soft light entering from a skylight and clerestory windows of stained glass. The lectern is located against the entry wall so that when people exit the sanctuary they will be walking toward the minister instead of away from him. The building is a fitting tribute to the Unitarian principles of the unity of worship and service.

NEARBY

➡ **The Oak Park Conservatory,** 617 Garfield Street. ☎ 708-386-4700 If you need an escape from viewing historic buildings, visit this botanical gem that is open all year around. It has desert, tropic, and fern houses and outdoor gardens.

Riverside

Southwest of Oak Park is the Riverside Landscape Architectural Dis-trict, a National Historic Landmark. Set alongside the Des Plaines River, the district is bounded by Harlem, Ogden, and First Avenues and 26th Street. Laid out by Olmsted and Vaux (see p. 125) in 1869, this is one of the nation's first planned model communities (see p. 188). Half of the dis-trict's sixteen hundred acres were set aside for parks, commons, and other public uses, creating what has been described as "a village within a park." Riverside remains almost exactly as it was when it was laid out, and many of its important buildings survive, including the **Coonley House** (281 Bloomingbank Road), designed in 1908 by Frank Lloyd Wright; Olmsted and Vaux's (ca. 1869) **Swiss (Dore) Cottage** (100 Fairbank Road), one of the oldest in the village; and the **Schermerhorn Residence,** designed by W. L. B. Jenney (124 Scottswood Road) and built (ca. 1869) for L. Y. Schermerhorn, Jenney's partner and the primary project engineer for Riverside.

Bartlett

Northwest of Oak Park at the intersection of routes 20 and 59 in the Fox River Valley, is the town of Bartlett, founded in 1834. Like so many small towns in the area, it has become an outer-ring suburb of Chicago, with a population of over 33,000. It is home to the largest worship center in North America for Jains (see pp. 59–60).

"Pillars of Glory" in a Midwestern Suburb
THE JAIN CENTER
435 N. Route 59. 1993. ☎ 630-837-1077

The Jain Center, Bartlett

Located on fifteen acres of rolling countryside, the Jain Center's three white marble towers, known as *sikhara* or "pillars of glory," rising fifty feet from the rooftop, are an unexpected sight in the Midwest. Jainism's architectural style borrows from traditional Indian forms. For example, its marble towers, decorated with intricately carved symbolic elements, were designed and fabricated in India and transported to Bartlett, where they were reassembled. The temple's interior, in the form of a cube, is very austere, reflecting the faith's principles of nonviolence, nonmaterialism, and purity.

Oak Brook

Oak Brook, near the intersection of I-88 and Route 83, is today a major financial center, but from 1852 until 1929 it was a milling center, the site of the area's largest gristmill.

More Than a Mill
THE GRAUE MILL AND MUSEUM (NR)
York and Spring Roads. 1852. ☎ 630-655-2090

The Graue Mill, built in the Federal style, sits on the south bank of Salt Creek, about one hundred feet west of York Road, at the edge of the Fullersburg Forest Preserve. Frederick Graue, a German immigrant who moved to York Township in Du Page County in 1833, built a sawmill that burned down in 1847. Rather than rebuilding it, he built a gristmill to grind grain that farmers were beginning to grow in the area. His descendants operated the mill until 1929. Restored in 1951 by the Du Page Graue Mill Association, the mill's upper two floors are a house museum. On the main floor the old milling machinery is once again producing stone-ground cornmeal, the only waterwheel gristmill still operating in Illinois. The mill appears much as it did in 1852, but it is not only the milling operations that make this site worth a visit. Graue Mill served as an Underground Railroad station before the Civil War. An exhibit in the museum documents the Mill's role in providing slaves with a safe haven in their flight to freedom.

Lisle

West of Oak Brook, at the intersection of I-88 and Route 53, is the town of Lisle, incorporated in 1852 and known today as "Arboretum Village" because of the famed seventeen-hundred-acre arboretum located north of town.

Salt Does More Than Season Food
MORTON ARBORETUM
4100 Illinois Route 53. ☎ 630-868-0074 🖥 www.mortonarb.org

Joy Morton, the founder of the Morton Salt Company and the son of Julius Sterling Morton, who was the originator of Arbor Day (1872), donated the land for the arboretum in 1922. Described as a "tree hugger's" paradise, the arboretum has over seventeen hundred acres of trees from all over the world arranged in geographic groups. Visitors can experience forests from regions as remote as Siberia and China, or as close as the Ozarks and the Appalachian Mountains. It has a variety of gardens, lagoons, wildlife refuges, and a reconstructed Illinois prairie. You can drive along thirteen miles of road, take a tram ride, or hike along twenty-five miles of trails to view this arboreal microcosm organized in four general categories: botanical groups, landscape groups, geographic groups, and special habitat groups.

Wheaton

Jesse and Warren Wheaton, two brothers from New England, founded Wheaton in 1838. In the 1850s Warren Wheaton gave land to a small struggling religious college, the Illinois Institute, established in 1854 by the Wesleyans. In gratitude, the college was renamed in his honor. In 1859 Jonathan Blanchard, a strong abolitionist and crusader for social justice, left his post as president of Knox College in Galesburg (see pp. 248–50) to lead the college. Due to his leadership, and that of those who followed him, Wheaton and Wheaton College became important centers for religious publications, organizations, and study. Several campus buildings are on the National Register of Historic Places, including **Blanchard Hall,** erected in 1858 with later additions.

The History and Impact of Evangelism in America
BILLY GRAHAM CENTER
501 E. College Avenue. 1980. ☎ 630-752-5909

The center is home to the Billy Graham Center Museum, Archives, and Evangelism Library, and the Wheaton College Graduate School. The museum provides a visual history of the growth of evangelism from the time of the early church fathers through the ministries of American evangelists. Erected in 1980 and renovated in 1994, the museum is entered through the Rotunda of Witnesses, hung with nine tapestries containing images of historic Protestant church figures. Evangelists such as Sojourner Truth, Charles Finney, Dwight Moody, and Billy Sunday are all represented in the museum's collection. A major part of the space is devoted to family photographs and personal memorabilia related to Billy Graham.

Promoting Harmony among All People
OLCOTT NATIONAL CENTER OF THE THEOSOPHICAL SOCIETY IN AMERICA
1926 N. Main Street. 1927, Claude Bragdon. ☎ 630-668-1571

Madame Helena Petrovna Blavatsky and Colonel H. S. Olcott founded the Theosophical Society in New York City in 1875. Four years later they moved to India, and in 1882 established the international headquarters of the Theosophical Society in Adyar, near Madras, where it remains. Sources are available at the Wheaton Center to explain Theosophy as it is revealed in the many writings of Madame Blavatsky. The center's mission statement sums up its goals: ". . . to promote harmony among all people and to encourage the comparative study of religion, philosophy, and science, so that people may better understand themselves and their place in the universe."

The Olcott Center was erected in 1927 to be the center for theosophical works in the United States. Designed by a theosophist, Claude Bragdon, the center's reception hall is decorated with murals by Richard Blossom Farley, a Philadelphia artist, that illustrate the unity of life through changing forms, including ancient religious and mythical symbols, ecclesiastical figures, and heavenly bodies. A brochure provides more detailed information about the murals. A library is accessible from the building's south corridor. On the north side of the building's central balcony is the Shrine Room, where visitors are invited to meditate with the staff, but you must arrive before 8:30 A.M., when the door closes. The Olcott Gallery on the third floor presents changing art exhibits with a spiritual theme.

Behind the main building is a labyrinth with seven circuits modeled after the one in Crete that appears in the myth of Ariadne, Theseus, and the Minotaur; it is open to the public during daylight hours. Walkers are asked to be mindful of others on the path and to respect their need for quiet concentration. A booklet is available that describes different ways to walk the labyrinth.

NEARBY

➥ **Cantigny Garden,** 151 Winfield Road. ☎ 630-668-5161

The garden is located on the five-hundred-acre estate of Robert McCormick, who was the editor and publisher of the *Chicago Tribune*. McCormick, the commanding officer of the First Division during World War I, named the garden for a small village in France that was the site of America's first victory of the war. In the early 1930s, McCormick and his wife renovated the small house on the site (now a museum) and in 1967 hired Franz Lipp, a landscape architect, to design the ten-acre garden. It is divided into a series of twenty-one different gardens and plant collections that have something to offer visitors year-round, from flowering trees and shrubs in spring, brightly colored beds of flowers in summer, autumn hues, to shades of green in the Green Garden in winter.

Aurora

New Yorkers Samuel and Joseph McCarty platted Aurora in 1837 and built a dam on the Fox River to provide energy for the town's first industry, a sawmill. The town became the central headquarters for the Chicago, Burlington and Quincy Railroad in the 1850s and has housed the machine shops since then. Today Aurora is a dynamic city with a diverse population of about 100,000 people.

A Blend of Ancient Tradition and Modern Architectural Technology
SRI VENKATESWARA SWAMI (BALAJI) TEMPLE OF GREATER CHICAGO

Hindu. 1145 W. Sullivan Road. 1986, Padmashri Muttaialstapathy and Sri Subhash Nadkarni. ☎ 630-844-2252 💻 www.balaji.org

Designed by an expert on temple architecture in India and a Chicago architect, the temple is one of three Balaji temples in the United States. The term *Balaji* refers to the temple's presiding deity, Lord Venkateswara, also known as Lord Balaji.

The brown brick building situated on a low hill is crowned with domes and a tall tower, a *Gopuram*, a symbol of Hindu spirit. It has transepts projecting beyond the main entrance and dwarf transepts at the opposite end. On the first floor is an auditorium that seats four hundred people and is used for cultural events and weddings. On the second floor are the shrines, including the one for the temple's major deity, Lord Venkateswara Swami. The temple's plan, which includes projecting transepts, is unique for a Hindu temple, but it does provide room for circumambulation on the interior, not only around the presiding deity, but also all the major shrines. The sculpture of Lord Venkateswara Swami is carved from a single unblemished stone; according to Hindu belief, the slightest blemish would render a stone unfit for consecration and worship.

NEARBY

➡ **The African-American Heritage Museum,** 126 S. Kendall Street. ☎ 630-375-0657 💻 www.net22.com/dreamtime/grotto/charlessmith

Founded in 1986 by Dr. Charles Smith, the mission of the museum is to preserve, collect, exhibit, and provide programs that educate the general public about the experiences and achievements of African Americans and people of African ancestry, including their role in the nation's armed forces. Dr. Smith, a folk artist, has created over four hundred figures portraying the African American experience, including figures from the period of the Great Migration to the North. It archives over forty thousand items.

Lemont

Nestled among the bluffs of the Des Plaines River in the southwest corner of Cook County, the history of Lemont is closely associated with the building of the Illinois and Michigan Canal (see also p. 202 and pp. 205–6). Its first settlers were Irish canal builders; later came Polish and

THE ILLINOIS AND MICHIGAN CANAL NATIONAL HERITAGE CORRIDOR (NHL)

(The corridor stretches from Navy Pier in Chicago to Locks 14 and 15 at LaSalle/Peru. For information, contact the National Park Service. ☎ 800-926-CANAL or 815-740-2047; Illinois and Michigan Canal Visitor Center, Gaylord Building, 200 W. 8th Street, Lockport. ☎ 815-838-4830 🖥 www.nps.gov/ilmi/)

As early as 1673, Louis Jolliet and Father Jacques Marquette (see pp. 2–3) recognized the feasibility of a canal linking the Great Lakes to the Illinois River and ultimately to the Mississippi, but nothing was done about it until 1823 when Illinois created a Canal Commission; however, a lack of financing forced it to quickly disband. A new commission was formed in 1835 and by selling land given to it by a federal grant, funds were raised to start canal construction on July 4, 1836. Thousands of Irish immigrants who worked fifteen hours a day for a salary of a dollar a day and a ration of whiskey dug the canal; it is estimated that upward of fifteen hundred of them died in the process. Financial difficulties plagued the entire process, but the canal was finally completed in 1848. In April of that year, a cargo of sugar and other goods from New Orleans reached the docks of Buffalo, New York, by boat, signaling a new era of growth for the United States. Chicago and other towns along the canal prospered, as did farmers whose grain and livestock could now be shipped directly to eastern markets. In addition, other industries along the corridor developed, including coal, zinc, and sand mining. But the heyday of the canal was short-lived; by the 1860s the nation's expanding network of railroads had rendered it all but obsolete, and by the early twentieth century it became an open sewer carrying wastes away from Chicago. As the canal began to deteriorate, several futile efforts were made to transform it into a recreational area, but it wasn't until the 1970s that redevelopment began. In 1984 an act of the United States Congress created the Illinois and Michigan Canal National Heritage Corridor, the nation's first national linear park. Since then the locks have been restored and canal era buildings have been put to a variety of uses.

German immigrants who found work on the railroad or in the nearby dolomite-limestone quarries that provided the stone for many of Chicago's earliest historic churches including Holy Name Cathedral (see pp. 164–65) and St. James Episcopal Cathedral (see pp. 162–63). Nicknamed the Village of Faith, Lemont is home to many churches and temples.

A Memorial to Those Who Built the Illinois and Michigan Canal
ST. JAMES AT SAG BRIDGE CATHOLIC CHURCH AND CEMETERY (NR)

106th and Archer Avenue (SR 171). 1859, 1882, Martin Carr.
☎ 630-257-7000

Located right outside Lemont at milepost 17 on the Illinois and Michigan Canal, St. James Church and Cemetery overlook what was once a thriving hamlet. The date *1833* inscribed on the keystone over the church's entrance commemorates the arrival of the parish's first resident priest; the church itself was not built until 1859. Immigrants from Wexford County, Ireland, purchased the land for use as a cemetery, which was desperately needed to bury those who died digging the canal, as well as others who fell victim to cholera, malaria, and malnutrition. The earliest recorded burial is that of a child who died in January 1837. The cemetery has a fine collection of locally carved tombstones recording the names of the deceased and their counties and parishes in Ireland.

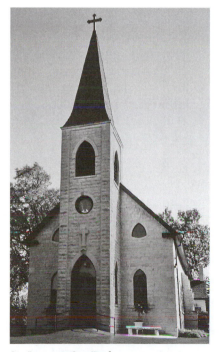

The parishioners, after working all day digging the canal, would return home at night to quarry stone for the masonry to build their church, whose steeple remains a beacon to those traveling along the Illinois and Michigan Canal National Heritage Corridor. The building was enlarged in 1882, and buttresses were added in the 1920s. More recently, stations of the cross were placed around its exterior and a

St. James at Sag Bridge

grotto was built across the road. St. James is a "pilgrim" church for visitors who come to pay homage to the memory of those who sacrificed so much for so little reward in expanding the nation's industrial growth.

A Symbol of Hindu Heritage in North America
THE HINDU TEMPLE OF GREATER CHICAGO

10915 Lemont Road. The Ganesha-Shiva-Durga Temple, 1985; sanctified in 1994. The Rama Temple sanctified in 1986. Architect Sri Sthapathi Ganapathi from Andhra Pradesh, India. ☎ 630-972-0300
🖳 www.ramatemple.org

Brochures are available that explain the temples' architecture and symbolism.

Two Hindu temples are situated on a bluff overlooking the Des Plaines River Valley. The eighty-foot tower (*Gopuram*) of the Rama Temple is clearly visible from Lemont Road. An impressive gate, the *Maha Dwara*, leads to a road that curves up to the temples passing by a statue of Swami Vivekananda (1863–1902), who officially introduced Hinduism into the United States at the Parliament of World's Religions held in Chicago in 1893. The smaller of the two temples, the Ganesha-Shiva-Durga Temple, is modeled after the Bhuvaneshar Temple in southern India, built during the Kalinga dynasty dating to the first century B.C.E. The larger Rama Temple is built in the authentic style of the Chola dynasty, dating to the tenth century C.E. Their interiors house shrines dedicated to various deities clothed and painted in vivid colors. The sound of prayers and temple bells contribute to an atmosphere that is both vibrant and meditative. Check the dates for the temple's annual *Greeshma Mela*, "summer fest."

NEARBY
➥ **Isle a la Cache Museum,** 501 E. 135th St., Romeoville.
☎ 815-886-1467

Located between Lemont and Lockport on an island in the Des Plaines River, this little museum documents the history of the region prior to the construction of the canal. It received its name, "Island of the Hiding Place," from French Canadian fur trappers, who for over two hundred years traveled along the region's many interconnected waterways. Native Americans lived nearby in permanent villages, including the Grand Village of the Kaskaskia, near present-day Utica, which stretched for two miles along the Illinois River across from Starved Rock State Park (see pp. 215–16). Other amenities on the island include picnic facilities, the Centennial Trail, which parallels the Des Plaines River, and canoeing. The soaring, billowing smokestacks of a huge power plant behind the museum disfigure this beautiful natural environment. They symbolize the price paid for progress.

Lockport

Lockport, considered the best-preserved town along the Illinois and Michigan Canal, was founded in 1836 as the canal headquarters. Located at Lock 1, Lockport quickly became a center for the canal's shipping and passenger activity. A map for a self-guided walking tour of Lockport and its downtown, which is on the National Register of Historic Places, is available at the Illinois and Michigan Canal Visitor Center located in the historic Gaylord Building.

NEARBY

➥ **Illinois and Michigan Canal Visitor Center, Gaylord Building,** 200 W. 8th Street. 1838, 1859.
☎ 815-838-4830
The Gaylord Building, owned by the National Trust for Historic Preservation, houses the visitor center, the Illinois State Museum Lockport Gallery, and a restaurant. Built of locally quarried limestone, the building was a canal warehouse and grain elevator. A three-story addition housed a dry goods store and offices for grain companies that occupied the building from 1848 to 1890.

The Illinois and Michigan Canal near Lockport

➥ **Illinois and Michigan Canal Headquarters Building,** 803 S. State Street. 1837, 1875. ☎ 815-838-5080
The one-story wing of the building dates back to 1837 and served as the canal's headquarters; it is the oldest surviving canal structure. In 1875 a two-story wing was added to provide housing for the canal manager. The Will County Historical Society Museum now occupies the building.

To facilitate your discovery of sacred sites and peaceful places in Illinois, we have divided the state into five regions:

Northeastern Illinois
Northwestern Illinois
West-Central Illinois
Southern Illinois
East-Central Illinois

After leaving Chicago, we suggest that you begin your journey through Illinois in the state's northeast region, and then move counterclockwise through the state, ending where the journey began, in Chicago.

Within each region, the places to visit are organized along the suggested travel itinerary; however, feel free to design your own itinerary. The initials "SR" refer to Illinois state routes; "CR" identifies county roads.

Brown highway signs direct travelers to Illinois' 262 state parks and recreational sites. All are free and the majority are open year-round except for Christmas and New Year's Day. For additional information, contact: IDNR Clearinghouse, 524 S. Second Street, Springfield, Ill., 62701. ☎ 217-782-7454 🖥 www.dnr.state.il.us. For information for visitors with disabilities: ☎ 815-929-1223; e-mail: pcrec@colint.com or cpangle@dnrmail.state.il.us.

··························· ✵ ···························

CHAPTER FOUR

*N*ortheastern Illinois

NORTHEASTERN ILLINOIS STRETCHES south from the Wisconsin border to SR 17 and west from Lake Michigan and the Indiana border to I-39. The greater part of the region has been covered in chapter 3. What follows are additional sites beyond Chicago's orbit.

Northeastern Illinois is "the gateway to the great prairie." It begins at the Lake Michigan lakeshore with its sand dunes and marshy bogs that give way to forested hills, winding rivers, and placid lakes. Then comes the vast prairie that is now mainly endless cornfields. We begin by traveling northwest to Belvidere.

Belvidere

A few miles north of I-90 on the banks of the Kishwaukee River is Belvidere, founded by settlers from New York state and New England in 1836. The city is known for its large Chrysler plant, but it was the stagecoach that contributed to its early development. Belvidere was an important stop on the stage route between Chicago and Galena. Many of its early residents had close social and economic ties to Chicago, including the family that erected Pettit Memorial Chapel.

Frank Lloyd Wright's Restored Masterpiece
PETTIT MEMORIAL CHAPEL (NR)
1100 N. Main Street. 1906; restored and rededicated in 1981, Frank Lloyd Wright. ☎ 815-547-7642

A map for a historic walking tour through the cemetery is available at the cemetery office.

According to Frank Lloyd Wright this was a "small, inexpensive burial chapel . . . a simple, not unhomelike room for services with shelter at rear and sides to accommodate people waiting for cars." The story of how this fine example of Wright's "Prairie period" came to be built in Belvidere, and its abandonment and ultimate restoration, parallels the changing attitude critics and the public have had toward his architecture. The chapel illustrates how a creative architect inspired by the challenge of an unusual commission can translate what is generally considered a domestic architectural vocabulary into a spiritual space.

The chapel is a memorial to Dr. William H. Pettit, a highly regarded physician who died suddenly in 1899. Set in the midst of a fifty-seven-acre cemetery, it is the only memorial or cemetery structure designed by Wright. Its Prairie School style, similar to the houses Wright was designing at this time, appears almost incongruous set in the midst of tombstones. The T-shaped building's long, low lines, rough-sawn shingle-hip roof with overhanging eaves, abstract geometric art-glass windows, and stucco exterior with cypress wood trim are all expressions of this style. It even has a large brick hearth on the interior, considered by Wright to be the heart of a home.

The popularity of funeral homes in the 1920s spelled the end of the chapel's usefulness, and it fell into neglect at about the same time that Wright's fame began to fade. Boarded up, its beautiful art-glass windows shattered, the little building was transformed into a storage shed. The Belvidere Junior Woman's Club made the restoration of the chapel its major undertaking in 1977. It is now restored to its original appearance and function.

Continue west to Rockford (see p. 221) and the northwest region, or continue through the northeast region by traveling south to De Kalb.

De Kalb

South of Belvidere and off I-88 and SR 23 is De Kalb, nicknamed Barb City for a simple, but important invention that transformed the West.

Joseph Glidden, a De Kalb resident, was aware of the need for an inexpensive product to fence in the vast, treeless prairies. He came up with a solution in 1873—barbed wire. Isaac Ellwood recognized the invention's potential and formed a partnership with Glidden to build the world's first barbed-wire factory in De Kalb in 1875. The next year Glidden sold out his interest to Elwood who then established the American Steel and Wire Company, which for years monopolized the production of the fencing. Glidden's role as the actual inventor of barbed wire is overshadowed by Ellwood's success in marketing the product. The **Glidden Homestead** at 921 W. Lincoln Highway, while listed on the National Register of Historic Places, is not open to the public. Elwood's Victorian mansion is now a museum.

The Mansion That Barbed Wire Built
ELLWOOD HOUSE MUSEUM (NR)
122 N. First Street. 1879; remodeled 1910. Original architect: George O. Garnsey of Chicago; 1910 architects: Perkins, Fellows, and Hamilton, Chicago; interior by George Terwilliger of Marshall Field.
☎ 815-756-4609 🖥 www.dios.niu.edu/ellwood

Ellwood's success is visible in the mansion and beautiful grounds he built at a cost of $50,000. The three-story brick house has an imposing presence on First Street. His son made alterations in 1910, but the mansion's general plan remains unchanged. The house's splendor is evidence of the wealth generated by the ingenuity and success of some of those who settled on the prairie.

Geneva

East of De Kalb on SR 38 is Geneva, located on the banks of the Fox River. The area was home to Pottawatomie Indians before white settlers displaced them following the Black Hawk uprising in 1832 (see p. 15). Geneva has more than two hundred buildings listed on the National Register of Historic Places.

The Oldest Unitarian Church Building in Continuous Use
West of New York
UNITARIAN UNIVERSALIST SOCIETY OF GENEVA
110 S. 2nd Street. 1843. ☎ 630-232-2350
🖥 http://www.uusg.org/pioneer.htm

Augustus Conant was twenty-one years old in 1832 when he set out from Vermont to seek new land for his family. He crossed the Great Lakes to Detroit and walked for six days across Michigan to Fort Dearborn (Chicago). From there he trekked farther west to the Mississippi River.

When he returned to Vermont he convinced his family to settle near the Des Plaines River; other New Englanders soon followed.

Conant went back east in 1840 to study at Harvard Theological Seminary. He returned to Geneva in 1842 to establish a Unitarian Society. The society's Greek Revival church was similar to the ones its members left behind in New England. Further linking the congregation to its New England heritage is its bell, inscribed: "Caste by G. H. Holbrook, East Medway, Mass., 1846." An addition completed in 1955 was designed by Chicago architect Jacques Brownson, a student of Mies van der Rohe (see p. 99).

Batavia

Immediately south of Geneva on SR 31 is Batavia, founded in 1833. The town was known for its manufacture of windmills; it is now the site of Tevatron, the world's most powerful high-energy particle accelerator.

From Harnessing the Wind to Smashing the Atom
FERMI NATIONAL ACCELERATOR LABORATORY (FERMILAB)
Pine Street and Kirk Road (take Farnsworth N. Exit off I-88).
☎ 630-840-3351 🖳 www.fnal.gov

The laboratory, named for Enrico Fermi (see p. 130), illustrates the enormous advances that have been made in the conquest of nature since the town manufactured its first windmills. Visitors can view an audiovisual program on the fifteenth-floor observation deck of the Robert Rathbun Wilson Hall (named for the laboratory's founding director) that explains the workings of the accelerator. There are models of the laboratory and the accelerator's circular tunnel (four miles in circumference) that allows scientists to study the nucleus of the atom.

Available at the Wilson Hall Visitor's Center is a pamphlet with a self-guiding tour of the Fermilab's 6,800-acre site; 1,100 acres are restored prairie. While deep beneath the ground scientists are at work, above-ground visitors can hike or bicycle along prairie trails and enjoy nature's unspoiled bounty, including a herd of bison.

Field Boulders Put to Practical Use
UNITED METHODIST CHURCH (NR)
8 N. Batavia Avenue. 1888, Solon S. Beman; 1991 addition, Dixon and Associates of St. Charles, Illinois. ☎ 630-879-7060

Boulders that broke many a plow had to be painstakingly removed from a field before it could be planted. One congregation, however, found a positive use for them.

Designed by the prominent Chicago architect, Solon S. Beman, the French Romanesque Revival church is constructed out of massive colored boulders collected from the fields surrounding Batavia. The church's deeply recessed arched entry, framed by a band of Bedford stone moldings, is repeated in the shape of its stained-glass windows, the carvings at the ends of the pews, and the ceiling that was constructed by hammering the wood into place while it was still wet.

The thoughtful design of an 113,000-square-foot addition maintains the architectural integrity of the original church.

Plano

South and west of Batavia on US 34 is Plano, home to two important and historic buildings: the "Stone Church," built by the Plano Branch of the Reorganized Church of Jesus Christ of Latter Day Saints (now the Community of Christ), and the Farnsworth House, the only house in the United States designed by Mies van der Rohe.

Where Joseph Smith III Gathered "Scattered Saints"
REORGANIZED CHURCH OF JESUS CHRIST OF LATTER DAY SAINTS (NR)
304 S. Center Avenue. 1868, architect unknown. ☎ 815-286-3270

This small stone Greek Revival church may appear ordinary, but it is important in the state's history as the original headquarters of the Reorganized Church of Jesus Christ of Latter Day Saints (RLDS; see p. 43).

Joseph Smith III, the eldest son of Joseph Smith, Jr., and the RLDS prophet and president, was actively involved in the design and building of the church. Dedicated in November 1868, it was the first church legally titled under the name of the RLDS and its central house of worship until 1881, when Smith transferred the church's headquarters to Lamoni, Iowa.

The church was Smith's personal base of operation during the early and critical years of the RLDS, when he traveled far and wide to regather "scattered Saints" to the fold. Smith's important role in reuniting his fragmented group of followers into a mainstream faith ensures his role, and the role of this small building, in America's religious history.

A "Paradigm of International Style Architecture in America" and a Source of Controversy
THE FARNSWORTH HOUSE ESTATE
On the outskirts of Plano; 14520 River Road. 1949–51, Mies van der Rohe. For information on its status call ☎ 217-785-4512.

This small house became a center of an international uproar at the intersection of art, politics, and to a degree, religion.

Surrounded by a sixty-acre estate, this "modern masterpiece" at the time of its completion was denounced by its owner as "not livable," described in *House Beautiful* as a "threat to the New America," and attacked by Frank Lloyd Wright as the work of "totalitarians . . . not wholesome people." Lurking beneath all these accusations was the fear of internationalism raised by the Cold War. "Foreign" architects like Mies van der Rohe, Walter Gropius, Le Corbusier, and other followers of the International style developed in Europe were suspected of harboring Communist ideals that found expression, according to *House Beautiful*, in their "grim" and "barren" buildings. According to Wright, "internationalism" and "Communism" "both must by their nature do this very leveling in the name of civilization." In his view there was no room for faith or nature in a building described by its supporters as a "pure expression of an idea that embodied the highest ideals of the new, utopian International style."

The Farnsworth House is austere and abstract; there are no organic forms to offset its rigid geometry, except the views of nature seen through its large expanses of glass. It is rectangular in plan with two parallel rows of eight steel columns supporting precast concrete roof slabs with windows spanning the distance between them. The house appears to float in its landscape and, contrary to the architect's intention, it is almost romantic in its effect, recalling eighteenth- and nineteenth-century garden architecture.

Dr. Edith Farnsworth, the house's owner, was right about one thing—the house is not livable, although she resided in it off and on for about twenty years. Illumination from the interior attracts flying insects that splatter against its pristine windows; its steel columns rust and require frequent painting; it has ventilation problems; and its location near a stream results in periodic flooding. With all of its problems, the house is well worth a stop. It allows visitors to experience the enormous impact that even the most simple and unadorned forms of architecture can have, and to arrive at their own conclusion whether it is a masterpiece or an abomination.

A Corridor of Historic Travel
ILLINOIS AND MICHIGAN CANAL NATIONAL HERITAGE CORRIDOR

Exit Plano on SR 47 and travel south to Morris. Take US 6 to Channahon to begin an exploration of the Illinois and Michigan Canal National Heritage Corridor.

Established by Congress in 1984, the corridor is a land-and-water trail that stretches nearly a hundred miles from Navy Pier in Chicago (see p. 102) to LaSalle/Peru (see p. 217). It includes over forty cities and towns, portions of five counties, and nearly twenty Chicago neighborhoods. Within its boundaries are state and local parks, forest preserves, and historic sites, many of which played an important role in the construction of the canal. Only a few of its major sites can be highlighted here. (For sites east of Morris, see pp. 201–5.) Maps and additional information on the Illinois and Michigan Canal National Heritage Corridor can be obtained through the National Park Service.
☎ 815-740-2047 or 1-800-926-CANAL 💻 www.nps.gov/ilmi

NEARBY
➥ **Channahon State Park** and **McKinley Woods,** off US 6; from Channahon State Park take Cemetery Road west to McKinley Woods.

This state park, located at the midway point of the Illinois and Michigan Canal National Heritage Corridor, is a good place to start an exploration of the western half of the canal. While the canal was hailed as a great human achievement, it spelled the end of the prairie and the way of life of the Native American people who lived off its bounty. The steep bluffs and deep ravines of the 473-acre McKinley Woods have never been plowed, allowing hikers to view more than four hundred native species of trees and plants.

The park and woods have hiking and biking trails, picnic areas, camping, and the Aux Sable and Dresden accesses to the **Illinois and Michigan Canal State Trail,** a sixty-one-mile hiking and biking path that ends at LaSalle (see p. 217).

Morris

....

NEARBY

➥ **Goose Lake Prairie State Natural Area,** 5010 N. Jugtown Rd.
☎ 815-942-2899

 Don't look for a lake in Goose Lake Prairie State Natural Area; it was drained a century ago for farms and for the clay deposits that gave Jugtown Road its name. Prairie View Trail leads to the top of a strip-mine spoil mound where you can view evidence of coal mining that began in the 1820s.

The park has the largest remnant of original prairie in Illinois—fifteen hundred acres. Walk along the one-and-a-half-mile Tallgrass Nature Trail to experience what the grassland was like before John Deere's "singing plow" (see pp. 219–20) transformed it into farmland. The Visitor Center has exhibits of native grassland and animals. Nearby is a replica of an 1834 log cabin built by one of the area's first white settlers that served as a station on the Underground Railroad.

➥ **Chief Shabbona's Grave,** Evergreen Cemetery, east of Morris on Cemetery Road. ☎ 815-942-1037

The graves of Chief Shabbona, a contemporary of Black Hawk, and members of his family are in this small cemetery located on the outskirts of Morris, near the Illinois and Michigan (I & M) Canal.

Ottawa

....

NEARBY

➥ **Illinois Waterway Visitor Center,** Route 1, Dee Bennett Road.
☎ 815-667-4054

When the I & M Canal was completed, it was considered a major engineering feat. Less then a hundred years later engineers were able to design and build a far more impressive system of locks and dams that transformed the shallow Illinois River into a major waterway, replacing the I & M Canal as the primary link between the Mississippi River and the Great Lakes. The Visitor Center has information and exhibits about the I & M Canal and two observation decks overlooking lock and dam operations on the Illinois Waterway. 327 miles long, it was completed in 1933.

➥ **Washington Park,** 100 W. Lafayette Street. ☎ 815-433-0084

A boulder in the park marks the site where on August 21, 1858, an estimated forty thousand people gathered to witness one of the famed Lincoln-Douglas Debates (see p. 19). A bronze sculpture of Lincoln and Douglas by Rebecca Childers-Caleel was dedicated in September 2002.

➡ **Reddick Mansion (NHL),** 100 W. Lafayette Street, 1856.
☎ 815-433-0084

Across from the park is one of the most expensive and ornate Italianate residences in the Midwest. Built by Sheriff William Reddick, the restored mansion now houses the Ottawa Chamber of Commerce and a tourist information center. Pick up a map for an auto tour of the town's historic sites and information on the Starved Rock Land Tour that begins in the nearby village of Naplate.

Utica

➡ **LaSalle County Historical Society Museum Complex,** Mill and Canal Streets, 1848. ☎ 815-667-4861

This stone warehouse located along the Illinois and Michigan Canal National Heritage Corridor has exhibits related to the history of the canal and pioneer settlements. Also on display are artifacts excavated from the site of the Grand Village of the Kaskaskia Indians, which existed near the Illinois River from 1678 to 1700. The archaeological excavations and the village's site are not open to the public.

➡ **Father Jacques Marquette Memorial,** St. Mary's Catholic Church, Johnson Street.

A memorial plaque commemorates Father Jacques Marquette, who founded the Mission of the Immaculate Conception nearby on April 14, 1675 (see pp. 291–92).

The Site of a Native American Legend of Injustice and Retribution
STARVED ROCK STATE PARK
Located on the south bank of the Illinois River one mile from Utica.
☎ 815-667-4726; visitor center ☎ 815-667-4906 🖳
http://www.dnr.state.il.us/lands/landmgt/parks/I&m/east/starve/park.htm

Surrounded by prairie except for the forested areas along the Illinois River and its tributaries, Starved Rock State Park with its spectacular rock formations, sandstone bluffs, stream-fed canyons, and waterfalls comes as a surprise to a visitor traveling along I-80. While its scenery is spectacular, the park is important historically. It is the site of a Native

American legend that accounts for its name, and a historical event that changed the face of the continent—the arrival of the first European explorers and missionaries in the region.

In 1673, French explorers Louis Jolliet and Father Jacques Marquette (see pp. 2–3) passed through the area on their way up the Illinois River from the Mississippi. When they returned two years later, Father Marquette established the Mission of the Immaculate Conception (see pp. 291–92) in the village of the Kaskaskia (a subtribe of the Illiniwek), located directly across the river on the north bank. Less than ten years later Robert Cavelier, Sieur de la Salle and his companion, Henri de Tonti (see p. 6), built Fort St. Louis atop a 125-foot sandstone bluff they called Le Rocher (the rock) overlooking the Illinois River. Several thousand members of the Illini Confederation established a village near the fort as protection from Iroquois war parties. However, continual raids by the Iroquois forced the French troops and their Illiniwek neighbors to abandon the fort in 1693. The site later became a safe haven for Native Americans and French trappers, including a band of Illiniwek who settled there in the 1760s. According to legend, Pontiac, chief of the Ottawa who lived upriver from Starved Rock, was slain in southern Illinois by an Illiniwek while attending a tribal council in 1769. A series of battles followed between the Illiniwek and the Ottawa and their allies the Potawatomi. During one of the battles, a band of Illiniwek sought refuge atop the 125-foot bluff. Ottawa and Potawatomi warriors quickly surrounded them and cut off their food supply. The Illiniwek died of starvation, thus giving the site its name, Starved Rock.

The park has over thirteen miles of well-marked hiking trails and camping or picnic sites, and boats and canoes can be rented.

NEARBY

➡ **Matthiessen State Park,** southeast of Starved Rock off SR 178.
☎ 815-667-4868

The park, named for a local industrialist and philanthropist who purchased the land at the end of the nineteenth century for a private park, has seven miles of well-marked trails through beautiful rock formations and forests. A restored French fort and stockade are at the start of the main trail to Cascade Falls, a spectacular area where a small stream drops forty-five feet to form the falls.

LaSalle

Just to the west of Starved Rock, near the junction of I-90 and I-39, is the town of LaSalle, which was established when plans for the I & M Canal were finalized in 1827. It marks the western end of the I & M Canal National Heritage Corridor (see p. 213).

A House Where Philosophy and Religious Thought Found Support
HEGELER CARUS MANSION (NR)
1307 Seventh Street. 1874, W. W. Boyington. ☎ 815-224-6543

This elaborate Second Empire–style residence is where the Open Court Publishing Company was founded in 1895. The mansion, designed by a well-known Chicago architect (see p. 162), belonged to one of the company's founders, the German-born zinc baron Edward C. Hegeler, who wanted to bring substantive works of science, religion, and philosophy to the general public. The Open Court Publishing Company was in business until the early 1960s, but its most productive time was under the leadership of Hegeler and his son-in-law, Dr. Paul Carus, a German-born scholar, who was the editor from 1895 until his death in 1919.

Since the company was bankrolled by a millionaire and was not affiliated with a church or established creed or doctrine, it could afford to publish whatever it wished. Works were solicited on ethnography, comparative religion, anthropology, philosophy, science, and mathematics. Dr. Carus attended the 1893 Parliament of World Religions in Chicago where he met Buddhist scholars whom he invited to the LaSalle mansion. As a result of their visit, Open Court became one of the first American publishers to produce English translations of Eastern religious texts. The meeting also led to Carus's employment of a young man, Daisetz Teitaro Suzuki (1870–1966), to assist in the translation of these works. Suzuki became one of the world's great Zen scholars, but few people know that he began his academic career in LaSalle. As a result of his association with Suzuki, who was assistant editor of Open Court for eleven years, Dr. Carus wrote his magisterial work, *The Gospel of Buddha,* which is considered to this day one of the best books on Buddhism.

CHAPTER FIVE

⁘

*N*orthwestern Illinois

NORTHWESTERN ILLINOIS STRETCHES west from I-39 to the Mississippi River, and south from the Wisconsin border to US 136. The region is bisected by I-80, which runs from LaSalle west to Rock Island. For convenience, the sites north of I-80 are covered first, followed by those south of the Interstate.

Unlike the flat prairie grasslands that once covered most of Illinois, glaciers didn't flatten the area that stretches from I-88 north to Rockford and west to the Mississippi River. Rolling hills, limestone cliffs, tumbling streams, and rivers define most of the landscape. It was along the Rock River that Black Hawk (see p. 15) and his warriors fought valiantly in the spring and summer of 1832 to save their land from encroachment by settlers.

From LaSalle/Peru, go northwest on CR 89 to Cherry Hill, population five hundred, the site of a dreadful mine disaster. Then take I-39 north and I-88 west to Grand Detour.

Cherry Hill

On November 13, 1909, almost five hundred men and boys were working underground in a coal mine near the town. Working conditions were deplorable, accidents and fatalities were numerous, and compensation for survivors nonexistent. On that fateful day, a young boy parked a wagon piled with hay next to an open kerosene lamp. His bad judgment caused an underground fire that took 259 lives. Bereaved families were destitute because Illinois lacked a workmen's compensation act. Each family finally received about $1,800 in donations from an outraged public and the coal company. The public outcry over the tragedy had two positive outcomes: the passage of stronger fire and safety regulations governing mines and the Illinois Workmen's Compensation Act.

➡ **Cherry Hill Public Library,** Main Street. ☎ 815-894-2919

The library has a model of the mine and displays of old mining tools and photographs related to the disaster.

➡ **Cherry Hill Cemetery,** SR 89 on the south edge of town.

The United Mine Workers of America erected a powerful monument in the cemetery in memory of the victims.

Grand Detour

The village of Grand Detour, located on an oxbow of the Rock River, just north of I-88, was given its name by French voyageurs. It was the traditional home of Black Hawk and the Sauk and Fox people. Black Hawk remembered his homeland in these words: "We always had plenty; our children never cried from hunger neither were our people in want. . . . The rapids of the Rock River furnished us with an abundance of excellent fish, and the land being very fertile, never failed to produce good crops of corn, beans, pumpkins, and squashes. . . . Here our village stood for more than a hundred years. If a prophet had come to our village in those days and told us that things were to take place which have since come to pass, none of our people would have believed him." Pioneers from the east began to arrive after the futile Black Hawk uprising (see p. 15). One was a blacksmith from Vermont named John Deere, who came here in 1836.

The Plow That "Sings" and the People That Sighed
JOHN DEERE HISTORIC SITE (NR, NHL)
8393 S. Main Street, Grand Detour. ☎ 815-652-4551

John Deere's services were sorely needed on the prairie. Unlike Native Americans who were satisfied with subsistence farming, pioneers tried to till the entire virgin prairie. Its rich, sticky soil refused to yield to their efforts and many of their iron plows ended up in Deere's blacksmith shop in need of repair. Deere quickly recognized that farmers needed a plow that would make a clean furrow. One year after he opened his shop he developed his first steel plow that farmers claimed they could hear "sing" as it broke the prairie. In partnership with a fellow New Englander, Leonard Andrus, he began to produce plows by the hundreds. After parting from Andrus, Deere built a new plant in Moline (see p. 235), where there was better waterpower and transportation. By 1856 the plant was producing over thirteen thousand plows a year—a simple invention that changed the face of the prairie.

The site includes Deere's restored home, a reconstruction of his blacksmith shop, an exhibit hall over the site of his original shop, a visitors' center in the 1843 home of the Dana family, Deere's neighbor, and two acres of natural prairie that illustrates the challenges faced by farmers.

Remembering Black Hawk
LOWDEN STATE PARK (EAGLES' NEST)
1411 N. River Road, Oregon. ☎ 815-732-6828

A Chicago patron of the arts purchased this land in 1898 to establish an artists' colony, Eagles' Nest, named after a tall, dead cedar tree that clung to the high riverbank. The colony attracted writers, musicians, and artists, including Lorado Taft (see p. 126).

At a time when monuments were dedicated to the "brave soldiers and pioneers" who died in the Black Hawk Wars (see p. 221), Taft created a sculpture that was a sympathetic portrayal of a Native American. Completed in 1910, the poured-concrete sculpture named *Eternal Indian* is nearly fifty feet tall and weighs a hundred tons. Taft's intention was to create a generic image of a Native American, but over time the majestic, melancholy figure with his arms folded over his chest sadly gazing over the Rock River has been identified as Chief Black Hawk. For an even more dramatic view of the figure, cross back over the Rock River to SR 2, north of Oregon, and look at it from the opposite bank.

Eagles' Nest, now known as the Lorado Taft Field Campus, is associated with Northern Illinois University at De Kalb. The park has picnic and camping sites and four miles of good foot trails.

Stillman Valley

From Oregon, continue north on SR 2 to Byron and then east on SR 72 to Stillman Valley, where a memorial commemorates the first battle of the Black Hawk War.

The Site of Black Hawk's Victory and Stillman's Run
BATTLEGROUND MEMORIAL PARK
218 W. Main Street. 1901. ☎ 815-645-2603

A tall granite column surmounted by a figure of an armed Illinois militiaman stands near the graves of a dozen fallen soldiers, a memorial to an event known as "Stillman's Run."

On May 14, 1832, Black Hawk sent out three messengers carrying a white flag to negotiate with a scouting party of Illinois Militia led by Major Isaiah Stillman. The militia responded by shooting one messenger and capturing the other two. In retaliation, Black Hawk and 40 warriors attacked the 275-man militia at this site. Terrified, Stillman and his troops panicked and ran from the field. His retreat signaled the start of the Black Hawk War. Among those who helped bury the dead was Abraham Lincoln.

Rockford

Two Yankees, Thatcher Blake and Germanicus Kent, and their African American slave, Lewis Lemon, founded Rockford in 1834–35. Other Yankees followed, but Irish laborers hired to build the Chicago Union Railroad soon outnumbered them. Swedish immigrants began to arrive by the trainload after the Civil War and quickly became the city's largest ethnic group. Many were skilled carpenters and craftsmen who formed socialist cooperatives that transformed Rockford into a major furniture-manufacturing center. It is now the second largest city in Illinois.

A Church Steeped in History and Tradition, and a Grotto for Meditation
ST. MARY'S SHRINE AND
OUR LADY OF LOURDES GROTTO
Catholic. 517 Elm Street. 1886, James Egan. ☎ 815-965-5971. Our Lady of Lourdes Grotto, 1928.
🖥 http://www.institute-christ-king.org/rockford.htm

St. Mary's, built for Irish immigrants, is a monumental Gothic Revival church that seats over seventeen hundred people. Its spire, a landmark in downtown Rockford, was almost lost following a disastrous fire in 1962 set by an eleven-year-old arsonist. While the church's interior was badly damaged, its beautiful stained-glass windows and altars were spared. At the time of the fire Hispanics had begun to replace the Irish who were moving out of downtown. Masses are now conducted in Spanish and English, and there is a traditional Latin mass.

LEWIS LEMON

A sculpture, *Founders: Pulling Together,* stands on a triangle of land across from Rockford's downtown post office. It depicts the city's three founders: Germanicus Kent, Lewis Lemon, and Thatcher Blake. Kent purchased Lemon in Alabama in 1829 for $450 and agreed to give him his freedom for $800, plus interest. It took Lemon four years and four months to pay off his debt. Meanwhile Kent went broke and left the town he founded to move to Virginia. Lemon's whereabouts from 1842 to 1871 remain unknown. He returned to Rockford in 1871 and was elected to membership in the Old Settlers Society. When he died in 1877 he was buried in an unmarked grave in **Greenwood Cemetery** at North Main and Auburn streets. In 1976 students in a Middle School raised funds for a black granite headstone engraved: "Born slave—died free. Lewis Lemon, 1812–1877, a founder of Rockford."

The grotto, modeled after the shrine in Lourdes, France, where the Virgin Mary allegedly appeared to Bernadette Soubirous in 1858, is open to all who seek a quiet place for meditation and prayer. Its cool and dimly lit rocklike setting was fashioned in Chicago and then reconstructed in Rockford. Note the ruby and dark blue stained-glass windows made from fragments of glass collected from church windows in Europe destroyed during World War I. Below the shrine is a flowing stream reminiscent of the miraculous stream in Lourdes. Additional shrines are dedicated to St. Theresa and St. Anthony.

Feel the Spirit through Art and Symbolism
EMMANUEL LUTHERAN CHURCH
920 3rd Avenue. 1923, church; 1958, chapel; both designed by Gilbert A. Johnson. ☎ 815-963-4815

A brochure of the church's art is available in the office.

According to a local tale, during the height of Swedish emigration in the nineteenth century, if a tag was put on someone in Sweden saying "Kishwaukee Street" the wearer would be faithfully deposited in Rockford, Illinois. Most settled on the city's east side, particularly along 7th Street or Kishwaukee Street, where the Swedish language was as common as English until the late 1920s. This is the neighborhood where the first Emmanuel Lutheran Church was erected in 1883.

Although forty years separate the building of St. Mary's (see above) and Emmanuel Lutheran, the two buildings share many similar exterior stylistic features: a corner tower, a large Gothic-arch window on the façade, and pointed-arch entryways. The similarities illustrate the continued popularity of the Gothic Revival style (see pp. 71–73) well into the twentieth century.

The interior is richly decorated with art; a few examples will give a sense of its beauty and symbolism.

The large stained-glass window set in the front façade is entitled *Come Unto Me*, based on a famous sculpture of Christ done by the Danish artist Bertel Alberto Thorwaldsen (1770–1884). Copies of the statue appear in many Scandinavian churches; it is more unusual to see it in stained glass. A window over the rear balcony, the *River of Life*, based on Revelations 22:1–2, was dedicated to the early pioneers who founded the church and have since crossed the river of life. The altar carving is by Louis Lang (1814–93), an American artist, and is based on Leonardo da Vinci's famous painting in Milan, Italy, the *Last Supper*.

The walls of the nave and ceiling are decorated with a variety of Christian symbols, including the Luther Rose, a black cross within a red heart set in the center of a white rose, designed by Martin Luther to summarize his faith.

The chapel, in a contemporary style, has three stained-glass windows crafted in Chartres, France, that symbolize God the Father, God the Son, and God the Holy Spirit.

NEARBY

➥ **Allen Chapel A.M.E. Church,** 206 S. Winnebago Street. Established in 1891 by five women and three men, the congregation worshiped in a small house until the present building was erected in 1917. Bishop Archibald J. Carey dedicated it as Allen Chapel African Methodist Episcopal Church in 1920.

A Quiet Place to Pray, to Grow, to Discover
ANDERSON JAPANESE GARDENS
340 Springcreek Road. Begun in 1978; designed by Hoichi Kurisu.
☎ 815-229-9390 🖥 www.andersongardens.org

The garden's brochure claims: "A person who can accept nature as it is can also accept one's self." But this garden, patterned after a traditional Japanese pond-strolling garden dating from the Kamakura period

Anderson Japanese Gardens, Rockford

(1185–1333), for all of its beauty and contemplative, tranquil places, is not "nature as it is," but rather nature as it was carefully manipulated by the landscaper who designed it. It is built around a natural spring-fed pond whose ring of bubbles is part of an aeration and filtration system that keeps the water clear. Japanese koi (carp), hardly native to Illinois, swim in the pond, along with other fish and amphibians. A viewing house, an ideal place to pause, is not to be entered. Neither is the guest house, or *geihinkan*, where all the elements related to the tea ceremony are laid out.

NEARBY

➥ **Sinnissippi Gardens, Greenhouse, and Lagoon,** 1300 N. Second Street. ☎ 815-987-8858

The garden has a paved ten-mile walk along the Rock River, a large floral clock, and a greenhouse that contains a small aviary.

➥ **Klehm Arboretum and Botanic Garden,** 2701 Clifton Avenue. ☎ 888-418-0782 ▣ www.klehm.org

A maze, interactive sundial, demonstration gardens, walking paths, and a botanical education center, all on over 150 acres of trees and plants, are available to the visitor. Go on one of the free self-guided tours or opt for a ride on the Blossom Buggy.

Available at the Education Center is a map of a garden walk that visits twelve gardens in Rockford.

Freeport

Continue west from Rockford on US 20, which follows the route of the Chicago-Galena Stagecoach Line to Freeport, a former stagecoach stop so-named because one of its founders, William "Tutty" Baker, offered travelers free ferry rides, meals, and lodging. Freeport's economy boomed with the development of lead mines near Galena, and it gained fame when it became the site of the second Lincoln-Douglas Debate.

Lincoln's Freeport Doctrine
LINCOLN DOUGLAS DEBATE SQUARE
Corner of Douglas and State Streets

Lincoln's proclamation on August 27, 1858, before an audience of fifteen thousand people that "this government cannot endure permanently half slave and half free," and Douglas's response, "I am not for the dissolution of the Union under any circumstances," brought to a head the issues that later carried Lincoln to the presidency and precipitated the Civil War. Both statements are inscribed on a bronze plaque affixed to a boulder that was dedicated by President Theodore Roosevelt in 1903. Nearby is the sculpture, *Lincoln and Douglas in Debate*, by a local artist, Lily Tolpo, dedicated in 1992.

A Monument Rededicated to the Dignity and Respect of All People
BLACK HAWK MONUMENT (NR)
Take Stephenson Street west out of Freeport to Kent Road and Kent.

Standing atop a hill overlooking the Yellow Creek Valley is a thirty-four-foot high limestone monument that marks the graves of militiamen who died fighting in the final Illinois battle of the Black Hawk War on June 25, 1832. In defeat, Black Hawk and his followers fled, and the dead militiamen were buried where they fell. It wasn't until fifty years later that farmers gathered up the soldiers' remains and buried them in a single enclosure at the battle site. The monument, dedicated on September 30, 1886, is in "memory of the brave men and true, who suffered death but not defeat at the hands of the red man."

One hundred years later a second dedication took place. The committee preparing the application to put the site on the National Register wrote a "Document of Principle" that stated: "This monument was erected to commemorate the brave soldiers and pioneers who died in the battle of

Kellogg's Grove area. But it is more than a memorial. It is a reminder that impatience and hatred lead to death. . . . This monument challenges all of us to treat men everywhere with the dignity and respect they deserve by guaranteeing their rights as human beings to equal justice and equal opportunity for all men are a part of God's 'Great Spirit.'" Descendants of Chief Black Hawk participated in the 1986 rededication ceremony.

Cedarville

Immediately north of Freeport on SR 26 is the town of Cedarville, where Jane Addams was born on September 6, 1860, and where she was buried following her death on May 21, 1935.

Honoring Cedarville's Nobel Prize Winner, Jane Addams
CEDARVILLE HISTORICAL MUSEUM
Cherry Street. ☎ 800-369-2955

Jane Addams, founder of Chicago's Hull-House (see p. 148), was the eighth of nine children of a prosperous miller, John H. Addams, and his wife. The museum, housed in an old stone jail, has a permanent exhibit honoring Jane Addams, including many of her personal items and memorabilia.

NEARBY
➥ **Jane Addams Burial Site, Cedarville Cemetery,** northwest of the village off Red Oak Road.

John H. Addams and four other settlers established Cedarville Cemetery in 1855. A monument marks the Addams family's lot. Jane's marker is a small stone engraved with an epitaph she selected that reveals not only her modesty, but what she considered her greatest accomplishments: "Jane Addams of Hull-House and the Women's International League for Peace and Freedom."

➥ **Jane Addams Trail** begins in downtown Freeport at the Tutty's Crossing trailhead. The scenic seventeen-mile Jane Addams Trail passes through several nineteenth-century settlements before it ends near the Wisconsin border at Orangeville. It crosses over twenty bridges and passes through a variety of natural environments, including wetlands, forests, prairies, limestone cliffs, and rolling farmland.

COULEE COUNTRY

Coulee (French for valley or ravine) Country was the name given by French voyageurs to a region that covers nearly fifteen thousand square miles of southwestern Wisconsin, southeastern Minnesota, northeastern Iowa, and the northwest corner of Illinois. Geologists refer to it as the Driftless Area because it remained ice-free during the last glacier stage of the Ice Age that ended about twelve thousand years ago.

Native Americans who lived in the region thousands of years ago hunted mastodons, mammoths, horses, camels, caribou, and giant beaver. As the glaciers receded, the prairies expanded westward and with them came bison. More settled Native American communities began to develop, particularly along the banks of the Mississippi River and on its islands. By the time French explorers arrived in the seventeenth century, Native Americans were mining lead ore in northwestern Illinois. The French continued to mine lead until all their land was ceded to the United States in the Louisiana Purchase. Shortly afterward, the United States Congress established the region as a federal mine district, and it began to attract speculators, scoundrels, and miners, all seeking to make their fortune.

A Fort Built in Terror
APPLE RIVER FORT INTERPRETIVE CENTER (NR)
West of Freeport on US 20 in the town of Elizabeth. ☎ 815-858-2028

A smelter established near the Fever River (renamed the Galena River) in 1825 attracted miners to Elizabeth. Fearful of Black Hawk and his warriors, the settlers hastily constructed the Apple River Fort, where forty-five men, women, and children found shelter when Black Hawk attacked on June 24, 1832. Black Hawk lost the brief skirmish (forty-five minutes long) and departed for Kent, where the last battle of the Black Hawk War in Illinois was fought (pp. 225–26). The original fort was torn down in 1847 and its lumber used to build a barn. Archaeological excavations began at the site in the 1990s and the fort was rebuilt in its original form. The Apple River Fort Interpretive Center contains a model of the fort, a timeline of the Black Hawk War, and exhibits illustrating the lives of the Sauk and Fox Indians and the Apple River settlers.

➥ **The Wedding Chapel of Elizabeth,** 113 S. Main Street.
☎ 815-858-3458 ▣ www.galenacountryweddings.com/chapel.htm

Built as a Presbyterian Church in 1875, this chapel was a haven for weary travelers on the stagecoach route between Chicago and Galena. After serving its community for many years, the church was put up for sale, and Elizabeth was faced with the possibility of losing one of its historic places of worship. Fortunately, an adaptive reuse was found for the building, one fitting its long history. It was purchased and transformed into a nondenominational wedding chapel. Restored to its original appearance, including the rebuilding of its steeple, the building is once again open to visitors, including weary travelers and, of course, those seeking a picturesque place to wed.

Galena

Further west on US 20 is Galena, a town that began as the LeFevre (Fever) River Settlement in 1819. The settlement began to flourish as a

GALENA'S AFRICAN AMERICAN HERITAGE

The Galena African-American Heritage Foundation's objective is "to promote the research, interpretation, preservation, and dissemination of Galena and Jo Daviess County's African-American cultural heritage."

Among Galena's earliest settlers were Upland southerners who brought with them their slaves or "bondsmen." One was Swansey Adams, the property of James Duncan, who took him to the slave market in St. Louis where he was sold for $100 to William Hempstead, who brought him back to Galena as a free man. In Galena's New City Cemetery, now known as Greenwood (see p. 232), a tombstone that marks the graves of John and Mernervery Hall simply reads, "Born and Raised in Slavery." An inscription on John Barton's marker is more explicit: "Deprived of the rights of a citizen by odious and unjust laws, yet his whole life vindicated." As H. Scott Wolfe, a local historian, has observed: "These were the people who helped create the Galena of history. People who worked the mines, thronged the bustling steamboat levee, staffed the local hotels, and served the wealthy merchants whose mansions still cling to Quality Hill."

port for Mississippi River steamboat traffic and as the market center for the area's expanding lead mines. In 1829 the settlement was renamed Galena, Latin for lead sulfite. Galena thrived as a wide-open frontier town described by one priest as a place where all a man needed to satisfy "any of his lower appetites was enough cash." Galena's population grew to four-teen thousand by the 1850s, when it was the busiest Mississippi River port between St. Louis and St. Paul.

Ulysses S. Grant, a former military man, arrived in Galena with his family in the spring of 1860 to work in his father's store. His timing was bad; the railroads had begun to replace steamboats and the lead mines were nearly exhausted. His salvation was the Civil War. Grant left Galena to join the United States Army as a colonel of the Twenty-first Illinois Volunteer Infantry Regiment; the rest is history (see p. 21). Following the war, Grant returned to Galena to accept a house presented to him by the city's grateful citizens, but by that time Galena had begun its long slumber from which it didn't awake for nearly a century. In recent years the town has been restored to appear much as it did in the mid-nineteenth century.

Preserving Galena's Days of Glory
GALENA/JO DAVIESS COUNTY HISTORICAL SOCIETY AND MUSEUM
211 S. Bench Street. 1858. ☎ 815-777-9129
🖳 www.galenahistorymuseum.org

Located in an Italianate-style mansion built for Daniel Barrows, a pros-perous merchant, the museum has an audio-visual presentation on the city's history, and exhibits about lead mining, smelting, and steamboats. On view is *Peace in the Union,* a painting by Thomas Nast (1840–1902) that depicts General Robert E. Lee's surrender to General Ulysses S. Grant at Appomattox in 1865.

A Gift to a President and His Wife from a Grateful City
ULYSSES S. GRANT HOME
STATE HISTORIC SITE (NR, LR)
500 Bouthillier Street. 1860, William Dennison. ☎ 815-777-0248

A group of local Republicans purchased the house in June 1865 and presented it to Grant when he returned to Galena in August of that year. His wife, Julia Dent Grant, described it "as a lovely villa exquisitely fur-nished with everything good taste could desire."

Grant actually spent little time in the house. He was elected president in 1868, and after he left for Washington the home was maintained by caretakers in anticipation of his visits. He died in 1885 at Mount McGregor, New York; Julia died in 1902. The Grants' children then gave the house to the city of Galena with the understanding that it would be kept as a memorial to their father. In 1931 it was deeded to the state of Illinois. A restoration project begun in 1955 returned the house to its 1870s appearance.

The Oldest Continuously Used Protestant Church Building in the Old Northwest Territory
FIRST PRESBYTERIAN CHURCH
106 N. Bench Street. 1838. ☎ 815-777-0229

A steamboat captain appalled by the "wickedness" he observed in Galena reported to his Presbyterian church that the town was in need of religious guidance. Guidance came when the Reverend Aratus Kent, a recent graduate of Yale and Princeton Universities who had requested an assignment to a place that was "so tough no one else would take it," arrived in 1829. Kent had to preach in taverns and other buildings until the fledging congregation could purchase the town's old log courthouse. Membership steadily increased, and the present church was erected in 1838. Built out of native stone, the original church exemplified the Greek Revival style until a vestibule and towering steeple were added in 1851. Stained-glass windows were installed between 1890 and 1910.

The church retains many of its original features, including the pews and the pulpit and four chairs in front of the sanctuary that were donated by Yale University. The two chairs on either side of the communion table and the two in the back of the sanctuary are from Kent's home.

The Cradle of Catholicism in Galena
ST. MICHAEL'S ROMAN CATHOLIC CHURCH
225 S. Bench Street. Begun 1856; dedicated 1863; designed by Reverend Charles Samuel Mazzuchelli. ☎ 815-777-2053

A request was sent to the diocesan office in St. Louis for a priest to provide spiritual guidance to Galena's Irish miners. One was quickly sent. A parish was organized in 1832 and work began on a church designed by the parish's third priest, Father Charles Samuel Mazzuchelli, in 1839. Completed in 1842, the building was destroyed by fire in 1856. Father Mazzuchelli was now a pastor in Benton, Wisconsin, but he agreed to design a second, much grander church for the parish.

Constructed of Galena brick, the Romanesque Revival church is 135 feet long, 60 feet wide, and the ceiling rises 35 feet from the floor. The measurements are important because of the uniqueness of Father Mazzuchelli's design. A complex system of trusses support the building's roof so the sanctuary is free of columns or pillars, thus providing all worshipers with an unobstructed view of the chancel area, a revolutionary concept for a nineteenth-century Catholic church. The building retains much of its original artwork, including statues of St. Michael and the Sacred Heart of Jesus. Behind the rectory are various shrines and religious statuary.

The Bells of St. Mary's
ST. MARY PARISH
Catholic. 406 Franklin Street. 1861–62, Reverend Charles Samuel Mazzuchelli. ☎ 815-777-0134

In this church designed by the same priest as St. Michael's, the bells of St. Mary's continue to ring as they have for well over one hundred years. The parish was founded in 1850 to serve the spiritual needs of German Catholics working in the lead mines. Additions include a steeple, stained-glass windows, and a high altar that was in use until 1928, when the church was remodeled. In 1878, the parish received its most impressive gift, a Swiss painting of the assumption that hangs over the high altar, donated by a fur trader, Leopold de Massuir.

NEARBY
➡ **Grace Episcopal Church,** Hill and Prospect Street. 1848, C. N. Otis. ☎ 815-777-2590

Built in 1848 for a parish that was formally organized in 1835, the stone Gothic Revival church was designed by C. N. Otis, an architect from Buffalo, New York, who was a student of Richard Upjohn (see p. 73). Built of native limestone quarried on the spot, its buttresses and trim are made of Niagara limestone that was taken from the top of nearby Horseshoe Mound. Stained-glass windows were added later and a half-ton bell placed in the tower.

➡ **First United Methodist Church,** 125 Bench Street, 1856. ☎ 815-777-0192

This was the church Ulysses S. Grant attended. The congregation began in 1829, when the first regularly appointed Methodist minister arrived in the region. By 1831, there were seventy-five members who worshiped in a small frame church on Bench Street that was destroyed in a fire in 1838. It was replaced by a brick building that remained in use until the present church was erected in 1856.

NEARBY

➥ **Linmar Gardens,** 504 S. Prospect Street. ☎ 815-777-1177

Nestled in a hillside overlooking Galena is a garden planted in the ruins of an African American Baptist Church erected in the mid-1850s, one of the earliest black churches in Illinois. Nearby in an empty lot are the foundations of an early African American Episcopal Church. The site will become the home of the Galena African-American Heritage Foundation.

➥ **Greenwood Cemetery,** Gear Street. Greenwood Cemetery was officially opened in 1857. Like all garden or "rural" cemeteries, it is designed for burials as well as for those seeking a peaceful place to stroll.

Four miles west of Galena is the Mississippi River and the **Great River Road,** a National Scenic Byway that travels from the source of the Mississippi River in Lake Itasca (Minnesota) to where it spills into the Gulf of Mexico at New Orleans. The Illinois section is over 550 miles long; in this region it is SR 84 that travels south from Galena to the Quad Cities (see p. 234). An alternative route from Galena to the Great River Road (SR 84) is Blackjack Road, one of the state's most scenic drives.

A short detour can be made into Wisconsin to visit the famed Dickeyville Grotto. Take US 20 from Galena to Dubuque and then travel north on US 61/151 for eight miles to Dickeyville.

Dickeyville

Dickeyville, a small village of 250 people, has become an important tourist destination, thanks to the efforts of a Roman Catholic priest and his many volunteers who, over a period of five years, 1925 through 1930, created one of the more beautiful and unusual religious sites in the United States.

Religion and Patriotism in Stone
DICKEYVILLE GROTTO
305 W. Main Street. 1925–30, Father Matthias Wernerus.
☎ 608-568-3119

Father Wernerus was born in 1873 in Kettenis in Germany and was ordained a Roman Catholic priest in 1918. That same year he became pastor of the Holy Ghost Church in Dickeyville, where he served until his death in 1931. Grotto building in the 1920s was one method a priest had at his disposal to create a sense of community among his parishioners at a time when there was little opportunity for them to participate in the liturgy. Father Wernerus began his grotto building with a Soldiers' Monument, dedicated to three parish men who had lost their lives in World War I. The memorial in the church cemetery was Wernerus's first attempt to work with embellished concrete. Pleased with the result, he, along with an army of volunteers, began using concrete in an increasingly elaborate manner for an entire complex of grottos and shrines that are set within a beautiful garden area next to the church. Narrow pathways winding throughout the complex function as an ambulatory leading visitors to the various sites. The narrowness of the paths and the lack of gathering spaces are deliberate. This is a place for private devotions, not group activity.

The first of the four major shrines is the **Grotto of the Holy Eucharist,** a small four-square building covered with concrete and embellished with a variety of materials, including shells, glass, and rocks. The **Grotto for the Blessed Mother,** a large grotto facing the street and flanked by encrusted columns supporting equally encrusted images of the papal and American flags, enshrines a statue of the Virgin Mary. The shrine and flags are intended to illustrate the entire complex's theme, described by Wernerus as "religion in stone and patriotism in stone." The third major **grotto** is dedicated to the **Sacred Heart** and was inspired by an altar that had been erected in Soldier Field in Chicago for the Eucharistic Congress held there in 1926. Its model was the baldachin covering the altar in St. Peter's in Rome: a dome supported by four twisted columns. Wernerus' last project was the **Patriotism Shrine,** situated behind the rectory and somewhat detached from the rest of the garden. It incorporates all the nation's most patriotic images and symbols: the eagle, images of Christopher Columbus, George Washington, and Abraham Lincoln, and two bells symbolic of Washington's gift of liberty and Lincoln's gift of emancipation.

Return to Illinois via US 61 south to East Dubuque and pick up the Great River Road, traveling south toward the Quad Cities.

The Father of Water
MISSISSIPPI PALISADES STATE PARK
On the Great River Road (SR 84), 3 miles north of Savanna.
☎ 815-273-2731

 The park, located near the confluence of the Mississippi and Apple rivers, is an ideal place to stop and enjoy the rivers' beauty. Pathways lead up to the lofty, wooded palisades that rise above banks of the Mississippi River. This area, untouched by glaciers, has beautiful rock formations carved by erosion, including ones named *Indian Head* and *Twin Sisters*. A portion of the park was designated a National Landmark in 1973.

The river was a formidable barrier to people seeking land beyond its west bank. Native Americans, forced to flee their lands in Illinois, Wisconsin, and elsewhere in the East faced this barrier, as did settlers hoping to homestead in lands opening in the West. By the end of the nineteenth century, the river was conquered. Complex locks and dams were built to control it, but every spring it gets its revenge when it once again tries to break free of its confines and flood the plain that for so many centuries was part of its domain.

Immediately south of the park on the Great River Road is the charming, small river town of **Savannah,** popular today for its antique shops. A plaque on the east side of the road marks the site of a Native American wigwam occupied in November 1828 by Aaron Pierce and his wife Harriet Bellows Pierce and their four children, the town's first white settlers. Other picturesque towns line the river's banks, including **Albany** and **Hampton.** The latter is the site of a forest preserve, founded in 1836, containing campgrounds.

The Quad Cities

The Quad Cities are Moline and Rock Island on the Illinois side of the Mississippi River and Bettendorf and Davenport on the Iowa side. Sauk and Fox Indian villages once occupied the area, including the one Black Hawk was living in when the first white settlers began to arrive.

Fort Armstrong was erected in a strategic location on the lower end of Rock Island following the War of 1812. It served as a trading post and a military installation to ward off attacks by Native Americans. Mills built along the river in the nineteenth century began to attract settlers, and the towns became major commercial and manufacturing centers.

Moline

Moline, (a corruption of the French word for "mill") began as a simple brush and stone dam in 1836. Settled by Yankees, the city prides itself on being at its core a New England village transplanted in the West. It was the area's water power and transportation that convinced John Deere (see pp. 219–20) to move his plow-manufacturing operation to Moline in 1848, the year the town was legally incorporated.

Modern Architecture and Ancient Hills
DEERE AND COMPANY ADMINISTRATIVE CENTER
Three miles off I-74 on John Deere Road East. Main office building, auditorium, display floor, 1964, Eero Saarinen. West Office Building, 1978, Roche and Dinkeloo. ☎ 877-201-3924; 800-765-9588

Set in the midst of a thousand acres of wooded hills overlooking the Rock River Valley, this elegant, but simple steel and glass main office building is considered one of Eero Saarinen's (1910–61) masterpieces. It was selected by the American Architectural Foundation for its exhibition, *The Substance of Style: 31 Buildings That Changed American Life*, because it has "forever changed the nature of suburban corporate design."

The building's display area houses a variety of Deere farm implements, including Deere's first steel plow. A three-dimensional mural created by Alexander Girard (1907–95) along one wall features a collection of souvenirs and memorabilia related to John Deere and life in the Midwest, from the development of Deere's first plow in 1837 to the company's entry into the tractor business in 1918.

NEARBY
➡ **John Deere Pavilion,** 1400 River Drive. ☎ 309-765-1000

Located in John Deere Commons near the first John Deere factory that is part of the city's newly renovated and restored riverfront, the pavilion is a glass-encased barnlike building that is home to the largest agricultural exhibit in the world. Many of the exhibits are interactive, teaching about the history of farming and farming in the future, and, of course, there are displays telling the John Deere story. You can also climb into tractors and combines and experience what farming is like today, as opposed to what it was 150 years ago, when the first settlers began plowing up the prairie.

Also in the commons are the city's mass transit station and the departure point for tours on the MetroLink Historic Trolleys. Reservations can also be made here for inside tours of the **Deere-Wiman** and **Butterworth Homes,** mansions lived in by members of the Deere family.

The Faith of Its Founders
FIRST CONGREGATIONAL CHURCH, UNITED CHURCH OF CHRIST
2201 7th Avenue. 1918; enlarged 1939. ☎ 309-762-0787

Among the Yankee settlers who established this congregation in 1844 were David B. Sears, the city's founder, and John Deere. Services were held in the town's schoolhouse until the congregation moved into its first church in 1851. The city prospered in the years following the Civil War, and the congregation made plans to erect a more impressive church that "was to be of brick, in the New England form . . . with a steeple a hundred and fifty feet high." Dedicated in 1870, it was referred to as the "Cathedral on Henry Street," the largest Congregational church in the state outside of Chicago.

The church underwent extensive remodeling in 1900, but within twenty years it was replaced by an even grander building that was further enlarged in 1938, thanks to the generosity of Mrs. William Butterworth, daughter of Charles H. and Mary Little Deere. One of the church's most striking features is a huge stained-glass Trinity window donated by Mrs. Butterworth that towers thirty feet above the altar. It illustrates the parable of Jesus as sower and Ruth and Naomi as the gleaners. Other symbols relate to agriculture and the seasons, appropriate for a window donated by a descendent of John Deere. The pulpit at the left of the chancel is decorated with an unusual selection of hand-carved figures: Jesus Christ, Abraham Lincoln, Louis Pasteur, Jane Addams, and David Livingstone.

The narthex was enlarged and a new entrance added in 1992 and 1993.

NEARBY
➡ **Riverside Cemetery,** 29th Street and 6th Avenue. ☎ 309-797-0790
Perched on a bluff overlooking the Mississippi River Valley is Riverside Cemetery, incorporated in 1851. Located on the crest of a hill are the graves of John Deere and many of his descendants, including all the men who headed the Deere company from 1837 to 1855. Also buried in this cemetery is Francis J. Dickens, son of English author Charles Dickens. Soldiers Hill is dedicated to veterans of the Civil War.

Rock Island

Do not confuse the city of Rock Island with the actual Rock Island in the Mississippi River that was the site of Fort Armstrong (see p. 239). Steamboat traffic and the Chicago and Rock Island Railroad's construction of the first railroad bridge across the Mississippi River in 1856 contributed to Rock Island's rapid growth. Evidence of its early settlers' prosperity remains visible in the fine homes surrounding Rock Island's downtown, and in the elegant mausolea and monuments in Chippiannock Cemetery.

A Garden Cemetery on the Site of a Native American Village
CHIPPIANNOCK CEMETERY (NR)
2901 Twelfth Street. 1855, Almerin Hotchkiss. ☎ 309-788-6622
A tour brochure is available at the cemetery entrance.

Chippiannock Cemetery, designed by Almerin Hotchkiss (see p. 188), is considered a significant example of a garden or "rural" cemetery. The name *chippiannock* in the Sacs and Fox dialect means "a village of the dead." The site chosen for the cemetery was a Sauk-e-nuk village, and it includes the western slope and crest of Manitou Ridge, named for the great Native American spirit.

Hotchkiss carefully manipulated the sixty-two-acre site's natural beauty by adding curving driveways that wend their way through carefully landscaped "natural" woods and gardens to vistas of the distant Mississippi River.

The style of many of the monuments and grave markers reflects changing attitudes toward death and mourning. Some dating to the Victorian era are quite moving, especially those of children, such as the stone cradle that marks the site of the infant Jamie Sax's grave. Others are extremely impressive, like Robinson's Sphere, atop the cemetery's hill, a six-ton polished granite sphere anchored to an equally heavy granite base. The sphere is said to come from the 1893 World Columbian Exposition in Chicago. Two monuments are the work of famous artists. The Harte Cenotaph (1905), by Alexander Stirling Calder (1870–1945), father of the famous mobile artist, is a Celtic cross carved with nautical motifs and symbols in memory of a naval officer. The Cable Monument (1891), by the French sculptor Paul de Vigne (1843–1901), is a bronze sculpture of a full-sized draped woman grieving beneath an elevated sarcophagus.

A Catholic Parish in a Historic Presbyterian Church
ST. JOSEPH PARISH
1316 Second Avenue. Purchased 1874; 1906 remodeling, George Stauduhar.
☎ 309-794-9793

Irish Catholics organized the city's first parish in 1840. The arrival of German-speaking immigrants resulted in a division of the parish by language. English-speakers founded St. Joseph's and purchased a former Presbyterian church whose ceiling was taken from Hassillingford Church in Cambridgeshire, England.

As the parish flourished the church was remodeled and enlarged. An impressive rededication ceremony held on November 4, 1906, was presided over by a bishop and twenty priests. Much to the parishioners' chagrin, however, the city decided to build a jail across the street from St. Joseph's. A protest was lodged through the courts, and finally the state legislature passed a bill stating that no jail could be erected within 300 feet of a church—the jail is 310 feet away.

Additional changes were made to the church in 1962 and 1963, including the installation of stained-glass windows illustrating the Hebrew Bible and New Testament, and a magnificent thirty-six-foot-high mosaic in the chancel depicting the Last Supper. Created by Peter Recker, a German artist based in Rome, it consists of one hundred thousand pieces of glass in four hundred different shades of color. The mosaic was completed in Rome and shipped to St. Joseph's, where Recker personally supervised its installation.

An Ancient Tradition in Modern Garb
ST. GEORGE GREEK ORTHODOX CHURCH
2930 31st Avenue. Consecrated 1975. ☎ 309-786-8163

The city's first permanent Greek settlers were single men who began to arrive in 1900. It was the Greek women, arriving about a decade later, who were responsible for establishing a Greek Orthodox congregation. A church was built in Moline in 1912 followed by a Greek school.

The Greeks purchased property in Rock Island for a new church in 1963. Ground breaking took place in 1970, and the church was consecrated in 1975. The building's exterior is modern, but its identity as a Greek Orthodox Church is clearly visible in the Greek crosses that adorn it, including one that crowns an unusual tower off to one side of the building.

The church's beautiful iconostasis is hung with mosaic icons that include St. George, the church's patron saint, the Theotokos (Mary with the Christ child), St. John the Baptist, and Christ the Teacher. The altar is behind the Royal Doors, which are decorated with a mosaic of the Last Supper, the four Evangelists, a double-headed eagle, and branches of wheat and grapes.

Remembering Black Hawk, One Hundred Years Later
BLACK HAWK STATE HISTORIC SITE
1510 46th Avenue, (SR 5). ☎ 309-788-0177

Sauk and Fox Indians farmed this land until the late 1820s, when the arrival of white settlers led to Black Hawk's rebellion (see p. 15). Fifty years later, the site became home to the Watch Tower amusement park. After the park's popularity declined in the 1920s, the state of Illinois purchased the land and renamed it Black Hawk State Park. The Civilian Conservation Corps (CCC) built hiking trails, picnic shelters, parking lots, and much of the present-day lodge that houses the Hauberg Indian Museum.

NEARBY

➥ **Hauberg Indian Museum,** Black Hawk State Historic Site.
☎ 309-788-9536

Dr. John Hauberg, a Rock Island philanthropist, donated much of the museum's collection of Sauk and Fox (Mesuakie) artifacts. Exhibits include full-size replicas of Sauk winter- and summerhouses and dioramas that show Sauk and Fox activities. In the lodge's main room are two murals that depict seasonal activities of the Sauk and Fox people, painted in 1936 by Otto Hake as part of the Works Progress Administration (WPA).

A monument in front of the lodge marks the site of the American Indian village of Saukenuk on the Rock River, where the westernmost conflict of the Revolutionary War was fought. American forces destroyed the village in the summer of 1780 in retaliation for the Native Americans' support of the British. The Sauk rebuilt their village and continued to live there until they were forced to move across the Mississippi River in 1828. Near this marker stands a statue of Black Hawk gazing off toward where his village once stood—now an ugly industrial site.

A Display of Armament and a Cemetery with the Remains of Soldiers
ROCK ISLAND ARSENAL
(U.S. Army Armament, Munitions and Chemical Command)
On the island. ☎ 309-782-5013

The Rock Island Arsenal, on an island in the middle of the Mississippi River, has manufactured arms for the United States Army since the 1870s. The island is also the site of the first railroad bridge to span the Mississippi River, and the Rock Island District United States Army Corps of Engineers Mississippi River Visitors Center, located next to Lock and Dam Number 15. There are tours of the lock and dam.

A replica of a blockhouse on the west end of the island marks the site of **Fort Armstrong,** occupied from 1816 to 1836. The 1833 Greek Revival **Colonel George Davenport Home** is the oldest building in the Quad City area. During the Civil War the island was transformed into a notorious prisoner-of-war camp that held about twelve thousand Confederate soldiers. In the center of the island is a **Confederate Cemetery** with the remains of over two thousand men who died while imprisoned in the camp. Construction of the limestone buildings began during the Civil War but was not completed until after hostilities ended. One is the **Clock Tower Building** that now houses the army's Corps of Engineers.

➡ **Rock Island Arsenal Museum,** Building 60. ☎ 309-782-5021

The museum has one of the world's most extensive collections of firearms. A Court of Patriots honors the memory of many of the nation's heroes. Exhibits document the history of the arsenal.

Take either US 6 or I-80 east toward Sheffield, located halfway between the Quad Cities and LaSalle. We leave behind the hilly Driftless area and the flood plain of the Mississippi River to travel through a landscape immortalized by Carl Sandburg in his 1918 poem "Cornhuskers": "I am the prairie, mother of men, waiting." The prairie may lack the grandeur of the Coulee Country, but there is beauty to be found in the gently waving fields of corn and in the distant houses and barns of those who labor, as Sandburg has so eloquently said, in "the sunburn of the day."

Sheffield

Irish and Danish immigrants who worked on the Rock Island Railroad, or broke the prairie, founded Sheffield. The poet John Greenleaf Whittier (1807–92), while visiting friends there in 1869, watched a young Danish immigrant boy hitch up horses to a wagon for the family to take to church. The boy inspired him to write one of his most popular poems, "The Barefoot Boy," that begins:

> Blessings on thee, little man,
> Barefoot boy, with cheek of tan!

The barefoot boy was Hans Peder Bertelsen, who went on to become a well-known Lutheran minister.

The First Evangelical Danish Lutheran Congregation in America
ST. PETER'S EVANGELICAL DANISH LUTHERAN CHURCH (OLD DANISH CHURCH; NR)
Corner of Cook and Washington Streets. 1880. ☎ 815-454-2788

St. Peter's, organized in 1869, is recognized as the oldest congregation of the Danish Evangelical Lutheran Church in America. The congregation's historic white clapboard Gothic Revival building with its seventy-five-foot steeple almost suffered the fate of many rural churches whose members have moved away, had it not been for the intervention of concerned citizens of all faiths. One was Margaret B. Schmitt, an Irish Catholic woman who was knighted by Queen Margrethe II of Denmark in 1994 for her efforts in restoring the church. The queen visited it in 1976 to view the restoration work in progress.

Entering the church's doors is to return to yesteryear. Its frescoes (wall paintings) and stenciling have all been restored. The large fresco of the crucifixion over the altar, painted by one of the church's early members, is considered an important example of American primitive art. The original kerosene chandeliers hang from the ceiling, and the old potbelly stove still warms visitors.

One new addition is the ship hanging from the ceiling with its prow pointing toward the altar. According to Danish tradition, sailors would make replicas of ships they sailed on to give to their church in thanksgiving for their safe voyages. For some reason, this church lacked one, but that was remedied in 1980 when a replica of the famous royal Danish ship *Danmark* was presented to the congregation at a ceremony attended by many Danish and American dignitaries.

The onset of World War II found the *Danmark* in a Florida harbor unable to return to its homeport in Denmark. The Danish government offered it to the United States Coast Guard to use for the duration of the war as a training vessel. One of the sailors who served on the ship made the replica that hangs in the church.

Princeton

The town's Congregational church, the first in Illinois, was organized in Northhampton, Massachusetts, on March 23, 1831, by eighteen pioneers prior to their move to Illinois. Its members supported Owen Lovejoy's abolitionist belief in the moral wrong of slavery.

A Major Stop on the Underground Railroad
THE OWEN LOVEJOY HOMESTEAD (NR, NHL)
East of the intersection of US 6 and SR 26. 1838, 1850s. ☎ 815-875-8491

Owen Lovejoy, who witnessed his brother's death by a proslavery mob on November 7, 1837, in Alton (see p. 280), swore he would "never forsake the cause that has been sprinkled with my brother's blood."

Although Lovejoy was not formally ordained, following his brother's death he accepted the call to be the minister of the Princeton Congregational Church. He married a local widow whose home was already a stop on the Underground Railroad and transformed it into the railroad's "main depot" in Princeton. As a result of his actions, Southern congressmen called Princeton the "nigger-stealing center of Illinois."

Lovejoy was elected to the House of Representatives in the Illinois General Assembly in 1854. He died in 1863 in Brooklyn, New York, while promoting the antislavery cause in the Northeast.

Except for hidden details on the inside, the Lovejoy house is unexceptional in appearance. A cramped space between a wall, floor, and roof at the top of a stairway was a hideaway where slaves would quietly huddle until it was safe for them to continue their flight to freedom.

Bishop Hill

Bishop Hill is located a few miles southwest of Kewanee. From Princeton and Sheffield, take US 34 south and turn right on CR 1670E, Bishop Hill Road. Look for the brown road signs pointing to the town, a State Historic Site.

Today, the 160 miles that separate Chicago and Bishop Hill is easily covered by car, but for four hundred Swedish immigrants who arrived in Chicago in the summer of 1846 after an exhaustive ocean voyage and journey from the East Coast, it was a very long walk. But they were highly motivated, for they were followers of Eric Jansson (also spelled Janson), a religious dissenter forced to leave Sweden, who promised them a better life in the New World. Their Utopia was named Bishop Hill, the English translation of Bishkopskulla, Jansson's hometown in eastern Sweden. An advance party had purchased eighty acres of land and built a log cabin on a wooded tract known as Red Oak Grove; the commune would eventually own eleven thousand acres.

The settlers dug in for the winter, but were unprepared for the harsh weather. Over ninety colonists died the first year from starvation and the cold. Undeterred, the survivors laid out a town around a public square and began to erect permanent buildings in 1847. In less than fifteen years, nineteen large structures and another thirty or more smaller buildings were constructed. Of the nineteen major colony buildings that face the town square, thirteen survive, including the church, school, hospital, hotel, administrative and residence buildings, and commercial/industrial structures.

By 1853 the colony had a peak population of between eight hundred to one thousand members and was incorporated as a business entity; it was one of the most important commercial centers in the region. Enthusiastic letters back to Sweden encouraged others to emigrate, although not all who came chose to live in the commune known as the Utopia on the Prairie. All, however, was not utopian in Bishop Hill. A former colonist, angered because his wife refused to leave the commune, murdered Jansson in 1850. His death proved to be both a spiritual and temporal loss. Lacking Jansson's spiritual leadership, the commune became more commercialized. Although many members retained their old-world customs and traditions, social and theological differences began to weaken the communal bond, and the colony was dissolved in 1861. The town continued to attract Swedish immigrants and became a way station for those moving westward to homestead in Minnesota and the Dakotas. However, by 1960 the population had dwindled to 130, and many of the buildings were going to ruin. A group of concerned citizens organized the Bishop Hill Heritage Association to oversee the restoration of key buildings. In the spirit of reconciliation, King Carl XVI Gustav and Queen Sylvia of Sweden visited the colony on September 14, 1996.

A brochure describing a walking tour of Bishop Hill is available at the museum or visitors' center. Of the numerous buildings, only two can be discussed here.

The Bishop Hill Colony's First Permanent Building
COLONY CHURCH (NR)
Opposite the northeast corner of the town square (Bishop Hill Park). 1848.

The colonists worshiped in a cruciform log-and-canvas church until this gambrel-roofed white frame building was erected. Because of the hous-

*Colony Church,
Bishop Hill*

ing shortage, the basement and first floor of the church were divided into ten rooms, each of which was used as living quarters, one family per room. They now house an office and museum.

Two exterior staircases lead up to the second floor and a door that opens onto a narthex or gathering space. Beyond is a broad, airy hall whose simplicity reflects the Janssonists' rejection of the elaborate accoutrements of worship. Light enters the space through large, clear-glass windows. Its black walnut pews have a center divider to separate men from women. The only decorative feature and the hall's focus is a large faux marble pulpit set behind a chancel rail. A unique feature that anticipates later developments in church architecture is the set of folding walls under the balcony that can be opened to the gathering space, thereby increasing the hall's size.

A "Steeple Building" without a Steeple
STEEPLE BUILDING
Opposite the southeast corner of the town square (Bishop Hill Park). 1853–54. ☎ 309-927-3345

Currently used as an administration office, museum, and archive of the Bishop Hill Heritage Association, this substantial Classical Revival building illustrates how rapidly the colony prospered. It was initially built to be a hotel to accommodate the many salesmen flocking to the colony to visit its various enterprises. However, the great influx of settlers resulted in its first floor being used as a school and its upper floors as living quarters.

The roof of the tan-stuccoed building is crowned with a two-story clock tower added in 1859. The clock's four faces are each four feet in diameter with one hand each. Produced in the colony's blacksmith and carpenter shops, it is modeled after a tall clock brought from Sweden, which is on exhibit in the building. Plans to add a tall steeple to stand atop the tower were never realized, but the hope for one remains in the building's name.

NEARBY
➥ **Cemetery,** west of Bishop Hill Park, at the edge of town.

Settlers who died the first winter (1846–47) are buried in mass graves at the north end of the cemetery. Many of the stones date to 1849, when a cholera epidemic killed another 143 colonists. Eric Jansson's grave, marked by a simple, unadorned tombstone, can be found nearby. The cemetery is still in use.

Andover

Andover is a few miles northwest of Bishop Hill and just east of I-74 (Exit 24). Three years after the conclusion of the Black Hawk War in 1832, a highly respected English Presbyterian minister, Ithamar Pillsbury, accompanied by Archibald Slaughter and Noah T. Pike, arrived in Henry County to establish a colony modeled after New Haven, Connecticut. It was to be a center of learning, religion, and commerce. They built a mill on the nearby Edwards River and awaited the arrival of settlers. Their dream of a Yale University in the Heartland never materialized, but they did establish a Presbyterian congregation in 1836 and erected a church in 1856 that has since been demolished. The only visible evidence of Andover's first settlers can be found in the **Presbyterian Cemetery,** between Ash and Beech Streets, where Pastor Ithamar Pillsbury and members of his flock are buried. It was Swedish immigrants, including some disillusioned Janssonites who had left Bishop Hill, that gave Andover its particular ethnic character. The letters these settlers sent back to Sweden led Pastor Lars Paul Esbjorn to depart for America in June 1849 to minister to those loyal to the Lutheran Church of Sweden.

A boulder set in the midst of fir trees on the right side of the road entering Andover bears a bronze plaque that honors Pastor Esbjorn and his wife. Their home was three blocks south of the marker.

A Historic Shrine of American Lutheranism
THE JENNY LIND CHAPEL
Southwest corner of Sixth and Oak Streets. 1851–54. ☎ 309-521-8127

Although Swedish Lutherans had established congregations in New England in the seventeenth century, there is no connection between those churches that later became Episcopal and this tiny church in Illinois. It

Jenny Lind Chapel, Andover

PASTOR LARS PAUL ESBJORN

Born in Delsbo, Sweden, in 1808 and ordained at Uppsala Cathedral in 1832, Pastor Esbjorn, like Eric Jansson, was dissatisfied with the established church in Sweden, whose increasingly formalized practices he viewed as distancing the church from the common people. However, unlike Jansson, Esbjorn did not want to disassociate himself completely from the church. Rather, he wrote in his diary, his reason for going to the New World was to "organize a Christian congregation according to His word in order that He might be served in true faith and love." Other more secular reasons why he and so many other Swedes left their homeland were crop failures and the economic crisis sweeping much of Europe in the nineteenth century.

Esbjorn and 146 of his followers departed Sweden on June 29, 1849. They arrived in New York City two months later. Still ahead was the long trek to Illinois. They traveled by steamboat through the Great Lakes, and from Chicago to Peru/LaSalle by canal boat. The women and children were then put on wagon trains, while the men walked the last seventy-five miles to Andover; they covered the total distance from New York City in a remarkable twenty-six days. Some died en route; others became discouraged and went their own way; only a handful remained in Andover to help Esbjorn establish a community and build a church that became the "mother church" of the Augustana Lutheran Church and Augustana Synod in America. Once the congregation was fully operational, Pastor Esbjorn left for Chicago to accept the position of president of Augustana College and Theological Seminary. But when he got there he learned that the seminary had moved to the small town of Paxton. Angered by the move, Esbjorn resigned from the presidency and returned to Sweden, where he became the pastor of one of his old parishes. He died on July 2, 1870, and is buried in a cemetery in Ostervala, Sweden.

can rightfully claim to be the first church building erected on American soil by Swedish immigrants, and is recognized by Lutherans as the "Cradle of Swedish Lutheranism in America."

The congregation was organized in 1850, but with a charter membership of only ten adults, funds were unavailable to erect a church. Pastor Esbjorn was undaunted, and in 1851 he began a 3,600-mile journey to older German Lutheran settlements in the East to seek building funds. William A. Passavant, a noted Lutheran missionary and philanthropist in Pittsburgh, made arrangements for Esbjorn to meet the famous Swedish singer Jenny Lind in Boston. Impressed with Esbjorn's story, Jenny Lind gave him $1,500. In gratitude, the congregation named its church after her.

It took over three years for the parishioners to erect their little church. Due to a cholera epidemic in 1853 that killed many settlers, the lumber intended for the church's steeple had to be used for coffins instead. Once the church was completed, it served its congregation until construction began on a new building in 1867 (see below).

Built of homemade brick and hardwood lumber cut from trees near Galesburg (see p. 248), the Greek Revival chapel is built on a gentle knoll framed by cornfields and a cemetery. It was dedicated as a synodical shrine in 1948 and underwent extensive restoration from 1973 through 1976, in time for the nation's bicentennial. Some of the chapel's original pews are now in the balcony; look for the initials carved into them by bored children. A museum in the basement displays documents, photographs, and memorabilia related to the congregation's history and the building of the chapel.

JENNY LIND,
THE "SWEDISH NIGHTINGALE"

Jenny Lind was born in 1820 in Stockholm, Sweden. Gifted with a three-octave vocal range and great beauty, she became the singing sensation of Europe. Even the great composer Felix Mendelssohn declared her the "greatest singer I know, in every style." Hans Christian Andersen was in love with her, and she supposedly inspired him to write some of his stories. The self-proclaimed world's greatest showman, Phineas Taylor Barnum, laid down a deposit of nearly $200,000 with Lind's London agent for her to tour the United States in 1850 and 1851. Lind was a sensation, and she and Barnum made a fortune from her American tour. Known for her generosity, Lind supported many causes while in the United States, including funding Lutheran congregations and the antislavery movement. Lind returned to Europe in 1852 and moved to London, where she died in 1887. She was the first woman to be buried in Westminster Abbey.

NEARBY
➥ **Augustana Lutheran Church,** 6th and Oak. 1867–70, Charles Ulrickson. ☎ 309-521-8127

Known as the Cathedral of the Prairie, this spacious red brick church seats over a thousand people. Its size and grandeur illustrate the community's prosperity in the years following Pastor Esbjorn's struggles to erect the Jenny Lind Chapel. When this church was built, the congregation was prepared to raze the chapel, but thanks to the efforts of the women in the congregation, it was saved.

Galesburg

A Presbyterian minister, George Washington Gale, who along with other pioneers from upstate New York, moved west to bring education, civility, and religion to the newly opened prairie, founded Galesburg in 1836. They established Knox College as a manual labor institute that became a liberal arts college in the 1850s. Knox later gained fame as the site of one of the Lincoln-Douglas Debates.

Swedish immigrants began to settle here in the mid-nineteenth century, joining the thousands of Swedes already living on Illinois' western prairie. Among those who arrived at this time were the parents of Carl Sandburg.

"I was born on the prairie. . . ."
CARL SANDBURG STATE HISTORIC SITE
331 East Third Street. ☎ 309-342-2361

Follow the signs; this is the only way to get through the maze of streets that wind through Galesburg's industrial area and railroad yards to reach the modest house where one of the nation's greatest poets was born on January 6, 1878. Every American school child knows the poem that begins with the unforgettable words: "The fog comes on little cat feet." But Sandburg's fame far exceeds the words in this poem, and this three-room cottage where he was born and lived for only one year and the adjoining visitors' center memorialize and encapsulate his entire illustrious career.

Behind the house is a small wooded park. A winding path paved with stones engraved with quotes from Sandburg's poetry leads to a large boulder, the "Remembrance Rock," named after his only novel, an epic saga of American life; beneath it lie the ashes of Sandburg and his wife Lillian Steichen Sandburg.

CARL SANDBURG

Carl Sandburg was the son of poor Swedish immigrant parents. The family's name was originally Johnson, but his father, August, changed it to Sandburg after arriving in America, where he found employment in Galesburg as a blacksmith and railroad worker. Carl's mother was Clara Anderson. Sandburg left school at thirteen to help support his family that numbered seven children, two of whom died of diphtheria in 1892. He enlisted in the Sixth Illinois Infantry at the outbreak of the Spanish-American War in 1898, but was not in combat. Returning to Galesburg, Sandburg entered Lombard College to study the classics, but instead was encouraged by one of his professors to write poetry. His first book, *In Reckless Ecstasy*, was privately printed in 1904.

Sandburg never lost sight of his working-class roots that were buried deep in prairie soil, serving first as a labor organizer for the Wisconsin Social Democrats and then as a journalist for the socialist *Milwaukee Leader*. More importantly, he acclaimed the working class in all of his writings. While working in Wisconsin he met Lillian Steichen, the sister of the famous photographer Edward Steichen, and married her in 1908.

Sandburg's writings celebrate the American spirit, often in the language of ordinary folk he met during his journeys: railroad men and factory workers, cowboys and hoboes. It seems particularly fitting that he chose to write a six-volume life of a fellow Illinoisan and son of the prairie, Abraham Lincoln, published between 1929 and 1939. The last four volumes, *Lincoln: The War Years* (1939), won the 1940 Pulitzer Prize for history. It was also during this period that Sandburg gained wide popular recognition for reciting his poetry at public readings, and singing folksongs while accompanying himself on a guitar.

In 1928 Sandburg moved to Harbert, Michigan, and in 1943 to a farm in Flat Rock, North Carolina, where he died on July 22, 1967.

The Only Surviving Site of One of the 1858 Lincoln-Douglas Debates
OLD MAIN, KNOX COLLEGE (NHL)
South Street. 1857, Charles Ulricksen. ☎ 309-343-0112

Charles Ulricksen, an architect from Peoria (who also designed Augustana Lutheran Church in Andover, see p. 248), was hired to design an imposing building for the campus. The fortress-style structure, known as

Old Main and crowned with a cupola, housed classrooms, a chemistry laboratory, and a chapel. The small town was rightfully proud of its new building; a year after its completion it was selected to be the site of one of the Lincoln-Douglas Debates. Held on October 7, 1858, before a crowd of more than ten thousand people, it was the first debate where Lincoln framed his objection to slavery in moral terms. The quote, inscribed on a bronze tablet near the building's north door, reads: "He is blowing out moral lights around us who contends that whoever wants slaves has a right to hold them."

Bronze tablets with images of Lincoln and Douglas flank Old Main's east door. The building was designated a National Historic Landmark in 1936 as the only debate site that remains as it was in 1858.

Where the United Voices of the Past Call the Present to Worship
CENTRAL CONGREGATIONAL CHURCH (NR)
Central Square. 1898, Grant Beadle. ☎ 309-343-5145

Central Church is located near the northern boundary of Knox College's campus on the site of "Old First Church of Christ," founded in 1837 by Gale and his companions. In the 1890s Old First merged with a neighboring Congregational church to become Central Church, a union that was symbolically expressed when the bells from both churches were melted down and recast to make a huge bell weighing 3,400 pounds, so that "united voices of the past might call the present to worship."

The new church is in the Richardsonian Romanesque style; its auditorium plan places the focus on the pulpit. An altar has replaced a large choir loft that was once behind the pulpit. Over the church's main entries is a magnificent nonfigurative rose window twenty-two feet in diameter composed of Bavarian glass. The great pipe organ was installed in 1912.

NEARBY
➡ Hope Cemetery, Main and Academy.

Established by the trustees of First Church of Christ in 1836, the cemetery, originally simply called the Burying Ground, contains about ten thousand graves, including those of the town's founders. Among those buried in the cemetery is Julia Fletcher Carney (1823–1908), a local schoolteacher who gained renown for her charming poem, "Little Things."

An Early Educational Enterprise in Illinois
JUBILEE COLLEGE STATE PARK AND HISTORIC SITE

The park, located off of I-74 and US 150, occupies the site of Jubilee College, founded in 1839 by Bishop Philander Chase (1775–1852), the first Episcopalian bishop of the Illinois diocese and the founder of Kenyon College in Ohio. Jubilee College closed in 1862. Several schools occupied the college's buildings until the entire complex, along with ninety-three acres of land, was presented to the state of Illinois in 1933. Since then the park's acreage has increased to 3,200 acres and includes a campground, picnic facilities, ten miles of beautiful hiking trails, and twenty-five miles of horseback-riding trails.

Chase selected the college's remote rural setting believing it would promote the college's financial independence (it could grow its own food) and remove students from the city's temptations. Chase purchased 2,500 acres of wilderness and made plans to erect a series of buildings, including what was to be the school's main quadrangle. Only half of the quadrangle was completed before a series of events led to the college's quick demise: Its wilderness location discouraged students; Bishop Chase died and funds dried up; and fire destroyed part of the quadrangle. In 1971, the Citizens Committee to Preserve Jubilee College was organized to raise funds to restore the quadrangle, a project that was completed in 1986. Visitors can see a restored chapel complete with box pews and an antique organ, a re-created schoolroom, dormitory, library, and more.

On the grounds is a cemetery that has graves dating to the period when the college was in operation. Bishop Chase and members of his family are buried here.

Peoria

Peoria is famous for its Caterpillar plant and for its citizens who, as many advertisers and pollsters believe, represent the mood and mind of middle-class Americans. Nicknamed the Corn Belt City, Peoria is one of the state's oldest settlements. Louis Jolliet and Father Jacques Marquette were here in 1673 (see p. 2). In 1680 Robert Cavelier, Sieur de la Salle and his lieutenant Henry de Tonti (see p. 216) built **Fort Crevecoeur** overlooking the Illinois River, the first fort in the region (see p. 6). It was abandoned a few months later but has since been restored. Every September it is the site of an annual reenactment of French/Indian trading.

Home of Illinois' Second Jewish Community
CONGREGATION ANSHAI EMETH
Reform Jewish. 5614 N. University Street. 1967, Gyo Obata.
☎ 309-691-3323

Peoria is the site of the first Jewish community in Illinois established outside of Chicago. There were few Jews in Peoria and money was scarce, but in 1859 they began to raise funds for a synagogue. The amount needed was $4,500; the congregation raised $1,500; the rest came from their Christian neighbors. A former Universalist church was purchased in 1863 and the congregation adopted the name Anshai Emeth (men of truth). It affiliated with the Reform movement and hired its first rabbi. By 1887 there were enough Jews from eastern Europe in the city to form a second congregation, the Orthodox Agudath Achim (fellowship of brothers).

Congregation Anshai Emeth dedicated a new synagogue in 1898 to replace the earlier one that was destroyed by fire. It remained in use until 1967, when a new building was erected. (The 1898 building at Monroe and Hancock Streets is now a church.) According to the architect, Gyo Obata, the synagogue was designed from the inside out, following Mies van der Rohe's dictate that form is to follow function. The sanctuary is a pleasant and intimate space with a sloping roof and wood paneled walls. Light filters into it through stained-glass clerestory windows designed by Samuel Wiener, Jr. Since the mid-1990s, congregation Agudath Achim, now affiliated with the Conservative movement, has shared the building with Anshai Emeth. Agudath Achim's synagogue at 3616 North Sheridan Road is now used by New Hope Church of the Deliverance.

"The world's most beautiful drive. . . ." —*President Theodore Roosevelt*
GRAND VIEW DRIVE (NR)
Bounded by N. Prospect Road, the Illinois River bluffs, Adams Street, and the west right of way of Grand View Drive. 1903–25, Oscar F. Dubuis.

Grand View Drive is a product of the City Beautiful movement that swept the United States in the latter part of the nineteenth and early twentieth centuries (see pp. 94–95). The Drive was designed by a student of Frederick Law Olmsted, Oscar F. Dubuis, the father of Peoria's park system. His parks feature lagoons, springs, waterfalls, pools, and winding walkways that incorporate elements of the natural landscape and are enhanced with plantings of native shrubs, trees, and flowering plants. Lining Grand View Drive are native trees that frame scenic overlooks of the Illinois River and the valley below. **Grand View Park,** at the south end of the Drive, is a beautiful place to stop for a picnic.

*An Awe-Inspiring Journey through Twelve Thousand Years
of Human Experience in the Illinois River Valley*
DICKSON MOUNDS AND
DICKSON MOUNDS MUSEUM

10956 N. Dickson Mounds Road, between Lewistown and Havana off SRs
78/97. ☎ 309-547-3721 🖳 www.museum.state.il.us

Fulton County has the greatest known concentration of prehistoric
archaeological sites in Illinois. The nearly three thousand mound and village sites represent every phase of prehistoric human habitation in central
Illinois. One of the more important sites is the Dickson Mounds Cemetery
where Native Americans had a village, gardens, and burial mounds
between approximately 1050 C.E. and 1350 C.E. (see below). The reason
for their disappearance remains unknown, but may be due to religious-
political changes, a major climatic shift, or disease. What is known is that
their disappearance coincides with the decline of another major prehistoric site, Cahokia, and may well be related (see pp. 282–83).

The ancient mounds were plowed up, bones were scattered, and artifacts kept as souvenirs by the area's first permanent white settlers. There
was little interest in the area's prehistory until 1927, when Don F. Dickson,
an amateur archaeologist, began the partial excavation of a Middle Mississippian (ca. 1250 C.E.) burial mound on land owned by his father. His
discoveries attracted the attention of archaeologists at the University of
Chicago, and scientific excavations of the area began in 1930. The state
purchased the site from the Dickson family in 1945, and in 1965 it became
part of the Illinois State Museum; the Dickson Mounds Museum was built
in 1972.

For years the museum left the skeletal remains of American Indians in
the burial grounds exposed for visitors to view. Following protests from
American Indian groups, they were covered up in a Native American ceremony. An impressive multimedia event has been produced in the space
above the burial ground that takes a visitor through the Mississippian people's cultural and spiritual life.

The drive onto the museum grounds passes the Eveland Site, an early
Mississippian ceremonial center, where it is possible to view the remains
of three early Mississippian (ca. 1100 C.E.) buildings that are preserved
within shelters. Nearby is a small "demonstration" garden planted with
crops known to have been part of the people's diet.

Lewistown

....

Founded in 1821, Lewistown is a small town located along the Spoon River Valley Scenic Drive, which wends its way for sixty miles through Fulton County.

"I stirred certain vibrations in Spoon River." —Edgar Lee Masters
OAK HILL CEMETERY (NR)
North Main Street.

For many years the folks living in Lewistown weren't certain how to respond to the notoriety they received with the 1915 publication of Edgar Lee Masters' masterpiece, *Spoon River Anthology*, a "novel" that consists of 244 poetic monologues by real and imagined dead inhabitants "sleeping on the hill" of a midwestern cemetery. Although most of the names he used are fictitious, the events related too often resonated with the truth. Nathan Beadles, for example, who arrived in Fulton County in about 1830, was the inspiration for Masters' poem "Nicholas Bindle," in which Bindle complains about how he was hounded all his life to donate money, especially to the church, and ended up dying practically broke. He could not have been too broke; he is buried along with his two wives within a fenced plot marked with an elaborate arched monument.

EDGAR LEE MASTERS

Masters' parents, Hardin W. Masters and Emma Dexter, were homesteading in Garnett, Kansas, when he was born on August 23, 1868. The family then moved near Petersburg (see pp. 264–65), before settling in Lewistown when Edgar was twelve years old. As a young adult Masters left Lewistown for Chicago, where he wrote and practiced law until 1920, when he moved to New York City. He died in 1950 in a convalescent home in Melrose Park, Pennsylvania. By that time the *Spoon River Anthology*, the only one of his more than fifty books to gain popular recognition, had been translated into at least eight languages.

Masters is buried on the hill in Oakland Cemetery, Petersburg, next to his grandparents, Squire Davis Masters and Lucinda Masters. His epitaph was chosen by his family and is taken from his poem "Tomorrow Is My Birthday"; it includes the poignant line, "I think I'll sleep. There is no sweeter thing."

The garden-style cemetery has winding roads that lead to hilltops with vistas of the Spoon River and the countryside. In the middle of the cemetery are two tall columns capped with urns that flank a cannon, a memorial to the Civil War dead. Take a copy of Masters' *Anthology* with you when you visit the cemetery and read some of the poems as you view the tombstones.

NEARBY

➥ **First United Presbyterian Church,** 101 N. Main Street. 1856, 1906. ☎ 309-547-2805

The congregation, organized in 1828, built its white brick church with its towering steeple in 1856. Additions made in 1906 include a rather strange looking projection on its façade. While it looks like an apse, it is actually a vestibule. The well-maintained sanctuary is a broad hall with curving pews and a balcony facing toward the pulpit. Light streams in through nonfigurative stained-glass windows. Across the street is the **County Courthouse,** built in 1897.

Table Grove

West of Lewistown on US 136 is Table Grove, a charming town with a picturesque white clapboard church. It was here that many of the battles for women's rights in Illinois were fought.

A Bully Pulpit for Two Pastors Who Fought for Women's Equal Rights
TABLE GROVE COMMUNITY CHURCH (NR)
Nondenominational. 204 N. Broadway. 1869, 1934. ☎ 309-758-5242

Founded as a Universalist church on February 22, 1868, Table Grove Community Church is important for the religious and societal influences generated by its clergy and members, beginning with its first pastor, Reverend John Hughes (1834–1916).

Reverend Hughes was born in Geddes, New York, but moved to Fulton County as an infant. He attended school in Table Grove and Lombard College in Galesburg before entering the ministry in 1860. After the death of first wife in 1879, Hughes married Catherine Matteson (1854–1921) of Bellevue, Michigan, who was a teacher there and in Grand Rapids. She was ordained a Universalist minister in 1895 and participated as a pastor in the Sharpsburg and Swan Creek churches in Illinois before she and her husband made Table Grove their permanent home. With support of their

Table Grove Community Church, Table Grove

congregation they used the church as a bully pulpit to preach equality for all people, and worked together toward women's suffrage, she as the president of the Illinois Equal Suffrage Association, and he as a member of the Illinois State Legislature, where he introduced bills supporting women's rights.

Carthage

Carthage, twelve miles east of the Mississippi River on US 136, was just a small market town when it became the site of an event in 1844 that gave it fame and notoriety. It was in the town's jail that Joseph Smith, Jr., the founder of the Church of Jesus Christ of Latter-Day Saints, his brother Hyrum, and two companions were imprisoned on charges of polygamy, riot, treason, and destroying a printing press. A lynch mob, angered because of the Mormons' practice of polygamy, and possibly jealous of their economic success, broke into the jail on June 27, 1844, and killed Joseph and Hyrum and wounded one of their companions.

➥ **Carthage Jail and Visitors Center,** 307 Walnut Street, 1839.
☎ 217-357-2989
The Church of Jesus Christ of Latter-Day Saints maintains the site. Leading up to the Visitors Center is an impressive brick walkway with over-life-size statues of Joseph and Hyrum Smith with their statements of

faith inscribed on plaques. Tours are given of the two-story limestone jail, including a videotape presentation on the life of Joseph Smith. However, the events leading up to the arrest and murder of the Smith brothers took place in Nauvoo, a few miles upriver from Carthage.

➡ **The Carthage Primitive Baptist Church,** 220 S. Scofield Street, 1997. ☎ 217-357-3723

This small plain building crowned with a small belfry echoes the style of the Greek Revival churches favored in the first decades of the nineteenth century. Its simple interior reflects a worship service that focuses on congregational singing, preaching, and family worship.

➡ **The Primitive Baptist Library,** 416 Main Street. ☎ 217-357-3723
🖳 www.carthage.lib.il.us/community/churches/primbap/pbl.html

Organized in 1988, the Primitive Baptist Library is a reference library with a collection of books and records for those who want to research Primitive Baptist sites throughout the nation.

Nauvoo

Joseph Smith, Jr. (1805–44), who founded the Church of Jesus Christ of Latter-Day Saints (also known as the Mormon Church) in Palmyra, New York, in 1830, thought he had finally found a safe haven for his followers when he arrived at the little settlement of Commerce on the Mississippi River in 1839. The Mormons were anxious to establish a permanent community that would serve as their religious, governmental, and cultural center after they had been forced to flee Kirtland, Ohio, where the church had established a headquarters in 1831, and later in Independence, Missouri, where they had hoped to build a temple. Smith renamed Commerce, Nauvoo, "beautiful" in Hebrew (actually pronounced nau-veh). The community prospered and grew, at one point rivaling Chicago in size. Construction began on a monumental temple that was to be one of the most beautiful and imposing structures in the Midwest; it was never completed. The Mormons' stay in Nauvoo was short-lived. Once again they faced persecution; their temple was burned and their leader murdered in the Carthage Jail (see above), resulting in a split of his followers. One group supported Brigham Young as Smith's successor, while others supported his son, Joseph Smith III. Young led his party farther west to the Great Salt Basin in Utah; Smith's followers established a church in Plano (see pp. 211–12) and changed their name to the Reorganized Church of Jesus Christ of Latter Day Saints (RLDS, now known as Community of Christ).

The Mormons returned to Nauvoo in the 1960s to restore their former community, rebuilding their temple in its original form and on its original site at Muholland and Wells Streets; it was rededicated in 2002. There are two visitor centers in Nauvoo, one operated by the Latter-Day Saints, the other, the Joseph Smith Historic Center, administered by the Community of Christ.

➥ **Latter-Day Saints Visitor Center,** Main and Young Streets.
☎ 888-453-6434 🖳 www.lds.org

Set in the center of the restored area, the center offers information about historic sites as well as films and musical performances that extol the virtues of the Church of Latter-Day Saints. Guided tours of restored homes and shops are available.

➥ **Joseph Smith Historic Center,** Off SR 96 on Water Street.
☎ 217-453-2246 🖳 www.joseph-smith.com

Operated by the RLDS (Community of Christ), tours focus on the Smith family: the Joseph Smith, Jr. Homestead and Smith Family Cemetery; Nauvoo Mansion House; and the Red Brick Store that belonged to Joseph Smith, Jr.

A Final Resting Place for
Weary Saints
THE PIONEER BURIAL GROUND

East on Parley Street several miles beyond Nauvoo State Park

🌿 Perhaps the most sacred and spiritual site in the Nauvoo area is this cemetery located high on a windswept wooded hill. Except for a recently built wooden shelter and a statue of a grieving family, the cemetery remains untouched by the passage of time. This is not a prettified garden cemetery; this is a burial ground where simple unadorned stones mark the graves of the deceased. Most of the graves are of mothers and their children who died while

The Pioneer Burial Ground, Nauvoo

trying to establish a new life in the wilderness. One stone expresses the sadness that permeates this hallowed place: "Here sleeps a mother and her child in friendships [*sic*] sweetest ties." The large bronze statue of a grieving family who gaze out at the graves of others who suffered and lost is a fitting memorial to those who lie here in peace.

CHAPTER SIX

❋

*W*est-Central Illinois

W EST-CENTRAL ILLINOIS STRETCHES south from US
136 to US 50. Its eastern border is US 51, and the Mississippi River forms
its western border. It encompasses the vast prairies of central Illinois,
including its former capital, Vandalia, and its present capital, Springfield,
many Lincoln-related sites, and the Mississippi River Bottom east of
St. Louis, Missouri, where the famed prehistoric Native American site
Cahokia is located (see pp. 282–83).

Leave Nauvoo and drive south along SR 96, part of the Great River
Road (see p. 232) and the Lincoln Heritage Trail. The first stop is Quincy,
a historic river town founded in 1818 by John Wood from Moravia, New
York, who was Illinois' twelfth governor.

Quincy

Named in 1825 after the nation's newly elected president, John
Quincy Adams, Quincy's first settlers were New Englanders. Joining them
briefly in 1838 were about five thousand Mormons fleeing persecution in
Missouri who stayed here until Joseph Smith, Jr., established a new settlement forty miles up the river at Nauvoo (see p. 257). German-speaking
immigrants who arrived at about the same time settled in what is now the
South Side German Historic District.

Illinois entered the Union as a free state and Missouri as a slave state;
all that separated them was the Mississippi River and a political gulf wider
than an ocean. Quincy roiled with conflicts between abolitionists and

slaveholders. Slavery was the main issue of Abraham Lincoln and Stephen Douglas's debate held in Washington Park (see p. 263).

Quincy prospered with the arrival of steamboats in the 1850s and the building of a massive railroad bridge across the Mississippi River following the Civil War. It became the area's major market center and for a time was the state's second-largest city. Today, with a population just under forty thousand, Quincy is a charming river town where one can stroll down quiet streets lined with many pre–Civil War buildings, thanks to the historic preservation vision of its civic leaders.

Early Jewish Settlers on the Prairie
B'NAI SHOLOM SYNAGOGUE
Reform Jewish. 427 N. 9th Street. 1866–70, Robert Bunce.
☎ 217-222-8537

Abraham Jonas, a lawyer, high priest, and grand master of a Masonic lodge and a close friend of Abraham Lincoln, moved to Quincy from Kentucky in 1832. He was one of the founders of Quincy's first Jewish congregation, B'nai Avraham (Children of Abraham), an Orthodox synagogue organized in 1856. The congregation split in 1864 when German-speaking Jews from Ohio decided to organize a Reform synagogue, B'nai Sholom (Children of Peace). Both congregations began to construct synagogues in 1866, but B'nai Avraham's frame structure was damaged by fire. Rather than rebuild, the congregation reunited with B'nai Sholom in 1872.

The synagogue's Moorish style, accented by elaborate onion domes supported on horseshoe arches that once crowned its octagonal corner towers, was consistent with the adoption of this style by Jewish congregations elsewhere in the nation (see pp. 75–76). Perhaps most important to this newly minted Reform congregation was the fact that Rabbi Isaac Mayer Wise in Cincinnati, Ohio, had chosen the Moorish style for his new synagogue (1866), considered the "mother temple" of Reform Judaism.

Damaged in a 1945 tornado, the elaborate horseshoe arches and onion domes had to be removed, leaving the building with a far less dramatic appearance. While the congregation's membership has diminished from its high of five hundred in 1870, it remains active.

The First Station on Illinois' Underground Railroad
DR. RICHARD EELLS HOUSE
415 Jersey Street. 1835, 1841, 1871–73. ☎ 217-222-1799

On a hot summer night in August 1842, a black man, soaking wet from swimming across the Mississippi River, knocked at the door of Dr. Eells's home, which was just a few blocks from the river. The home was station number one in Illinois on the Underground Railroad to Chicago. "Charley" had just escaped from a farm near Monticello, Missouri, and was being pursued by his owner and a posse. Dr. Eells gave Charley dry clothes, stowed him in the back of his carriage, and drove at top speed toward the Mission Institute, a known safe haven (see below). Unfortunately, he drove into an ambush. Charley jumped out of the carriage and ran for his life but was eventually caught and returned to his owner. Dr. Eells managed to get home but was arrested two days later on the charge of harboring, secreting, and assisting a slave to run away from his rightful owner. The *Quincy Whig* described Dr. Eells as "a well known abolitionist; in fact one of the principal head men of his misguided sect in this county. . . ." Missouri wanted the doctor extradited, and the Illinois governor signed the papers, forcing Dr. Eells to make his own escape along the Underground Railroad to Chicago. The extradition order was finally rescinded, but the case went to trial before then Circuit Court Judge Stephen A. Douglas. The jury found Eells guilty of violating Section 149 of the Criminal Code of Illinois, harboring a slave. Eells's attorneys appealed the case all the way to the United States Supreme Court. In 1853, seven years after Eells's death in the Bahamas, where he is buried in a pauper's grave, the Supreme Court upheld the lower court's ruling.

The only evidence of this historic episode is the simple four-room Greek Revival house that Dr. Eells built for his family in 1835. The house was in a neglected state when the Friends of the Richard Eells House acquired it in 1990 and subsequently restored it.

THE MISSION INSTITUTE

Dr. David Nelson, a Congregational minister from Missouri who was forced to move to Quincy because of his antislavery views, founded the Mission Institute to prepare young men to be foreign missionaries. His faculty included Dr. Richard Eells, who had come from Simsbury, Connecticut, to practice medicine and teach medical courses. According to one observer, the Institute "soon became the special object of hatred by the slaveholders of Missouri."

The Madison School and Madison Park at 24th and Maine Streets now occupy the land where the Mission Institute once stood. A plaque at the northeast corner of the park commemorates the abolitionist activities that once took place here.

NEARBY

➼ **Woodland Cemetery,** 5th and Jefferson Streets, 1846.

Considered one of the most beautiful garden cemeteries in the Midwest, Woodland Cemetery was founded by John Wood in 1846 on a forty-acre plot on his own property. Additional land has since been added. The cemetery's wooded hills and curving roadways provide scenic vistas toward the Mississippi River. The cemetery's mausoleum is located on the site of a city hospital that was used during the Civil War as an army hospital and later as a "pesthouse."

➼ **Calvary Cemetery,** 1730 N. 18th Street.

It was in the late 1990s that someone first noticed what appeared to be a life-size image of Jesus Christ holding a lamb on the side of a pink birch tree. The tree has since attracted visitors from around the world who believe it is the site of a miracle.

➼ **Washington Park,** 5th and Hampshire Streets.

A monument decorated with a bas-relief created in 1936 by Lorado Taft (see p. 126) commemorates the sixth debate between Lincoln and Douglas held here on October 13, 1858. To the right of the monument is a chunk of granite simply engraved, "Lincoln-Douglas Debate, Oct. 13, 1858."

An African American Daniel Boone
FREE FRANK MCWORTER GRAVE SITE (NR)
Site of New Philadelphia

I-172 leads south out of Quincy and becomes I-72 near Fall Creek where it turns east toward Springfield (see p. 266). New Philadelphia, an inaccessible but important historical site located four miles east of Barry on the north side of I-72, was a town founded in 1836 by a freed slave, Free Frank McWorter, who is buried in its overgrown cemetery. The site is now privately owned, and an effort is currently underway by the Free Frank Historical Preservation Foundation to restore the town and cemetery and to erect a visitors' center that will tell Free Frank's remarkable story.

Free Frank was born a slave in Union County, South Carolina, in 1777, and moved with his owner to Pulaski County, Kentucky, in 1795. His first step toward freedom was taken when his owner allowed him to hire out his own time for pay. When his owner moved to Tennessee in 1810 he left Free Frank to manage his farm and to hire out his own time. Sensing the onset of the War of 1812, Free Frank began to manufacture and market saltpeter, the key ingredient in gunpowder. His successful enterprise enabled him to purchase his wife Lucy's freedom in 1817 for

$800 and his own freedom two years later for the same amount. In 1829 Free Frank traded his saltpeter business for his son's freedom, and the next year headed to Illinois, where he settled in Pike County. He platted the town of New Philadelphia in 1836 on 620 acres of land he acquired. Unlike other agricultural colonies started by free blacks, New Philadelphia was open to everyone. The town became a stagecoach stop, had a post office, and even a Baptist teacher. Because it was bypassed by the railroad, New Philadelphia began to decline, eventually returning to farmland. All that remains today is a sign commemorating a town that was founded by a black man in pre–Civil War America.

Petersburg

Petersburg is located twenty miles northwest of Springfield. It serves as the gateway to New Salem, a small village that thrived for a brief period in the 1830s. It has been rebuilt as a tourist attraction and historic site.

Where Lincoln Went from Being an Unskilled Laborer to a Lawyer and Politician
LINCOLN'S NEW SALEM STATE HISTORIC SITE (NR)
Two miles south of Petersburg on SR 97. ☎ 217-632-4000

In 1828 John M. Cameron and his uncle, James Rutledge, received permission from the state legislature to dam the Sangamon River to power a saw and gristmill. It was here that the village of New Salem was platted. A young Abraham Lincoln became acquainted with New Salem in 1831 when his flatboat, loaded with produce for the New Orleans market, became stuck on the dam. Rescued by locals, he continued his journey south, but upon his return decided to settle in the prospering village. He worked in the mill and split rails before becoming a shopkeeper. After failing in business, Lincoln decided to be a surveyor and to study the classics and law. He served as the village postmaster, enlisted in the Black Hawk War (see p. 15), and was elected to the Illinois General Assembly in 1834 and 1836 after an unsuccessful try in 1832. It was in New Salem that Lincoln launched his career as a politician, and as one tour guide at the site observed, "From a rail-splitter, he traveled to the White House."

New Salem began to decline when Petersburg was named the county seat in 1839. It was all but abandoned until about 1910 when a renewed interest in Lincoln inspired efforts to preserve sites associated with his life.

William Randolph Hearst, the famed newspaper publisher, purchased New Salem and in 1917 the Old Salem Lincoln League was formed to keep interest in the site alive. Two years later the site was given to the state of Illinois, and in 1932 work began on reconstructing some of the buildings. The village appears as it did when Lincoln lived there. Costumed interpreters portray historic figures.

NEARBY
➡ **Edgar Lee Masters' Home,** corner of 8th and Jackson Streets, Petersburg. ☎ 217-632-7013

The house is where Edgar Lee Masters, the author of *Spoon River Anthology* (see p. 254), lived as a boy. Members of the Masters' family, including Edgar Lee Masters and his wife Ellen Coyne Masters, are buried in Petersburg's **Oakland Cemetery,** as is Ann Rutledge, Abraham Lincoln's first love who died in 1835 at the age of twenty-two.

Pleasant Plains

Pleasant Plains, on SR 125 fourteen miles south of Petersburg, is the site of the Peter Cartwright Church, an official Heritage Landmark of the Worldwide United Methodist Church. There are five historic sites in and around Pleasant Plains related to Peter Cartwright, who preached the gospel from Galena to St. Louis and westward as far as the prairies extended.

"The Lord's Breaking-Plow"
PETER CARTWRIGHT UNITED METHODIST CHURCH
205 W. Church Street. 1857; additions and restoration in the 1960s.
☎ 217-626-1087 or 217-245-0266
🖥 www.ashland.lib.us/community/churches/petercartwrightumc

Moving west with pioneers who broke the prairie with John Deere's "singing plow" (see pp. 219–20) were Christian missionaries like Peter Cartwright, whose effort to save souls earned him the nickname, the Lord's breaking-plow.

Cartwright was born in Virginia, the son of a Revolutionary War veteran. His family moved to Kentucky, where Peter joined the Methodist Episcopal Church. Bishop Frances Asbury ordained him as a deacon in 1806 and two years later he became an elder. In 1812 he was appointed a presiding elder and served in that office for fifty years, longer than any other minister in the Methodist Church at the time.

In 1808 Cartwright married Frances Gaines. Her dramatic death while attending church was memorialized by Carl Sandburg in his poem "Waiting for the Chariot." The Cartwrights moved to Illinois from Kentucky in 1824 so their children would not have to be brought up in a slave state. Cartwright began to organize Methodist class meetings in his home, and then throughout Illinois. He was elected a representative to the state legislature in 1828, and he defeated Abraham Lincoln to be reelected in 1832. In 1846 he ran unsuccessfully against Lincoln for Congress.

The Peter Cartwright United Methodist Church, a simple Greek Revival structure, was erected in 1857, three years after the town was laid out. The sanctuary remains nearly untouched. Two additions have been made; one is a museum housing Cartwright family memorabilia.

Peter Cartwright died at his home on September 25, 1872. He is buried alongside his wife in the Pleasant Plains Cemetery.

NEARBY
➤ **The Pleasant Plains Cemetery,** one-half mile south of the church.

A double stone joined by a sculptured arch marks the gravesite of Peter and Frances Cartwright. Carved on Peter's tombstone is the text of Isaiah 26:4, from which he preached his first sermon: "Trust ye in the Lord forever; for in the Lord Jehovah is everlasting strength." Following it is a stanza of an old hymn often used by circuit riding ministers at camp meetings; it begins with, "Tis done; thou dost this moment save. . . ."
➤ **Bethel Cemetery,** one and a half miles west and one-third mile north of Pleasant Plains.

The cemetery is located on the former site of Bethel Methodist Church, which was torn down in 1953. A monument now stands where the church once stood. Jane Cartwright, one of the Cartwrights' daughters, is buried here.

Springfield

Springfield abounds with sites immortalizing Abraham Lincoln's personal life and as a martyr in the fight to save the Union and emancipate slaves. Paradoxically, the city was also the site of a major race riot in 1908, which led to the creation of the National Association for the Advancement of Colored People (NAACP).

Springfield became the state's capital in 1839, thanks to the lobbying efforts of legislators like Abraham Lincoln, who was living in nearby New Salem. Springfield is where a young woman, Mary Todd, caught the eye of both Lincoln and his future political and debate opponent, Stephen Douglas. Douglas may have won the senate seat in 1858, but Lincoln won Mary Todd. They married in 1842 and two years later purchased a home in Springfield, the only home Lincoln ever owned (see below).

Many of Springfield's historic sites are within easy walking distance. Brochures are available from the Springfield Convention and Visitors Bureau, 109 N. Seventh Street, Springfield, Illinois 62701. ☎ 800-545-7300 🖳 www.springfield.il.us/visit

". . . to this place, and the kindness of these people,
I owe everything. . . ."
LINCOLN HOME NATIONAL HISTORIC SITE (NHL)
Visitor Center, 426 S. 7th Street. ☎ 217-492-4241 🖳 www.nps.gov/liho

Lincoln said the words quoted above to the crowd gathered at the Springfield station when he and his family left for his inauguration in Washington, D.C., on February 11, 1861. It was in Springfield that Lincoln launched his career as a lawyer and a politician, where he met and married Mary Todd, and where three of their four children were born, and one died. It was here that Lincoln purchased his only home, a small Greek

Lincoln Home, Springfield

Revival cottage. As their family grew, the Lincolns enlarged the house, expanding it to a full two stories. Following his election the Lincolns sold or gave away most of their furnishings and rented the house to the president of the Great Western Railroad. The house was draped for mourning following his assassination in 1865, and on May 4, 1865 his grand funeral procession passed in front of it on its way to Oak Ridge Cemetery (see p. 269). In 1887, the Lincolns' only surviving son, Robert, donated the house to the people of Illinois to be preserved as a memorial. It 1972 it was given by the state of Illinois to the United States; the National Park Service and the U.S. Department of the Interior now administer it.

Lincoln's house is in a neighborhood of restored homes; some are offices and others are private residences. Lincoln is experienced on a personal level in his home; as one writer remarked, "His presence is here." But it is not only Lincoln's presence you sense, but also that of his entire family. The parlor is where Lincoln was formally notified that he was to be the Republican Party's candidate for president; the bedrooms echo with the sounds of four lively boys and their dog Fido; the wallpaper, carpets, and furnishings reveal Mary Lincoln's taste. You depart the house with a deeper understanding of Lincoln, not just as a martyr, but also as a husband and father, the extraordinary everyman who had the vision to save a nation.

"A house divided against itself cannot stand. . . ."
OLD STATE CAPITOL STATE HISTORIC SITE
Downtown Mall. 1839, John Rague. ☎ 217-785-7961

It was at the Republican state convention in the Representatives Hall in the Old State Capitol that Lincoln began his campaign for the senate by delivering his immortal "House Divided" speech on June 16, 1858. While he lost the election to Stephen Douglas, that speech catapulted Lincoln onto the national political stage and ultimately into the presidency.

Lincoln's association with the Old State Capitol dates back to December 7, 1840, the year the building opened. He was serving his last year in the state legislature when it convened for the first time in the Representatives Hall. In the years to follow he pleaded over three hundred cases in the supreme court's first-floor chambers and made ample use of the building's law libraries. In May 1860, following his presidential nomination, he moved into the governor's office on the second floor to receive well-wishers and to plan his campaign. And, finally, on May 3 and 4, 1865, his body lay in an open casket on a velvet-covered catafalque in Representatives Hall as thousands of people passed by to pay their last respects. It was from here that the casket was placed on a hearse for the trip to his final resting place in Oak Ridge Cemetery.

The Old State Capitol was replaced by a new statehouse a few blocks away in 1876. It lost most of its historic attributes during a complete remodeling at the turn of the nineteenth century. As early as the 1920s, Lincoln admirers tried to raise funds to restore the building, but it wasn't until 1961 that legislation was signed to purchase it and return it to its Lincoln-era appearance. The structure was completely dismantled in 1966 and rebuilt; it was rededicated on November 15, 1969.

"Now he belongs to the ages." —Edwin M. Stanton
LINCOLN TOMB STATE HISTORIC SITE (NHL)
Oak Ridge Cemetery, entrance on SR 29 and Monument Avenue. 1874, Larkin Mead. ☎ 217-782-2717

The cemetery was designed in 1855 by landscape architect William Saunders, a follower of the garden cemetery movement. You are facing in the direction of the Lincoln tomb when you enter the cemetery. It was at Mrs. Lincoln's request that the president was buried here.

The National Lincoln Monument Association was formed by a small group of Lincoln's friends and political associates to raise funds for an appropriate memorial to the fallen president. Children sent their pennies and veterans' groups collected funds, and within three years following Lincoln's death enough money was raised to hire an artist, Larkin Mead (1835–1910), to design the tomb that was dedicated on October 15, 1874. In 1895, the Monument Association deeded the property to the state of Illinois.

Mary Todd Lincoln and three of the Lincoln's four children are interred with the president; Robert Todd Lincoln, the only child to reach adulthood, is buried in Arlington National Cemetery, near Washington, D.C.

Lincoln's tomb has undergone two reconstructions: one in 1899 when the obelisk was increased fifteen feet in height, and a second in 1930 when a large porphyry (red marble) stone was placed under the dome to mark the president's grave.

The giant obelisk crowning Lincoln's tomb is remindful of the Washington Monument in Washington, D.C. However, Lincoln's obelisk stands on a high terrace reached by flanking staircases. In front of the obelisk is a statue of Lincoln standing on the Constitution, a symbol of his authority for deploying troops in defense of the Union; military statues are placed at the corners of the terrace. The tomb's designer, Larkin Mead, created all of these figures.

A pathway leads to the tomb's ground-level entrance, where there is a large bronze bust of Lincoln by the sculptor Gutzon Borglum (1867–1941), famous for the monumental heads of four presidents (George Washington, Thomas Jefferson, Abraham Lincoln, and Theodore Roosevelt) he carved out of Mount Rushmore in South Dakota.

Throughout the tomb are bronze statues of Lincoln and plaques engraved with quotes from his speeches, including the entire Gettysburg Address. Surrounding the president's porphyry burial marker are flags representing the states where he and his family dwelt. Above a window behind the marker are the words spoken by Secretary of War Edwin M. Stanton upon hearing of Lincoln's death, "Now he belongs to the ages."

NEARBY
➥ **Vietnam Veterans and Korean War Memorials**
Two impressive war memorials are located to the right of the cemetery's Walnut Street entrance: the Illinois Vietnam Veterans Memorial and across from it, the Illinois Korean War Memorial. They are both inscribed with the names of servicemen killed in the conflicts.

"Each blade of grass is a study." —Abraham Lincoln
ABRAHAM LINCOLN MEMORIAL GARDEN AND NATURE CENTER (NR)
2301 East Lake Drive. Dedicated 1938, Jens Jensen. ☎ 217-529-1111
🖳 www.imgnc.com
In 1932, Mrs. T. J. Knudson of the Springfield Civic Garden Club came up with the idea for a garden that would be a living memorial to Abraham Lincoln. It was to be "a site for meditation on Lincoln, his principles and thoughts, and the role of man in the overall scheme of nature." The concept received widespread support, and by 1934 the landscape architect, Jens Jensen (1860–1951), agreed to design the garden pro bono. It was to be his last great public work. Although the garden was dedicated in 1938, it took over seventeen years to implement Jensen's Prairie-style plan. His goal wasn't to replicate nature, but to capture its essence by carefully selecting and overseeing the placement of nearly every tree and plant. Thus, while all of the garden's natural beauty may appear to be as it was for centuries, it has all been carefully laid out to provide a sequence of landscape designs held together by eight council rings and punctuated by benches, fountains, bridges, and shelters. The benches are all inscribed with pithy quotes, like the one above by Abraham Lincoln.

NEARBY

➥ **Ostermeier Prairie Center,** on the garden's southern boundary.
A thirty-acre farm includes additional trails through restored prairie and reforestation areas. A restored farm pond is being developed as wetland habitat.

➥ **Vachel Lindsay Home (NR),** 603 S. 5th Street. 1846; 1893 addition by Bullard and Bullard. ☎ 217-785-7290

Known as the Prairie Troubadour, the poet Vachel Lindsay (1879–1931) spent much of his life as a pilgrim walking throughout the nation to

THE SPRINGFIELD RACE RIOT OF 1908

Vachel Lindsay witnessed the Springfield Race Riot of 1908. It led him to lecture on race at the local YMCA and to write and publish at his own expense the first of five *War Bulletins* that included an article opposing racial prejudice.

Racial issues that simmered in Springfield in the years following the Civil War were exacerbated by the arrival of numerous southern blacks seeking increasingly scarce jobs in factories and coal mines. Tensions led to episodes of extreme violence, such as the infamous Virden Massacre of 1898 (see below) and the race riot that rocked Springfield.

A black man was jailed on July 4, 1908, for allegedly murdering a white man and raping his wife. A second black man was accused of raping a white woman on August 14. These two arrests were enough to incite many in the white community to take the law into their own hands. Fearing violence, the police moved the prisoners to Bloomington. This enraged a mob of nearly twelve thousand people who descended upon black businesses and neighborhoods in Springfield and destroyed property valued at over $200,000 at the time. Thousands of black citizens were forced to flee the city and at least seven people were killed before five thousand National Guard troops quelled the rioters. Although 107 indictments were handed down by a special grand jury, no one was ever convicted. The fact that a race riot could occur in Lincoln's hometown spurred a group of white and black businessmen in New York City to establish an organization that would fight for the civil rights of African Americans. This organization became the National Association for the Advancement of Colored People (NAACP).

present and sell his visionary poetry to the "masses." Lindsay was born in Springfield to followers of the immigrant Scotch-Irish clergyman Alexander Campbell, who promoted individual spirituality and envisioned a nondenominational Christian church in the United States. While attending art schools in Chicago and New York, Lindsay came to believe that art began with a vision, an idealization of what an artist sees. After experiencing his own visions, he began to spread his "gospel of beauty," promoting the belief that a person could be redeemed through great art. Many of Lindsay's poems and writings had their origins in visions he experienced, including "Abraham Lincoln Walks at Midnight," which describes Lincoln's mystical return to Springfield, and "I Heard Immanuel Singing," based on a vision he had of Christ singing in heaven.

Mr. and Mrs. Clark M. Smith, Mary Lincoln's sister and brother-in-law, originally built the home that was later purchased by Lindsay's family. Some argue that the same architect who built Abraham Lincoln's home designed this house. The original house is Greek Revival; the Lindsays' addition is Victorian. The house is restored to look as it did at the height of Lindsay's popularity in 1917. He committed suicide at home in 1931.

Virden

Twenty miles south of Springfield on SR 4 and west of I-55 is the site of the infamous Virden Massacre of 1898. Thousands of union workers came to Virden in 1998 to commemorate the centennial of the massacre.

It is believed that the tragedy was precipitated by the unwillingness of the owners of the Chicago-Virden Coal Company to honor an agreement worked out by mine operators and mine workers that guaranteed an eight-hour work day, a mutually agreed upon wage, and the elimination of company stores. Instead, the owners chose to lock out union workers and to surround the mine with a stockade. What led to violence was the mine operator's decision to import black strikebreakers from Alabama. Fearing a riot, the mine operator went to Governor Tanner to request he send in troops to protect the strikebreakers; the governor refused. The train carrying one hundred black workers and their families arrived at Virden at 12:40 P.M. on October 12, 1898, and the feared violence broke out. Several people, including armed guards and union miners, were shot. Not satisfied, the union miners followed the train to the mine stockade, where further rioting occurred. At least six union members and five company guards were killed. Fearing for his life, the train's engineer took the strikebreakers to St. Louis, where he dumped them without money or shelter. The violence prompted Governor Tanner to order the National Guard to Virden to prevent the offloading of a second trainload of strikebreakers. It was the first time in the nation's history that a governor had ordered troops to the support of labor. The incident in Virden did have two positive outcomes: Mining companies quit the practice of recruiting blacks to be strikebreakers and, after a six-month lockout, management finally conceded to the union's demands. "Remember Virden" became a union rallying cry.

The union members killed in the turmoil were denied burial in the local cemeteries, so the union purchased an acre of land in Mount Olive and turned it into a union miners' cemetery.

Mount Olive

The town is about forty miles south of Virden, just off I-55.

A Pilgrimage Site for All Union Members
THE UNION MINERS' CEMETERY (NR)
One-half mile north of the city park. ☎ 312-663-4107

A wrought-iron gate leads into the small cemetery that is dedicated to those who fought for the rights of union workers. Beyond the gate is a granite obelisk bearing the likeness of Mother Jones (see pp. 22–23), who dedicated her life to "those brave boys," coal miners who had died fighting for the union and among whom she asked to be buried. On each side of the obelisk is a large bronze sculpture of a coal miner with his sledge. A crowd estimated at fifty thousand attended the dedication of the monument on October 11, 1936, the day before Miners Day, October 12, a date selected to commemorate the Virden Massacre.

Hillsboro

Located northeast of Mount Olive on SR 16 is Hillsboro, settled in the 1820s by pioneers of German descent from North Carolina.

A Church Grows in the Wilderness
ST. PAUL'S LUTHERAN CHURCH
103 N. Main Street. 1897, R. C. Gotwald of Springfield, Ohio.
☎ 217-532-2353 or 217-532-5284

In the early 1830s the Reverend Daniel Scherer, a circuit-riding Lutheran minister from North Carolina known as the Patriarch of Lutheranism in Illinois, gathered with thirty others to formally organize a congregation known as Zion Evangelical Lutheran Church; its name was changed to St. Paul's Evangelical Lutheran Church in 1867.

The congregation gathered in the town's courthouse until its first house of worship, arguably the state's first frame church, was erected in 1834. Five years later it was the site of the Fifth Annual Convention of the Evangelical Lutheran Synod of the West.

The 1834 church served the congregation until a two-story brick building was erected at a cost of $7,000. Dedicated in 1857, the new church was described by its pastor as comparing "favorably with any house of like dimensions in the State; and will we trust, stand long as a monument to the self-denying liberality of the little band that have reared it." When the pastor left in 1861, the congregation had a debt of $4,000; its council recorded the church's position as "sad, gloomy and discouraging." A new pastor was called who revitalized the congregation, and an even grander church was erected at a cost of $15,000, including furnishings. Unlike the previous building, however, this one was almost completely paid for when it was dedicated on April 4, 1897.

The congregation considered building a new church in the 1960s, but chose instead to remodel the 1897 structure and add an educational wing. St. Paul's is the oldest Lutheran congregation in Illinois with continuous active weekly worship.

Vandalia

When Kaskaskia (see p. 289) was flooded by the Mississippi River in 1818, the statehouse was moved to a more central location, Vandalia. Erected in 1820, the new statehouse was a frame structure that according to one historian was "plain and primitive"; it burned down in 1823 under circumstances that were considered "suspicious." Anxious for Vandalia to remain the capital, its citizens contributed $3,000 to repair and remodel the Old State Bank building as a statehouse. It served six general assemblies, and it was here that Lincoln began his political career in 1834. Unhappy with the sorry condition of the remodeled statehouse, legislators led by Abraham Lincoln lobbied to move the capital to Springfield (p. 266). Vandalians once again put up money to keep the capital in town and built yet another statehouse. It was completed in 1836. Regardless, in July 1839, the senate declared that Springfield would be the new seat of government and the supreme court. Vandalia went into a decline but was revitalized in the 1850s when the Illinois Central Railroad came through the town.

The Oldest Surviving Illinois Capitol Building
VANDALIA STATEHOUSE STATE HISTORIC SITE (OLD STATE CAPITOL) (NR)
315 W. Gallatin Street. 1836; remodeled in 1859, 1889; restored in the 1970s, McDonald and Mack. ☎ 618-283-1161

Dominating Vandalia's public square, the tall white brick Greek Revival building served as the state capitol from 1836 through 1839. It was then used for various purposes and has undergone many alterations over the years, including the addition of a balcony and porticos to its front and rear façades. It was about to be razed in the early 1900s when it was sold to the state to be used for county offices. Its interior has been recently restored to resemble its original appearance.

The Start of a Historic Journey
LEWIS AND CLARK STATE HISTORIC SITE
SR 3 at Poag Road. ☎ 618-251-2680. From Vandalia return to I-70 and travel west toward St. Louis, continue onto I-270, taking Exit 3 A-B north onto SR 3. Go north for approximately four miles and follow signs for "Lewis and Clark State Historic Site."

A peaceful oasis set in the midst of an industrial wasteland, this monument commemorates where the Lewis and Clark expedition trained and made preparations for their excursion into the wilderness. The actual site has been obliterated by river channel migration. Plans are underway by the National Park Service to erect an interpretive center and museum at this site that will be the starting point for the Lewis and Clark National Historic Trail.

A plaque on a rock reads: "Near here at Camp DuBois the Lewis and Clark detachment spent the winter of 1803–04. They left on May 14, 1804 and ascended the Missouri River to the source where it crossed the Great Divide reaching the Pacific on November 7, 1805. They returned to Illinois on September 23, 1806 having concluded one of the most dramatic and significant episodes in our history."

Fifty Mythical Miles
MEETING OF THE GREAT RIVERS SCENIC ROUTE
☎ 800-258-6645 💻 www.visitalton.org

Stretching fifty miles from Kampsville in the north to Alton in the south is one of the nation's most scenic roads. Magnificent bluffs tower over the roadway as it follows an unusual bend in the Mississippi River that causes it to run west to east for a while. The road travels through many historic river towns and passes the confluence of the Mississippi and Illinois Rivers and the Mississippi and Missouri Rivers.

From the Lewis and Clark State Historic Site, go north to Pere Marquette State Park, then head back south to visit several picturesque and historic river towns before driving to Cahokia (see pp. 282–83).

A Nature Lover's Paradise
PERE MARQUETTE STATE PARK
Five miles west of Grafton on SR 100 (the Great Rivers National Scenic Byway). ☎ 618-786-3323

A large white stone cross east of the park's entrance on SR 100 marks the spot where Father Jacques Marquette and Louis Jolliet are thought to have landed in 1673 following their exploration of the Mississippi River (see pp. 2–3). Although no documented historic Native American sites have been found in the park, it is believed the area was occupied by the Illinois Confederation. Evidence of prehistoric American Indians was uncovered when the Pere Marquette Lodge was constructed in the 1930s and again when it was expanded in 1985.

The nine-thousand-acre park lies on high bluffs that overlook the confluence of the Mississippi and Illinois Rivers. Some of the more spectacular views can be reached by hiking up some moderately steep pathways to McAdams Peak and Twin Mounds.

A small white clapboard church and a cemetery are located next to the park's trailer camping area. The **Hartford Methodist Episcopal Church** was established in 1876 in a region where death was not an uncommon visitor. A walk through the cemetery reminds visitors how fragile life was on the frontier. A low concrete wall surrounds the grave site of the Journey family. Between 1889 and 1896 the parents lost four children, ages two weeks to eight years old. Nearby is another grave; the name of the child inscribed on the marker is no longer legible, but a poignant inscription set within a small glass case reads: "Birdie, two years, eleven months and six hours. Two little words, yet they bring the tears that alas are near the surface. Never again in after years will I hear our little darling say, 'take baby.'"

Elsah (NR)

Elsah, once an important steamboat stop on the Mississippi River, is now a quaint village nestled in a valley. Time has stood still here. Elsah's cozy cobblestone cottages surrounded by white picket fences, flower-lined narrow brick streets, and rustic bridges spanning flowing streams all contribute to its picturesque character. The **United Methodist Church,** built in 1874, was the only house of worship in Elsah until the 1940s. It is the first town to be listed in its entirety on the National Register of Historic Places (1973).

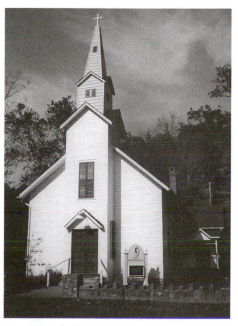

United Methodist Church, Elsah

Dedicated to the Educational Needs of Young Christian Scientists
PRINCIPIA COLLEGE (NHL)
Maybeck Place. 1931–46, Bernard Maybeck, Henry Gutterson.
☎ 618-374-5236

Please call before visiting. The campus is not always open to the public.

Located on the bluffs above Elsah, this is the only college in the world dedicated to educating young Christian Scientists. Bernard Maybeck (1862–1957), a highly regarded San Francisco architect whose First Church of Christ, Scientist, Berkeley (1910), is also a National Historic Landmark, designed the campus to resemble an English village. He believed this plan embodied Principia's educational system that aimed to produce "constructive thinkers." As one writer observed, "[the campus] reveals the way in which a romantic architect and his sympathetic client were able to design and locate buildings that were intended to embody and transmit ideals." Maybeck and his successor, Henry Gutterson (1884–1954), were responsible for the design of many of the buildings on the campus.

Godfrey

Captain Benjamin Godfrey, a retired Cape Cod fisherman, founded the town as the site of the Monticello Female Seminary, which he established in 1835. The seminary promoted Godfrey's philosophy that "when you educate a woman you educate a family." Its first class graduated in 1838. Until its final commencement in 1971, the seminary educated thousands of women from all over the country. It was then transformed into the Lewis and Clark Community College, and the seminary's chapel was moved onto the campus from its original site across the street.

A House of Worship for All
BENJAMIN GODFREY MEMORIAL CHAPEL (CHURCH OF CHRIST; NR)

On the campus of Lewis and Clark Community College. 1854.
☎ 618-466-3411 or 800-500-5222

The Benjamin Godfrey Memorial Chapel is one of only six churches outside of the northeastern United States considered to be an authentic copy of a New England church. The white Greek Revival church was organized by Presbyterians, Dutch Reformed, and Congregationalists as a nondenominational congregation. It served as a religious umbrella under which students, teachers, and community members of various faiths who lived in a sparsely populated area could come together to worship. The chapel is considered the finest example of Greek Revival architecture in the Midwest. A broad flight of stairs on the front façade of the one-story "frame over stone foundation" church lead up to a porch that has six grand pillars supporting a pediment; its tower, capped by a white spire, is a local landmark. Although religious services and weddings are occasionally performed in the

Benjamin Godfrey Memorial Chapel, Godfrey

chapel, the college uses it primarily as an auditorium. The basement is used for classrooms.

Alton

Alton is located along bluffs just north of the confluence of the Mississippi and Missouri Rivers. Colonel Rufus Easton, who named the town after his son, founded it in 1818. The Eagle Packet line of boats manufactured in Alton made it an important steamboat port. For a time it even rivaled nearby St. Louis, thanks to newspaper advertisements that promoted it as the prime location of a ferry site and "surrounded by the richest

THE PIASA BIRD LEGEND

High on a river bluff, one mile west of the Alton Visitors Center on SR 100, is a giant image of the Piasa Bird (meaning "the bird that devours men"), originally painted by Native Americans. Marquette and Jolliet reported seeing a painting on the bluff of two reptilian-like figures with red eyes, beards, and scales. It was probably this painting, which was destroyed in 1870 by quarry operations. The original painting was recreated on the bluff in 1998. Once again the Piasa Bird is a visible part of the region's local history and legends.

According to a Native American legend, there was a time when a huge birdlike creature swept through the area to snatch up victims to eat. Hundreds of brave warriors tried to slay the creature, but failed. The Illini people lived in great fear of the bird. One of their chiefs, Ouatoga, went off alone to fast for a whole moon, praying to the Great Spirit for protection for his people. On the last night of his fast, the Great Spirit appeared in a dream and directed Ouatoga to select twenty warriors, arm them with bows and arrows and conceal them while another warrior was to stand in open view as bait for the Piasa. After telling his people of the dream, the warriors were selected and hidden, while Ouatoga offered himself as the victim. The Piasa saw his prey and swooped down on the chief who was chanting the death song of a warrior. As the Piasa neared Ouatoga, the concealed warriors let loose with their arrows that pierced the body of the beast; it died uttering a blood-chilling scream. Thus were Ouatoga and the Illini people saved.

soil and best settlements to be found in the Illinois country." The city's Federal, Greek Revival, and Victorian houses attest to its prosperity in the years leading up to and immediately following the Civil War.

St. Louis, one of the largest slave-owning areas north of New Orleans, was the site of a large slave market. Many slaves en route to auction escaped by crossing the Mississippi River to Illinois, where they could begin their flight to freedom along the Underground Railroad (see p. 14). They received assistance from many local people, including the abolitionist minister and journalist Elijah Parish Lovejoy, who was murdered on November 7, 1837, by a proslavery mob.

A Martyr to Human Rights and a Champion of Free Speech
ELIJAH PARISH LOVEJOY MONUMENT
Alton Cemetery at Monument Avenue. Dedicated Nov. 7, 1897.

Lovejoy's monument is the most imposing one in the cemetery. Its ninety-three-foot-tall column, topped by the Winged Victory, makes it the tallest monument in Illinois, surpassing even Abraham Lincoln's in Springfield (see pp. 266–72).

WHO WAS ELIJAH PARISH LOVEJOY?

Elijah Parish Lovejoy, born in Albion, Maine, in 1802, was a brother of Owen Lovejoy, whose home in Princeton was a principal stop on the Underground Railroad (see pp. 241–42). Elijah Lovejoy moved to St. Louis in 1827 to teach school and work as a journalist. He enrolled in the Princeton Theological Seminary in New Jersey in 1832 and after completing his studies returned to St. Louis. In November 1833 he began to edit a religious newspaper, *The St. Louis Observer*, whose fierce antislavery views enraged many Missourians, who demanded he cease attacking slavery. After a mob destroyed his press in 1836, Lovejoy moved across the river to Alton, where he started another religious abolitionist newspaper, *The Alton Observer*. Lovejoy continued to meet stiff opposition to his views, even in the free state of Illinois. Three more of his presses were destroyed, but Lovejoy, in his fight for freedom of the press and freedom for slaves, continued to publish his newspaper. He was shot dead on November 7, 1837, his thirty-fifth birthday, while defending a warehouse where a fourth press was stored. The press that Lovejoy died protecting is on display in *The Alton Telegraph* building.

From street level, a visitor ascends a grand staircase leading to the huge monument. Inscriptions on flanking stones record Lovejoy's biography and accomplishments; one reads: "Elijah Parish Lovejoy was the publisher and editor of the *Alton Observer*, a social reformer, and Presbyterian minister whose death at the hands of an angry mob in Alton, Illinois made him an enduring symbol of the fight for human liberty and freedom of the Press. He was shot dead defending his fourth press."

Following his murder, Lovejoy was buried in an unmarked grave until he and his wife were moved and interred on a hillside north of his monument. A wrought-iron fence encloses their tombs. Next to the fence is a stone marker set in 1997 that lists the names of members of Alton's African American community who continue to provide perpetual care to the Lovejoys' graves.

NEARBY

➡ **Lincoln-Douglas Square,** corner of Broadway and Landmarks Streets.

Over six thousand people attended the final Lincoln-Douglas Debate that took place on October 15, 1858, in front of Alton's city hall. The city hall burned in 1923, but life-size statues of Lincoln and Douglas shown in debate are on the original site.

Peace at Last
CONFEDERATE CEMETERY AND MEMORIAL

Rozier and Hill Streets (2 blocks west of State Street). Dedicated in 1910.

Nestled away in a suburban neighborhood is a tall granite pylon "erected to the memory of the Confederate soldiers who died in the Alton Prison, 1862–1865" by the Sam Davis Chapter of the United Daughters of the Confederacy. Affixed to it is a tablet that reads: "Erected by the United States to mark the burial place of 1,354 Confederate Soldiers who died here and at the Smallpox Hospital on the adjacent island while prisoners of war and whose graves cannot now be identified." On four sides of the base are bronze plaques engraved with the names, companies, and regiments of the soldiers buried here. Many were from Missouri, separated from Illinois by the Mississippi River, and by differences in an ideology that brought about their deaths.

NEARBY

➡ **Alton Prison (1831–33),** Williams Street at Broadway.

Alton Prison was Illinois' first penitentiary and the first building funded by public money in the state. Because of unsanitary conditions, the prison was abandoned in 1860 and a new penitentiary was built at Joliet. Although deemed unsuitable for civilian prisoners, the dark, dank Alton Prison was transformed into a military prison during the Civil War. Over the course of three years, more than eleven thousand Confederate prisoners were housed there. All that remains of this notorious place are remnants of a restored cellblock and a historical marker.

City of the Sun
CAHOKIA MOUNDS STATE HISTORIC SITE (NR, NHL)
One mile southwest of Collinsville, near the intersection of I-255 and I-55/70. ☎ 618-346-5160 🖳 www.cahokiamounds.com

Henry Brackenridge, a friend of Thomas Jefferson, was interested in American Indian sites, especially mounds he found scattered near St. Louis. However, few shared his excitement when he encountered ". . . a stupendous pile of earth" that struck him with the same degree of astonishment as one would experience contemplating the Egyptian pyramids. As he complained in a letter to Jefferson in 1813: "When I examined it [Monks Mound, the largest mound at the site] in 1811, I was astonished that this stupendous monument of antiquity should have been unnoticed by any traveler . . . but this, which I . . . considered a discovery, attracted no notice."

Nearly two hundred years later, many travelers who visit St. Louis are unaware that one of the world's most important archaeological sites is just a few miles east of St. Louis. Fortunately, others have come to recognize

Cahokia Mounds

the site's importance. In 1982, UNESCO designated Cahokia Mounds a World Heritage Site for its importance in understanding the prehistory of North America. The site of the largest prehistoric city north of Mexico, it joins an elite group of cultural and natural landmarks that include the Great Wall of China, the Pyramids in Egypt, and the Taj Mahal in India.

Exhibits and models in the Cahokia Mounds Interpretive Center provide an excellent introduction to the story of the great prehistoric Mississippian Indian civilization that developed at Cahokia. From the top of Monks Mound, the largest prehistoric earthenwork in North and South America, you have an awesome view of the entire site and the surrounding rich American Bottom Land, and if the pollution isn't too bad, the Arch in St. Louis. Monks Mound receives its name from the French Trappist Monks who moved there in 1809 and grew vegetables on its terraces, totally oblivious of the mound's historic significance.

The name *Cahokia* (wild geese) is taken from a subtribe of the Illinois Confederation that lived in the area when the French arrived in the late seventeenth century. Cahokia's earlier prehistoric inhabitants did not leave written records, so much of what is known comes from material remains. Unfortunately a great deal of that evidence was picked over by collectors in the nineteenth century or destroyed by plows and urban sprawl. What is known is that for about five hundred years, from about 800 C.E. to about 1300 C.E., Cahokia was, according to one scholar, "the central community of the American heartland." At its height, from about 1100 to 1200 C.E., the city covered nearly six square miles and had a population of about twenty thousand. It was laid out in a carefully conceived plan, with Monks Mound at its center surrounded by four plazas, one at each of the cardinal directions. It is likely that the ruler of Cahokia, the "Great Sun," lived on top of Monks Mound. Another mound (# 72), south of Monks Mound and west of the interpretive center, was used for the burial of sacrificial victims, including one high-ranking victim who was found resting on a bed of twenty thousand shell beads. Nearby is Woodhenge, a circle of reconstructed wooden poles whose alignment suggests that it was used to make calendrical observations.

❀

CHAPTER SEVEN

Southern Illinois

THE "LAND BETWEEN THE RIVERS" is bounded by the Mississippi on the west, the Wabash on the east, and the Ohio on the south. Its northern boundary is US 50, the Old St. Louis Trace that runs from the Wabash River near Vincennes, Indiana, to St. Louis, Missouri. The region includes prairies and coal mines, early French sites along the Mississippi river, and the wooded hills of the Shawnee National Forest. According to John M. Coggelshall, southern Illinois always had an identity distinct from other regions of the state, a reflection of the western Appalachian culture of many of its first settlers (see p. 9). He argues that even Poles, Italians, and Slovakians who began to settle in the region in the late nineteenth century adopted this identity, a result of pressures to assimilate. However, at the same time they held onto many of their old world traditions, and the result was, according to Coggelshall, "ethnic diversity within a unified regional identity."

Southern Illinois is known as "Egypt," but no one seems certain why. Some argue that the name came from Baptist missionaries seeking a new Zion in the wilderness who compared the Mississippi River and its fertile valley to the Nile in Egypt, the breadbasket for the Roman Empire. "Egypt" was Illinois's breadbasket when the "Winter of Deep Snow" (1830–31) caused crops to fail in the north and farmers had to journey south to purchase grain and seed. According to one legend, when asked where they were going, the farmers would reply, "We are the sons of Jacob, going into Egypt to buy corn."

Cahokia

The town of Cahokia is located off I-255, Exit 13. Its ideal location a few miles below the confluence of the Illinois, Missouri, and Mississippi Rivers made it a strategic fur-trading center. The presence of Native Americans and French-Canadian fur traders prompted French priests to open a mission in 1699 that became the town of Cahokia, considered the state's oldest established community. At the end of the French and Indian War in 1763 (see pp. 6–7), many French Cahokians fled across the Mississippi River, where they helped found the cities of St. Genevieve and St. Louis. Rather than turn the church and other church holdings over to the British, the priest in charge, without the consent of his congregation, sold everything at a public auction and returned to France. The Catholics who remained later swore allegiance to the United States, and Cahokia became the first seat of St. Clair County in 1787.

The Oldest Active Catholic Parish in the United States
HOLY FAMILY CATHOLIC CHURCH (NR, NHL)
120 East First Street. 1799; 1833; 1949–51 restoration, Guy Study.
☎ 618-337-4548 ▣ hfamily1699@aol.com

The Cahokia parish, organized by French missionaries at the same time as the town, has remained active since that date, giving it the distinction of being the oldest continuously active Catholic parish in the nation. Beautifully restored and maintained, Holy Family Catholic Church is one of the oldest extant colonial buildings west of the Appalachian Mountains. Dedicated in 1799 as a replacement for the church sold by its priest (see above), it remained in use until a large "rock" church was erected next to it in 1891. That building was demolished in 1972 and replaced by a smaller chapel. Father Robert Hynes, who arrived in Cahokia in 1912, is responsible for the preservation of the little log church. Further restoration was carried out from 1949 through 1951, and additional preservation of the site is ongoing.

Originally rectangular in plan (seventy-four feet long by thirty-two feet wide), small rectangular wings similar to transepts were added to the church's east and west sides in about 1833, giving it its present cruciform plan. A belfry was added at the north ridge of the roof during restoration work between 1949 and 1951. Along with the Cahokia Courthouse (see below), Holy Family is an example of an early French log construction technique known as *poteaux-sur-sole*, post-on-sill foundation: Vertical heavy hewn black walnut logs are seated on horizontal sill logs that rest on a stone foundation. The spaces between the logs are filled with rubble stone set in clay, a technique known as *pierrotage*. The church's simple elegance is a reminder to visitors that spiritual sites do not have to be dependent upon lavish displays of wealth.

NEARBY

➤ **Cahokia Courthouse State Historic Site (NR),** 107 Elm Street. Ca. 1737; 1814–1939; moved and remodeled several times. ☎ 618-332-1782

Built in about 1737 as a private residence for François Saucier, who supervised the construction of Fort de Chartres (see p. 289), the government purchased the house in 1793. It served as the St. Clair County courthouse and center of political activity for the Northwest Territory until the county seat moved to Belleville in 1814. The building was used for a variety of purposes before it was dismantled and reerected in 1904 at the St. Louis World's Fair. When the fair was over it was moved to Chicago and reconstructed on Wooded Island in Jackson Park, where it stayed until 1920. Cahokians then asked it be returned, and it was accurately reconstructed on its original site in 1939.

Belleville

Belleville, located on SR 15 a few miles east of Cahokia, was founded by the French in 1814, but the city has a predominantly German character, thanks to the discovery of coal in 1827, which attracted German miners, and the arrival of a number of liberals and freethinkers, known as Forty-Eighters, fleeing Germany after the 1848 revolution.

The Largest Cathedral in Illinois
CATHEDRAL OF ST. PETER
Catholic. 200 W. Harrison Street. 1866, 1913, 1957, 1968.
☎ 618-234-1166

A booklet that describes the interior decoration, including the symbolism of the stained-glass windows, is available in the cathedral office.

German Catholics formally established a parish in 1842, and the following year they erected a small wooden church just east of the present cathedral. It was replaced in 1866 by a larger, red brick church that became a cathedral when the southern part of Illinois became the Diocese of Belleville in 1887. All but the red brick outer walls of the cathedral was destroyed by fire on January 4, 1912. The interior was entirely rebuilt in an English Gothic style modeled after the famed Exeter Cathedral in England. Another fire damaged the interior in 1937 and it was completely redecorated, but the brick walls survived until they were sheathed with stone in the 1950s. The most dramatic change to the building occurred in the 1960s, when its length was extended, the chancel area expanded, and new sacristies, shrines, and the Blessed Sacrament Chapel were added.

A tower and lofty spire, two hundred feet high, guide visitors toward the expansive cathedral that seats approximately fourteen hundred people. The interior is elaborately decorated with plasterwork, statuary in marble and bronze, and stained-glass windows. Two of the windows depict the early history of the Catholic Church in Illinois and include images of Pere Marquette and local Native American tribes. An Italian artist, Raffo Figli, who also designed the stations of the cross, designed the Italian marble main altar in the chancel. Its top weighs about three tons and is considered one of the most perfect pieces of marble in the country. A museum located outside of the Bishop's Chapel displays many historical documents and artifacts.

A Spiritual Oasis
NATIONAL SHRINE OF OUR LADY OF THE SNOWS
Catholic. 442 S. DeMazenod Drive (SR 15 at SR 157). Founded in 1958. ☎ 618-397-6700 or 314-241-3400 🖥 www.snows.org

Father Edwin J. Guild, of the Missionary Oblates of Mary Immaculate, founded the shrine to carry out the order's missionary work. It is one of the largest outdoor shrines in North America, covering over two hundred beautifully landscaped and wooded acres.

The shrine has a choice of pathways, many lined with memorials and sculptures leading to devotional sites, such as the Lourdes Grotto, a replica of the famed grotto in France, or the Way of the Cross, which has full-color statues of the fourteen stations of the cross. The Main Shrine, nestled in a gentle valley, is an amphitheater that can accommodate 2,400 people. On the grounds is the Church of Our Lady of the Snows. Round in design to symbolize the universality of the Catholic Church, its plan allows all worshipers to easily participate in liturgies and celebrations.

SR 156 south from Belleville passes through other towns that have a German heritage. Wartburg, for example, is named after the Castle of Wartburg, where Martin Luther translated the Bible into German. South of it is the village of Maeystown, located on CR 7.

Maeystown

A nineteenth-century one-lane stone bridge leads into this tiny, picturesque village. The hundred-acre hilly wooded tract of land bisected by streams and studded with limestone deposits was first claimed by James McRoberts, a Revolutionary war soldier whose eldest son, Samuel, became the first native-born Illinoisan to be elected to the United States Senate. McRoberts died in 1844, and in 1848 Jacob Maeys, an immigrant from Oggersheim in Germany, purchased his land. Maeys built a sawmill and log cabin and established the village of Maeystown in 1852, which was settled by Germans fleeing the outcome of the 1848 revolution. Once settled, they began to erect stone buildings and bridges similar to those in their homeland. Because so many of their buildings have survived, the entire village is listed on the National Register of Historic Places.

A Historic Stone Church
ST. JOHN'S CHURCH (NR)
United Church of Christ. 1865–67; remodeled several times.
☎ 618-458-6940

Situated atop a hill overlooking Maeystown is a charming church built of limestone quarried from nearby hills by its members. Founded in 1858 by a German Lutheran minister, the congregation's current affiliation reflects denominational mergers that occurred in the twentieth century (see p. 44).

St. John's originally was a simple structure, somewhat Greek Revival in style, until a stone entrance tower capped with a steeple was added to its front façade in the 1880s. Other changes include extending its length and the addition of a balcony. German was used exclusively for services until 1935, when English was introduced, but German services continued to be offered once a month until 1942 when, according to the congregation's history, they were discontinued "because of the war and its pressures." Maeystown and St. John's now take pride in their German heritage. The village publishes a periodic newspaper, *Maeystown Volksblatt,* and celebrates *Fastnacht,* a German carnival the Tuesday before Ash Wednesday, and *Oktoberfest* on the second Sunday in October.

The cemetery is on a wooded hillside east of the church. One of its members, Wilhelm Feldmeier, who retained a large lot on the top of the hill for himself, his family, and two friends who came over with him on the same boat from Germany, donated the land.

Leave Maeystown on SR 7 and head south into Randolph County, whose motto is "Where Illinois began." It was the center of French colonial power and control in Illinois Country.

The Center of French Authority
FORT DE CHARTRES STATE HISTORIC SITE (NHL)

Located south of SR 3 on SR 155. 1720–63. ☎ 618-284-7230

"About a musket shot" from the Mississippi River is the massive stone Fort de Chartres, which looms as an almost alien presence on the empty prairie. Between 1720 and 1763, the French constructed three forts on or near this site that were named in honor of Louis duc de Chartres, son of the regent of France. The first two forts were built of logs, but due to flooding and bad repair, they deteriorated rapidly. A stone fort, built in 1760 under the direction of François Saucier, engineer general in the French army, was handed over to the British at the end of the French and Indian War. The British renamed it Fort Cavendish but abandoned it following a flood in 1771. The unrelenting Mississippi River soon swallowed what remained of the fort, except for its powder magazine, which was restored in 1913 after the Illinois legislature purchased the site. Additional restoration was undertaken in the 1920s and 1930s. The river took its toll again during the great flood of 1993, when the fort was inundated by fifteen feet of water; it has since been refurbished.

A path leads to the gate in the fort's north wall. The roof of its gatehouse serves as a lookout. Climb to its top to see why the site was selected: It affords unobstructed views of the prairie and the levees holding back the Mississippi. The original powder magazine, considered the oldest building in Illinois, is located in the east bastion. The king's storehouse and museum and a guards' building with a **chapel** are near the north wall. Two "buildings" appear to be simply wood frames; this is a reconstruction technique called "ghosting"—the frames outline the buildings' dimensions.

Kaskaskia

Mark Twain once remarked, "ten thousand river commissions . . . cannot tame that lawless stream . . . cannot say to it, 'Go here,' or 'Go there,' and make it obey. . . ." His sense of the river was reconfirmed when levees could not hold it back in 1993. Over a century earlier, an equally devastating flood wiped out historic Old Kaskaskia, site of the Jesuit mission founded in 1703 and a French bastion in the New World, and Illinois' first capital from 1818 to 1820.

In the spring of 1881, the Mississippi River broke through a narrow strip of land north of Kaskaskia, changed course, and flowed into the Kaskaskia River channel, thus destroying town and mission.

Kaskaskia Island

The tiny, isolated village of Kaskaskia Island, population eighteen, the only Illinois community located west of the Mississippi River, is accessible only from Missouri, via the Chester Bridge. Go west on Missouri Highway 51 to Highway H, north to St. Mary, Missouri, then follow the signs to the village.

When it became apparent that Old Kaskaskia would not survive the recurrent flooding of the Mississippi River, its residents began to dismantle its buildings, brick by brick, and rebuilt them here in 1894. The first Randolph County Courthouse, built in 1795 and now located west of the Bell Shrine, was used as a school until 1946. The reconstructed rectory is located between the Bell Shrine and the rebuilt Immaculate Conception Church.

The buildings are in a parklike setting, with a campground and picnic tables. For years Missouri officials claimed Kaskaskia Island because it was on the west side of the Mississippi River. Illinois officials disagreed and argued that the original river channel was the correct boundary and Kaskaskia Island was part of Illinois. The dispute continued until 1970, when the United States Supreme Court, in a decision worthy of King Solomon, divided the land between the two states, with the village of Kaskaskia Island and a large area of the disputed territory going to Illinois.

The Liberty Bell of the West
KASKASKIA BELL STATE HISTORIC SITE
Kaskaskia Island. Bell, 1741; building erected in 1948 (press button on the right to open doors to view bell). ☎ 618-859-3741

The 650-pound bell, cast in La Rochelle, France, in 1741, was a gift to the Catholic Church at Kaskaskia from King Louis XV. It is decorated with the royal lilies (fleur-de-lis) of France and a cross and pedestal. A French inscription reads: "Pour l'église des Illinois par les Soins du Roi Doutre Lea" (For the church of Illinois, by the gift of the King across the water). It was shipped to New Orleans and then transferred to a raft that was pulled up the Mississippi River by men walking along its banks. It arrived at Kaskaskia in 1743 and was hung in the tower of Immaculate Conception Church, where it remained until it was replaced by a new set of bells in 1874. Kaskaskians rang the bell on July 4, 1778, to celebrate their liberation from the British; thus its name, "the Liberty Bell of the West" (see p. 6). It rang again to celebrate the visit of the Marquis de Lafayette in 1825, and it continues to be rung each Fourth of July to celebrate the nation's independence.

A Symbol of a People's Faith and Dedication
IMMACULATE CONCEPTION CHAPEL
Kaskaskia Island. 1843; rebuilt in 1894. ☎ 618-366-2633 or 618-826-2667

Immaculate Conception began as a mission established by Father Jacques Marquette in 1675 near Starved Rock for the Kaskaskia Indians (see pp. 215–16). It was moved in 1703 to a peninsula about six miles north of the confluence of the Mississippi and Kaskaskia Rivers that became the site of Old Kaskaskia.

The Gothic Revival brick church, erected in 1843 in Old Kaskaskia to replace the mission's small stone church (since destroyed), had to be dismantled and rebuilt on higher ground to protect it from flooding. But even this didn't save it from the 1993 flood that inundated it with over ten feet of water after the river breached forty- and fifty-foot levees. Descendants of families who have cared for the mission for three hundred years repaired the church. Its bell tower with a golden cross atop its spire remains a local landmark.

The church houses many important artifacts. The hand-carved black walnut and cottonwood altar, dated to around 1736, has in its center an altar stone imbedded with a relic that allegedly was brought to the New World from France in the seventeenth century and then carried in a canoe to Kaskaskia by Father Marquette. At the back of the apse hangs an oil painting, *The Immaculata*, installed by Jesuit priests in the early eighteenth century as a symbol of the parish's name. It is a copy of a painting by the Italian artist Guido Reni (1575–1642) that hangs in the Metropolitan Museum of Art in New York City. A carved walnut pulpit and canopy dating to 1860 are to the left of the altar. Local craftsmen did all the woodcarving. The parish's most precious object is "Father Marquette's Chalice." The cup and base are original and have the hallmarks of a Spanish silversmith named Gonzales. The nineteenth-century Jackson Pipe Organ, built in nearby Chester, is one of three surviving Jackson Organs. Constructed of wood, leather, and copper tubing, it was rebuilt after the flood of 1881. It has recently undergone restoration.

Two sites on the east bank of the Mississippi River are closely related to Kaskaskia's history, the Pierre Menard Home and Fort Kaskaskia. They are both located between Chester and Ellis Grove, off SR 3.

The Mount Vernon of the West
PIERRE MENARD HOME
STATE HISTORIC SITE (NHL)
Five miles north of Chester off SR 3. 1800–1802. ☎ 618-859-3031

Pierre Menard, born at St. Antoine-sur-Richelieu near Montreal, Canada, in 1766, built this house known locally as the Mount Vernon of the West. Menard joined a trading expedition to Illinois Country when he was fifteen and became a successful fur trader and entrepreneur. His second wife was Angelique Saucier, granddaughter of François Saucier, the supervisor of construction for the nearby Fort de Chartres (see p. 289). Menard was the state's first lieutenant governor.

His home, built using the *poteaux-sur-solle* (post and sill) technique (see p. 285), is considered the finest example of French colonial architecture in the central Mississippi Valley. Untouched by the 1881 flood, it is the only surviving vestige of Old Kaskaskia.

The house and grounds have been restored to their original appearance. A museum has displays and artifacts related to the area's history.

High on a bluff above the Menard home is Fort Kaskaskia.

Views of a Sunken City
FORT KASKASKIA STATE HISTORIC SITE
Fort Kaskaskia Road. 1759–66. ☎ 618-859-3741

Fearful of being attacked by the British during the French and Indian War, Kaskaskians petitioned the French government for permission to erect a fort on the hill across the Kaskaskia River (see p. 6). The fort stood until 1766, when townspeople destroyed it rather than have it occupied by the British. All that remains are earthworks that supported the heavy logs that formed a palisade wall.

Located high on a magnificent river bluff, the park has many splendid and awesome views of the Kaskaskia and Mississippi Rivers and the site of flooded Kaskaskia. An overlook with a covered picnic pavilion has bronze tablets inscribed with the sonnet "To a Sunken City" and the history of the area, written by a local blind poet, Louis William Rodenburg (1891–1966), the superintendent and printer-in-charge of the Illinois Braille and Sight-Saving School.

Kaskaskia's residents tried heroically to move the bodies from the flooded town's three cemeteries to a new resting place. They selected a quiet hillside just north of Fort Kaskaskia, the Garrison Hill Cemetery, dedicated in 1891 to the "heroes buried here." Simple concrete crosses replace many of the tombstones that were lost in the flood.

Carbondale

It was along the banks of Big Muddy River west of Carbondale that coal mining began in Illinois in about 1810. The city was incorporated in 1856 and is home to Southern Illinois University, founded in 1869, and Woodlawn Cemetery, where the first Memorial Day service was observed.

"Let no . . . ravages of time testify to the present or the coming generations that we have forgotten as a people the cost of a free and undivided republic." —John A. Logan, Commander-in-Chief of the Grand Army of the Republic, May 5, 1868

WOODLAWN CEMETERY (NR)

405 E. Main Street. 1853, Daniel Brush. ☎ 800-526-1500

Right off Main Street, shaded with trees, is a small cemetery designed by the founder of the city, Daniel Brush. Opened in 1853, the cemetery is the final resting place for many Union and Confederate soldiers whose graves were the focus for the nation's first community-wide observance of Memorial Day in 1866. Earlier that year, three Carbondale veterans proposed that the entire community gather on April 29 to clean and decorate the graves of their fallen comrades. General John (Black Jack) A. Logan, a Jackson County native, in an address to the crowd, proclaimed: "Every man's life belongs to his country and no man has a right to refuse when his country calls for it." The success of the observance led to a second ceremony in 1867. The following year, as commander-in-chief of the Grand Army of the Republic, Logan issued G.A.R. General Order Number 11 that decreed on May 30, 1868, and on successive May 30ths, "for as long as survivors of the War of the Rebellion live," people should gather to decorate the soldiers' graves, thus ensuring that Memorial Day would become a traditional national observance.

From Carbondale, go east and north for a loop tour of the Mount Vernon hill country, one of "Egypt's" major coal mining regions. It is here that Coggelshall's observation that this region "displays ethnic diversity within a unified regional identity" (see p. 284) is most evident. Immigrants, who could not express their ethnicity in the design of their homes that were usually built by the mining companies, could do so collectively in their houses of worship. The accents of the people may be southern, but the age-old traditions made visible in their churches reveal their particular ethnic and religious identity.

Upland southerners who survived on subsistence farming and hunting began to establish small homesteads in the region in the 1820s (see p. 12). German immigrants who came to farm or work in the coal mines followed them in the 1850s. Soon outnumbering them were Poles recruited by the Illinois Central Railroad (see p. 24). Towns with names like Radom and Posen, Americanization of the names of Polish cities Radomsko and Poznan, began to appear. As deposits of coal were mined on a larger scale, the demand for workers increased, and more immigrants poured in from eastern and southern Europe. Southern Illinois began to enter a period of tremendous growth and prosperity that in turn led to ethnic and religious tension. The Protestant Upland southerners felt threatened by the newcomers, most of whom were Catholic. The Ku Klux Klan, reborn in the early decades of the twentieth century, began to expand its terror to include "foreigners," particularly Catholic immigrants. One result of the tension was the infamous Herrin Massacre.

Herrin

Herrin is west of I-57 (Exit 59) and north of SR 13 in the heart of coal country. It was already an established town when Catholic immigrants came to work in the coal fields. Shunned by the townspeople, the immigrants settled in their own separate ethnic neighborhoods and formed their own organizations and corporations, and as a result they were accused of being "clannish."

A Cross of Coal
OUR LADY OF MOUNT CARMEL
Catholic. 316 W. Monroe Street. 1925. ☎ 618-942-3114

Hanging over the altar of this beautiful red brick and limestone church is a large cross inlaid with coal mined near Herrin. It represents the one

THE HERRIN MASSACRE, JUNE 22, 1922

Mining in the late nineteenth and early twentieth centuries was a dangerous and often fatal occupation. Efforts to unionize were met with resistance by mine owners and often led to violent confrontations such as the Virden Massacre in 1898 (see pp. 272–73). By the 1920s the thirty thousand men who worked in the mines around Herrin were unionized, but many were dissatisfied with their pay and working conditions. The United Mine Workers of America called a nationwide strike on April 1, 1922, that led to the cessation of coal-mining operations throughout the country. The timing was particularly bad for the owner of the Southern Illinois Coal Company who had just opened a new strip mine near Herrin and was deeply in debt from loans. The union agreed to let him hire union miners to remove coal with the understanding he would not ship it out on rail lines until after the strike. Eager to profit by the strike-induced shortages of coal, he broke the agreement, fired the union miners, and brought in strike-breakers and guards from Chicago to move the coal out. The miners, aware that if his action succeeded other owners would follow, prepared to assault the mine. Anticipating trouble, the owner set up his own fortifications. Trigger-happy, the guards shot and killed three protesting miners on June 21. The next day the strikebreakers became aware that they were outnumbered by angry armed miners and agreed to surrender. Several enraged miners opened fire on the unarmed men, killing at least nineteen and wounding many more. A number of miners were arrested and three trials were held but not one person was ever convicted.

thing all the Catholics in Herrin shared—they were all coal miners. Otherwise they represented an array of national and ethnic groups. If they wanted a place to worship, they would have to set aside their differences, pool their resources, and organize one parish. That is what they did.

Father Bernard Hilgenberg, a German priest from Carbondale, was invited to Herrin in 1898 to celebrate mass. Two years later the impoverished miners raised enough money to purchase land for the construction of a first church that was dedicated in 1901. While the parish was primarily Italian, Father Hilgenberg, a gifted linguist, would preach the sermon in at least three languages each Sunday. Even in the face of overt acts of prejudice and violence, including an arson fire in 1917 that destroyed nearby

Immaculate Conception Church in Carterville, the parish grew and a school, rectory, and convent were built.

The Herrin Massacre of 1922 receives no mention in the parish's published history, but one year after that event fund raising began for the present church, which was dedicated in 1925. Built in the Italian Renaissance style with a square campanile (bell tower) off to one side, Our Lady of Mount Carmel appears to have been transported to "Egypt" directly from the hills of Italy, the homeland of many of its parishioners. The church's barrel-vaulted nave underwent changes in 1963 dictated by Vatican II (see p. 83). The altar was turned to face the congregation and the communion rail was removed. Additional changes in 1977 include a new altar, pulpit, mosaic stations of the cross, baptismal font, and organ. A large nonfigurative wheel window graces the front façade. A large Celtic cross represents the Irish parishioners, who also donated one of the stained-glass windows.

DuBois

Continue north on SR 148, and west in Waltonville to reach DuBois.

Like elsewhere in southern Illinois, the Poles were the last to settle in DuBois and its surrounding area. As their farms flourished, Poles began to replace their log houses with frame structures, complete with statues of the Virgin Mary in their gardens. Their success in the New World is reflected in their monumental church, which stands in stark contrast to its neighbor, the modest **St. Mark's United Church of Christ,** founded by German Protestant pioneers as an Evangelical and Reformed Congregation.

The "Cathedral of the Prairie"
ST. CHARLES BORROMEO CATHOLIC CHURCH
223 S. Third Street. 1908–10, Father Joseph Ceranski; 1968, 1998.
☎ 618-787-2171

Poles organized the parish in 1868. Their first church, built in 1877, was replaced by this monumental building designed by Father (later Monsignor) Joseph Ceranski, who served the parish for sixty-four years. Certain of the parish's continued growth, Ceranski designed a church that would seat at least nine hundred people. While the church's patron saint, St. Charles Borromeo (whose statue is above the entrance), is Italian, the church is proudly Polish, attested to by the Polish inscription above the entrance. The red brick church is decorated with horizontal bands of limestone that emphasize its broad eighty-foot-wide front façade. A lantern on

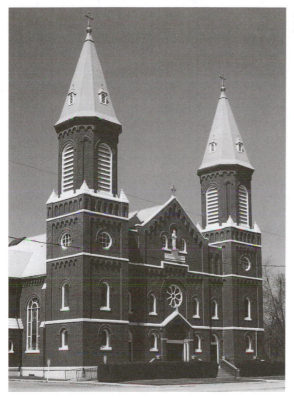

*St. Charles Borromeo,
DuBois*

the roof ridge marks the crossing of its shallow transepts. Visible for miles are its two towers surmounted by 116-foot-high steeples crowned with crosses.

In contrast to the building's rather austere exterior is its beautifully appointed interior. Immediately behind the double doors that open into the broad nave is a large baptismal font that symbolizes entry into the church through the act of baptism. The interior has undergone several renovations, first in 1968 to conform to Vatican II (see p. 83), and again in 1998 when the chancel rail was removed and the altar table placed into the nave. The old altar that holds the tabernacle is now at the rear of the apse. Above it hangs a large crucifix. Cruciform in plan, the church's domed and vaulted ceiling is supported by faux marble columns crowned with capitals decorated with gold leaf. Beautiful stained-glass windows pierce the walls and the upper level of the apse. They include depictions of Polish saints and Polish historical events, including an image of the "Black Madonna," a revered Polish religious and national symbol.

THE BLACK MADONNA

Legend has it that the icon known as the Black Madonna was painted by St. Luke the Evangelist on a piece of cypress wood from the table used by Mary in Nazareth. While painting the image, Mary told him about the life of Jesus, and he incorporated those remembrances into his gospel. The icon was discovered in Jerusalem in 326 C.E. by Queen Helena, who gave it to her son, Emperor Constantine, who in turn built a shrine for it in Constantinople. For a thousand years the fate of the icon was unknown, until 1382 when invading Tartars attacked a fortress where the icon was located. Although damaged by an arrow, it survived and was transferred to a church in Czestochowa, Poland. Known as Our Lady of Czestochowa and considered the Queen and Protector of Poland, the original icon is at the Jasna Gora (Bright Hill) monastery in Czestochowa, where it is visited by millions of pilgrims every year.

Royalton

From DuBois take US 51 back south to Royalton, located east of US 51 on SR 149.

The promise of jobs in the Franklin County Coal Company mine attracted immigrants. Among the last to arrive were Slovakians, who settled in a neighborhood that became known as Russian Row. They were considered outsiders by their neighbors because of their Orthodox faith.

An Orthodox Oasis in "Egypt"
HOLY PROTECTION ORTHODOX CHURCH
112 N. Fairdale. 1914–18. ☎ 618-984-2144

To pay for their church, each family was to contribute $25 at the start of construction and another $25 when work was completed, a considerable sum at the time for miners who labored long hours for little pay. Work began on October 14, 1914, the feast of the Protection of the Theotokos, thus the church's name, and was completed four years later. To hold down costs, the parishioners actually built the church themselves. The building's three-part plan is typical of Byzantine Orthodox churches. Proclaiming its identity are the traditional three-bar Orthodox crosses on its roof. The simple white clapboard exterior of the building is in dramatic contrast to its interior, which is lavishly decorated with stained-glass windows and beautiful traditional Orthodox icons.

In front of the church hall (to the left of the church) is the Bell Memorial Monument, dedicated in memory of the Orthodox Christians who attended the now-closed Saints Peter and Paul Orthodox Church in nearby Dowell. Behind the Mosaic Grotto is the **Cross Monument** commemorating the thirteen Orthodox men who died in the Franklin County Coal Company mine disaster on October 27, 1914.

The Slovakians were in high spirits that day as work progressed on their new church when an earth-shattering explosion rocked the mine, killing fifty-two men, thirteen of them parishioners. One miner miraculously survived, Frank Derbak, a founder of the parish, who from that day forward fasted every day for the rest of his life. The thirteen men were buried on land owned by the mining company that was later given to the parish for use as an Orthodox cemetery. Each year on October 27, a solemn requiem service is celebrated in memory of the dead.

Return to US 51 and a drive south toward Carbondale to Shawnee National Forest.

Illinois' Largest Forest
SHAWNEE NATIONAL FOREST
☎ 800-699-6637

The forest's 270,000 acres, the largest, most diverse natural area in Illinois, lie in an unglaciated area known as the Ozark and Shawnee Hills. Situated between the Ohio and Mississippi Rivers, its landscape stands in stark contrast to the vast farmlands to the north that gave Illinois its nickname, the Prairie State. Only the Coulee Country around Galena (see p. 227) is similarly unglaciated, but it encompasses a much smaller area and is more populated.

Shawnee National Forest was witness to one of the many tragic episodes in Native American history, the *Nunna-da-ul-tsun-yi* (Trail of Tears), the forced march of thousands of Cherokee people during the winter of 1838 and 1839 from southeastern states to reservations in Oklahoma. Their trek is now designated a National Historic Trail; in Illinois it runs through the Shawnee National Forest from the Ohio River to the eastern banks of the Mississippi River (see p. 301).

Sharecroppers from the Upland South cleared the forest and used the wood to build their houses, furniture, and tools. It was a hardscrabble life, and by the 1930s erosion had taken its toll. As people moved on, the government began to acquire the land, replanting trees and designating the area a national forest.

An Ancient Stone Wall on Top of a Cliff
GIANT CITY STATE PARK (NR)
Makanda. ☎ 618-457-4836

South of Carbondale off US 51 is the village of Makanda, the gateway to Giant City State Park. Pioneers from Kentucky and Tennessee thought the park's massive sandstone rock formations separated by canyons looked like the streets of a city built by giants. But it wasn't giants, it was nature that built these enormous sandstone cliffs over two hundred million years ago. Evidence of human habitation dating to 10,000 B.C.E. can be found in rock shelters whose ceilings are blackened by age-old fires. Near the park's entrance is the Stone Fort Trail that leads up to an 80-foot sandstone cliff holding the remains of a 285-foot-long stone wall dating back from 600 to 800 C.E. It is uncertain whether the wall served as part of a fort or was used as an impoundment in which deer and bison were herded and later killed for food.

By the 1850s, much of the area's native vegetation had been replaced by fruit trees cultivated by the first white settlers. Many fled during the Civil War, when the cliffs and canyons became hiding places for soldiers from both sides. Scientists and tourists, intrigued by the area's unusual geology and its wide variety of plant and animal life, found the area to be a peaceful place to study and relax; it then became a state park.

A Postman with a Dream
BALD KNOB CROSS
Four miles outside of Alto Pass, off SR 127. Dedicated in 1963, Victor J. Kunz. ☎ 618-893-2344

Wayman Presley, a son of sharecroppers, was a postman with a dream. He wanted to erect a giant cross atop Bald Knob Mountain as a symbol of peace where Easter sunrise services could be held. The first Easter service held at the site in 1937 was such a success that Presley knew the cross had to be built. After twenty-six years of creative fund raising, including a project known as "the Pig Program," which raised hogs for the cross, Presley's dream became a reality. At its dedication, he proclaimed that the cross was to be ". . . our guiding light and banner while we pray, work and even fight, if necessary, for peace."

The cross is 111 feet tall, 22 feet square at the base, and 16 feet square at the top; its arms extend out 63 feet. Designed by Victor J. Kunz of St. Louis, it is covered with reinforced white porcelain steel panels and stands on a base of Illinois marble. It is lit with forty 1,000-watt bulbs that can be seen over an estimated area of 7,500 square miles. As impressive as the cross are the views of the Shawnee National Forest from atop Bald Knob Mountain.

A Shameful Event in Our Nation's History
TRAIL OF TEARS STATE FOREST
South of Bald Knob Mountain off SR 127. ☎ 618-833-4910

Native Americans once lived in this rugged area but were pushed out by settlers moving west. They returned involuntarily in 1838 and '39, when it became the winter camp for thousands of Cherokee Indians forced by the United States Army to move from their homes in the Great Smokies to reservations in Oklahoma Territory. The roundup of between fifteen thousand and seventeen thousand Cherokee began in May 1838, but due to bad weather and illness, the eight-hundred-mile trek west was delayed until October. Famished and ill equipped, they had to trek across Tennessee, Kentucky, and through the treacherous Shawnee Forest region of Illinois to reach the Mississippi River near Jonesboro (see p. 303) in November. Ice floes prevented them from crossing the river, and they were forced to winter over in makeshift camps two miles south of today's state forest. The winter was unusually harsh, and starvation claimed perhaps as many as four thousand lives. The march was memorialized in 1978 when Union State Forest was renamed Trail of Tears State Forest.

Limestone cliffs, clear streams, stands of old trees, and beautiful wildflowers make the forest a place of beauty where one might almost forget the tragic events that happened nearby. Hiking trails range from moderately difficult to difficult, including a trail that runs through the 222-acre **Ozark Hills Nature Preserve,** which remains much as it was before the arrival of Europeans.

South of Alto Pass and east of SR 127 is farmland that was settled between 1803 and 1850 by pioneers of German descent, mainly Lutheran and Reformed (Calvinistic) Protestants. On their heels came Germans fleeing the 1848 revolution in their homeland who preferred to establish their own communities, such as Kornthal (see p. 303). For those who were believers, one of their first acts was to organize a congregation and build a church. Since their numbers were few and money was scarce, alliances had to be made. As a result, many of the early Protestant congregations in the area were a union of Lutheran and Reformed Germans, who would share pastors and the same building until they could afford to go their separate ways. Three pioneer churches survive: St. John's Evangelical Church outside of Dongola (see pp. 304–5), the Kornthal Church south of Jonesboro (see p. 303), and Campground Cumberland Presbyterian Church near Anna.

Anna

A Place to Rest
CAMPGROUND CUMBERLAND PRESBYTERIAN CHURCH

Near Anna. 1907. ☎ 618-833-8216. Located off I-57 (Exit 30) south of the Trail of Tears State Forest.

Campground Church is on the trail that led from the Ohio River to the Mississippi River near where it intersects with the trail running north from Fort Massac (see p. 308). The church is set on a knoll to escape being flooded during high water. Travelers would pause here to rest before continuing their trek north or west, and it was near here that three thousand Cherokee Indians camped during their Trail of Tears (see p. 301). Some are buried in an adjacent cemetery.

The Cumberland Presbyterians who formed the congregation were Upland southerners from North Carolina and Tennessee. According to one historian, the congregation chose the name "Cumberland" for its church because they had passed through the Cumberland Gap in Maryland on their way to southern Illinois. Another explanation is that they were Presbyterians who had broken away from the Kentucky Synod of the Presbyterian Church in the U.S.A. in 1810 (see p. 52).

The congregation, organized in 1847, worshiped in a brush arbor before a small shed was erected that also served as a schoolhouse. It was replaced by a log building that was in use until a two-story frame church was built in 1882. Initially named the Union Church (because it was shared with a Lutheran congregation), the building was totally destroyed by fire in 1906; only the organ miraculously survived. The white clapboard Gothic Revival church capped with a three-stage entry tower and steeple was dedicated the next year. Sunday school rooms were added in 1980 and the sanctuary was remodeled in 1982.

Jonesboro

··

A Church Built in the "Valley of Grain"
KORNTHAL CHURCH (ST. PAUL'S
EVANGELICAL LUTHERAN CHURCH [NR])
Kornthal Church Road. 1861, Charles Theodore Fettinger.
☎ 618-833-2689. Drive through Jonesboro and continue two and one-half miles south to Kornthal. Take a right on Old Cape Road and then a left on Kornthal Church Road.

A group of Austrian Lutherans who arrived at the Port of New Orleans in 1852 traveled by flatboat up the Mississippi River to Illinois, landing near Ware. They then began a trek eastward in search of fertile land before finally settling in a valley they called Kornthal, "valley of grain." They were fleeing religious persecution in Catholic-dominated Austria where, among other practices, restrictions were placed on the appearance of their churches. They had to be modest in size, could not have bell towers or spires, and their entrances could not open onto the street. Upon settling in Kornthal, the immigrants built a *betsaal* (house of prayer) in 1853, designed by one of its members, Charles Theodore Fettinger that, ironically or intentionally, conformed to those restrictions. The small frame rectangular church had a door in the center of each long wall that did not open onto the main street. One door was for women, the other for men; the sexes were also separated on the inside. There was no steeple or bell tower. A surprising bequest was made to the church in 1889 when a widow willed her estate to the congregation for the purpose of purchasing a bell. Her request suggests that the congregation now felt secure enough in the New World to erect a handsome bell tower. Rising from ground level to a height of eighty-five feet at the top of the spire, the tower not only housed an eight-hundred-pound bell, it also provided a gable-end entrance into the church from the main street.

The dominating features on the interior are its U-shaped balcony, altar, and elevated pulpit. Fettinger is credited with designing and executing the beautiful carved wood decorations found throughout the sanctuary. Three steps lead up to the altar that is decorated with a line in German script: "Halte Im Gedaechtnis Jesum Christum," (Keep Jesus Christ in Memory). Twelve steps on the side of the altar, symbolic of the apostles, lead up to the high pulpit that is at the same level as the balcony; it is embellished with panels, pilasters, and moldings and capped by a beautifully carved wooden canopy. According to a local legend, if one of the steps collapses, then that step is the one that symbolizes Judas Iscariot.

A decline in the rural population led to a drop in church membership, and services were discontinued in 1949. The state of Illinois acquired the property in 1960, repaired it, and gave it to the Kornthal Union County Memorial, Incorporated. It is now open to the public and has periodic services and weddings.

NEARBY

➥ **Lincoln Memorial Picnic Grounds,** Main Street north of the Public Square, Jonesboro.

A plaque set on a large boulder commemorates the Lincoln-Douglas Debate held here on September 15, 1858. The crowd, estimated at about fifteen hundred people, was the smallest for any of the debates. According to one observer, "The people showed some interest, but there was a lack of enthusiasm." Southern Democrats did not support Stephen Douglas; furthermore, Lincoln's famous "House Divided" speech (p. 19) had made him intensely unpopular in "Egypt." In an attempt to appeal to the hostile crowd, Lincoln argued, "I was raised just a little east of here. I am a part of this people." But he wasn't, and the crowd knew it.

Dongola

The Oldest Lutheran Congregation in Illinois
ST. JOHN'S EVANGELICAL LUTHERAN CHURCH
St. John's Road. 1856, 1888, 1976. ☎ 618-827-3810 or 618-995-2882

St. John's Evangelical Lutheran Church is located south of Jonesboro, near the village of Dongola. Drive through the Dongola "downtown" area and turn right at the end of a parking lot onto St. John's Road. Follow the hilly, curving road for about four miles to the church and cemetery.

On a hill outside of Dongala is a small white clapboard Lutheran church with Greek Revival details whose modest appearance belies its historical importance. It is Illinois' oldest Lutheran congregation. (St. Paul's in Hillsboro is the oldest Lutheran congregation that still has a weekly prayer service; see pp. 273–74.) In 1816, a group of German Lutherans from North Carolina traveled to Illinois Territory to establish a community and a congregation. They held prayer meetings in their homes and barns until about 1823, when they joined with a Reformed congregation to erect a small church.

The two congregations built a second church in 1856 that was extensively remodeled and rededicated in 1888. Further renovations made in

1976 include the placement of a bell in its tower that came from the closed Mill Creek Lutheran Church nearby.

The cemetery dates back to the founding of the congregation. In it is a grove of large spruce trees that marks the site of the first church. The pioneers brought the seeds from North Carolina and planted them here as a reminder of the home they had left behind.

Cairo

The only two characteristics that Cairo, Illinois, and its namesake in Egypt share are their river locations and a propensity for their rivers to periodically flood. Their name is not even pronounced the same; in Illinois it is "Kayrow."

Magnolia trees still bloom along the boulevard once known as Millionaire's Row, but Cairo, once a rival to Chicago, is now a sleepy little town of less than five thousand people. According to the National Register of Historic Places, "Cairo . . . remains to this day the history of promise unfulfilled." The city once echoed with the sounds of train and steamboat whistles, the tramping boots of soldiers, and the bustle of social and commercial activity. Now storefronts are empty and once beautiful homes are decaying; all is quiet except for the occasional sound of barges and towboats that still glide along the rivers.

Strategically located on the tip of a peninsula at the confluence of the Mississippi and Ohio Rivers, the area was first visited by French explorers and missionaries in the late seventeenth century, but its humid weather, frequent flooding, and malaria-carrying mosquitoes made it unattractive for permanent settlement. Easterners who recognized the area's potential as a river port began to arrive in the 1830s. They built costly levees so the city could develop, and once completed, Cairo began to grow. It was incorporated in 1855, the same year the Illinois Central Railroad linked river traffic with the railroad to open a commercial link between Cairo and Chicago. Within a year Cairo's port was shipping millions of tons of cotton and wool to northern mills, as well as thousands of barrels of molasses and hogsheads of sugar.

Union and Confederate leaders were quick to recognize Cairo's strategic location. Home to many southern sympathizers and in control of access to major waterways and railroads, Cairo was immediately fortified by Union soldiers, who transformed it into what the *New York Times* called the Gibraltar of the West. The city became a military outpost complete with a parade ground, barracks, and the usual bawdy houses and saloons. Fort Defiance (originally named Fort Prentiss after a Mexican War hero) was built at Cairo Point, a flat-topped mound that was subject to constant flooding (see p. 307). It was from this fort that General Ulysses S. Grant launched his invasion of the South in 1862. Over the course of the war, millions of soldiers passed through Cairo: Union soldiers going to battle and Confederate soldiers heading to prisoner-of-war camps further north. Many did not get further than Mound City National Cemetery, four miles north of town, which houses the graves of over five thousand Union and Confederate soldiers (see p. 307).

Cairo continued to prosper in the years immediately following the war. Lavish homes, opera houses, theaters, and churches catering to the wealthy and saloons and gambling casinos along the wharf contributed to Cairo's reputation as a curious mixture of violence and gentility. And then it collapsed. The transcontinental railroad that bypassed the city began to carry increasing amounts of freight and passengers that resulted in a decline in river traffic. Chicago became the region's major market and industrial center, and Cairo, after having experienced phenomenal growth, went into an equally phenomenal decline.

A Bit of the Glory That Once Was Cairo
MAGNOLIA MANOR (NR)
2700 Washington Avenue. 1869. ☎ 618-734-0201

This magnificent Italianate mansion symbolizes Cairo's glorious past, when great wealth was displayed in the homes built along "Millionaire's Row." All that is left is this fourteen-room estate that was built for Charles Galigher, a friend of General Grant, who made his fortune supplying flour to the Union armies. Decorated with many of its original furnishings, the house echoes with memories of Cairo's brief moment of glory.

NEARBY

➡ **St. Patrick Catholic Church,** 9th and Washington, 1894.
☎ 618-734-2061

This stone Romanesque-style church was built in 1894 for Cairo's oldest congregation, founded in 1838.

➡ **Church of the Redeemer Episcopal Church,** Sixth and Washington, 1886. ☎ 618-734-1819

A congregation organized in 1840 erected this stone Gothic Revival church. It houses a solid silver bell allegedly cast from a thousand silver dollars. It was on the steamboat *James Montgomery*, which was used to transport Civil War troops. When the ship sank in 1861, the ship's captain salvaged the bell and gave it to the church.

At the Confluence of Two Great Rivers
FORT DEFIANCE PARK (NR)
Immediately south of Cairo on US 51. ☎ 618-776-5281

Fort Defiance was the command post for General Grant during the Civil War. The rivers' course has changed and the peninsula's point has extended southward over a mile from the fort's original site at the confluence of the Mississippi and Ohio Rivers. Damage caused by frequent flooding finally contributed to the fort's abandonment. It became what the *Chicago Tribune* once described as "probably the ugliest park in America, the park no one wants." In response, the citizens of Cairo leased the park from the state and renovated it.

The Boatmen's Memorial, a concrete building that is supposed to look like a boat, is dedicated to those who lost their lives on the river. You can observe the confluence of the two rivers from its decks. Their magnitude and power are visible as they meet but refuse to merge. The Ohio is a strand of blue in the midst of the mighty, muddy Mississippi.

"The muffled drum's sad roll has beat the soldier's last tattoo.
No more on life's parade shall meet that brave and fallen few."
MOUND CITY NATIONAL CEMETERY
Four miles north of Cairo.

The quote is from "Bivouac of the Dead" by Theodore O'Hara (1820–67), written in memory of the Kentucky troops killed in the Battle of Buena Vista in 1847 during the Mexican War. It appears on stones that line the cemetery's pathways. The bodies of over five thousand Confederate and Union soldiers are buried here, joined together in death. Poignantly, the vast majority of Confederate tombstones carry the simple inscription, "unknown" (except for one that reads "Confederate Spy").

East of SR 37 begins southeastern Illinois, a sparsely populated area that includes broad swatches of the Shawnee National Forest. Many sites are along the **Ohio River Scenic Byway,** which begins at Fort Defiance and follows the river north to the confluence with the Wabash River. It crosses the Wabash Memorial Bridge north of Shawneetown in Gallatin County and enters Indiana. As quiet as the land appears, it has been witness to many important historical events.

Illinois' First State Park: "A captivating reminder of days gone by. . . ."
FORT MASSAC STATE PARK (NR)
Southeast of Metropolis on US 45. ☎ 618-524-9321

The Daughters of the American Revolution (DAR) are responsible for having saved this site. It is Illinois' oldest state park.

The French built a fort here in 1757 that they abandoned at the end of the French and Indian War. The British changed its name to Massac, but did not rebuild it. They came to regret this when Colonel George Rogers Clark and his "long knives" (see p. 7) crossed into Illinois and camped at the site before continuing north to capture Kaskaskia (see p. 289). A statue of Clark commemorates the event.

President Washington ordered the fort to be rebuilt in 1794, but after being damaged in a series of earthquakes known as New Madrid Earthquake of 1811 and 1812, it was dismantled. It served briefly as a training camp during the Civil War until it was abandoned in 1862, not because of the war, but because of a measles epidemic that claimed many soldiers' lives.

The park has replicas of the 1757 and 1794 timber forts, and a museum. Several hiking trails loop through the park, including the 2.5-mile Hickory Nut Ridge Trail that takes you along the scenic Ohio River.

Golconda

The Ohio River Scenic Byway continues east along CR 6 and CR 4 toward New Liberty and then turns north on CR 1 toward Golconda, situated on the banks of the Ohio River. Its first settlers were Major James Lusk, a Revolutionary War veteran, and his wife, Sarah. Lusk operated a ferry across the Ohio River until his death in 1803. Sarah continued the ferry service and in 1805 married Thomas Ferguson, who had acquired land from the government for a new town. He donated the ground for the county's courthouse with the understanding that the new town was to be named Sarahsville in honor of his wife. Soon after he acquired title to the land he sold it and the town's name was changed to Golconda. A plaque set in a large boulder on the grounds of the 1872 Pope County Courthouse commemorates Sarah Lusk as "the brave pioneer woman who founded Golconda." Almost the entire village is on the National Register of Historic Sites.

A Historic Presbyterian Congregation
FIRST PRESBYTERIAN CHURCH
189 Main Street. 1869. ☎ 618-683-3383

The congregation was founded in 1819 by sixteen people under the leadership of Nathan B. Errow, a Presbyterian missionary from Connecticut. It is the oldest Presbyterian congregation in continuous service in the state of Illinois.

The two-story brick structure with a tall bell tower has survived a flood in 1937, several high windstorms, and a fire in 1967. An exterior staircase leads to the second-floor sanctuary, which is bathed in light filtering through ten stained-glass windows. Above its entrance is an inscription that reads: "The master is here and calls for you." Today the church has thirty-three members who are called to worship by the ringing of a century-old bell purchased from a defunct female seminary.

The Oldest Church Building in Golconda
OUR REDEEMER LUTHERAN CHURCH
Madison and Franklin Streets. 1867. ☎ 618-683-8621

Situated on the rise of a hill is a little white clapboard church organized in 1865 by German immigrants who named it St. Peter's Evangelical Lutheran Church. It was later renamed Our Redeemer Lutheran Church and affiliated with the Lutheran Church-Missouri Synod. The building has been remodeled over the years but still retains many of its original features, including a bell that was cast in Germany. A lovely stained-glass window depicting the gospel-inspired image of Christ with the children was added over the altar in 1925, and all the original clear-glass windows were replaced with stained-glass in 1960.

NEARBY

➡ **English United Methodist Church,** Northwest corner of Washington and Market Streets. ☎ 618-683-4061

This brick church was erected in 1886 to serve English-speaking Methodists. (A German Methodist church was erected in 1897 in Sloan's Addition, a Golconda neighborhood, and was sold in 1912 for use as a private residence.) It was partially destroyed by a fire in 1897, but was immediately rebuilt in its original form.

The Site of a Good Soak
DIXON SPRINGS STATE PARK
Near the crossroads of SR 146 and SR 145.
☎ 618-949-3304 or 618-949-3394

The Shawnee and Algonquin Indians, aware of the springs' healing effects, called them *Kitch-mus-ke-nee-be*, "Great Medicine Waters." White settlers, including William Dixon, who built a home here in about 1848, transformed the area into a popular health spa. Although it is no longer a resort, visitors can still swim in the park's outdoor pool or simply enjoy its pleasant surroundings. Follow Park Drive and the signs saying "church" to a cul-de-sac where three small white clapboard churches are nestled. The **Dixon Spring Independent Methodist Church,** erected in 1913 for a congregation that was established in 1856, remains in use, its bell tolling every hour. The other two churches are not in use.

A Place of Beauty, Quiet, and Calmness
SAN DAMIANO RETREAT CENTER AND SHRINE
Opened in 1992. ☎ 618-285-3507

Ten miles from Golconda and two miles south of the intersection of SR 146 and SR 34, San Damiano is operated as a not-for-profit facility by the Catholic Shrine Pilgrimage and is open to people of all faiths. Covering two hundred acres on the bluffs of the Ohio River and surrounded by the Shawnee National Forest, San Damiano is on the site of one of the state's oldest towns, Shetlerville. The only remnant of the village is the old restored **Civil War Cemetery,** containing the graves of fifty Union and Confederate soldiers. San Damiano's buildings, all constructed in the style of Italian Umbrian and Tuscan architecture, include a visitors' center with a dining room, a conference building with a chapel and theater, and guest cottages overlooking the river. There are hiking trails along the river bluffs, and walkways lead to the XXIII Psalm Granite Monolith and Prayer Garden, the Saint Francis Shrine and meditation area, and the Shrine of the Good Shepherd. The latter is a 35-foot cast-bronze statue of Jesus as the Good Shepherd that stands on a 225-foot limestone bluff above the river.

One of the Best Preserved Prehistoric Settlements in the Midwest
MILLSTONE BLUFF ARCHAEOLOGICAL AREA (NR)
One mile west of the intersection of SRs 145 and 147, on SR 147.

Millstone Bluff is considered one of the most important archaeological sites in the Midwest. Here are the remains of a prehistoric settlement that was first occupied in approximately 500 C.E. by Woodland Indians. Five hundred years later, a permanent settlement was established and later was abandoned at about the same time as Cahokia (see pp. 282–83). Evidence of dwellings, a stone wall, and petroglyphs carved into the bluff survive. Centuries later settlers began to quarry the area's large boulders for millstones, thus the site's name. A half-mile path leads up to the bluff, which offers spectacular views of the forest and evidence of a nearly lost past.

Cave-in-Rock

Located on the north bank of the Ohio River, the village of Cave-in-Rock was settled in the early nineteenth century but wasn't incorporated until 1901. The village operates the only ferry service on the Ohio River.

A Pirate's Lair
CAVE-IN-ROCK STATE PARK (NR)
Located a half mile north of town. ☎ 618-289-4325 or 618-289-4545

The park is named for a fifty-five-foot-wide cavern overlooking the Ohio River that once was a shelter for Native Americans. French explorers visited the site in 1729, but it gained notoriety following the Revolutionary War when it became a hiding place for river pirates who preyed on travelers on the Ohio River. One of the most infamous was Samuel Mason, a "Kentucky long knife" who had fought with General George Rogers Clark (see p. 7) and then decided to stick around and terrorize settlers. Pirating finally ended in 1834, and the cave became a rest stop for pioneers moving west.

Equality

The town of Equality, at the crossroads of SRs 13 and 142, derives its name from the motto of the French Revolution, "Liberty, Equality and Fraternity." However, this name is sadly ironic. Nearby are saline springs that were a source of salt for Native Americans and the French before it became Illinois' first industry. Its success was dependent upon slave laborers, many of whom were freedmen or escaped slaves that were kidnapped by slave hunters and transported to the salt works via a perverse "reverse underground railroad." The importance of salt to early pioneers cannot be overemphasized; among its many uses were the preservation of food and as a component for tanning hides. The need for cheap labor to produce salt was one of the factors that almost led Illinois to enter the Union as a slave state.

About one and a half miles east of Equality is the **Hickory Hill Plantation** (🖥️ www.illinoishistory.com/oshpage.html), a house that is on the National Register and has been recently acquired by the Illinois Preservation Agency; it is not yet open to the public. John Hart Crenshaw, the "Salt King of Southern Illinois" and a wealthy and influential businessman, built the house between 1834 and 1838. Recent scholarship suggests that he was involved in the illegal kidnapping of free blacks for the purpose of selling them back into slavery to work in the salt mines. Allegedly the slaves were kept shackled and imprisoned in cells on the third floor of his house, while white visitors (possibly including Abraham Lincoln) dined and danced in the ballroom on the second floor.

Lake View

Lake View is west of Equality and south of Carrier Mills, off US-45. Known at first as "the Pond Settlement" due to its many bogs, it was later renamed Lake View by its settlers after the bogs were drained for farmland. Following the War of 1812, four African American families began a dangerous journey. Leaving North Carolina in ox-drawn wagons, they crossed over the Ohio River at Shawneetown and headed west to settle on land along the northern edge of the Shawnee Hills. By 1830 there were twenty-four people in the community. Lake View is actually a group of farmsteads in a two-square-mile area. It has its own distinct identity and currently is home to fifty people, all descendants of the original pioneers.

It is remarkable that this community could exist during a time when slave hunters were swarming through the area kidnapping blacks and selling them back into slavery. When asked how Lake View was able to survive under those conditions, a descendant of one of the founders responded: "A few slave hunters came. They never got out."

The Hub of a Community
MT. ZION BAPTIST CHURCH
Taborn Road (Route 2). 1869. ☎ 618-994-2589

One of the oldest black churches in the nation, this white clapboard church serves as Lake View's religious and social hub. Zachariah Taborn, one of the community's founders, donated the land for the church and cemetery. A book published in 1976 by Russell Cofield, *Memories of Lake View,* inspired three sisters who are descendants of Taborn's to spearhead an effort to preserve the church and cemetery. Lucille Mooreland, who lives in Detroit, led the successful effort to have Saline County erect a Settlers Monument in front of the church. Dedicated on Memorial Day in 1992, the nine-foot-high pylon commemorates the thirty-three families who settled in Lake View from 1820 to 1920 and honors the memory of its young men who died while serving in the military. Another sister, Artie Lenora Chachere, who lives in Los Angeles, lobbied to

Monument for settlers in unmarked graves, Mt. Zion Baptist Church, Lake View

have the town's main thoroughfare, Route 2, named Taborn Road after Zachariah Taborn. The third sister, Lina Witherspoon, still lives in Lake View and is the community's historian. She, along with her husband, Sam, tends to the upkeep of the church and cemetery.

The cemetery is entered through a beautiful brick and wrought-iron gateway that was dedicated in 1992. Sadly, two years later, looters stole over four hundred of the cemetery's tombstones. Although a reward was offered, the culprits were never found. A large, granite cross has been erected in the cemetery to honor those who now lie in unmarked graves; it is inscribed: "Lest we forget."

The First Presbyterian Church in Illinois
OLD SHARON PRESBYTERIAN CHURCH
Near Norris City on RR 1. 1864. ☎ 618-265-3258

Founded in 1815 by settlers from Kentucky, including the father of Abraham Lincoln's first love, Ann Rutledge, this was the first Presbyterian church established in the Illinois Territory. Its members worshiped in a series of log buildings until they were able to erect a church in 1864; the adjoining cemetery was dedicated at the same time. The church remained in use until the congregation was dissolved in 1896. For years it stood derelict until descendants of the founders restored it. The church is now used for revival meetings and Memorial Day services.

The building appears much as it did when well-known pastors, such as Benjamin R. Spilman, the founder of a number of Presbyterian churches in the region and the brother of Jonathon Spilman, the composer of "Flow Gently, Sweet Afton," preached from its pulpit. A simple white clapboard building, it has a small raised lectern set against the short wall opposite its entrance and an old upright piano in one corner. A big pot-bellied stove in the center of the hall is still in use.

CHAPTER EIGHT

·············· ❀ ··············

$\mathcal{E}$ast-Central Illinois

The "Grand Prairie" was described by one of the founders of Dwight as "a sight to behold with all the reds, purples, pinks . . . of the wildflowers . . . and with prairie grass over sixteen feet tall." Within a century the prairie was tilled and three major urban centers were established: Decatur, Bloomington-Normal, and Champaign-Urbana. The region stretches from SR 17 south to US 50; US 51 is to the west and the Indiana border on the east.

US 40, which follows the path of the National Road, or "Cumberland Road," authorized by Thomas Jefferson in 1806, crosses the region at a diagonal from Terre Haute, Indiana, to the state's second capital, Vandalia (see pp. 274–75). Among the many pioneers who trekked west along this route were Thomas and Sarah Lincoln and their family in 1830. Abraham Lincoln's father and stepmother farmed near Charleston and are buried at Shiloh Cemetery.

To reach the Lincoln Log Cabin and Shiloh Cemetery, take US 40 or I-70 west from Marshall to Exit 119 at Greenup and go north on SR 121 and right on Lincoln Highway Road.

Pioneer Life at Goosenest Prairie Farm in 1845
LINCOLN LOG CABIN STATE HISTORIC SITE
Lincoln Highway Road. ☎ 217-345-6489 🖳 www.lincolnlogcabin.org
The site is a living-history farm where first-person interpreters perform the chores and answer questions relating to life on the prairie in 1845. Adjoining Lincoln's farm is the restored farm of his neighbor, Stephen Sargent.

In 1830, traveling in wagons pulled by oxen, Thomas and Sarah Lincoln, Thomas's son from a previous marriage, Abraham, and Sarah's two daughters and sons-in-law left the National Road near the Lincoln Trail State Park (see below) to head northwest toward Decatur in Macon County, where they erected a log cabin (see pp. 319–20). Their first year in Illinois was a disaster. Cold weather and disease forced them to abandon their homestead and begin the long trek back to their old homestead in Indiana. On the way they stopped in Coles County to visit family members who convinced Thomas to stay and try farming there. Meanwhile Abraham, together with his stepbrother, John D. Johnston, and John Hanks, hired themselves out to take a flatboat from Beardstown, Illinois, to New Orleans. Later, Lincoln settled in Decatur, where he became a circuit-riding lawyer and entered politics. With the financial help of his son Abraham, Thomas was able to purchase eighty acres of land near the town of Charleston.

Thomas Lincoln built a barn, smokehouse, and a two-room cabin that in 1845 housed as many as eighteen people, but life was difficult and he died in 1851. Sarah continued to live on the farm with her grandson, John J. Hall, until she died in 1869. John stayed on until 1892, when the cabin was dismantled and sent to Chicago for display at the 1893 World's Columbian Exposition. Inexplicably, it disappeared following the close of the Exposition. By the time the state of Illinois acquired the Lincoln farm in 1929, all of its original buildings were gone. The Civilian Conservation Corps reconstructed an accurate replica of the cabin on its original site in 1935; all the other farm buildings were either moved from elsewhere or were built by staff and volunteers.

Like many Upland southerners, Thomas Lincoln was suspicious of new-fangled gadgets (like steel plows) and barely survived as a subsistence farmer. In contrast, his neighbor, Stephen Sargent, an ambitious and successful Yankee farmer from New Hampshire, utilized all available modern technology to farm his four hundred acres and care for his six hundred head of livestock.

NEARBY
➥ **Shiloh Cemetery (Thomas Lincoln Cemetery),** off of S. Lincoln Highway Road. ☎ 217-345-1845

At the entrance to Shiloh Cemetery stands the **Shiloh Presbyterian Church,** built in 1921. A stained-glass window on the south side of the church's nave has an image of the original Lincoln cabin. The cemetery is the final resting place of Thomas and Sarah Lincoln, father and stepmother of Abraham Lincoln. Their original tombstone and a new monument mark the site of their graves.

A grove of Cedar trees mark the common grave of over thirty victims of cholera who died between 1840 and 1851. A monument was erected in their memory in 1984. The dreaded disease was introduced into the area by troops brought in to fight in the Black Hawk War in 1832 (see p. 15). Ironically, more settlers in Illinois died from cholera than at the hands of Native Americans.

➡ **Reuben Moore Home State Historic Site,** 400 S. Lincoln Highway Road. ☎ 217-345-1845

One mile north of Lincoln Log Cabin Historic Site is the home of Reuben and Matilda Hall Moore. Matilda was one of Sarah Lincoln's daughters. Moore purchased this small frame house in the now abandoned village of Farmington in 1856. It has been restored to its original appearance and is intended to represent the living conditions of a middle-class family after the Civil War. Sarah was staying with her daughter when her stepson, President-elect Lincoln, stopped by the house in January 1861 for a dinner in his honor before visiting the grave of his father in Shiloh Cemetery.

➡ **Lincoln Trail State Park,** 16985 E. 1350th Road, near US 40 and Marshall. ☎ 217-826-2222
🖳 www.netins.net/web/creative/lincoln/sites/decaturock.htm

The American Beech Woods Nature Preserve within the park is a virtually untouched forest that allows visitors to experience what the wooded areas of the prairie were like when the Lincoln family passed through here in 1830.

Charleston

A series of historic outdoor murals account for Charleston's nickname, City of Murals. Charleston began to prosper in the 1840s as pioneers came in response to advertisements placed in eastern newspapers that promised fertile farmland and riches to those willing to work. Charleston was the site of the fourth Lincoln-Douglas Debate.

A Day of Infamy in Charleston
COLES COUNTY COURTHOUSE
Courthouse Square, Monroe and 7th Street, Charleston. 1898; remodeled 1951. ☎ 217-348-0430

The Richardsonian Romanesque courthouse presides over the heart of Charleston, but at its heart is darkness, for it harbors memories of an infamous moment in history. The city linked to the Lincolns is also the location of the infamous Charleston Riot that occurred in March 1864. A historical marker on the southeast corner of the courthouse's lawn recounts how over three hundred Union soldiers and citizens who favored the Lincoln administration fought local southern sympathizers over a speech to be given by a Democratic congressman who was going to urge the country to reunite. Six soldiers and three civilians were killed in the riot, one of the most disastrous encounters that ever occurred between soldiers and civilians in the North during the Civil War. A mural located one block west of the courthouse at the corner of 6th and Jackson Streets illustrates this infamous event.

NEARBY
➥ **Coles County Lincoln-Douglas Debate Museum,** 416 W. Madison Avenue, Charleston. ☎ 217-348-0430

The debate took place on the Coles County Fairgrounds. The museum is the only one in Illinois that retraces the history of the famed 1858 senatorial debates. Outside the museum is a life-size bronze sculpture of Lincoln titled *A House Divided*, named for one of Lincoln's most famous speeches (see p. 19).

Amish Towns in Douglas County

From Charleston take SR 16 west, then I-57 north and take Exit 203 at Arcola to visit Amish towns in Douglas County, where tourism is a multi-million-dollar industry. (For a history of the Amish, see pp. 39–40.) It began about forty years ago when Elvan Yoder, an Amish farmer (who later became a Mennonite), bought Rockome gardens, a private flower and rock garden near Arcola and opened it to visitors. The gardens did not have an Amish theme until Yoder decided to furnish a house on the grounds in an Amish fashion. Over the years other attractions were added, causing an Amish bishop to wish "the attraction was out in the middle of the Atlantic Ocean."

While the Amish recognize that tourism brings work into the community at a time when agricultural prices are dropping, many still lament that they "feel like exhibits in a zoo." Another downside is that "as more people come in to observe the Amish way of life, they are—in a way—changing it."

As you travel through this area please be respectful of your hosts: Drive slowly because of their buggies and honor their request not to be photographed. There are no Amish churches; they conduct religious services in their homes (see p. 40).

The First Museum Dedicated to the Old Order Amish of Central Illinois
ILLINOIS AMISH INTERPRETIVE CENTER

111 S. Locust Street, Arcola. ☎ 217-268-3599 or 888-45AMISH
🖥 www.amishcenter.com (Note: A second center with similar exhibits and schedule is located at 139 S. Vine Street, Arthur, nine miles west.)

The center's purpose is "to provide visitors with accurate and sympathetic information about the Amish faith and way of life." An introductory video and exhibits depict various aspects of Amish and Mennonite history, art, and culture. The center also offers a paid guided tour of the Amish countryside, a meal in an Amish home, and tours of Amish homes and farms.

The Lincoln Family's First Home in Illinois
LINCOLN TRAIL HOMESTEAD STATE MEMORIAL PARK

Take SR 36 west from Decatur for ten miles to Lincoln Trail Memorial Parkway; turn south and go four miles. ☎ 217-864-3121

The Lincoln family left Indiana on March 1, 1830, and arrived in Macon County later that same month. Abraham Lincoln recalled that they built a log cabin on the north side of the Sangamon River "at the juncture of timberland and prairie about ten miles west from Decatur." The cabin disappeared years ago, but a bronze plaque on a large boulder on the park road marks its site overlooking the Sangamon River, which flows down to Springfield. The 162-acre park has hiking trails and picnic facilities.

Decatur

Since its founding in 1829 as the seat of Macon County, Decatur has been called the Pride of the Prairie, the commercial and cultural hub for central Illinois. It later became the "Soybean Capital of the World" thanks to a new industry that began to develop there following A. E. Staley's success in processing soybeans. Contributing to the city's growth and prosperity was the arrival of the Great Western Railroad in 1854.

After his family departed for Coles County, Abraham Lincoln moved to Decatur, where he became a circuit-riding lawyer and launched his political career. It was in Decatur that Lincoln was given the nickname the Railsplitter, and it was at the Illinois Republican Convention held there in 1860 that he received his first formal presidential endorsement. Decatur made another important contribution to American culture: George Halas and his team the Decatur Staleys were charter members of the National Football League when it was formed in 1919. The team later moved to Chicago and changed its name to the Chicago Bears.

A Living-History Museum
MACON COUNTY MUSEUM COMPLEX
5580 North Fork Road, Decatur. ☎ 217-422-4919

A log courthouse erected in Decatur soon after the town was founded was where a young Abraham Lincoln tried some of his first cases as a frontier lawyer. That courthouse, plus other historic buildings, is now in the Prairie Village on the grounds of the Macon County Museum Complex. The complex includes a variety of indoor and outdoor exhibits that bring to life the county's early prairie years and prosperous Victorian era.

NEARBY

➡ **Rock Springs Center,** 3839 Nearing Lane, Decatur. ☎ 217-423-7708
 The goal of the Rock Springs Center, operated by the Macon County Conservation District, is to put people "in touch with the environment." Visitors can experience life on an 1860s farm, hike along wilderness trails, and view pristine ponds and woods from a lookout tower.

➡ **Anna Bethel Fisher Rock Garden,** in Nelson Park, Nelson Park Boulevard and Lake Shore Drive, Decatur. ☎ 217-422-4911
This beautiful park overlooking Lake Decatur was built in 1927 and restored in 1993. Visitors can walk along its secluded pathways that wend through rocky terraces planted with colorful flowers in the summer and evergreens that are dusted with snow in winter.

➡ **Scovill Oriental Garden,** in Scovill Park, 71 S. Country Club Road, Decatur. ☎ 217-421-7435
A stone Chinese fu dog by the entrance plaza guards the Oriental Garden. Other Asian sculpture is set in the midst of rocks and

greenery, sand and water. A sod bridge leads to a view of a serene waterfall and a pavilion surrounded by flowers.

Oreana

From Decatur take SR 48 northeast for seven miles to the small farming community of Oreana. It was first settled in the late 1820s, but it didn't begin to grow until the 1850s, when the railroad built a depot and made it a water stop for their steam engines. By 1910 it had a population of 110 people. Not far from Oreana is a historic white clapboard church built in 1876.

Where Time Stands Still
UNION CHURCH (NR)

Nondenominational. Take SR 47/48 north; just before Oreana turn right at East Forest Parkway, then left onto North Kirby Road for one mile. 1876. ☎ 217-468-2338

Set on a rise in rolling hill country is a small white clapboard church erected by its members. Organized on March 25, 1865, by the Reverend J. Blake as a United Brethren Church Society, its members would invite circuit-riding ministers to preach regardless of their denomination. Thus Union Church, as its name implies, has been from its inception a nondenominational Protestant congregation.

The frame rectangular church set on a foundation of bricks molded on site by its members has not been renovated, remodeled, or restored. It still lacks electricity and running water, and its original potbellied wood stove continues to provide warmth. It is decorated with Greek Revival and Italianate features that indicate its members were aware of current architectural styles. Italianate features include its high ceiling, tall narrow windows, and the arched four-pane fan window over the central double-door entry. Except for one pane, all the glass windows in the church are original. Greek Revival features are its simple "temple-front" façade and wide cornice, as well as decorative motifs such as dentils found on the interior.

A central aisle leads from the entry to a podium set against the opposite wall. On it is a lectern covered in its original green velvet. The carpet on the risers is "relatively" new—it was installed in 1914. To the right of the podium is one of the church's prized possessions, a pump organ and stool given to the congregation in 1879 by the local Temperance Society that has been carefully maintained. The pews are not fixed in place and can be moved around to accommodate various functions.

Union Church is the property of the Whitmore Township Board and is used for a variety of functions. While it may no longer have a "union" congregation, it continues to fulfill its original mandate of being "free to all."

Next to the church is **Union Cemetery,** laid out in an irregular shape with the oldest graves on a grassy knoll in the center. A family mausoleum built in 1915 is located to the right of the main gate.

One of the Best-Kept Secrets in Illinois
ROBERT ALLERTON PARK

Entry off Allerton Road. ☎ 217-762-2721 or 217-244-1035
🖳, www.ceps.uiuc.edu. From Decorah take I-72 north to Exit 166, then take SR 105 into Monticello and follow the Allerton Garden markers along Allerton Road for 3.5 miles to Robert Allerton Park.

Most of the natural and manmade beauty found in this fifteen-hundred-acre park is due to the vision of one individual, Robert Henry Allerton, an art collector and philanthropist who inherited the land from his father, Chicago livestock baron Samuel Waters Allerton. Robert Allerton gave the land, including his forty-room Georgian-style red brick mansion, to the University of Illinois in 1946 "for research and educational purposes, as a wildlife and plant life reserve, and as an example of landscape gardening."

It takes at least a day to explore the park's formal landscape gardens and the more than twenty miles of trails that wind through its natural areas. It includes elaborately landscaped gardens filled with more than one hundred sculptures and garden ornaments, including a limestone copy of Auguste Rodin's (1840–1917) famous bronze, *Creation of Man;* a sixteen-foot sculpture of the Greek god Apollo named *The Sun Singer* by the Swedish artist Carl Milles (1875–1955); and a two-story summerhouse that shelters two teakwood Buddhas and a limestone Brahmin god.

The wilderness area of the park includes a six-hundred-acre flood plain created by the Sangamon River and two of its major tributaries and four hundred acres of upland forest. The combined one thousand acres were declared a National Natural Landmark in 1971. In addition, seventy-five acres in the park are reclaimed prairie. Allerton also gave the University of Illinois 3,775 acres of fertile farmland with active farms located north of the park and an additional 250-acre tract that is set aside for 4-H youth activities.

Champaign-Urbana

The county was given its name in 1822 by pioneers from Champaign County, Ohio. Urbana was incorporated in 1833 and another community known at first as the Depot was established closer to the railroad tracks. It was incorporated in 1860 and renamed Champaign. The two cities prospered from their position along the railroad and as the site of the state's largest educational institution, the University of Illinois, chartered in 1867.

The Oldest Congregation Established in Champaign-Urbana
URBANA FIRST UNITED METHODIST CHURCH
304 S. Race Street, Urbana. Dedicated 1927. ☎ 217-367-8384

The congregation organized in 1836 and worshiped in a small frame structure until a second church was built in 1856 at a cost of $10,000. The brick church with a white frame steeple was the first to stand at the present church's location. Peter Cartwright (see pp. 265–66), the famed Methodist minister, conducted the dedication services in 1858. An even grander edifice was erected in 1893 that was replaced by an even more monumental church. Dedicated in 1927 at the onset of the Depression, the building's great cost wasn't paid off until 1945.

The Gothic Revival church exemplifies the concept of the church as both a spiritual space and a community center that began to develop among some Protestant denominations in the mid-nineteenth century (see p. 25). A 132-foot-high tower houses the church's main entrance and is a beacon in its neighborhood. The sanctuary space on the second level is rectangular in shape with the pulpit, choir loft, and choir room on the wall opposite the entrance; a balcony provides additional seating space. Also on this floor are a parlor with a stone fireplace, two more large assembly rooms, and five classrooms. On a third floor above the sanctuary are more classrooms, offices, and even a gymnasium. In 1970 an education wing, children's library, and day-care center were added.

A Center of Jewish Life in Champaign-Urbana
SINAI TEMPLE
Reform Jewish. 3104 W. Windsor Road, Champaign. 1975 building, Walter H. Sobel; 1999 addition, Gary L. Olson. ☎ 217-352-8304

A booklet available in the synagogue office provides an excellent commentary on the congregation's many religious artifacts and works of art.

Jewish settlers of German descent organized Ahavath Achim (Brotherhood Association), a benevolent burial society, in 1867. A year later land was purchased for a cemetery. The first recorded public Jewish religious service occurred on Yom Kippur, the Jewish Day of Atonement, in 1895. It was held above a store, but a formal congregation was not organized until 1904 when Sinai Temple was founded as the Champaign and Urbana Hebrew Congregation. Its name was changed in 1914 to Sinai Temple when it affiliated with the Reform Movement (see p. 62).

Temple Sinai's first building, located at the corner of Clark and State Streets, was built in 1918 and partially destroyed in a fire in 1971. Rather than rebuild on its original site, the congregation moved to the suburbs and built a brick and cedar one-story building dedicated in 1975. Several elements from the 1918 building are in the present synagogue, including brass chandeliers in the Litman Library and stained-glass windows mounted in vertical panels in the wall between the Levin Lounge and the 1975 sanctuary. The original Eternal Light now hangs over the *Yad Vashem*, a hammered-copper bas-relief that memorializes the Holocaust, in the Levin Lounge.

To the left of the *bimah* and Ark in the 1999 sanctuary is a bronze seven-branched menorah designed by Sante Fe artist Ted Egri (1913–). The bronze Eternal Light over the Ark is by Ludwig Wolpert (1900–81), who escaped from Hitler's Germany and for many years was the artist-in-residence at the Jewish Museum in New York City. The Ark curtain is woven with an image of the Tree of Life, and the finials of several of the congregation's Torah scrolls are covered with sterling silver ornaments (*rimonim*) in the shape of pomegranates, the fruit of the Tree of Life.

Among the congregation's sacred objects is the small Torah scroll in the Ark. On it is an engraved brass plate that reads: "Number 786 Czech Memorial Scrolls, Westminster Synagogue, London, 1964—5725." This scroll is one of 1,564 Torah scrolls that once belonged to Jewish communities in former Czechoslovakia. The Nazis gathered the Scrolls and other Jewish religious artifacts with the perverse idea of displaying them in a museum in Prague that would document a "lost" people. Following the war, the artifacts were rescued and the scrolls were sent to the Westminster Synagogue in London for safekeeping. Many have since been loaned to congregations throughout the world, where they were carefully repaired by Jewish scribes, and are once again being read by vibrant Jewish congregations.

A Religious Counterpart to Democratic Education
CHANNING-MURRAY FOUNDATION TAGORE CENTER (URBANA UNITARIAN CHURCH; NR)
1209 W. Oregon Street, Urbana. 1908, Walter C. Root. ☎ 217-344-1176

From the exterior this small building does not appear to be very impressive, but appearances can be deceptive. The history of the Urbana Unitarian Church makes clear why it is an important site.

Experimental farms surrounded the building when it was erected in 1908. The small two-story Tudor Revival–style building, renamed the Channing-Murray Foundation Tagore Center, remains essentially unchanged, except today it is surrounded by fraternity and sorority houses and parking lots.

Congress passed the Morrill College Land-Grant Act in 1862, which established public tax-supported universities where equal weight would be given to the sciences, technical studies, and the liberal arts. This was a far different approach to higher education than that offered by traditional church-based institutions. Many denominations opposed secular universities, fearing that their teachings would undermine the authority of the Bible and traditional values. The University of Illinois, chartered in 1867 as the Illinois Industrial University to teach mechanical and agricultural arts, was one of the nation's first land-grant institutions. It was committed to providing its students with a modern, secular education. Not unexpectedly, this led to tensions in the community, with some clergy calling it "the Godless State University." At the opposite pole were academics who wanted to establish a "rational religious" center that would support secular educational values. Many of the university's professors were Unitarians who received support from the American Unitarian Association (AUA), headquartered in Boston, which was promoting missionary work "in the West." With the AUA's help, funds were raised to purchase land, erect a building, and hire a full-time minister. The university, in support of a campus ministry that would not undermine a public university, sold the Unitarians a desirable corner lot and also contributed money for the church's construction.

The Unitarian Church, according to one observer, became a "refuge for students who were disoriented by a sudden exposure to scientific ideas, which contradicted the Bible." Its first minister, the Reverend Albert R. Vail, introduced readings from the Qur'an, Hindu texts, and other scripture at gatherings known as the Unity Club, which attracted many international students at the university.

Walter Root, the younger brother of John Wellborn Root (see p. 96) of

Burnham and Root in Chicago, designed the building. Its plan and appearance were based upon designs published in a 1903 pamphlet, *Plans for Churches,* distributed by the AUA that set aesthetic standards for Unitarian missions in the west. Features approved by the AUA and still visible in this building are its domestic scale, the use of native stone simply dressed in combination with wood and stucco on the exterior, a vertical sliding partition on the interior to divide the chapel from the side parlor that is graced with a fireplace, and diamond leaded-glass windows.

Site of the First Muslim Students' Association (MSA) in North America
CENTRAL ILLINOIS MOSQUE AND ISLAMIC CENTER (CIMIC)
106 S. Lincoln Avenue, Urbana. ☎ 217-344-1555
🖳 www.http://cimic.prairienet.org/

Muslim students at the University of Illinois formed the first Muslim Students' Association in North America in 1963. CIMIC now has sixty members and is under an umbrella organization, the Islamic Society of North America (ISNA). The center is a nonprofit religious organization whose goals are to assist Muslims in carrying out their religious obligations and to convey information about Islam to non-Muslims through educational programs and interfaith forums.

CIMIC initially received support from local churches until funds were made available for it to erect a million-dollar facility, a white structure with a colonnaded arched entry. The building houses a full-time Islamic preschool, a weekend Islamic school, an Islamic resource center and library, and a *musalla,* or prayer hall, oriented toward Mecca.

Visitors are welcome, but it is suggested you call ahead to ensure that someone is available to guide you through the facility. It is requested that visitors dress conservatively.

A Museum of World History and Culture
SPURLOCK MUSEUM
600 S. Gregory Street, University of Illinois Campus. ☎ 217-333-2360
🖳 www.spurlock.uiuc.edu

The Spurlock Museum opened in 2002 and is affiliated with the University of Illinois' College of Liberal Arts and Sciences. It houses the university's World Heritage Museum's 45,000 ethnographic and cultural artifacts from six continents that tell the story of civilizations past and present, and the administrative offices of the Museum of Natural History.

A significant percentage of the museum's collections document religious and spiritual rites, ceremonies, art, and architecture. These include Buddhist statues; diviners' bags and masks from Africa; an entire gallery dedicated to Islam, Judaism, and Christianity; and displays of indigenous North and South American cultures, including a large collection of artifacts associated with the Plains Indians.

NEARBY

➥ **Bethel African Methodist Episcopal (AME) Church,** 401 E. Park Avenue, Champaign. ☎ 217-356-0323

This church was founded two years before the end of the Civil War by a small group of African Americans. A few of its members owned farms or small businesses, but most worked on the railroad or in other domestic or day-labor jobs. By 1877, the parishioners had raised enough money to move into their own church, where their descendants continue to worship.

➥ **Salem Baptist Church,** 500 E. Park Avenue, Champaign. ☎ 217-356-8176

According to one source, Salem Baptist Church would have been organized in 1856 if it weren't for the state's Black Laws (see p. 13). Instead it wasn't until after the conclusion of the Civil War that the congregation was founded. Its present church building dates to 1899.

➥ **Prairie Zen Center,** 515 S. Prospect Avenue, Champaign. ☎ 217-355-8835 🖥 www.prairiezen.org

Housed in a remodeled Prairie-style home, the center is part of the Ordinary Mind Zen School established by Joko Beck of the Zen Center of San Diego. Call for times of meditation sessions and the dates of *Sesshin*, or retreats, that are offered five times a year. The center is open to the public and welcomes visitors.

➥ **First United Methodist Church of Champaign,** 210 W. Church Street, Champaign. 1907, 1965. ☎ 217-356-9078

Champaign was still "the Depot" when three families began to meet in their homes for prayer services in 1855. A year later they organized the Methodist Church Society. A lot was purchased in 1860 and the society's first church was dedicated in 1863. Construction began on a brick church in 1889 that was replaced in 1907 when the present building was dedicated. The congregation numbered nearly four thousand in 1965, when the sanctuary was remodeled and a chapel and an educational building were added. Since then many of its members have moved elsewhere and its numbers are diminished, but the small congregation housed in a monumental Gothic Revival church continues to play an important role in its downtown neighborhood.

Telling the Story of Pioneer Life on the Prairie
THE EARLY AMERICAN MUSEUM AND GARDEN
Near Mahomet. ☎ 217-586-2612. From Champaign-Urbana go west on
I-74 and take Exit 172 (ignore the sign to the museum at Exit 174). Go
north to SR 47, which leads directly to the museum.

The mission of the museum, located in the midst of the famed
"Grand Prairie," is to "nurture an appreciation of history, in particular the history of Champaign County and east-central Illinois . . . , to make
the connection between the past and the present, [and] more importantly,
how the decisions and changes we make today influence the future."

Using tools, implements, personal belongings, and other artifacts of
domestic life, the museum traces the story of the development of the
Grand Prairie, beginning with Native Americans who made their homes
along its waterways until they were displaced by pioneers moving westward. It illustrates the role the railroad played in altering the prairie forever, and the changes brought about by advances in technology from
Deere's "singing plow" to tractors, automobiles, the telephone, and rural
electrification. The museum also explores the very timely and at times
controversial issue of preservation by asking the question: "What evidence
of our heritage should we be preserving today?"

Bloomington-Normal

These twin cities lie in the heart of Illinois' fertile corn belt. Normal,
the smaller of the two, is named after the State Normal University,
founded in 1857, which is now Illinois State University. How Bloomington got its name is a flowery story. Traders and trappers called their settlement Keg Grove, a reference to their custom of hiding kegs of whiskey in
thick groves of trees. This name didn't appeal to the first pioneers, who
named their settlement Blooming Grove after the fields of blooming wildflowers that greeted them. It was later changed to Bloomington. The city is
home to Illinois Wesleyan University, established in 1850 by thirty civic
and Methodist church leaders as a secondary school. One of the more
exceptional buildings on the campus is Evelyn Chapel, dedicated in 1984.

"An Expression of Faith in Brick and Stone"
EVELYN CHAPEL
Methodist. 1301 N. Park Street, Bloomington. 1984, Ben Weese.
☎ 309-556-3161

An alumnus of Illinois Wesleyan University attending the dedication of Evelyn Chapel on May 4, 1984, described the new building as "an expression of faith in brick and stone." That is what this building represents, for it took 134 years before the university had a chapel in which to hold prayer service. Its dedication marked the two hundredth anniversary of the establishment of the Church of John Wesley in the United States.

Named for a major donor to the university, Evelyn Sheean, the chapel's design is derived in part from Moravian churches erected in eastern colonies by followers of Jan Hus, the Christian reformer executed in Prague in 1415 as a heretic. The reason given by the architect for his use of this style is the influence that Hus and other Anabaptists had on John Wesley, the founder of Methodism.

The chapel does reflect exterior stylistic elements found in Moravian colonial architecture. These include its jerkinhead roof (a gable roof with its ends clipped off) and its brickwork laid in a Flemish bond pattern (headers, or the short ends of bricks, and stretchers, the long ends, laid alternately). The small open octagonal tower set on its roof ridge is similar to a tower on the Bethabara Moravian Church in Bethabara, North Carolina, built in 1788. The interior, however, is in the traditional basilica plan. Clear-glass windows and the simplicity of its decoration reflect the sparseness of Moravian churches. A small chapel can be found above the narthex, and in 1987 a Casavant-Freres organ with more than 1,650 pipes was placed in the west gallery of the balcony.

NEARBY

➡ **McClean County Historical Society,** 200 N. Main Street, Bloomington. ☎ 309-827-0426

The society's museum is in the **Old McClean County Courthouse** (NR) completed in 1904. Its roof is crowned with a limestone drum and copper dome that is allegedly modeled after Michelangelo's dome for the Basilica of St. Peter's in the Vatican. The interior of the building has a central three-story rotunda over one hundred feet high that is decorated with an allegorical painting, *Peace and Prosperity*. Marble walls, mosaic floors, mahogany doors, and bronze screens are only some of the decorative features that greet visitors. The museum's permanent exhibit, *Encounter on the Prairie*, tells the story of the people who settled in the county.

➡ **Evergreen Cemetery,** 302 E. Miller Street, Bloomington. ☎ 309-827-6950

 Buried in this cemetery are three generations of one of Bloomington's most famous families: the Stevensons, including Adlai Stevenson I, the nation's vice-president under Grover Cleveland, and Adlai Stevenson II, the governor of Illinois who was the Democratic candidate for president in 1952 and 1956, and the American ambassador to the United Nations in 1961. Also buried here are the wife of Adlai I, Letitia Green Stevenson, who was the second national president-general of the Daughters of the American Revolution, and her sister, Julia Green Scott, who was the seventh national president-general.

Funks Grove

Leave Bloomington and travel south on I-55. Take Exit 154 at Shirley and at the stop sign turn left onto the overpass to SR 41, and go for about a mile and a half to Funks Grove and the Funk Prairie home.

Anyone growing up in the Midwest was familiar with the words "Funk's G Hybrid" that were made popular on highway billboards and radio commercials, although most city kids had no idea what it was. In rural Illinois, on the other hand, the name *Funk* was closely linked with the state's history and agriculture. E. D. Funk, the grandson of Isaac Funk, the founder of Funks Grove, developed Funk's G Hybrid in 1916, the first commercially produced hybrid corn that went on to revolutionize corn production and to transform the nation into a food superpower.

Isaac Funk settled here in 1824 and by the 1860s had accumulated 25,000 acres of land, making his farm the largest in the nation at the time. As a feeder of cattle and hogs, he was known as the Cattle King and played an important role in the development of Chicago's stockyards. His son LaFayette, heir to the Cattle King title, was a founder and director of the Chicago Union Stockyards. A popular product still produced by the Funks from trees on their land is maple "sirup" that Hazel Funk Holmes began to make in the 1820s as a "sweet bonus" for her grandchildren. (Hazel insisted on using the spelling "sirup" that appeared in a Webster's dictionary rather than the more popular "syrup.")

Funks Grove provides visitors with an opportunity to visit a site that has been continuously occupied by the same family for over 175 years.

Home of a Pioneer Family
THE FUNK PRAIRIE HOME AND GEM AND MINERAL MUSEUM
10875 Prairie Home Lane. 1864. ☎ 309-827-6792

Isaac Funk was the descendant of German immigrants who had arrived in the New World in 1733 and settled in Pennsylvania. For nearly a century the Funks were on the move, living in Virginia, Kentucky, and Ohio before Isaac settled in Illinois in 1824. The Prairie Home was built by one of Isaac's sons, Marquis de LaFayette, who was named after the famous French general and Revolutionary War hero. LaFayette went on to serve as an Illinois state senator. He built the Prairie Home in 1863 and '64 with timber felled in Funks Grove, and the year it was completed married Elizabeth Paullin in its parlor. Their son, Marquis DeLoss, electrified the home and entire farm in 1910, the first private farm in the world to be so extensively electrified. The house, restored to its original condition, contains historic memorabilia and artifacts of the Funk family and the first-ever electric kitchen island.

Located next to the home is the **Funk Gem and Mineral Museum** erected by LaFayette Funk II, grandson of LaFayette I, to house his extensive collection of gems and minerals, considered one of the largest individual collections in the world.

NEARBY

➥ **Funks Grove Chapel,** 1864–65.

A small sign on the front of the little white clapboard church relates that it was erected in 1864 and '65 by Robert Stubblefield and Isaac Funk and Sons. The Stubblefields were descendants of English Methodists who married into the Funk family. The church was Methodist but is now nondenominational and is used in the summer by various visiting congregations. The Funk family has been holding annual family reunions at the church since 1884.

➥ **Funks Grove Cemetery**

Members of the Funk family are buried here, as are the remains of fifty Irish railroad workers. No one is sure why these workers are buried here, but according to a Funk family story, in the 1850s when the Chicago and Alton Railroad was being built south of Funks Grove, a number of Irish Catholic railroad workers became ill and died. Because people in nearby towns feared the sickness to be contagious (and possibly because the workers were Catholic), they refused to allow the bodies to be buried in their cemeteries. The Funk family offered their family cemetery and the bodies were buried in a twelve-foot by seventy-five-foot grave. For years the gravesite went unmarked until the McClean County Historical Society and individuals of Irish descent donated money for a marker.

Dwight

....

Dwight is located fifty miles northeast of Bloomington-Normal at the intersection of I-55 and SRs 17 and 47.

The Alton and Sangamon (later the Chicago and Alton) railroad line linking Chicago and St. Louis built a water stop at a site about eighty miles south of Chicago that had the somewhat ironic name West New York. Settlers renamed the town that began to develop in honor of Henry Dwight who, according to one of his friends, "lost his fortune building this railroad." The community flourished, and attracted many notable visitors including the Prince of Wales (later King Edward VII) in 1860. En route from Chicago to St. Louis, the prince decided to accept an invitation to do some shooting in Dwight and to attend Sunday church services at the local Presbyterian church.

A Rare Surviving Example in Illinois of a Frame Gothic Revival Church
PIONEER GOTHIC CHURCH
(DWIGHT TOWNSHIP HALL [NR])
Presbyterian. 201 N. Franklin Street, Dwight. 1857.
☎ 815-584-1959 or 800-554-6635

By the mid–nineteenth century, the Gothic Revival style had begun to replace the Greek Revival as the style of choice for many churches. Missionaries and pioneers brought this style with them, often in the form of planning books, such as the one published in 1852 by the English architect Richard Upjohn entitled *Rural Architecture*. The style was quickly translated into an American idiom in rural areas where carpenters and craftsmen had to rely on available material and technology to replicate the style of the monumental Gothic Revival churches being built in urban areas such as Chicago.

Wood was scarce on the prairie and it was also subject to fire, a lesson well learned in Dwight, which experienced four fires between 1869 and 1891. The town finally passed zoning regulations that required all new buildings to be constructed of brick or iron-covered wood. The frame Pioneer Gothic Church survived all the fires and today is one of only a handful of nineteenth-century "Carpenter" Gothic Revival churches surviving in Illinois. "Carpenter" refers to its frame structure characterized by vertical board-and-batten walls, lancet (pointed arch) windows, an off-center tower, and large amounts of decorative wood trim.

The church was sold to the Keeley Institute (the first clinic in the

United States to treat alcoholism as a disease) in 1891 for use as a club-room. Various other congregations used it until it was sold to the Dwight Historical Society in 1966. After restoring the building and adding a small kitchen and restroom, the society gave the building to Dwight Township for use as a community hall.

❀

This concludes our spiritual journey through Illinois, a state that in all of its diversity represents our nation's magnificent ethnic and religious mosaic. By traveling north and south, east and west on the freeways, state routes, county roads, avenues, streets, and alleys of Chicago and Illinois, we have become aware of the numberless sacred and peaceful places this city and state are blessed with, and how they are all, in many different ways, worthy of our visit and contemplation.

GLOSSARY

Adhan (Azan) Arabic term for call to prayer.

Altar In Christian churches, a table on supports consecrated for the celebration of the sacrament.

Ambulatory An aisle encircling the apse or choir.

Apse A semicircular space that often projects off the eastern end of a church.

Aron Ha Kodesh Hebrew term: "the Holy Ark." Refers to the cabinet that holds the Torah scrolls (*Sefer Torah*) in a synagogue.

Ashkenazi A Hebrew term that is applied to Jews (and their descendants) from German-speaking areas of Europe and areas farther east where Yiddish was spoken.

Ashlar Masonry Hewn blocks of stone.

Baldachin Canopy over the altar that represents the dome of heaven.

Barrel Vault A continuous arched stone roof or ceiling.

Basilica Originally, a Roman colonnaded hall. Later applied to oblong churches with nave, aisles, and, often, galleries and possibly an apse on a short wall opposite the main entrance. Also, an honorific title conferred by the pope to particular Catholic churches.

Bimah Greek term for platform. In a synagogue, it is the platform from which the service is conducted.

Cathedra Throne for presiding bishop, hence the word cathedral.

Chancel The east end of a church where the liturgy is performed. Traditionally houses the altar.

Clerestory Clear story: windows in the upper story of a wall, usually above lower side aisles in a basilica-plan building.

Colonnade A row of columns.

Colonnaded Portico A porch or portico with a roof supported on columns.

Corbel A stone bracket.

Crossing The center of a church where the nave, transepts, and eastern arm meet.

Crucifix Cross with crucified Christ figure.

Cruciform *See* Latin-Cross Plan.

Dais Platform located against a broad wall opposite the main entrance.

Entablature Horizontal beams resting on columns or pilasters, usually associated with a classical order.

Ephod Hebrew term: "breastplate." Refers to the breastplate worn by the high priest in the Temple and the breastplate often used to decorate the Torah scroll.

Etz Hayyim Hebrew term: "Tree of Life." Refers to the wooden rollers that the Torah scroll is wound around.

Eucharist Principal act of worship of the Christian religion; also known as the Divine Liturgy, Holy Communion, Lord's Supper, or mass.

Façade Front or principal face of a building.

Federal Architectural style that refers to the period following the conclusion of the War for Independence until about 1840.

Flying Buttress A masonry half-arch on the exterior of a building that transmits the thrust of a vault or roof from the upper part of a wall to an outer support or buttress.

Gable The triangular upper portion of a wall at the end of a pitched roof.

Garbha Griha Womb chamber in a Hindu temple that houses the temple's most sacred divinity.

Georgian Architectural style that dates from 1733 to 1776. Also known as English Colonial.

Greek Cross A cross with four arms of equal length.

Greek Orders Refers to the three types of Greek capitals: Doric, Ionic, and Corinthian.

Icon Religious images in an Orthodox church. They are objects of veneration and treated with respect.

Iconostasis In an Orthodox church, a screen displaying icons that separates the priest's area and the altar from the congregation.

Keter Torah Hebrew term: "Crown of Torah." Refers to one of the three crowns of Judaism. Also refers to the silver crown placed atop the Torah scroll's wooden finials.

Kippot Hebrew term: a small skullcap worn by men in Orthodox and Conservative synagogues.

Latin-Cross Plan Cross-shaped (cruciform), with one arm longer than the other three. Created when transepts or cross-arms intersect the nave, creating a crossing between the nave and chancel.

Liturgical Referring to a form of public worship. In Christian churches, it pertains to denominations whose focus is on the altar where the Divine Liturgy (Eucharist) is performed.

Mandala A geometric diagram considered by Hindus to be holy.

Masjid Arabic term: "prostration." Another term for mosque.

Menorah Hebrew term for candelabrum. In particular, refers to the seven-branched candelabrum found in the Tabernacle and the Temple in Jerusalem.

Mihrab Arabic term for the empty niche on the *Qibla* wall in a mosque.

Minaret A tall slender tower next to a mosque with a balcony from which the *muz'azzin* calls the faithful to prayer.

Minbar Arabic term for pulpit in a mosque.

Minyan Hebrew term that refers to the quorum of ten men over the age of thirteen necessary for public prayer in Orthodox and some Conservative synagogues.

Multistage Tower A tower divided into telescoping sections.

Narthex An enclosed porch that stretches across the entire width of a façade.

Nave Great central space in a house of worship, often flanked by aisles.

Ner Tamid Hebrew term: "perpetual light." Refers to the lamp that hangs above the *Aron ha Kodesh* in a synagogue.

Nonliturgical Referring to Protestant denominations whose focus is on the pulpit, not the altar.

Pediment The triangular gable at the end of the roof, usually of a portico.

Pedimented Portico A porch with a triangular gable end.

Pilaster A rectangular column projecting only slightly from a wall.

Portico A roofed space, open or semiclosed, often with columns and a pediment.

Pradakshina To circle clockwise while praying in a Hindu temple.

Prasada Sacred interior of a Hindu temple.

Purusha In Hinduism, the Universal Man.

Qibla Arabic term for the direction of prayer toward Mecca; the wall in a mosque oriented toward Mecca.

Reredos Screen behind the altar often decorated with images of saints.

Ribbed Vault A stone ceiling or roof where the groins, or edges of the vault are outlined by stone.

Rimonim Hebrew term: "pomegranate." Refers to the removable ornaments, usually silver, placed on the tops of the Torah scroll's wooden finials.

Ritual System of actions and beliefs that has a beginning, a middle, and an end, and is directed toward superhuman beings.

Sanctuary Location of altar in liturgical churches; the worship space. In the Orthodox Christian faith, the body of the church.

Sefer Torah Hebrew for "the Scroll of the Law," the first five books of the Hebrew Bible: Genesis, Exodus, Leviticus, Numbers, Deuteronomy. Written in Hebrew on parchment (Ashkenazi) or leather (Sephardi) and mounted on two rollers. Stored in the synagogue's *Aron ha Kodesh*.

Sephardi Refers to Jews from the Iberian peninsula and their descendants.

Shikhara Tower associated with a Hindu temple.

Steeple A tall structure usually topped with a spire.

Stupa A dome-shaped monument associated with Buddhist temples. Can be free-standing, a pagoda on a temple roof, or small and enclosed within a temple.

Tabernacle In churches, a decorated receptacle that holds the conse-crated hosts.

Trabeated Post-and-lintel (beam) construction.

Tracery Ornamental stonework that holds glass in a window.

Transept Cross-arms that intersect the nave, creating a crossing between the nave and chancel. The cross-arms usually project beyond the nave. *See* Latin-Cross Plan.

Transubstantiation The Christian belief that the consecration of the host by ordained clergy changes bread and wine into the body and blood of Christ.

Vernacular A distinctive style evident in buildings erected by local crafts-men.

Vestibule Entry-way.

Yad Hebrew term: "hand." Refers to the pointer used to point at words when reading from the Torah scroll.

BIBLIOGRAPHY

Architecture

Andrews, Wayne. *American Gothic: Its Origins, Its Trials, Its Triumphs*. New York: Vintage Books, 1975.

Barrie, Thomas. *Spiritual Path, Sacred Place: Myth, Ritual, and Meaning in Architecture*. Boston and London: Shambhala, 1996.

Bluestone, Daniel. *Constructing Chicago*. New Haven: Yale University Press, 1993.

Blumenson, John J. G. *Identifying American Architecture: A Pictorial Guide to Styles and Terms: 1600–1945*. Rev. ed. New York: W. W. Norton, 1981.

Bruegmann, Robert. *The Architects and the City: Holabird and Roche of Chicago, 1880–1918*. Chicago: University of Chicago Press, 1997.

Chiat, Marilyn J. *America's Religious Architecture: Sacred Places for Every Community*. New York: John Wiley and Sons, 1997.

Crosbie, Michael J. *Architecture for the Gods*. New York: Watson-Guptill Publications, 2000.

Davies, J. G. *Temples, Churches and Mosques: A Guide to the Appreciation of Religious Architecture*. New York: Pilgrim Press, 1982.

Dobbins, John K. "Sacred Meaning in Historic Religious Architecture of Southern Illinois," in *Illinois Historic Symposium*, n.d.

Frazier, Nancy. *Louis Sullivan: And the Chicago School*. Albany: Knickerbocker Press, 1999.

Garner, John S. *The Midwest in American Architecture*. Urbana: University of Illinois Press, 1991.

Gowans, Alan. *Styles and Types of North American Architecture: Social Function and Cultural Expression*. New York: Icon Editions, 1992.

Gruber, Samuel D. *Synagogues*. New York: Metro Books, 1999.

Hanumadass, Marella, ed. *A Pilgrimage to Hindu Temples in North America*. Hickory Hills, Ill.: Council of Hindu Temples of North America, 1994.

Hayes, Bartlett H. *Tradition Becomes Innovation: Modern Religious Architecture in America*. New York: Pilgrim Press, 1983.

Hines, Thomas S. *Burnham of Chicago: Architect and Planner*. Chicago: University of Chicago Press, 1979.

Kennedy, Roger. *American Churches*. New York: Steward, Tabori and Chang, 1982.

Kilde, Jeanne Halgren. *Church Becomes Theater: The Transformation of Evangelical Architecture and Worship in Nineteenth-Century America*. New York: Oxford University Press, 2002.

Lane, George, and Algimantas Kezys. *Chicago Churches and Synagogues*. Chicago: Loyola University Press, 1981.

Mayer, Harold M., and Richard C. Wade. *Chicago: Growth of a Metropolis*. Chicago: University of Chicago Press, 1969.

Nabokov, Peter, and Robert Easton. *Native American Architecture*. New York: Oxford University Press, 1989.

Norman, Edward. *The House of God: Church Architecture, Style and History*. London: Thames and Hudson, 1990.

Rifkind, Carole. *A Field Guide to American Architecture*. New York: Penguin, Plume Books, 1980.

Saliga, Pauline G. *The Sky's the Limit: A Century of Chicago Skyscrapers*. New York: Rizzoli, 1998.

Schulze, Franz. *Mies van der Rohe: A Critical Biography*. Chicago: University of Chicago Press, 1985.

Schulze, Franz, ed. *Chicago's Famous Buildings*. 5th ed. Chicago: University of Chicago Press, 2003.

Sinkevitch, Alice. *AIA Guide to Chicago*. San Diego, New York, London: Harcourt Brace and Co., Harvest Originals, 1993.

Siry, Joseph M. *The Chicago Auditorium Building: Adler and Sullivan's Architecture and the City*. Chicago: University of Chicago Press, 2002.

Sprague, Paul E. *Guide to Frank Lloyd Wright and Prairie School Architecture in Oak Park*. Oak Park, Ill.: Oak Park Landmarks Commission, 1976.

Stone, Lisa, and Jim Zanzi. *Sacred Spaces and Other Places: A Guide to Grottos and Sculptural Environments in the Upper Midwest*. Chicago: The School of the Art Institute of Chicago Press, 1993.

Turak, Theodore. *William Le Baron Jenney: A Pioneer of Modern Architecture*. Ann Arbor, Mich.: UMI Research Press, 1966.

Whiffen, Marcus. *American Architecture Since 1780: A Guide to the Styles*. Rev. ed. Cambridge, Mass.: MIT Press, 1992.

Williams, Peter W. *Houses of God: Region, Religion, and Architecture in the United States*. Urbana and Chicago: University of Illinois Press, 1997.

Wischnitzer, Rachel. *Synagogue Architecture in the United States: History and Interpretation*. Philadelphia: Jewish Publication Society, 1955.

Zukowsky, John, ed. *Chicago Architecture: 1872–1922: Birth of a Metropolis*. Chicago: The Art Institute of Chicago, 1987.

Chicago and Illinois History and Geography

Abrams, Isabel S. *The Nature of Chicago: A Comprehensive Guide to Natural Sites in and Around the City*. Chicago: Chicago Review Press, 1997.

Carrier, Lois A. *Illinois: Crossroads of a Continent*. Urbana and Chicago: University of Illinois Press, 1993.

Coggelshall, John M. "Carbon-Copy Towns? The Regionalization of Ethnic Folklife in Southern Illinois' Egypt," in *Sense of Place: American Regional Culture*, ed. Barbara Allen and Thomas J. Schlereth. Lexington: University of Kentucky Press, 1990.

Cronon, William. *Nature's Metropolis: Chicago and the Great West*. New York: W. W. Norton and Co., 1992.

Gathier, Vincent A., and Janet Gates Conova. "Richard Eells, Quincy Abolitionist," in *Historic Illinois*, October, 1990.

Halli, Melvin, and Peter d'A. Jones. *Ethnic Chicago*. Rev. ed. Grand Rapids, Mich.: Wm. B. Eerdmans, 1984.

Huckle, Matt, and Ursula Bielski. *Graveyards of Chicago*. Chicago: Lake Claremont Press, 1999.

Meyer, Douglas. *Making the Heartland Quilt: A Geographic History of Settlement and Migration in Early-Nineteenth Century Illinois*. Carbondale: Southern Illinois University Press, 2000.

Miller, Donald L. *City of the Century: The Epic of Chicago and the Making of America*. New York: Touchstone Books, 1997.

Pacyga, Dominic, and Ellen Skerrett. *Chicago: City of Neighborhoods*. Chicago: Loyola University Press, 1986.

Walker, Juliet E. K. *Free Frank: A Black Pioneer on the Antebellum Frontier*. Lexington: University of Kentucky, 1983.

Woods, Nyssa. "The Virden Massacres," in *Illinois History Magazine*, December 1997.

General History and Geography

Allen, James Paul, and Eugene James Turner. *We the People: An Atlas of America's Ethnic Diversity*. New York: Macmillan, 1988.

Blockson, Charles L. *The Underground Railroad*. New York: Prentice-Hall, 1987.

Fagan, Brian. *The Great Journey: The Peopling of America*. New York: Thames and Hudson, 1987.

Johnson, Paul. *A History of the American People*. New York: HarperCollins, 1998.

Josephy, Jr., Alvin. *The Indian Heritage of America*. Boston: Houghton Mufflin, 1968.

Madison, James H., ed. *Heartland*. Bloomington: Indiana University Press, 1988.

McLuhan, T. C., ed. *Touch the Earth: A Self-Portrait of Indian Existence*. New York: A Touchstone Book, 1971.

McNickle, D'Arcy. *They Came First: The Epic of the American Indian*. Rev. ed. New York: Harper and Row, 1975.

Meyer, Richard E., ed. *Cemeteries and Gravemarkers: Voices of American Culture*. Ann Arbor, Mich.: U-M-I Research Press, 1989.

Morrison, Samuel Eliot, and Henry Steele Commager. *The Growth of the American Republic*, vols. 1 and 2. New York: Oxford University Press, 1951–52.

Noble, Allen G. *To Build in a New Land: Ethnic Landscapes in North America*. Baltimore: Johns Hopkins Press, 1992.

Renshaw, Patrick. *The Wobblies: The Story of Syndicalism in the United States*. New York: Doubleday, 1967.

Shortridge, James R. *The Middle West: Its Meaning in American Culture*. Lawrence: University of Kansas Press, 1989.

Religion

Albanese, Catherine L. *America, Religion and Religions*. 2nd ed. Belmont, Calif.: Wadsworth Publishing, 1981.

————. *Nature Religion in America: From Algonkian Indians to the New Age*. Chicago: University of Chicago Press, 1990.

Bodin, Wes, and Lee Smith. *Religion in Human Culture*. Allen, Tex.: Argus Communications, 1978.

Bradley, Martin B., et al. *Churches and Church Membership in the United States and Canada*. New York: John Wiley and Sons, 1992.

Chidester, David. *American Sacred Space*. Bloomington: Indiana University Press, 1995.

Eck, Diana L. *A New Religious America: How a "Christian Country" Has Become the World's Most Religiously Diverse Nation*. HarperSanFrancisco, 2001.

Gaustad, Edwin Scott. *A Religious History of America*. Rev. ed. HarperSanFrancisco, 1990.

Hirschfelder, Arlene, and Paulette Molin. *The Encyclopedia of Native American Religion: An Introduction*. New York: Facts on File, 1992.

Hoffman, Lawrence. *The Journey Home: Discovering the Deep Spiritual Wisdom of the Jewish Tradition*. Boston: Beacon Press, 2002.

Irwin, Lee, ed. *Native American Spirituality: A Critical Reader*. Lincoln and London: University of Nebraska Press, 2000.

Kasmin, Barry A., and Seymour P. Lachman. *One Nation Under God: Religion in Contemporary American Society*. New York: Harmony Books, 1993.

Livezey, Lowell W., ed. *Public Religion and Urban Transformation: Faith in the City*. New York: New York University Press, 2000.

Marty, Martin. *Pilgrims in Their Own Land: 500 Years of Religion in America*. Boston: Little, Brown, 1984.

Myers, David G. *The American Paradox: Spiritual Hunger in the Age of Anxiety*. New Haven: Yale University Press, 2000.

Neusner, Jacob, ed. *World Religions in America: An Introduction*. Louisville, Ky.: Westminster/John Knox Press, 1994.

Smith, Jonathan Z., and William Scott Green, eds. *The HarperCollins Dictionary of Religion*. HarperSanFrancisco, 1995.

Vecsey, Christopher. *Handbook of American Indian Religious Freedom*. New York: Crossroad, 1991.

Walsh, Michael, ed. *Butler's Lives of the Saints*. Rev. ed. HarperSanFrancisco, 1991.

Wind, James. *Places of Worship: Exploring Their History*. The Nearby History Series, vol. 4. American Association of State and Local History. Walnut Creek, Calif.: Alta Mira Press, 1997.

Wybrew, Hugh. *The Orthodox Liturgy: The Development of the Eucharistic Liturgy in the Byzantine Rite*. Crestwood, N.Y.: St. Vladimir's Seminary Press, 1990.

ACKNOWLEDGMENTS

Writing a book of this scope could not be accomplished without the generous assistance and support of many individuals and organizations. My heartfelt thanks to all of you who were so helpful in providing me with understanding and insight into the history of Illinois, its people, and its many spiritual sites and peaceful places. I would especially like to thank the following individuals who took time out from their busy schedules to answer my many questions and requests for information, and when necessary, to guide me to particular sites.

Charles Kiefer, my guide to many of Chicago's houses of worship, who generously shared with me his vast reservoir of knowledge about the buildings. His contributions to this book's final form cannot be adequately acknowledged, but all errors remain my own.

Al Walovich, my informative guide to Chicago's cemeteries.

Lisa Stone and Jim Zanzi, coauthors of *Sacred Spaces and Other Places*.

Tim Samuelson, the architectural archivist for the Chicago Historical Society.

Jon Austin, former executive director of the Illinois State Historical Society.

David Bahlman, executive director, Landmarks Preservation Council of Illinois.

Vince Michael, from the School of the Art Institute of Chicago.

Sherry Williams, founder, Bronzeville/Black Chicagoan Historical Society.

Gina Speckman, Chicago Convention and Tourism Bureau.

Amy Easton, assistant coordinator, Illinois Historic Preservation Agency.

Dr. Michael D. Wiant, anthropology chair, Illinois State Museum's Research and Collection Center.

Daniel Sack, associate director, Material History of American Religion Project, who guided me to sites outside of Chicago.

Jon Musgrave, for his extensive research on the Old Slave House.

Sarah Peveler, Partners for Sacred Places, for helping me understand "Egypt."

Kim Sheahan, Spurlock Museum, University of Illinois.

The following congregational historians and clergy generously provided me with information about their houses of worship. To those of you who sent me material but not your name, please accept my sincere thank-you and apology for not including you here.

Sue Brown, Christ Church, Lake Forest.

Anne Steinmetz, University of St. Mary of the Lake.

The Very Reverend Glen Nelson, J.C.L., chancellor, Diocese of Rockford, Illinois.

Ronald Beam, Cedarville Cemetery.

Stephen Rapp, Galena Public Library.

Harry Shuemaker, Unitarian Universalist Society of Geneva.

Reverend Kenneth Sandlin, St. Paul's Lutheran Church, Hillsboro.

Reverend Mike Jones, Peter Cartwright United Methodist Church, Pleasant Plains.

Emily Lyons, Immaculate Conception Catholic Church, Kaskaskia.

Reverend Paul Thompson, St. John's United Church of Christ, Maeystown.

Stan Palmer, St. John's Evangelical Lutheran Church, Dongola.

Reverend Kenneth Schaefer, Our Lady of Carmel Catholic Church, Herrin.

May E. Ksycki, St. Charles Borromeo Catholic Church, DuBois.

Father John Peck, Holy Protection Orthodox Church, Royalton.

Cindy Birk Conley, Old Sharon Presbyterian Church, Norris.

Lucille Mooreland and Lina Witherspoon, Mount Zion Baptist Church, Lake Wood.

Robert Webb, director, Primitive Baptist Historical Library.

Alice Ledbetter, First Presbyterian Church, Golconda.

Reverend Gary K. Harroun, Our Redeemer Lutheran Church, Golconda.

Richard Allen Avner, Sinai Temple, Champaign.
Steven Funk and Bill Case, Funk Prairie Home.
Millicent Kreischer, First Presbyterian, Lake Forest.

Three special notes of gratitude are necessary: to Jana Riess for vetting the subchapter on faith groups and for allowing me to use excerpts from her chapter on faith groups that appear in her book, *The Spiritual Traveler: Boston and New England*; to Jeanne Holgren Kilde for her many constructive suggestions and wise council; and to Frank DeSiano, C.S.P., for his many beautiful photos of Chicago sites.

There is one individual who deserves a great deal of credit for this book—Jan-Erik Guerth, the founder and editor of The Spiritual Traveler series. While the errors and omissions that appear herein are my responsibility, this volume's heart and soul reflect Jan-Erik's vision; it is the fruit of his wisdom, guidance, support, and excellent editing.

No one lives in a vacuum; we all depend on others for help when we are engaged in what at times may appear to be an endless task. My efforts were made easier by the support of my family, Bill, Penny, Paul, Jim, Heidi, and my husband, Harvey, to whom this book is dedicated. He has been my traveling companion for many years in the journey called life and in the journey that culminated in this book.

INDEX

✿

Numbers in **bold** indicate illustrations.

Abraham Lincoln Memorial
Garden and Nature Center,
270
Addams, Jane, 26, 148–49, 182,
226; birthplace, 28; burial
site, 226; historical museum,
226; trail, 226
Adler, Dankmar, 97–98, 143;
Auditorium Building, 96;
Charnley-Persky House, 168;
Eliel House, 119; Pilgrim
Baptist Church, 31, 67, 77,
82, 107, 113–**14**, 115, 122, 127
Adler Planetarium, 113
African-American Heritage
Museum, 201
African Methodist Episcopal
Church, 51, 111; Allen
Chapel, 223
African Methodist Episcopal
Zion Church, 51
Agudath, Achum, 26, 252
Ahavath Achim, 324
Ahlschlager, James, 146
Albany, 234
Allen, Richard, 51
Allen Chapel African Method-
ist Episcopal Church, 223
Allerton, Robert Henry, 322
Alschuler, Alfred S., 123, 126,
127, 128, 176, 177
Alton, 13–14, 19, 21, 241,
279–83
Alton Prison, 281–82
A.M.E. Zion Church. See
African Methodist Episcopal
Zion Church
American Baptist Educational
Society, 129
American Baptist Missionary
Union, 18
American Social Gospel, 25
American Unitarian
Association, 54, 195, 325
Amish (people), 25, 39–40
Amish towns, 318–19

Anderson Japanese Gardens,
223–24, **224**
Ando, Tadao, 99
Andover, 70, 245–48
Andrew R. Dole Memorial
Organ, 149
Andrus, Leonard, 220
Angel, John, 172
Anglicans. See Episcopalians
Anna (town of), 302
Anna Bethel Fisher Rock
Garden, 320
Annunciation Greek Orthodox
Cathedral, 154
Anshai Emeth, 252
Anshe Emet, 88
Anshe Emet Synagogue, 123,
128, 176–77
anti-Semitism, 25
Apple River Fort Interpretive
Center, 227
Arao, Hideaki, 175
"Arboretum Village," 198
Archbishop Quigley Preparatory
Seminary, 167
Archbishop's Residence, 161
architecture, 67–82; Beaux-
Arts, 76–77; building plans,
78–83; Byzantine "revival,"
75; Gothic Revival, 71–73,
74; Greek Revival, 68, 70,
71, 72–73; modern
architecture, 77–78; Moorish
"revival," 75–76; neoclassical
architecture, 68–69;
Romanesque Revival, 74–75.
See also churches
Arcola, 25
Area (town of), 191
Argon Ballroom, 177
Armour Institute, 116;
School of Architecture, 177;
see also Illinois Institute of
Technology
Art Institute of Chicago,
99–100; South Garden, 100

Arthur (town of), 25
Arts and Crafts Movement, 110
Asbury, 51
Asbury, Francis, 50
Atwood, 25
Auditorium Building, 96, 98
Augustana Lutheran Church,
246, 248
Aurora, 200–201
Azaz, Henri, 105

Bacon, Henry, 169, 181
Badgley, David, 11
Baha'i faith, 37, 184–85;
House of Worship, 184–85;
temple, 81
Bald Knob Cross, 300–302
Ballou, Hosea, 55
Baltimore and Ohio Railroad, 16
Baptists, 9, 11, 34, 40–41;
slavery, 18, 41
Bartlett, 60, 197
Bartlett, Frederic Clay, 110
Bartlett, Nathan F., 136
Batavia, 210–11
Battleground Memorial Park,
221
Beaux-Arts, 76–77
Bell Memorial Monument, 299
Belleville, 17, 79, 286–87
Belmont Harbor, 172
Belvidere, 207–8
Beman, Solon, 42, 74, 117, 120,
136, 180, 211
Benjamin, Asher, 69
Benjamin Godfrey Memorial
Chapel, **278**, 278–29
Bennett, Edward H., 95
Benson, Olaf, 172
Bertelson, Hans Peder, 240
Bethel African Methodist
Episcopal Church, 327
Bethel Cemetery, 266
Beth-El/Ridgelawn Cemeteries,
161
Bettendorf, 234

Billy Graham Center, 199
Bishop Hill, 20, 242–44; cemetery, 244
Black Hawk, 4, 14–15, 218, 219, 221, 226, 227; statue, 4, 220; state historic site, 30, 238–39; war monument, 225–26
Black Madonna, 297, 298
Blair Chapel, 166
Blake, J., 321
Blake, Thatcher, 221, 222
Blanchard Hall, 199
Blashfield, Edwin H., 173
Blavatsky, Helena Petrovna, 199–200
Bloomington-Normal, 315, 328–30
B'nai Avraham, 261
B'nai Sholom Synagogue, 261
Boatmen's Memorial, 307
Bohemian National Cemetery, 159–60, 160
Borglum, Gutzon, 270
Bosnian American Cultural Association, 187
Bourgeois, Louis, 185
Boyington, William W., 129, 162, 181
Brackenridge, Henry, 282
Bragdon, Claude, 200
Bridgeport, 139, 141–42
Bronzeville, 28, 115, 117, 121
Brooks, Gwendolyn, 28
Brotherhood of St. Andrew, 163
Brownson, Jacques, 210
Buckingham Fountain, 100–101
Buddhism, 34, 37–39; temples, 90–91
Buffalo Trace, 12
"Bughouse Square," 167
Burnham, Daniel Hudson, 95, 96, 97, 113, 123–24, 125, 140, 195; grave, 179
Burnham Park, 108, 113
Butterworth Home, 235
Byrne, Francis Barry, 29, 133–34
Byzantine "revival" architecture, 75

Cable Monument (De Vigne), 237
Cabrini, Francis Xavier, Mother, 145–46, 147; statue, 145
Café Brauer, 171
Cahokia, 3, 4, 6, 36, 68, 253, 285–86, 311
Cahokia Courthouse State Historic Site, 285, 286
Cahokia Mounds State Historic Site, 5, 282, 282–83
Cairo, 16, 21, 305–8

Cairo Point, 306
Calder, Alexander Stirling, 237
Caldwell, Alfred, 172
Calvary Cemetery, 263
Calvin, John, 52, 54
Camp Robert Smalls, 31
Campground Cumberland Presbyterian Church, 302
Canaryville, 134
Cancer Survivors Garden, 101
Cantigny Garden, 200
Capone, Alphonse, 30
Carbondale, 293–94
Cardinal's Villa, 192
Carl Sandburg State Historic Site, 248
Carlson (Dr. Margery) Greenhouse, 183
Carpenter Chapel, 149
Carraciolo, Louis, 106
Carroll, John, bishop, 53
Carthage, 43, 256–57
Carthage Jail and Visitors Center, 256–57
Carthage Primitive Baptist Church, 257
Cartwright, Peter, 10, 265–66, 323
Carus, Paul, 39, 217
Casady, William L., 106
Casavant Freres, 85, 165, 329
Cascade Falls, 216
Cathedral of St. James, 48
Cathedral of St. Peter, 79, 286–87
Catholics, 24, 34, 52–54; anti-Catholicism, 24; "holy tramps," 16; slavery, 18
Cave-in-Rock, 311; state park, 311
Cavelier, Robert, Sieur de la Salle, 216, 251
Cedarville, 226–28; historical museum, 226
Central Congregational Church, 250
Central Illinois Mosque and Islamic Center, 326
Ceranski, Joseph, 296
Champaign and Urbana Hebrew Congregation, 324
Champaign-Urbana, 315, 323–28
Channahon State Park, 213
Channing-Murray Foundation Tagore Center, 325
Chapel of St. Saviour, 99, 116–17
Chapel of the Immaculate Conception, 191–92
Charleston, 19, 317–18
Charnley-Persky House, 161, 168

Chase, Philander B., 251
Chase, Thornton, 185
Cherry Hill, 218–19; cemetery, 219; public library, 219
Chicago: architecture and architects, 95–99; Bronzeville, 117; environs of, 183–206; Great Fire, 24, 94; history of, 93–95; Hyde Park, 123, 129; Lincoln Park, 101, 172–73, 181; the Loop, 95–107; name and nicknames, 93– 94; North Side, 161–82; Northwest Side, 144–61; population, 33; South Side, 107–37; Southwest Side, 138–44
Chicago Board of Trade building, 129
Chicago Botanic Garden, 187
Chicago Community Trust, 28
Chicago Fire Academy, 151
Chicago Historical Society, 173
Chicago Loop Synagogue, 72, 104, 104–5
Chicago Portage National Historic Site, 102
Chicago School of Architecture, 24, 77, 96, 98, 157
Chicago Sinai Congregation, 123
Chicago Temple, First United Methodist Church, 103–4
Chicago Theological Seminary, 132, 149
Chicago Water Tower, 129
Chief Shabbona's Grave, 214
Childers-Caleel, Rebecca, 215
Chinatown, 111
Chippiannock Cemetery, 188, 236, 237
Chisholm, Proctor, 112
Christ Church (Lake Forest), 78, 188–89
Christ of the Loop (Strauss and Watts), 106
Christian Methodist Episcopal Church, 51
Christian Science, 34, 41–42
Christianity, 39–55; see also specific headings, e.g.: churches; Presbyterians
Chronic, I., Dr., 181
Church of Christ (Godfrey), 278, 278–79
Church of Christ, Scientist. See Christian Science
Church of Jesus Christ of Latter-Day Saints. See Mormons
Church of Jesus Christ of Latter-Day Saints, Chicago Illinois Temple, 185–86

Church of Our Lady of the Snows, 287
Church of Our Savior, 172
Church of the Epiphany, 150
Church of the Holy Family, 68
Church of the Redeemer Episcopal Church, 306–7
Church of the St. Sava, 189–90
churches: auditorium plan, 81–82, 88; basilica plan, 79–80; building plans, 78–82; central plan, 81; interiors, 83–84; location, 65–67; meetinghouse plan, 80; megachurch, 82; organs, 84–85; skyscraper construction, 96. *See also* architecture
Cicero, 31, 32
Civil War Cemetery, 310
Clarence Darrow Memorial Bridge, 124
Clarence Sidney Fund Cloister, 132–33
Clarke, Henry B., 107, 108; house, 107, 108
Cleaver, Charles, 119
Cleveland, H. W., 123
Clock Tower Building, 240
C.M.E.C. *See* Colored Methodist Episcopal Church
Coggelshall, John M., 284, 294
Coles County Courthouse, 318
Coles County Lincoln-Douglas Debate Museum, 318
Colonel George Davenport Home, 239
Colony Church, **243,** 243–44
Colored Methodist Episcopal Church, 51
Commerce (town of), 257
Community of Christ, 20, 43, 257, 258
Conant, Augustus, 209–10
Confederate Cemetery (Rock Island), 239–40
Confederate Cemetery and Memorial (Alton), 281
Congregation Anshai Emeth, 252
Congregation of the Men of the West, K.A.M. *See* Kehilath Anshe Ma'ariv
Congregation Rodfei Zedek, 134
Congregational Christian Church, 44
Congregationalists, 12, 18, 44–45, 132; slavery, 45
Connick, Charles J., 131, 132, 166
Construction in Space in the 3rd and 4th Dimension (Pevsner), 130
Coolidge, Charles A., 177

Coonley House, 196
Cornell, Paul, 129, 135
Corpus Christi Church, 123
Coulee Country, 227
Court of the Presidents, 101
Cram, Ralph Adams, 166
Crenshaw, John Hart, 312
Cross Monument, 299
Crunelle, Leonard, 118
Cumberland Presbyterian Church, 52
Cumberland Presbyterians, 11, 302
Cumberland Road, 15

Damen, Arnold, 145
Daniel H. Flaherty Rose Garden, 101
Danish Evangelical Lutheran Church in America, 240–41
D'Arcy McNickle Center for American Indian History, 36, 167
Darst, M. C., 150
Davenport, 234
David and Alfred Smart Museum of Art, 131
De Kalb, 208–9
De Vigne, Paul, 237
Decatur, 315, 319–21
Deere, John, 17, 214, 219–20, 234–35, 265; grave, 236
Deere and Company Administrative Center, 235
Deere-Wiman Home, 235
Deists, 54
Delle, William H., 112
DePaul University, 171
DeSell, Lee, 186
Dickeyville, 232–34; Dickeyville Grotto, 232–33
Dickson Mounds, 4, 36, 253; museum, 253
Disciples of Christ, 18
Dixon Chapel, 103
Dixon Spring Independent Methodist Church, 310
Dixon Spring State Park, 310
Dr. Margaret Carlson Greenhouse, 183
Dr. Richard Eells House, 261–62
D'Ogiers, Valentine, 134
Dongola, 11, 49, 304–5
Dorney, Maurice, 140
Dorsey, Thomas, 115, 116
Douglas, Stephen, 16, 18, 262, 267; estate, 21, 107; grave, 115–16; statues, 116, 215, 225. *See also* Lincoln-Douglas debates (1858)
Douglas (neighborhood of), 113–19

Douglas Community Area, 107
Douglas County, 40; Amish towns, 318–19
Douglas Park, 96, 158
Douglas Tomb State Historic Society, 115–16
Du Sable, Jean Baptiste, 94, 101, 102, 125–26; homesite, 101
Du Sable Museum of African American History, 102, 125–26
DuBois, 24, 66, 296–97
Dubuis, Oscar F., 152, 252
Dwight, 332–33
Dwight, Timothy, 10
Dwight Township Hall, 332–33

Eagles' Nest, 220
Early American Museum and Garden, 328
East Garfield Park, 151–52
Eastern Orthodox Christians. *See* Orthodox Christians
Eastern Rite Catholics, 53
Ebenezer Baptist Church, 122
Eck, Diana L., 29, 39, 58
Eddy, Mary Baker, 41–42, 120
Eells, Richard, 261–62
Egrim, Ted, 324
"Egypt," 11, 24, 284, 294, 304
Elam House, 121
Eliel House, 119
Elijah Paris Lovejoy Monument, 280–81
Eliot, John, 124
Elizabeth (town of), 227, 228
Elks National Memorial and Headquarters, 173
Ellis Grove, 6
Ellwood House Museum, 209
Elsah, 277
Elwood, Isaac, 208–9
Emmanuel Lutheran Church, 222–23
Engelbrecht, Herman H., 144
Englewood, 138–39
English United Methodist Church, 309
Episcopal Church Center and Cathedral House, 163–64
Episcopal Church of St. James, 162–63
Episcopalians, 12, 46–48; slavery, 18
Equality, 311–12
Ernest Magerstadt House, 126
Errow, Nathan B., 309
Esbjorn, Lars Paul, 245, 246–47, 248
Eternal Light Monument, **135,** 135–36
Eucharistic Congress (1926), 192, 233

Evangelical and Reformed Church, 44
Evangelical Covenant Church, 159
Evangelical United Brethren, 50
Evanston, 183–84
Eveland Site, 253
Evelyn Chapel, Illinois Wesleyan University, 85, 328–29
Evergreen Cemetery, 329–30

Faggi, Alfeo, 134
Fard, Wallace D., 58
Farley, Richard Blossom, 200
Farnsworth House Estate, 9, 211, 212–13
Father Jacques Marquette Memorial, 215
Feeham Memorial Library, 192
Fermi, Enrico, 130; grave, 135
Fermi National Accelerator Laboratory, 210
Fettinger, Charles Theodore, 303
Field, Marshall, 181
Field Museum of Natural History, 77, 113
Fifth Church of Christ, Scientist, 120
Figli, Raffo, 287
Finney, Charles, 82
First Baptist Church of Chicago, 119, 131
First Baptist Congregational Church, 78, 81, 85, 86, 149, 150
First Church of Christ, Scientist, 120
First Congregational Church, United Church of Christ, 235–36
First Congregational Church of Evanston, 183
First Methodist Church, 11, 85
First Presbyterian Church (Galena), 230
First Presbyterian Church (Golconda), 309
First Presbyterian Church (Lake Forest), 189
First Presbyterian Church and Society of Chicago, 109
First United Methodist Church, Chicago Temple, 103–4
First United Methodist Church (Galena), 231
First United Methodist Church of Champaign, 327
First United Presbyterian Church, 255
Ford, Henry, 28
Forest Home Cemetery, 151, 193

Forest Park, 193
Fort Armstrong, 234, 236, 239
Fort Crevecoeur, 6, 251
Fort de Chartres, 6, 286, 292; State Historic Site, 289
Fort Dearborn, 3, 10, 12, 13, 94, 109, 163; site, 101
Fort Defiance, 21, 306; Fort Defiance Park, 307
Fort Gage, 6, 7
Fort Kaskaskia State Historic Site, 292–93
Fort Massac State Park, 308
Fort Prentiss, 306
Fort Sackville, 7
Fort St. Louis, 6
Fountain of Time (Taft), 125
Fourth Presbyterian Church, 85, 165–66
Frances E. Willard House Museum, 184
Frank Lloyd Wright Home and Studio, 194
Fraser, James Earle, 173
Fraser, Laura Gardin, 173
Free Frank McWhorter Grave Site, 263–64
Freeman, Augusta, 163
Freeport, 19, 225–26
French, Daniel Chester, 124, 181
Fullerton Presbyterian Church, 172
Fulton County Courthouse, 255
Fulton Market, 140
Funk, Clarence Sidney, 132
Funk Gem and Mineral Museum, 331
Funk Prairie Home, 330–31
Funks Grove, 330–31; cemetery, 331; chapel, 331

Gale, George Washington, 248
Galena, 16, 21, 80, 228–32, 299
Galena & Chicago Union Railroad, 94, 193
Galena African-American Heritage Foundation, 228, 232
Galena/Jo Daviess County Historical Society and Museum, 229
Galesberg, 19, 65, 247, 248–51
Ganesha-Shiva-Durga Temple, 204
Garden, Hugh M. G., 150
Garfield Park, 96, 152, 158
Garrison Hill Cemetery, 293
Gaylord Building, Illinois and Michigan Canal Visitor Center, 205
Geller, Todras, 176
Geneva, 209–10

George, Francis Cardinal, 169
Getty Tomb, 98
Giant City State Park, 29, 300
Gibbs, James, 69
Giles, Robert, 72, 167
Gilson Park, 185
Girard, Alexander, 235
Glencoe, 32, 77, 186–87
Glessner, John J., 108
Glidden, Joseph, 17, 208–9
Glidden Homestead, 209
Godfrey, 70, 278–79
Goff, Charles Ray, 104
Golconda, 308–11
Gold Coast, 161
Golden Lady, 124
Goldman, Emma, 193
Goodhue, Bertram Grosvenor, 73, 130–31, 163; statue, 131
Goose Lake Prairie State Natural Area, 214
Goshen, 11
Gothic Revival architecture, 71–73, 74
Grace Church and Community Center, 106–7
Grace Episcopal Church, 81, 106, 231
Graceland Cemetery, 178–79, **179**
Graceland, 137, 170
GracePlace, 106–7
Grand Boulevard, 118, 121–23
Grand Crossing Park, 136
Grand Detour, 219–20
Grand View Drive, 252
Grand View Park, 252
Grant, Ulysses S., 229, 231, 306; home, 229–30
Grant Memorial A.M.E. Church, 42, 77, 120
Grant Park, 100–101
Graue Mill and Museum, 198
Great Lakes Naval Air Base, 31
Great River Road, 65, 232
Great Rivers Scenic Route, 276
Greater Grand Crossing, 135–36
Greek Revival architecture, 68, 70, 71, 72–73
Greeley, Andrew, 52, 53
Greenstone Church, 137
Greenwood Cemetery, 222, 228, 232
Grosse Point Light Station, 183
Groveland Park, 113
Guide to Frank Lloyd-Wright and Prairie Schoo Architecture in Oak Park (Sprague), 194
Guild, Edwin J., 287
Gutterson, Henry, 277

Hake, Otto, 239
Halloway, Charles, 150
Hampton, 234
Hands of Peace (Azaz), 105
Hardscrabble, 141
Harmen, Robert, 139
Harold Washington Library
  Center, 101–2
Harte Cenotaph (Calder), 237
Hartford Methodist Episcopal
  Church, 276
Hauberg Indian Museum, 30,
  239
Haymarket Riot (1886), 22, 23,
  145, 151, 193
Haymarket Square, 151
Haytown, 16
Heart of Chicago, 142
Hegeler, Edward C., 217
Hegeler Carus Mansion, 217
Henry B. Clarke House, 107, 108
Heritage Garden, 187
Hernandez-Avila, Ines, 35
Herrin, 30, 294–96
Hickory Hill Plantation, 312
Hilgenberg, Bernard, 295
Hillsboro, 273–74
Hindu Temple of Greater
  Chicago, 32, 57, 91, 204
Hinduism, 55–57, 59; temples,
  66, 91–92
Hodgdon, Charles, 177
Holcomb, 191
Holy Angels Church, 121–22
Holy Cross Church, 140–41
Holy Family Catholic Church
  (Cahokia), 6, 285–86
Holy Family Church (Chicago),
  73, 85, 145–46
Holy Family Mission, 3
Holy Family Preservation
  Society, 146
Holy Name Cathedral, 80, 85,
  153, **164**, 164–65, 203
Holy Protection Orthodox
  Church, 24, 85–86, 298–99
"holy tramps," 16
Holy Trinity Cathedral, 27, 75,
  157
Holy Trinity Russian Orthodox
  Cathedral, 27, 75, 85, 97, 157
Home Insurance Building, 96
Hope Cemetery, 250
Horner, Henry, 17
Hotchkiss, Almerin, 188, 237
Hughes, John, 255–56
Hull, Charles, 148, 181–82
Hull-House, 28, 182, 226;
  museum, 148–49
Humboldt Park, 158–59
Hyde Park, 129; Hyde Park area,
  107, 123–26

Hyde Park Union Church, 131
Hynes, Robert, 285

I Will (Kelly), 172
Iannelli, Alfonso, 133
Illinois: faith groups in, 33–63;
  history, 2–33; name, 4
Illinois Amish Interpretive
  Center, 319
Illinois and Michigan Canal,
  94, 139, 140, 141, 201, 205,
  205, 214, 217; Headquarters
  Building, 205; National
  Heritage Corridor, 102, 203,
  213, 215; State Trail, 213;
  Visitor Center, Gaylord
  Building, 205
Illinois Centennial Memorial
  Monument, 169
Illinois Central Railroad, 16, 24,
  113, 117, 129, 294
Illinois Confederation, 4
Illinois Country, 6, 7
Illinois Industrial University,
  325
Illinois Institute of Technology,
  99, 116, 177; chapel, 77, 116,
  118; School of Architecture,
  99
Illinois Korean War Memorial,
  270
Illinois Street Independent
  Church, 174
Illinois Territory, 10, 12
Illinois Vietnam Veterans
  Memorial, 270
Illinois Waterway Visitor
  Center, 214
Illinois Wesleyan University,
  328–29; Evelyn Chapel,
  328–29
Immaculate Conception
  Chapel, 291–92
Indians. *See* Native Americans
Ira Couch Mausoleum, 170
Ireland, John, archbishop of
  St. Paul and Minneapolis, 34
Isaiah Israel, 127, 128
Islam, 34, 57–59; mosques, 66,
  76, 89–90
Islamic Cultural Center of
  Greater Chicago, 76, 89, 90,
  187–88
Isle a la Cache Museum,
  204–5
Ives, Chauncey Bradley, 182

Jackson, Jesse, 32
Jackson Park, 95, 123, 124,
  124, 129
Jackson Pipe Organ, 291–92
Jain Center, 60, 197, **197**

Jainism, 59–60
Jane Addams Burial Site, 226
Jane Addams Trail, 226
Jansson, Eric, 20, 80, 242–43,
  246; grave, 244
Janssonites, 20, 80, 242–43, 244,
  245
Japanese Garden, 187
Jean Baptiste Point Du Sable
  Homesite, 101
Jehovah's Witnesses, 34
Jenney, William Le Baron, 77,
  96, 152, 158, 196; grave, 179
Jenny Lind Chapel, 70, **245,**
  245–47
Jensen, Jens, 152, 154, 158–59,
  270
Jews, 17, 24–25, 34; slavery, 18;
  synagogues, 66, 75–76, 79,
  81, 82, 87–89, 115
Jo Daviess County Historical
  Society and Museum, 229
John Deere Historic Site,
  210–20
John Deere Pavilion, 235
John G. Shedd Auditorium,
  113
John Hancock Center, 161–62
John Jacob Glessner House, 74,
  107, 108
Jolliet, Louis, 2–3, 183, 202,
  216, 251, 276
Jonas, Abraham, 261
Jones, Absalom, 51
Jones, Jenkin Lloyd, 195
Jones, John, 25
Jones, Mary Harris "Mother,"
  22–23, 273
Jonesboro, 19, 49, 301, 303–4
Joseph Bond Chapel, 131–32
Joseph Smith Historic Center,
  258
Jubilee College State Park and
  Historic Site, 251
Judaism, 60–63; synagogues, 66,
  87–89
Judson, Sylvia Shaw, 189
Julius Rosenwald Fund, 28
Julius Rosenwald House, 126

K.A.M.—Isaiah Israel Temple,
  76, 77, 122, 123, 126–28,
  127, 176, 177
Kampsville, 36
Kaplan, Mordecai, 63
Kaskaskia, 3, 6, 7, 11, 13, 216,
  289–90, 308
Kaskaskia Bell State Historic
  Site, 290–91
Kaskaskia Island, 290–93
Katz, A. Raymond, 176
Keeley, Patrick C., 153

Kehilath Anshe Ma'ariv Synagogue, 31, 67, 82, 97, 107, 113–14, **114**
Kellogg's Grove, 226
Kelly, Ellsworth, 172
Kent, Aratus, 230
Kent, Germanicus, 221, 222
Kenwood, 107, 123, 126–29
Kenwood Evangelical Church, 128–29
Kenwood United Church of Christ, 128–29
Kilgen Organ, First Methodist Church, 85
Kimball (W. W.) and Company, 149
King, Martin Luther, Jr., 32, 41, 123
Klehm Arboretum and Botanic Garden, 224
Kline, William Fair, 110
Knox, John, 52
Knox College, 248
Kolbe, Maximilian, 191
Korean War Memorial, 270
Kornthal, 301, 303
Kornthal Church, 302, 303–4
Kosmin, Barry A., 25
Ku Klux Klan, 24, 29, 294
Kunz, Victor J., 301

Lachman, Seymour P., 25
Lake Forest, 188–89
Lake Park, 170
Lake View, 312–14
Lake View (North Side), 175–77
Lancashire & Marshall, 85
Lang, Alois, 104
Lang, Louis, 223
LaSalle, 39, 213, 217
LaSalle County Historical Society Museum Complex, 215
Latrobe, Benjamin Henry, 69
Latter-Day Saints Visitor Center, 258
Lawndale, 142
Lawson, Victor Fremont, 181
Le Fevre River Settlement, 228–29
Learning Garden for the Disabled, 187
Lemon, Lewis, 221, 222
Lemont, 16, 32, 57, 91, 201–5
Levee, 111
Lewis and Clark State Historic Site, 275
Lewis Institute, 116
Lewistown, 254–55
"Liberty Bell of the West," 7, 29
Libertyville, 189–91

Lighthouse Nature Center, 183
Lincoln, Abraham, 20, 21, 317; in Chicago, 163, 174; Lincoln Tomb State Historic Site, 269–70; Memorial Garden and Nature Center, 270; National Historic Sites, **267**, 267–68, 269–70; in New Salem, 264, 265; in Peoria, 18; in Springfield, 19, 267, 266, 267–70; statues, 101, 215, 225, 270, 318; in Vandalia, 274
Lincoln Douglas Debate Square, 225
Lincoln-Douglas debates (1858), 19, 115, 215, 225, 248, 250, 261, 263, 268; Coles County Lincoln-Douglas Debate Museum, 318
Lincoln-Douglas Square, 281
Lincoln Home National Historic Site, **267,** 267–68
Lincoln Log Cabin State Historic Site, 315–16
Lincoln Memorial Picnic Grounds, 304
Lincoln Park, 101, 172–73, 181; Lincoln Park area, 170–75
Lincoln Square, 181–82
Lincoln Tomb State Historic Site, 269–70
Lincoln Trail Homestead State Memorial Park, 319
Lincoln Trail State Park, 317
Lincoln's New Salem State Historic Site, 264–65
Lind, Jenny, 247
Lind University, 189
Lindsay, Vachel, 271
Linmar Gardens, 232
Lipp, Franz, 200
Lisle, 198
Little Village, 142
Lockport, 205–6
Logan Square, 168–69
Longman, Evelyn Beatrice, 169
Loop, 95–107
Loop Christian Ministries, 106
Loop Synagogue, 72, **104,** 104–5
Lorado Taft Field Campus, 220
Lovejoy, Elijah Parish, 14, 280–81; monument, 281
Lovejoy, Owen, 14, 241–42
Lowden State Park, 220
Loyau, Marcel F., 100
Loyola University, 146
Loza, Julio A., 144
Luther, Martin, 48, 52, 223
Lutherans, 11, 48–49; slavery, 18

Macon County Museum Complex, 320
Madison County, 50
Madison Park, 262
Madison School, 262
Maeys, Jacob, 288
Maeystown, 288–89
Magnificent Mile, 161, 162
Magnolia Manor, 306
Maher, George, 126
Makarenko, Boris, 155
Making the Heartland Quilt (Meyer), 11
Makom Shalom, 106, 107
Mallary, Peter T., 80
Marquette, Jacques, 2–3, 6, 202, 216, 251, 276, 291; memorial, 215
Marshall Field Wholesale Warehouse, 74, 108
Martin Luther King, Jr. Drive, 117, 121
Marytown Eucharistic Adoration Chapel, 190–91
Masters, Edgar Lee, 128–29, 254–55; grave, 254; home, 265
Matthiessen State Park, 216
Maybeck, Bernard, 277
Mazzuchelli, Charles Samuel, 230, 231
McCarthy, Joseph, 190
McCarty, Joseph, 200
McCarty, Samuel, 200
McCormick, Cyrus, 17, 151; grave, 181
McCormick, Robert, 200
McCormick Harvester Company, 22
McKinley Woods, 213
McLean County Historical Society, 329
McWhorter, Free Frank, 263–64
Mead, Larkin, 269
Mechanic's Grove, 191
Meeting of the Great Rivers Scenic Route, 276
Menard, Pierre, 292
Mennonites, 39–40
Merchant Tailors Building, 42
Mesmer, Franz Anton, 41
Methodist Church, 50
Methodist Church Society, 327
Methodist Episcopal Church, 18, 50
Methodist Episcopal Church South, 18, 50
Methodist Protestant Church, 50
Methodists, 9, 11, 49–50; African American denominations, 51; slavery, 18, 50

Metropolitan Community Church, 120
Metropolitan Missionary Baptist Church, 150
Mexican Fine Arts Center, 144
Meyer, Douglas, K., 11
Michigan Canal, 15
Midway Plaisance, 123, 125, 129
Midway Studios, University of Chicago, 126, 130
Midwest Buddhist Temple, 90–91, 174–75, **175**
Mies van der Rohe, Ludwig, 77, 98, 99, 116, 118, 161; grave, 179
Mill Creek Lutheran Church, 305
Millennium Park, 100
Millet, Louis J., 100
Millstone Bluff Archaeological Area, 310–11
Minnekirken, 168–69
Mission Institute, 262
Mission of Chicago, 16
Mission of the Immaculate Conception, 3, 6, 216
Mission of the Immaculate Virgin Mary, 3
Mississippi Palisades State Park, 233–34
Moline, 220, 234–36, 238
Monadnock Building, 96, 112
Monks Mound, 283
Montauk Block, 96
Montrose Cemetery, 159, 160
Montrose Harbor, 172–73
Moody, Dwight Lyman, 25, 174
Moody Memorial Church, 25, 173–74
Moore, Henry, 130
Moore, Reuben and Matilda Hall, 317
Moorish "revival" architecture, 75–76
Mormons, 19–20, 34, 42–43; Visitor Center, 285
Morris, William, 72, 110
Morris (town of), 214
Morton Arboretum, 198
Morton B. Weiss Museum of Judaica, 128
Mosques, 66, 76, 89–90
Mother Jones. See Jones, Mary Harris "Mother"
Mound City National Cemetery, 21, 306, 307
Mount Olive, 273
Mt. Pisgah Missionary Baptist Church, 123
Mount Vernon hill country, 294
Mt. Zion Baptist Church, 312–13, **313**

Mozart Baptist Church, 150
Mundelein, 191–93
Mundelein, George Cardinal, 134, 151, 165, 167, 191, 192; crypt, 192
Murray, John, 54–55
Museum of Science and Industry, 124
Muslims. See Islam
Mveng, Englebert, 122

Nabokov, Peter, 35
Nanak, Guru, 60
Naplate, 215
Nation of Islam, 58
National Lincoln Monument Association, 269
National Road, 15
National Shrine of Our Lady of the Snows, 287–88
National Vietnam Veterans Art Museum, 112
Native Americans, 3–10, 14–15; spirituality, 35–36
Nauvoo, 19, 43, 257–59, 260
Navy Pier, 102
Near North Side, 161–70
Near South Side, 107, 108–13
Nelson, David, 262
Nelson, Swain, 172
neoclassical architecture, 68–69
Neusner, Jacob, 62
New City, 139
New City Cemetery. See Greenwood Cemetery
New Design, 11, 68
New Hope Church of the Deliverance, 25
New Philadelphia, 264
New Religious America, A (Eck), 29
New Salem, 264–65; State Historic Site, 264–65
Newberry Library, 167; D'Arcy McNickle Center for American Indian History, 36
Newhouse, Henry, 121
Nickel, Richard, 100
Nimmons and Fellows, 126
Normal. See Bloomington-Normal
Norske Lutherske Minnekirken, 168
North Lake Shore Drive Apartments, 99, 161
North Park, 159–61
North Park University, 159
North Shore Congregation Israel, 32, 77, 85, 186–87
North Side, 161–82
Northbrook, 187–88
Northern Illinois University, 220

Northside Tabernacle, 174
Northway, Dennis, 85
Northwest Side, 144–61
Northwestern University, 183
Norwegian Lutheran Memorial Church, 168–69
Notre Dame Catholic Church, 151
Nuclear Energy (Moore), 130
Nyden, John A., 118

Oak Brook, 197–98
Oak Hill Cemetery, 254
Oak Park, 98, 194–96; Oak Park Conservatory, 196
Oak Ridge Cemetery, 268, 269
Oak Woods Cemetery, **135,** 135–36, 170
Oakenwood, 113
Oakland, 119–20; cemetery, 265
Obata, Gyo, 252
O'Gara, Thomas, 123
Ohio River Scenic Byway, 307
Olcott National Center, Theosophical Society in America, 199–200
Old Colony Church, 80
Old Danish Church, 25, 240–41
Old Kaskaskia, 289–90, 291
Old Main, Knox College, 249–50
Old McClean County Courthouse, 329
Old School Baptists. See Primitive Baptists
Old Sharon Presbyterian Church, 11, 313–14
Old St. Patrick's Catholic Church 75, 146–47
Old State Capitol (Vandalia), 275
Old State Capitol State Historic Site (Springfield), 268–69
Old Stone Gate, 140
Old Town, 170, 171
Olivet Baptist Church, 41, 119
Olmsted, Frederick Law, 121, 123–24, 125, 163, 196
100 Great Organs of Chicago (Northway and Schnurr), 85
One Nation Under God (Kosmin and Lachman), 25
Open Court Publishing Company, 217
Operation Breadbasket, 32, 128
Operation PUSH, 128
Opus Dei, 158
Ordinary Mind Zen School, 327
Oreana, 321–22
Organs, 84–86
Oriental Institute, 131

Orthodox Christians, 45–46; architecture, 75, 81; church interiors, 85–86
Osaka Garden, 124, **124**
O'Shaugnessy, Thomas A., 147
Ostermeier Prairie Center, 271
Otis, C. N., 231
Ottawa, 19, 214–15
Ouilmette, Antoine, 184
Our Lady of Lourdes Grotto, 222
Our Lady of Mount Carmel, 294–95
Our Lady of Sorrows Basilica, 79, 152
Our Redeemer Lutheran Church, 309
Owen Lovejoy Homestead, 241–42
Owens, Jesse, 135
Ozark Hills Nature Preserve, 301

Palace of Fine Arts, 124
Parsons, Lucy E., 23
Pelikan, Jaroslav, 46
Peoria, 251–53
Pere Marquette State Park, 6, 276
Perry, David, 33
Peshigo, 94
Peter Cartwright United Methodist Church, 265–66
Petersburg, 264–65
Pettit Memorial Chapel, 207–8
Pevsner, Antoine, 130
Piasa Bird legend, 279
Pierre Menard Home State Historic Site, 6, 292
Pilgrim Baptist Church, 31, 67, 77, 78, 82, 86, 97, 107, 113–14, **114,** 115, 122, 127
Pilgrims, 44
Pillsbury, Ithamar, 245
Pilsen, 142–43
Pioneer Burial Ground, 258–59
Pioneer Court Plaza, 101
Pioneer Gothic Church, 332–33
Plano, 99, 211–13, 257
Plano Stone Church, 20, 43
Plans for Churches, 326
Pleasant Plains, 265–66; cemetery, 266
Polasek, Albin, 159–60
Polish Museum of America, 154
Portage Park, 169–70
Prairie School (architecture), 77, 96, 97, 195
Prairie Zen Center, 327
Presbyterian Cemetery (Andover), 245
Presbyterian Church in the Confederate States, 18, 52

Presbyterian Church in the U.S., 18, 52
Presbyterians, 11, 12, 44–45, 52; slavery, 18, 45, 52
Presley, Wayman, 300–301
Prairie du Roche, 6
Priestley, Joseph, 54
Primitive Baptist Library, 257
Primitive Baptists, 11, 41, 68
Prince Memorial Gallery, 103
Princeton, 241–42
Principia College, 277
Pulaski Park, 154
Pullman, George, 136, 180
Pullman (town of), 107, 136–37
Pullman United Methodist Church, 137
Pumping Station, 129, 162
Puritans, 44, 47, 188; meetinghouse plan, 80

Quad Cities, 234–40
Quigley, James, archbishop, 167
Quimby, Phineas Parkhurst, 41
Quincy, 19, 260–64
Quinn, William Paul, 112
Quinn Chapel A.M.E. Church, 14, 51, 111–12, **111**

Rainbow Push Coalition (K.A.M. Synagogue), 128
Rama Temple, 204
Rand, Archie, 177
Randolph County Courthouse, 290
Rattner, Abraham, 72, 105
Recker, Peter, 238
Reddick Mansion, 215
Renwick, James, 73, 109
Reorganized Church of Jesus Christ of Latter Day Saints, 20, 43, 257, 258
Reorganized Church of Jesus Christ of Latter Day Saints (Plano), 211–12, 257, 258
Republic, The, 124
Reuben Moore Home State Historic Site, 317
Richardson, Henry Hobson, 74, 108
Rifkind, Carole, 70
River Forest, 194
River North, 162
Riverside, 188, 196
Riverside Cemetery (Moline), 236
Robert Allerton Park, 322
Robert F. Carr Memorial Chapel of St. Saviour, 116, 118
Robie House, 98, 107, 129, 131
Robinson's Sphere, 237

Rock Island, 21, 30, 188, 236–40
Rock Island Arsenal, 234, 239–40; museum, 240
Rock Springs Center, 320
Rockefeller, 191
Rockefeller Memorial Chapel, 73, 130–31
Rockford, 221–24
Rodenburg, Louis William, 293
Rodfei Zedek (Congregation), 134
Roman Catholics. *See* Catholics
Romanesque Revival architecture, 74–75
Rookery, 97
Root, John Wellborn, 96, 97, 140; grave, 179
Root, Walter, 325–26
Rosehill, 170, 181–82; cemetery, 181–82
Royalton, 24, 86, 298–302
Ryerson Conservation Center, 189

Saarinen, Eero, 130, 235
St. Adalbert's Catholic Church, 141, 144
St. Alphonsus Catholic Church, 80, 175–76
St. Andrew's Chapel, 163
St. Bartholomew Catholic Church, 169
St. Benedict the African Catholic Church, 81, **138,** 138–39
St. Charles Borromeo Catholic Church, 24, 66, 296–97, **297**
St. Clement Catholic Church, 83, 171–72
St. Gabriel Catholic Church, 97, 140, 146–47
Saint-Gaudens, Augustus, 101, 172
St. George Greek Orthodox Church, 238
St. Ignatius College Prep, 146
St. James at Sag Bridge Catholic Church and Cemetery, 16, 65, **203,** 203–4
St. James Chapel, 72, 166–67
St. James Episcopal Cathedral, 83, 85, 203
St. John's Church (Maeystown), 288–89
St. John's Evangelical Lutheran Church, 11, 49, 302, 304–5
St. John's Lutheran Church, 11
St. Joseph Parish, 237–38
St. Joseph's Catholic Church, 140–41
St. Lucas Cemetery, 159

St. Luke's Episcopal Church, 184
St. Mark's United Church of Christ, 66, 296
St. Mary of Perpetual Help Church, 83, 141–42, **142**
St. Mary of the Angels Catholic Church, 155, 158
St. Mary of the Lake Church, 178
St. Mary of the Lake Seminary, 191
St. Mary Parish (Galena), 231
St. Mary's Catholic Church, 17, 96, 146, 223
St. Mary's Shrine, 221
St. Matthew Lutheran Church, 144
St. Michael's Church (Lincoln Park), 170–71, 176
St. Michael's Roman Catholic Church (Galena), 80, 230–31
St. Nicholas Ukrainian Catholic Cathedral, 66, 80, 154–55, **155**
St. Pascal Catholic Church, 169–70
St. Patrick's Catholic Church, 75, 79, 146–47
St. Patrick Catholic Church (Cairo), 306
St. Paul Catholic Church (Chicago), 143
St. Paul Church of God in Christ, 108
St. Paul's (Hillsboro), 403
St. Paul's Evangelical Lutheran Church (Jonesboro), 303–4
St. Paul's Lutheran Church (Hillsboro), 273–74
St. Peter's Church, 105–6
St. Peter's Evangelical Danish Lutheran Church (Sheffield), 25, 240–41
St. Peter's Evangelical Lutheran Church (Golconda), 309
St. Sava Monastery, 189–90
St. Stanislaus Kostka Catholic Church, 24, 80, 153–54
St. Thomas the Apostle Catholic Church, 29, **133,** 133–34
St. Vincent de Paul Church, 171
St. Vincent's College, 171
SS. Volodymyr and Olha Greek Catholic Church, 75, 81, 156, **156**
Salem Baptist Church, 327
San Damiano Retreat Center and Shrine, 310

Sandburg, Carl, 65, 93, 240, 248–49, 266
Saunders, William, 269
Savage, Eugene Francis, 173
Savannah, 234
Scherer, Daniel, 274
Schermerhorn, L. Y., 196
Schermerhorn Residence, 196
Schlacks, Henry J., 143, 144
Schmitt, Margaret B., 241
Schnurr, Stephen, 85
Schroeder, Ernst, G., 172
Science and Health with Key to the Scriptures (Eddy), 42
Scovill Oriental Garden, 320–21
Sears, David B., 235
Sears Tower, 162
Second Presbyterian Church (Chicago), 86, 109–10, **109**
Second Presbyterian Church (congregation), 73, 189
Selva, Attilio, 165
Separatists, 40, 44
Serbian Orthodox Monastery, 190
Seventh Day Adventists, 34
Sevetus, Michael, 54
Shabbona, Chief, 3, 214
Shakers, 34
Shannon, Thomas Vincent, 133–34
Shaugnessy, Thomas A., 147
Shaw, Howard Van Doren, 110, 166
Shawnee Hills, 11
Shawnee National Forest, 299–300, 301
Shawneetown, 12
Shedd, John G., 182
Shedd Aquarium, 77
Sheffield, 25, 240–41
Sheldon Business School, 191
Sherer, J. J., 166
Shiloh Cemetery, 316–17
Shiloh Presbyterian Church, 316–17
Sikhism, 60
Simonds, Ossiam C., 172
Sinai Temple, 323–24
Sinnissippi Gardens, Greenhouse, and Lagoon, 224
Sixth Church of Christ, Scientist, 120
Skinner, E. M., 120
Sky Chapel, 103
Sloan's Addition, 309
Smalls, Camp Robert, 31
Smith, Amanda Berry, 26
Smith, Charles, 201
Smith, Hyrum, 20, 43, 256–57

Smith, James, 11
Smith, Joseph, Jr., 19–20, 42–43, 211, 256–57
Smith, Joseph, III, 43, 211–12, 257
Smith Museum of Stained Glass Windows, 72
Snow, George Washington, 17, 95
Social Gospel movement, 28
Society for the Advancement of Judaism, 63
Soldiers Field, 108
South Side, 107–37
South Side German Historic District, 260
Southern Illinois University, 293
Southwest Side, 138–44
Spertus Museum, 102–3
Spilman, Benjamin R., 314
Spilman, Jonathon, 314
Spoon River Valley Scenic Drive, 254
Sprague, Paul E., 194
Springfield, 266–72; race riot (1908), 271
Spurlock Museum, 326–27
Sri Venkateswara Swami (Balaji) Temple of Greater Chicago, 201
Stained glass, 71–72
Starbuck, Henry F., 112
Starr, Ellen Gates, 148
Starved Rock, 6; land tour, 215; state park, 35–36, 215–16
Steeple Building, 244
Steinbeck, Gustav, 167
Stent, Edward Neville, 163
Stillman Valley, 220–21
Stock Exchange Building, 100
Stone Fort Trail, 300
Strauch, Adolph, 135
Strauss, Arvid, 106
Street in Bronzeville, A (Brooks), 28
Streeterville, 162
Sufism, 57
Sullivan, Louis, 27, 97–98, 143, 180, 194, 196; Auditorium Building, 96; Charnley-Persky House, 168; Eliel House, 119; grave, 179, 180; Holy Trinity Cathedral, 75, 157; Pilgrim Baptist Church, 31, 67, 77, 82, 107, 113–14, 115, 122, 127; Stock Exchange Building, 100
Suzuki, Daisett Teitaro, 217
Swarthout, Egerton, 173
Swedish Evangelical Mission Covenant, 159

Swiss (Dore) Cottage, 196
Synagogues, 66, 75–76, 79, 81, 82, 87–89, 115

Table Grove, 55, 255–56
Table Grove Community Church, 255–56, **256**
Taft, Lorado Z., 100, 125, 126, 152, 130, 180, 182, 220, 263
Tagore Center, Channing-Murray Foundation, 325
Tallmadge, Thomas, 180
Temple Building: Sky Chapel, 103
Temple Isaiah Synagogue, 122
Temple Sholom of Chicago, 88, 176, 177
Temples: Buddhist temples, 90–91; Hindu temples, 91–92
Theosophical Society in America, Olcott National Center, 65, 199–200
Third Church of Christ, Scientist, 150
Thomas Lincoln Cemetery, 316–17
Thorndike Hilton Memorial Chapel, 132–33
Tiffany, Louis Comfort, 110, 131, 189
Tolpo, Lily, 225
Tonti, Henri de, 216, 251
Trail of Tears State Forest, 301–2
Tribune Tower, 161

Ulricksen, 249–50
Ulysses S. Grant Home State Historic Site, 229–30
Underground Railroad, 14–15, 111, 132, 198, 214, 242, 262
Union Cemetery, 322
Union Church, 321–22
Union County, 48–49
Union Miners' Cemetery, 22, 273
Union Park Congregational Church, 149–50
Union Stockyards, 97, 139, 140
Unitarian Universalist Association, 54–55
Unitarian Universalist Society building, 70
Unitarian Universalist Society of Geneva, 209–10
Unitarians, 18, 54–55
United Church of Christ (Congregational), 44–45, 131
United Methodist Church, 50, 51

United Methodist Church (Batavia), 211
United Methodist Church (Elsah), 277, **277**
United Society of Believers in Christ's Second Coming, 34
Unity Temple, 27–28, 55, 72, 77, 98, 194–96
Universalists, 18, 54–55
University of Chicago, 107, 123, 129–30; David and Alfred Smart Museum of Art, 131; Joseph Bond Chapel, 131–32; Midway Studios, 126, 130; Rockefeller Memorial Chapel, 73
University of Illinois, 325, 326
Upjohn, Richard, 73, 231
Uptown, 177–81
Urbana. *See* Champaign-Urbana
Urbana First United Methodist Church, 323
Urbana Unitarian Church, 325–26
Utica, 2, 215–16
Utopian communities, 19–20, 43, 242–43

Vachel Lindsay House, 271
Vail, Albert R., 325
Valesko, Adolph, 141
Vandalia, 15, 274–76
Vandalia Statehouse State Historic Site, 275
Vatican Council II, 81, 83, 85, 132, 296, 297
Vaux, Calvert, 121, 123–24, 125, 196
Vedanta Society, 57
Victory Monument, 118, **118**
Vietnam Veterans Memorial, 270
"Village of Faith," 203
Vinchessi, Carolo, 106
Vinci, John, 100
Virden, 272–73
Virden Massacre (1898), 22, 271, 272–73, 295
Vivehananda, Swami, 56–57
Volk, Leonard W., 116

Walker, Jesse, 11, 103
Walker, Nelly Verne, 182
Walking Death (Polasek), 160
Wall, John J., 147
Wartburg, 287
Washington, Harold, 101, 135
Washington Park (Chicago), 107, 123, 125, 129
Washington Park (Ottawa), 214–15

Washington Park (Quincy), 261, 263
Washington Square Park, 167
Water Tower, 129, 162
Waterfalls Garden, 187
Watts, J., 106
Webb, Mohammed Russell Alexander, 58
Wedding Chapel of Elizabeth, 228
Weinert, Albert, 193
Wells-Barnett, Ida B., 26
Wernerus, Matthias, 232–33
Wesley, John, 49–50
West Town, 153–59
Wheaton, 65, 199–200
Wheelock, Otis, 149
Whitehouse, Frances, 150
Whittier, John Greenleaf, 240
Wicker Park, 153
Wiener, Samuel, Jr., 252
Wildflower Garden (Grant Park), 101
Will County Historical Society Museum, 205
Willard, Francis E., 184
Williams, Roger, 40, 44, 61
Wilmette, 81, 184–85; Wilmette Wildflower Garden, 185
Wise, Isaac Mayer, 76, 261
Wolfe, H. Scott, 228
Wolpert, Ludwig, 324
Woodland Cemetery, 263
Woodlawn Cemetery, 293–94
Woodruff, Howard Walker, 103
World Community of Al-Islam in the West, 58
World Outreach Conference Center, 106
Wright, Frank Lloyd, 29, 98; Charnley-Persky House, 168; on Farnsworth House, 212; home and studio, 194; Pettit Memorial Chapel, 207–8; Robie House, 107, 129, 131; Unity Temple, 27–28, 55, 72
Wrigley Building, 161

Yamasaki, Minoru, 77, 186
Yoder, Elvan, 318
Young, Brigham, 20, 32

Zettler, F. X., 131, 143, 153
Zimmerman, William Carbys, 154, 159
Zion Evangelist Lutheran Church, 274
Zukotynski, Thaddeus, 153

PICTURE CREDITS

.... ✦ ....

Permission to use copyright material is gratefully acknowledged to the following. While every effort has been made to trace all copyright holders, the publisher apologizes to any holders possibly not acknowledged.

Marilyn J. Chiat: 104, 114, 142, 156, 205, 224, 243, 245, 256, 258, 267, 277, 278, 282

The Commission on Chicago Landmarks and the Chicago Department of Planning and Development: iv

Frank DeSiano: 109, 111, 118, 124, 127, 133, 135, 138, 155, 160, 164, 175, 179, 203

Mary Ksycki: 297

Lucille Mooreland: 313

Suresh Shah: 197